Artificial Intelligence in
BEHAVIORAL AND MENTAL HEALTH CARE

To Chris,

It was a pleasure to meet you last week & I hope you enjoy this book, as a compilation of the work of my colleagues. Most of which, being Chapter 9!

Best Regards,

[signature]

Artificial Intelligence in
BEHAVIORAL AND MENTAL HEALTH CARE

Edited by

David D. Luxton PhD., M.S.

Department of Psychiatry and Behavioral Sciences,
University of Washington School of Medicine, Seattle, WA, USA
and
Naval Health Research Center, San Diego, CA, USA

AMSTERDAM • BOSTON • HEIDELBERG • LONDON
NEW YORK • OXFORD • PARIS • SAN DIEGO
SAN FRANCISCO • SINGAPORE • SYDNEY • TOKYO
Academic Press is an imprint of Elsevier

Academic Press is an imprint of Elsevier
125, London Wall, EC2Y 5AS
525 B Street, Suite 1800, San Diego, CA 92101-4495, USA
225 Wyman Street, Waltham, MA 02451, USA
The Boulevard, Langford Lane, Kidlington, Oxford OX5 1GB, UK

Notices

Knowledge and best practice in this field are constantly changing. As new research and experience broaden our understanding, changes in research methods, professional practices, or medical treatment may become necessary.

Practitioners and researchers must always rely on their own experience and knowledge in evaluating and using any information, methods, compounds, or experiments described herein. In using such information or methods they should be mindful of their own safety and the safety of others, including parties for whom they have a professional responsibility.

To the fullest extent of the law, neither the Publisher nor the authors, contributors, or editors, assume any liability for any injury and/or damage to persons or property as a matter of products liability, negligence or otherwise, or from any use or operation of any methods, products, instructions,
or ideas contained in the material herein.

British Library Cataloguing-in-Publication Data
A catalogue record for this book is available from the British Library.

Library of Congress Cataloging-in-Publication Data
A catalog record for this book is available from the Library of Congress.

ISBN: 978-0-12-420248-1

For Information on all Academic Press publications
visit our website at http://store.elsevier.com/

**Working together
to grow libraries in
developing countries**

www.elsevier.com • www.bookaid.org

Publisher: Nikki Levy
Acquisition Editor: Nikki Levy
Editorial Project Manager: Barbara Makinster
Production Project Manager: Nicky Carter
Designer: Matthew Limbert

Typeset by MPS Limited, Chennai, India
www.adi-mps.com

Printed and bound in the USA

CONTENTS

8. Robotics Technology in Mental Health Care   185

Laurel D. Riek

9. Public Health Surveillance: Predictive Analytics and Big Data   205

Chris Poulin, Paul Thompson and Craig Bryan

10. Artificial Intelligence in Public Health Surveillance and Research   231

Yair Neuman

LIST OF CONTRIBUTORS

Michael Anderson
Department of Computer Science, University of Hartford, West Hartford, CT, USA

Susan Leigh Anderson
Department of Philosophy, University of Connecticut, Stamford, CT, USA

Casey C. Bennett
School of Informatics and Computing, Indiana University, Bloomington, IN, USA;
Department of Informatics, Centerstone Research Institute, Nashville, TN, USA

Timothy Bickmore
College of Computer and Information Science, Northeastern University, Boston,
MA, USA

Craig Bryan
Department of Psychology, The University of Utah, Salt Lake City, UT, USA

Sidney K. D'Mello
Departments of Psychology and Computer Science, University of Notre Dame, Notre
Dame, IN, USA

Thomas W. Doub
Department of Informatics, Centerstone Research Institute, Nashville, TN, USA

Eric Forbell
University of Southern California Institute for Creative Technologies, Los Angeles,
CA, USA

Jonathan Gratch
University of Southern California Institute for Creative Technologies, Los Angeles,
CA, USA

Nancy Hanrahan
School of Nursing, University of Pennsylvania, Philadelphia, PA, USA

Lina Huang
Electrical and Systems Engineering, University of Pennsylvania, Philadelphia, PA, USA

Eva Hudlicka
Psychometrix Associates, Inc. and School of Computer Science, University of
Massachusetts, Amherst, MA, USA

Jennifer D. June
National Center for Telehealth & Technology, WA, USA; Department of Human
Centered Design and Engineering, University of Washington, Seattle, WA, USA

Samuel Lim
Electrical and Systems Engineering, University of Pennsylvania, Philadelphia, PA, USA

David D. Luxton
Naval Health Research Center, San Diego, CA, USA; Department of Psychiatry and Behavioral Sciences, University of Washington School of Medicine, Seattle, WA, USA

Louis-Philippe Morency
University of Southern California Institute for Creative Technologies, Los Angeles, CA, USA

Yair Neuman
Department of Education, Ben-Gurion University of the Negev, Israel

Chris Poulin
Patterns and Predictions, Portsmouth, NH, USA

Emilia Flores Rabinowitz
School of Nursing, University of Pennsylvania, Philadelphia, PA, USA

Laurel D. Riek
Department of Computer Science and Engineering, University of Notre Dame, Notre Dame, IN, USA

Albert Rizzo
University of Southern California Institute for Creative Technologies, Los Angeles, CA, USA

Akane Sano
MIT Media Lab, Massachusetts Institute of Technology, Cambridge, MA, USA

Stefan Scherer
University of Southern California Institute for Creative Technologies, Los Angeles, CA, USA

Russell Shilling
University of Southern California Institute for Creative Technologies, Los Angeles, CA, USA

Barry G. Silverman
Electrical and Systems Engineering, University of Pennsylvania, Philadelphia, PA, USA

Paul Thompson
Institute for Security, Technology, and Society, Dartmouth College, Hanover, NH, USA

ABOUT THE EDITOR

David D. Luxton, Ph.D., M.S. is a Research Health Scientist at the Naval Health Research Center in San Diego California and an Affiliate Associate Professor in the Department of Psychiatry and Behavioral Sciences at the University of Washington School of Medicine in Seattle. Prior to moving to San Diego, he served as a Research Psychologist and Program Manager at the U.S. Department of Defense's National Center for Telehealth & Technology (T2) in Tacoma Washington. He has previous experience as an electronics technician and technical writer in the semiconductor manufacturing industry and as a Secure Communications Systems Technician while serving in the United States Air Force. Dr. Luxton's research and writing is focused in the areas of military and veterans' health, telehealth, mobile health technologies, artificial intelligence, and emerging technology applications in health care. He serves on several national committees and workgroups and he provides training and consultation regarding the use and development of technology in behavioral healthcare. He is a licensed clinical psychologist and member of IEEE and the American Psychological Association.

PREFACE

We have entered a very exciting era for behavioral health and mental health care. Advances in artificial intelligence (AI) make it possible to build intelligent machines that enhance the quality, accessibility, and efficiency of care, while also providing entirely new capabilities. For example, the integration of natural language processing and virtual reality has allowed for the creation of interactive intelligent virtual humans that can provide training, consultation, and treatments. Artificial intelligent agent systems can also assist with clinical decision-making and healthcare management. Advances in sensing technologies and affective computing have enabled machines to detect, assess, and respond to emotional states. Robots capable of patient and medical provider interaction are now commercially available for use in the home and medical settings. Moreover, the use of machine learning and pattern recognition is improving public health surveillance while brain mapping initiatives now underway provide opportunities to model behavior and better understand normal and abnormal functions of the brain. The current and forthcoming advances in AI will transform behavioral and mental health care in the years ahead. Given these advances, it is important for healthcare professionals and AI systems designers and developers to be aware of the current and emerging capabilities, challenges, and opportunities that AI brings to the behavioral and mental healthcare arenas.

This book brings together multidisciplinary experts with specific experience in the development and study of intelligent technologies in health care. Our goal is to share some of the latest developments and to present the basic theoretical, technical, and practical aspects regarding the design and use of these technologies in behavioral and mental health care. We hope that this book will be informative to those who are interested in developing intelligent technologies and to healthcare professionals (e.g., counselors, psychologists, social workers, nurses, physicians, pharmacists, healthcare technicians, administrators, etc.) who use these technologies. This book should also interest the broader audience of persons interested in current and emerging technologies as well as ethical issues associated with the use of these technologies.

Any book that reports on current technological developments is destined to become outdated within just a short time. Between planning this book in 2013 and going to press in mid-2015, new and exciting technological innovations worthy of mention in this book emerged. Not only is it difficult to keep up with all of these impressive developments, it is impossible to cover all AI technologies and approaches in just one volume. Any one chapter of this book could easily be the subject of an entire book on its own. The aim of this book is thus to provide a wide-ranging but highly useful presentation of pertinent AI applications in behavioral and mental health care and to do so in a way that is accessible to a broad audience of readers.

I am grateful to the chapter authors for their willingness to share their knowledge and insight into the topics presented in this book. I wish to thank my publisher Nikki Levy and project managers Barbara Makinster and Nicky Carter at Elsevier for their assistance and support along the way. I also wish to acknowledge the assistance of Eva Hudlicka, Jennifer June, Laurel Riek, and Rudy Rull. I dedicate this book to my brother Matthew, for his courage to overcome adversity, his kindheartedness, and his thoughtful conversations about the stories of Isaac Asimov.

David D. Luxton
February 2015
Olympia, Washington, USA

CHAPTER 1

An Introduction to Artificial Intelligence in Behavioral and Mental Health Care

David D. Luxton[1,2]
[1]Naval Health Research Center, San Diego, CA, USA
[2]Department of Psychiatry and Behavioral Sciences, University of Washington School of Medicine, Seattle, WA, USA

INTRODUCTION AND OVERVIEW

Artificial intelligence (AI) is the field of science concerned with the study and design of intelligent machines. For people unfamiliar with AI, the thought of intelligent machines may at first conjure images of charismatic human-like computers or robots, such as those depicted in science fiction. Others may think of AI technology as mysterious computers confined to research laboratories or as a technological achievement that will occur at some far off time in the future. Popular media reports of the use of aerial surveillance drones, driverless cars, or the possible perils of emerging super-intelligent machines have perhaps increased some general awareness of the topic.

AI technologies and techniques are in fact already at work all around us, although often behind the scenes. Many applications of AI technologies and techniques have become so commonplace that we may no longer consider those applications as involving AI. For example, AI technology is used for predicting weather patterns, logistics planning, manufacturing, and finance functions (e.g., banking and monitoring and trading stocks). AI technology is also deployed in automobiles, aircraft guidance systems, smart mobile devices (e.g., voice recognition software such as Apple's Siri), Internet web browsers, and a plethora of other practical everyday functions. AI technologies and techniques enable us to solve problems and perform tasks in more reliable, efficient, and effective ways than were possible without them.

The behavioral and mental healthcare fields are also benefiting from advancements in AI. For example, computing methods for learning, understanding, and reasoning can assist healthcare professionals with clinical decision-making, testing, diagnostics, and care management. AI technologies and techniques can advance self-care tools to improve the lives of

Artificial Intelligence in Behavioral and Mental Health Care.
DOI: http://dx.doi.org/10.1016/B978-0-12-420248-1.00001-5

1

people, such as interactive mobile health applications (apps) that learn the patterns and preferences of users. AI is improving public health by assisting with the detection of health risks and informing interventions. Another example is the use of artificially intelligent virtual humans that can interact with care seekers and provide treatment recommendations. As each chapter of this book will demonstrate, the opportunities to apply AI technologies and techniques to behavioral and mental healthcare tasks abound.

The purpose of this introductory chapter is to provide basic background and context for the subsequent chapters of this book. I first provide an overview of essential AI concepts and technologies with emphasis on their relevance for behavioral and mental health care. Although the review is not by any means exhaustive, it will provide readers who are new to AI with basic foundational information. I also highlight recent technological developments in order to demonstrate emerging capabilities and to provide a glimpse of innovations on the horizon. I then discuss the many practical benefits that AI brings to behavioral and mental health care along with some additional considerations. A list of foundational texts is included at the end of the chapter to serve as a resource for readers seeking more in-depth information on any given topic.

KEY CONCEPTS AND TECHNOLOGIES

What Is AI?

The goal of AI is to build machines that are capable of performing tasks that we define as requiring intelligence, such as reasoning, learning, planning, problem-solving, and perception. The field was given its name by computer scientist John McCarty, who, along with Marvin Minsky, Nathan Rochester, and Claude Shannon, organized The Dartmouth Conference in 1956 (McCarthy, Minsky, Rochester, & Shannon, 1955). The goal of the conference was to bring together leading experts to set forward a new field of science involving the study of intelligent machines. A central premise discussed at the conference was that "Every aspect of learning or any other feature of intelligence can be so precisely described that a machine can be made to simulate it" (McCarthy et al., 1955). During the conference, Allen Newell, J.C. Shaw, and Herbert Simon demonstrated the Logic Theorist (LT), the first computer program deliberately engineered to mimic the problem-solving skills of a human being (Newell & Simon, 1956).

Over the last 60 years AI has grown into a multidisciplinary field involving computer science, engineering, psychology, philosophy, ethics, and more. Some of the goals of AI are to design technology to accomplish very specialized functions, such as computer vision, speech processing, and analysis and prediction of patterns in data. This focus on specific intelligent tasks is referred to as *Weak AI* (sometimes called Applied AI or Narrow AI) (Velik, 2012). An example of a Weak AI machine is IBM's Deep Blue chess-playing system that beat the world chess champion, Garry Kasparov, in 1997. Rather than simulating how a human would play chess, Deep Blue used the process of *brute force* techniques to calculate probabilities to determine its offensive and defensive moves. The term "Strong AI," introduced by the philosopher John Searle in 1980 (Searle, 1980), refers to the goal of building machines with Artificial General Intelligence. The goal of Strong AI is thus to build machines with intellectual ability that is indistinguishable from that of human beings (Copeland, 2000). The overall aim of AI is not necessarily to build machines that mimic human intelligence; rather, intelligent machines are often designed to far exceed the capabilities of human intelligence. These capabilities are generally narrow and specific tasks, such as the performance of mathematical operations.

The term AI is also sometimes used to describe the intelligent behavior of machines such that a machine can be said to possess "AI" when it performs tasks that we consider as intelligent. AI can be in the form of hardware or software that can be stand-alone, distributed across computer networks, or embodied into a robot. AI can also be in the form of intelligent autonomous agents (e.g., virtual or robotic) that are capable of interacting with their environment and making their own decisions. AI technology can also be coupled to biological processes (as in the case of brain—computer interfaces (BCIs)), made of biological materials (biological AI), or be as small as molecular structures (nanotechnology). For the purposes of this chapter, I use the term *AI* to refer to the field of science and *AI technologies* or *intelligent machines* to refer to technologies that perform intelligent functions.

Machine Learning and Artificial Neural Networks

Machine learning (ML) is a core branch of AI that aims to give computers the ability to learn without being explicitly programmed (Samuel, 2000). ML has many subfields and applications, including statistical learning methods, neural networks, instance-based learning, genetic algorithms, data mining, image recognition, natural language processing (NLP), computational learning theory, inductive logic programming, and reinforcement learning (for a review see Mitchell, 1997).

Essentially, ML is the capability of software or a machine to improve the performance of tasks through exposure to data and experience. A typical ML model first learns the knowledge from the data it is exposed to and then applies this knowledge to provide predictions about emerging (future) data. Supervised ML is when the program is "trained" on a pre-defined set of "training examples" or "training sets." Unsupervised ML is when the program is provided with data but must discover patterns and relationships in that data.

The ability to search and identify patterns in large quantities of data and in some applications without *a priori* knowledge is a particular benefit of ML approaches. For example, ML software can be used to detect patterns in large electronic health record datasets by identifying subsets of data records and attributes that are atypical (e.g., indicate risks) or that reveal factors associated with patient outcomes (McFowland, Speakman, & Neill, 2013; Neill, 2012). ML techniques can also be used to automatically predict future patterns in data (e.g., *predictive analytics* or *predictive modeling*) or to help perform decision-making tasks under uncertainty. ML methods are also applied to Internet websites to enable them to learn the patterns of care seekers, adapt to their preferences, and customize information and content that is presented. ML is also the underlying technique that allows robots to learn new skills and adapt to their environment.

Artificial neural networks (ANNs) are a type of ML technique that simulates the structure and function of neuronal networks in the brain. With traditional digital computing, the computational steps are sequential and follow linear modeling techniques. In contrast, modern neural networks use nonlinear statistical data modeling techniques that respond in parallel to the pattern of inputs presented to them. As with biological neurons, connections are made and strengthened with repeated use (also known as Hebbian learning; Hebb, 1949). Modern examples of ANN applications include handwriting recognition, computer vision, and speech recognition (Haykin & Network, 2004; Jain, Mao, & Mohiuddin, 1996). ANNs are also used in theoretical and computational neuroscience to create models of biological neural systems in order to study the mechanisms of neural processing and learning (Alonso & Mondragón, 2011). ANNs have also been tested as a statistical method for accomplishing practical tasks in mental health care, such as for predicting lengths of psychiatric hospital stay (Lowell & Davis, 1994), determining the costs of psychiatric medication (Mirabzadeh et al., 2013), and for predicting obsessive compulsive disorder (OCD) treatment response (Salomoni et al., 2009).

ML algorithms and neural networks also provide useful methods for modern *expert systems* (see Chapter 2). Expert systems are a form of AI program that simulates the knowledge and analytical skills of human experts. Clinical decision support systems (CDSSs) are a subtype of expert system that is specifically designed to aid in the process of clinical decision-making (Finlay, 1994). Traditional CDSSs rely on preprogrammed facts and rules to provide decision options. However, incorporating modern ML and ANN methods allows CDSSs to provide recommendations without preprogrammed knowledge. Fuzzy modeling and fuzzy-genetic algorithms are specific ancillary techniques used to assist with the optimization of rules and membership classification (see Jagielska, Matthews, & Whitfort, 1999). These techniques are based on the concept of fuzzy logic (Zadeh, 1965), a method of reasoning that involves approximate values (e.g., some degree of "true") rather than fixed and exact values (e.g., "true" or "false"). These methods provide a useful qualitative computational approach for working with uncertainties that can help mental healthcare professionals make more optimal decisions that improve patient outcomes.

Natural Language Processing

The capability of machines to interpret and process human (natural) language is called NLP. NLP is a sub-field of AI that combines computer science with linguistics. The use of computational techniques to specifically examine and classify language is referred to as "computational linguistics" or "statistical text classification" (Manning & Schütze, 1999). One of the earliest examples of a NLP user interface was the ELIZA program, which was created by MIT computer scientist Joseph Weizenbaum in 1966 (Weizenbaum, 1976). ELIZA was created using a simple programming language called *SLIP* (Symmetric *LI*st *P*rocessor) and employed language syntax to provide formulated responses based on a programmed model to imitate the empathic communication style of psychologist Carl Rogers (Rogers, 1959). Users would type a question or statement on a keyboard and the program would rephrase the statements into new questions or statements and therefore only mimicked human conversation. In the early 1970s, Stanford University psychiatrist Kenneth M. Colby developed a program called PARRY that simulated a person with paranoid schizophrenia. Like ELIZA, the program could converse with others via a text interface (Güzeldere & Franchi, 1995) and tests of

PARRY showed that expert psychiatrists were unable to distinguish between PARRY and real patients with paranoid schizophrenia (Teuscher & Hofstadter, 2006). The NLP techniques used in these systems were later adapted for use in the simple precursors of today's virtual agents, known as "chatbots" or "chatterbots."

An example of a much more sophisticated NLP system is IBM's *Watson* (IBM, 2015). The system, named after IBM's founder Thomas J. Watson, uses advanced NLP, semantic analysis, information retrieval, statistical analysis, automated reasoning, and ML. In 2011, Watson famously defeated the American TV quiz show *Jeopardy!* champions, Brad Rutter and Ken Jennings, during a televised exhibition match.

Watson makes use of what is called *DeepQA* (QA stands for question and answering). It works by analyzing data, generating a wide range of possibilities, assessing evidence that is based on available data for each possibility, and developing a confidence level for every possible solution. The system can then deliver a ranked list of responses and can describe the supporting evidence which is weighted by DeepQA algorithms (IBM, 2015). IBM has now developed an expanded, commercially available version of Watson that has learned the medical literature. Watson can also analyze data about patient-reported family history, electronic health records, medication use, and results from tests to help healthcare professionals make optimal decisions about diagnoses and treatment options (IBM, 2015).

NLP has many practical uses for behavioral and mental health care. For instance, NLP combined with ML can allow virtual humans to interact with people through text or voice communication (see Chapters 3, 4, and 6). NLP is also used for scanning and semantic analysis of text and voice (audio data) and can be used for predictive analytics for health surveillance purposes (see Chapters 9 and 10). NLP, combined with ML techniques, can also be used to scan treatment sessions and identify patterns or content of interest. For example, Imel, Steyvers, and Atkins (2015) tested such techniques to identify relevant semantic content in psychotherapy transcripts for the purpose of recognizing semantically distinctive content from different treatment approaches and interventions (e.g., psychodynamic vs humanistic/experiential). These researchers propose that this technique could be useful in training and fidelity monitoring in clinical trials or in naturalistic settings to automatically identify outlier sessions or therapist interventions that are inconsistent with the specified treatment approach.

Machine Perception and Sensing

Machine perception is a form of AI that aims to provide computer systems with the necessary hardware and software to recognize images, sounds, and touch, and even smell (i.e., machine olfaction) in a manner that enhances the interactivity between humans and machines. Some examples include visual sensing in automobiles (e.g., Google Car, Honda's Lane Assist) and video camera software that is capable of identifying human faces. Sensors can be embedded into the environment or onboard mobile devices such as smartphones. Examples of these types of sensors include accelerometers, digital compasses, gyroscopes, GPS, microphones, and cameras. Other biosensor technologies and techniques enable measurement of physiological characteristics such as blood pressure and respiration as well as the assessment of brain and heart activity (see Chapter 6).

Affective Computing

The term *affective computing* was coined from the title of the seminal book by Rosalind Picard of MIT (Picard, 1997). Affective computing is a sub-discipline of computer science which focuses on emotion recognition by machines, emotion modeling, affective user modeling, and the expression of emotions by robots and virtual agents. Affective human—computer interaction (affective HCI) aims to develop machines that have the ability to detect, classify, and respond to the user's emotions and other stimuli. Affective computing makes use of various technologies, including multimodal sensors, ML, and NLP.

An example of an affective detection system is the Defense Advanced Research Projects Agency (DARPA) Detection and Computational Analysis of Psychological Signals (DCAPS) system. This system uses ML methods, NLP, and computer vision to analyze language, physical gestures, and social signals to detect psychological distress cues in humans (DARPA, 2013). The intent of the system is to help improve the psychological health of military personnel as well as to develop and test algorithms for detecting distress markers in humans from other data inputs including sleep patterns, voice and data communications, social interactions, Internet use behaviors, and nonverbal cues (e.g., facial gestures and body posture and movement). Other affective detection systems have been developed to be worn on people or embedded in an environment (ambient sensors) for commercial purposes, such as for observing people's reactions to television commercials or political candidates (McDuff, Kaliouby, Kodra, & Picard, 2013). Emotion-sensing technology is becoming increasingly commercially available and is already a feature on gaming platforms such as Microsoft's Xbox One Kinect (Microsoft, 2015).

Virtual and Augmented Reality

Virtual reality is a human−computer interface that allows the user to become immersed within and interact with computer-generated simulated environments (Rizzo, Buckwalter, & Neumann, 1997). Clinical virtual reality is the use of this technology for clinical assessment and treatment purposes (Rizzo et al., 2011; Schultheis & Rizzo, 2001), and it has been used in the treatment of various psychological disorders (see Gorrindo & Groves, 2009; Krijn, Emmelkamp, Olafsson, & Biemond, 2004; Riva, 2005). Virtual reality is an enabling technology that is used to create virtual humans or other simulated life forms (e.g., virtual pets) that humans can interact with in virtual environments (such as in computer games) or on personal computers and mobile devices. For example, virtual human systems have been developed and tested to provide healthcare information and support (Rizzo et al., 2011), help improve medication adherence among patients with schizophrenia (Bickmore & Pfeifer, 2008), provide patients with hospital discharge planning (Bickmore et al., 2010), provide skills training for people with autistic spectrum disorder (Parsons & Mitchell, 2002), and provide training and treatments in therapeutic computer games (see Chapter 4). AI techniques such as ML, NLP, and affective computing make these artificial beings more life-like, interactive, and engaging.

Augmented reality (AR) or *mixed reality* combines virtual reality with the real world by superimposing computer-generated graphics with live video imagery (Caudell & Mizell, 1992; Craig, 2013). This technology allows information about the surrounding world of the user to be available for interaction and digital manipulation. The technology can also be paired with GPS capabilities that can provide real-time location data to the user. AR can be applied to mobile devices such as smartphones, tablet PCs, and other wearable devices (see Chapter 6). Google's Glass (wearable intelligent glasses), for example, provides users with access to the Internet for real-time data access and sharing and AR experiences. Cutting-edge research has tested AR technologies that can project images and information into contact lenses (Lingley et al., 2011) and directly onto the retina of the human eye (Viirre, Pryor, Nagata, & Furness, 1998). This allows for the user to see what appears to be a conventional video display floating in space in front of them.

AR has useful applications in health care, including training and assisting surgeons (Shuhaiber, 2004) and healthcare education (Zhu, Hadadgar, Masiello, & Zary, 2014). For example, it can enable users to scan the Internet and have access to medical data on demand (Lingley et al., 2011). Clinical uses of AR in behavioral and mental health care include helping children with autism to learn facial emotions (Kandalaft, Didehbani, Krawczyk, Allen, & Chapman, 2013), reminding people to take medications on schedule, and creating virtual stimuli that provoke anxiety in the patient's real-world environment during prolonged exposure therapy (Chicchi Giglioli, Pallavicini, Pedroli, Serino, & Riva, 2015; Powers & Emmelkamp, 2008). AR can also assist patients with real-time therapeutic virtual coaching via screen projection or to train mental health clinicians by having supervisors, who are observing treatment sessions in real-time, provide prompts and recommendations while the student is working with a patient/client.

Cloud Computing and Wireless Technologies

Cloud computing is another relatively new technology whereby computing and data storage are not based on one local computer, but accessed via a network such as the Internet. The concept of cloud computing is an extension of the ideas of J.C.R. Licklider, who was an experimental psychologist and professor at MIT who helped create the ARPANET, the predecessor of the Internet. Cloud computing is important for the development and application of AI because it leverages the advantages of distributed processing and storage and therefore provides access to vast amounts of processing power and data. The use of wireless technologies, such as wi-fi, Bluetooth, and cellular (4G, LTE, etc.) allows multiple types of hardware devices, such as smartphones and intelligent wearables, to connect to and integrate with other devices and data "in The Cloud."

Robotics

The field of robotics is experiencing a boom in several healthcare areas including surgery, diagnostics, prosthetics, physical therapy, monitoring, simulation, and mental health support (see Chapter 8). In behavioral and mental health care, robotics has enormous potential to improve how care is provided. One example, *robot therapy*, replaces animals used in animal-assisted therapies and activities with robots (Shibata & Wada, 2011). Various types of robot have been developed and adopted for use in robot therapy. *Paro*, for example, is a robotic baby seal designed to provide therapy for patients with dementia (Shibata & Wada, 2011). Additionally, the FDA has approved a robot called RP-VITA for use in hospitals that can maneuver from room to room to connect healthcare providers to patients or to other healthcare providers via wireless video teleconferencing (InTouch Health, 2012). Given the pace of innovation, it is possible that one day people will be able to seek mental healthcare counseling and treatments directly from AI embodied in robots in medical settings or in the home.

While robots can have all-in-one central processing units for the performance of intelligent functions, the combination of cloud comput-ing and wireless technologies creates new possibilities for robot learning and navigation. The *RoboBrain* project, for example, is a large-scale computational system intended to serve as an online "brain" that could assist robots with navigation and understanding of the environment around them (Saxena et al., 2014). The development of RoboBrain is supported by funding from the National Science Foundation, the Office of Naval Research, Google, Microsoft, and Qualcomm, and collabora-tions with researchers from the University of California at Berkeley, Brown University, and Cornell University.

BCIs and Implants

BCIs are technological devices that provide direct communication between the brain and external hardware (i.e., a computer). The coupling of AI technology directly with the human brain via invasive or noninva-sive means creates numerous useful capabilities. For example, BCIs have been used to communicate with and control devices such as robots (Wolpaw, Birbaumer, McFarland, Pfurtscheller, & Vaughan, 2002) and video games (Fitzpatrick, 2006). In the medical domain, BCIs have been used to control prosthetic limbs (Wolpaw et al., 2002) and treat noncon-genital (acquired) blindness (Naam, 2010; Naumann, 2012). Coupling AI technologies with the brain has the potential to one day help to repair or improve general cognitive abilities in humans or restore function to areas in the brain damaged by strokes, traumatic brain injuries, and aging (Grübler & Hildt, 2014; Kurzweil, 2005; Naam, 2010; Naumann, 2012).

Deep-brain stimulation is another highly exciting and promising techno-logical advance involving brain implants. This is a neurosurgical procedure where electrodes are implanted into the brain to stimulate targeted areas of the brain. The technique can have therapeutic benefits for conditions such as depression, chronic pain, OCD, Parkinson's disease, and Tourette's syndrome (Williams & Okun, 2013). In support of President Obama's BRAIN Initiative, DARPA awarded two large contracts in 2014 to Massachusetts General Hospital and the University of California, San Francisco, to create electrical brain implants capable of treating seven psychiatric conditions, including addiction, depression, and borderline personality disorder (DARPA, 2014). Deep-brain implants could be used as part of a system that combines external sensors and AI control systems that invoke desired responses to stress triggers in a person's environment.

Supercomputing and Brain Simulation

Computer processing power continues to be one of the major driving forces of advancements in AI. Faster and larger memory capabilities of computers combined with improved design and software processes allow computer systems to accomplish more operations in less time and with greater efficiency. Recent advancements in supercomputing hardware that have the potential to greatly advance AI include IBM's neuromorphic (brain-like) computer chip TrueNorth, which has 5.4 billion transistors, making it one of the largest and most advanced computer chips ever made (Modha, 2015). Researchers at Stanford University have also recently engineered a new circuit board called *Neurogrid* that simulates 1 million neurons and 6 billion synapses (Abate, 2014).

There are several research and development programs underway that are capitalizing on supercomputing advancements to map and model the human brain. The idea behind some of these projects is to create software versions of the individual neurons and neural circuits that make up the human brain. For example, the *Blue Brain Project*, founded in May 2005 by the Brain and Mind Institute of the École Polytechnique Fédérale de Lausanne (EPFL) in Switzerland, was initiated to study and create a soft-ware brain by modeling the mammalian brain down to the molecular level. The project makes use of a supercomputer called Blue Gene and software called NEURON that allows for the simulation of a biologically realistic model of neurons. In 2009, the project team announced that they had suc-cessfully developed a model of the rat cortical column (Neild, 2012).

The Human Brain Project (HBP) was established in 2013 as the next phase of the Blue Brain Project (https://www.humanbrainproject.eu). The goal of the HBP is to develop the technology to enable full human brain simulation. In the United States, the Obama administration announced a billion-dollar investment in a brain-mapping consortium consisting of private (e.g., Howard Hughes Medical Institute, Allen Institute for Brain Science) and public organizations (e.g., DARPA, National Institutes for Health, National Science Foundation; Markoff, 2013; National Institutes of Health, 2014). Like the HBP, this project aims to create a functional map of neural networks of the human brain (see Alivisatos et al., 2012).

The mapping of the brain at the neuron level has the potential to increase understanding of complex neurocognitive processes such as memory, perception, learning, and decision-making. Computer systems that simulate the human brain thus have the potential to improve understanding of both normal and abnormal human brain functioning. One future possibility is that they will make it possible to model psychiatric illnesses and test models of the development, courses, and outcomes associated with these illnesses at a level far more sophisticated than previous computer models. Simulated brains can also be "implanted" into virtual bodies such that simulated environmental changes can be manipulated, thus allowing researchers to test how the simulated brain will interact, learn, and adapt within a given environment. This could allow for complex tests of diathesis—stress models of psychopathology (Luxton, 2014a). For example, researchers could model a brain with genetic or other predispositional factors associated with depression and then run simulations of environmental stressors that may trigger the onset of the condition. These simulations could be time-accelerated in the laboratory to quickly model outcomes. Of note, in 2011, researchers at the University of Texas at Austin and Yale University modeled the development of schizophrenia on a supercomputer that used ANNs to simulate the excessive release of dopamine in the brain (Hoffman et al., 2011).

Mapping of the human brain may also greatly accelerate the development of AI and perhaps move the field closer to simulating human general intelligence. Some believe that this work will eventually lead to computers with intelligence that vastly transcends that of human beings (Kurzweil, 2005; Vinge, 1993). Ray Kurzweil, the futurist, inventor, and Director of Engineering at Google since 2012, predicts that by 2045, AI technology will exponentially advance to a point called the technological singularity (Kurzweil, 2005; Vinge, 1993; von Neumann, 2012). This singularity refers to the unpredictability of what will happen when machines develop super-intelligence. Whether or not machine super-intelligence presents an existential threat to humanity has been the topic of several books and media articles in recent years (Boström, 2015; Kurzweil, 2005; Rawlinson, 2015). Nonetheless, the quest to build machines with human general intelligence has the potential to help us to learn more about the "mind" of AI and even the nature of consciousness itself – a topic that has perplexed mystics, philosophers, and scientists for centuries. It would certainly be interesting to examine whether an artificial human brain will develop a subconscious mind, unwanted thoughts, or repressed memories.

The Turing Test

Any synopsis of AI would be remiss to not mention Alan Turing and the Turing Test. Alan Turing was the brilliant British mathematician considered by some to be the father of computer science (Beavers, 2013). In the article, *Computing Machinery and Intelligence*, published in 1950 in the philosophy journal *Mind*, Turing asked the question "Can a Machine Think?" and proposed what is now called the *Turing Test* (Turing, 1950). This test that Turing himself called "the imitation game" is a method for judging the intelligence of machines – and essentially, whether machines are capable of "thinking." To pass the test, a computer program must sufficiently impersonate a human in a written conversation with a human judge in real-time such that the human judge cannot reliably distinguish between the program and a real human. The test suggests that if a machine can answer *any* question presented to it using the same words that an ordinary person would, then we would conclude that the machine is capable of intelligent thinking.

The Turing Test has been an inspiration throughout the history of AI and it has also been subject to significant philosophical debate (Shieber, 2006). Much of this debate has centered on whether the Turing Test is a sufficient or necessary criterion for testing intelligence (Dennett, 1985; Saygin, Cicekli, & Akman, 2000; Shieber, 2006). Other philosophical debate has focused on the definition of intelligence (and consciousness) and what intelligent machines should be expected to do (see Newell & Simon, 1956; Searle, 1980). Of note, the Loebner Prize is an annual contest for AI that is based on the Turing Test (for more information, visit: http://www.loebner.net/Prizef/loebner-prize.html). There are now machines that have passed the Turing Test based on the basic rules of the test (BBC News, 2014).

Of particular interest to us is the use of Turing Test concepts to evaluate the ethical decision-making of intelligent care-providing machines. Moral Turing Tests (MTTs), for example, have been proposed as a way to judge the success of autonomous intelligent agents at ethical behavior (Allen, Varner, & Zinser, 2000; Anderson & Anderson, 2011). This topic is discussed in regards to intelligent care-providing machines in Chapter 11.

Technological Barriers

Throughout the history of AI, the field has experienced periods of high enthusiasm and achievement as well as discouraging setbacks. The 1970s, for example, were considered to be "AI winter" — a period when development slowed because the high expectations raised for AI in the previous decade failed to come to fruition and thus research funding was cut significantly (Warwick, 2012). Innovations in technology as well as renewed interest in practical applications of AI, such as in expert systems in the 1980s, have also ignited periods of incredible growth and innovation.

While we are currently experiencing a period of rapid advancement in technologies, multiple technological barriers remain a challenge for the field of AI and associated disciplines such as robotics. In general, AI technology is good at the things humans find difficult to do but not so good at things that are natural for humans. For example, solving complex mathematical problems is easy for computers, but a basic task such as recognizing a human face, understanding language, or having a robot cross a room without bumping into something is very difficult. Part of this problem has been described as Moravec's Paradox, which asserts that high-level reasoning requires very little computation, but low-level sensorimotor skills require enormous computational resources (Moravec, 1988). Moreover, humans have innate ability to apply commonsense knowledge to everyday situations, such as to reason about another person's internal emotional states or intentions. The design of intelligent machines with commonsense abilities would require them to be human-like in intelligence, an achievement which remains a challenge for the field of AI.

Some of the existing limitations are attributable to hardware resources that will be overcome in the not-so-distant future. Advances in hardware, software design, and materials used to make computers continue to improve, and Moore's Law (Moore, 1965), which has reliably demonstrated that both the speed and memory capacity of computers double about every 2 years, is expected to hold true for at least a while. The substantial research and development investments by federal agencies, private companies (e.g., Google, IBM, etc.), and academic institutions are compelling indicators of the commitment to advance AI and other technologies. We can expect innovation to continue and make much of what is now imagined into reality.

BENEFITS OF AI FOR BEHAVIORAL AND MENTAL HEALTH CARE

Intelligent Machines Are Better at Some Things

Intelligent machines have several advantages over human healthcare professionals. Modern expert systems and other intelligent machines can help with highly complex tasks and do so with greater efficiency, accuracy, and reliability than humans are able to do (Bindoff, Stafford, Peterson, Kang, & Tenni, 2012; McShane, Beale, Nirenburg, Jarell, & Fantry, 2012). Machines that provide care services are not susceptible to fatigue, boredom, burnout, or forgetfulness (Luxton, 2014b). Intelligent machines may also be perceived as being immune to personal biases that human therapists may have. Some patients may prefer encounters with intelligent machines, such as virtual humans rather than human therapists for this reason, and care seekers may experience less anxiety when discussing intimate, private issues with a machine than they would with another person. This notion is supported by initial evidence indicating that some people may be more comfortable disclosing information to virtual humans during clinical interviews and prefer to interact with virtual humans than with medical staff (Gratch, Wang, Gerten, Fast, & Duffy, 2007; Kandalaft et al., 2013; Lucas, Gratch, King, & Morency, 2014). One reason for this preference is that virtual humans are able to spend more time with patients, are always friendly, and do not make users feel rushed or judged (Bickmore et al., 2010).

Improved Self-Care and Access to Care

AI technologies can also greatly improve self-care options for persons seeking self-treatment or health-related information. In the United States, the majority of adults and children with behavioral health needs who may benefit from care do not receive any services (Merikangas et al., 2011; SAMSHA, 2013, 2014). Furthermore, nearly 80 million Americans reside in areas without a sufficient number of mental healthcare practitioners to meet the needs of those communities (US Health and Human Services Health Resources and Services Administration, 2013). This resource gap could be addressed through interactive virtual human care providers accessible anywhere and at any time on mobile devices to provide information about health conditions, conduct question-and-answer assessments, provide self-care counseling, and deliver therapeutic interventions. This application of AI can provide a more interactive experience than a simple informational website or scripted video. The use of intelligent care-providing machines also extends the benefits of telehealth services by providing services to care seekers in remote geographical areas and provide access to specialty care services that may not be available in the patient's area. Moreover, intelligent mobile and wearable devices can increase the amount of data that are available to users and can provide them with more information to assess health and monitor progress toward individualized health goals.

Integration and Customization of Care

Intelligent care providing machines have the potential to greatly improve health outcomes among care seekers by customizing their care. These systems could be programmed with the knowledge and skills of diverse evidence-based approaches and then deliver the most appropriate therapy or integrate different approaches based on a patient's diagnostic profile, preferences, or treatment progress. Intelligent care-providing machines may also be capable of sensitivity and adaptation to specific aspects of a patient's culture such as race/ethnicity or socioeconomic status. For example, a virtual human psychotherapist could change its mannerisms (e.g., eye contact), speech dialect, use of colloquialisms, and other characteristics to match a given cultural group and thus develop and enhance rapport with a patient and improve overall communication. By integrating data from other intelligent devices such as environmental sensors, wearables, and biofeedback devices, intelligent systems can further customize services to the clinical needs of patients. These capabilities will only improve as technology continues to become smaller in size, more integrated with other technologies, and more ubiquitous in everyday life.

Economic Benefits

The development of intelligent machines in healthcare has the potential to provide significant economic benefits for healthcare providers and consumers of mental health services. By speeding up decision-making processes, CDSSs can reduce demands on clinical staff time and therefore improve the overall efficiency of medical care. Computational modeling and simulation techniques can be used to help complex healthcare systems to become more efficient (see Chapter 7). AI systems can also help to reduce overall health-care costs via the stepped-care approach. Stepped care is the process whereby the least resource-intensive care is provided to the most people first, with more intensive care provided to patients who need it the most (Bower & Gilbody, 2005). For example, care seekers can take self-assessments with a virtual care provider and be transferred, if necessary, to full therapy with a human care provider. This would improve efficiency and ultimately reduce economic burdens on healthcare systems. Furthermore, because intelligent machine care providers can be easily replicated (especially software-based ones), they will bring an economy of scale to care delivery. The increased accessibility and lower costs of intelligent machines that provide care may provide opportunities for longer-term treatments that are currently restricted by managed-care costs (Luxton, 2014b). Thus, patients will have the opportunity to participate in longer-term therapies and also receive periodic check-ups at greatly reduced costs to healthcare providers.

On a societal level, applications of AI technology in the provision of care could lead to significant reductions in the long-term costs from untreated behavioral and mental health conditions as well as improved productivity resulting from a healthier population (Luxton, 2014a). The global cost of mental illness was estimated to be nearly $2.5 trillion dollars (US) (two-thirds in indirect costs) in 2010 and is projected to exceed $6 trillion dollars by 2030 according to a report from the World Economic Forum (Bloom et al., 2011). This same report also states that mental health costs are the largest single source of health-related global economic burden, exceeding the respective burdens of cancer, cardiovascular disease, chronic respiratory disease, and diabetes. Moreover, the World Health Organization (WHO, 2011) reported that mental illnesses are the leading causes of disability-adjusted life years worldwide, accounting for 37% of healthy years lost from noncommunicable diseases (Bloom et al., 2011; WHO, 2008). It is hoped that AI technologies and techniques will help mitigate the skyrocketing costs of health care by providing evidence-based and effective alternatives that address the current limitations of modern health care.

ADDITIONAL CONSIDERATIONS

The AI technologies and methods that are presented in this book are intended to augment the work of professionals and to enhance the care of patients — not to replace the need for human professionals. However, concern about whether some advances in AI could eventually pose a threat to jobs held by behavioral and mental health professionals is rational given that a move towards automation has occurred in just about all industries when technology and economics have made it feasible and advantageous. According to a 2013 report from the Oxford Martin School's Programme on the Impacts of Future Technology, 45% of jobs in the United States are at risk of being replaced by computers in the next two decades (Frey & Osborne, 2013). Moreover, an increasing number of "knowledge jobs" held by skilled professionals have already begun to be replaced by AI technologies, including jobs in the banking sector, semiconductor design, customer service, and the law profession (Brynjolfsson & McAfee, 2011; Markoff, 2011).

It is difficult to assess what impact AI may have on the job market for healthcare professionals. The advent of many technologies applied to health care, such as the Internet (e.g., eHealth) and mobile devices (e.g., mHealth), has been creating economic opportunities for mental healthcare professionals, rather than eliminating their jobs. Mental healthcare professionals can benefit from involvement in businesses that develop these technologies or through the expansion of their practices via use of these technologies. What may be the most worrisome thought for healthcare professionals, however, is whether continued technological advances will make it possible to build and deploy intelligent machine systems that equal or exceed the social and intellectual capabilities of human care providers.

The *super clinician* concept (Luxton, 2014a) is a proposed intelligent machine system that would integrate many of the technologies that are described in this book. The system could use facial recognition technology to verify the identity of patients and also advanced sensory technologies to observe and analyze nonverbal behavior such as facial expressions, eye blinking, vocal characteristics, and other patterns of behavior. Computer sensing technology could also assess internal states that are not detectable by the human eye, such as by observing changes in body temperature with infrared cameras or blood flow in the face with high-resolution digital video processing techniques. The system could be capable of accessing and analyzing all data available about patients from electronic medical records, previous testing results, and real-time assessments collected via mobile health devices. Knowledge acquisition and NLP technology such as that used by IBM's *Watson* could allow the system to learn every therapeutic approach, and with the use of predictive analytics, the system would know how and when to apply the best treatment or intervention. Human interaction with the system could be accomplished via a robot, a virtual human, or perhaps as a voice-only entity with ambient sensors strategically placed within an office.

The basic foundational technologies that could make up a machine such as this presently exist. As noted earlier in this chapter, however, there are technological barriers that limit our ability to build intelligent machines as fully capable as the imagined super clinician. Such a system would require reliable integration of the component technologies and the ability to process complex and ambiguous meaning from conversations in order to function autonomously. When it comes to traditional therapeutic encounters with patients, human care providers will for now maintain their edge over the machines.

Another concern worth mentioning is whether healthcare insurance companies or governments will one day require the use of intelligent machine care providers without providing consumers with choice to seek services from people (Luxton, 2014a). A ramification of this is the loss of something inherent to the helping professions: human-to-human expression of empathy, care, and compassion. Another consequence is the loss of the benefits of basic human physical presence and contact, such as shaking hands before and after a session with a patient, placing a hand on the shoulder of a person who is overcome with grief, or handing a patient a tissue to dry their tears. Virtual humans and robots are being improved in their capability to recognize, respond to, and express emotions (and in the case of a robot provide touch). Whether or not simulated acts of empathy and caring kindness are experienced as analogous to the real thing, or whether it matters if they are, are questions that will require further study as we continue to develop intelligent care-providing machines.

CONCLUSION

The practical application of AI technologies and techniques in behavioral and mental health care is a rapidly advancing area that presents many exciting opportunities and benefits. Intelligent machines can help to tackle many of the challenges that are facing health care throughout the world by providing useful tools that improve the efficiency and quality of health care. Advances in AI also help humankind to raise the bar of its potential for creativity and function. That is, technological advances can help enhance our intellectual and physical capabilities and increase our overall productivity.

Individual practitioners, small group practices, large hospitals, and entire healthcare systems all stand to benefit from these technologies, as do consumers who seek ways to improve their health and wellbeing.

Mental healthcare professionals, ethicists, technologists, engineers, healthcare administrators, entrepreneurs, and others must work together to accomplish the full potential of what AI and other technologies can bring to behavioral and mental health care. Psychologists and other mental healthcare professionals can assist system developers by providing the theoretical and practical expertise of implementing evidence-based treatments and therapeutic approaches to these technologies. Ethicists can assist with the design of these systems to enable them to function in an ethical manner and ethicists and mental healthcare professionals can work together to address practical mental healthcare ethics requirements. Involvement of the end user (i.e., patients) is also essential when planning the design and implementation of these technologies.

There is much research that needs to be done. In order to optimize intelligent machine systems for interaction with care seekers, research on human—computer and human—robot interaction in the context of health care is required. In particular, research is needed to understand people's attitudes and preferences for using intelligent machines for health care. This should also include examination of demographic and cultural differences regarding the preferences for using these systems. Randomized controlled trials are especially needed to examine how well emerging intelligent-machine-delivered treatments compare to traditional treatments.

AI is bringing about a paradigm shift for behavioral and mental health care. No longer will knowledge and skills of the medical professional be limited to the physician, psychologist, counselor, social worker, or other professionals; the knowledge and skills will be built into intelligent machines that we will interact with. The use of these machines also requires us to reconsider the therapeutic relationship as it now involves the patient's relationship with technology. There are also emerging ethical issues that need to be carefully considered, such as new risks to patient privacy. As we build and deploy these technologies, we must not forget about the importance of the relationship between care providers and care seekers and the responsibilities we have to each other and the communities in which we live. We must build these machines to always serve the well-being of people, to alleviate suffering as much as possible, and to do so in a fair and ethical manner.

REFERENCES

Abate, T. (2014). *Stanford bioengineers create circuit board modeled on the human brain*. Stanford News Service. Available from: <http://news.stanford.edu/pr/2014/pr-neurogrid-boahen-engineering-042814.html>.

Alivisatos, A. P., Chun, M., Church, G. M., Greenspan, R. J., Roukes, M. L., & Yuste, R. (2012). The brain activity map project and the challenge of functional connectomics. *Neuron, 74*, 970–974.

Allen, C., Varner, G., & Zinser, J. (2000). Prolegomena to any future artificial moral agent. *Journal of Experimental and Theoretical Artificial Intelligence, 12*, 251–261.

Alonso, E., & Mondragón, E. (Eds.), (2011). *Computational neuroscience for advancing artificial intelligence: Models, methods and applications*. Hershey, PA: IGI Global.

Anderson, M., & Anderson, S. L. (Eds.), (2011). *Machine ethics*. New York, NY: Cambridge Univesity Press.

BBC News. (2014). Computer AI passes Turing test in "world first". <http://www.bbc.com/news/technology-27762088>.

Beavers, A. (2013). Alan turing: Mathematical mechanist. In S. B. Cooper, & J. van Leeuwen (Eds.), *Alan turing: His work and impact* (pp. 481–485). Waltham, MA: Elsevier.

Bickmore, T., & Pfeifer, L. (2008). Relational agents for antipsychotic medication adherence. In *HI'08 workshop on Technology in Mental Health*. Florence, Italy. Available at: <http://relationalagents.com/publications/CHI08-mentalhealth.pdf>.

Bickmore, T. W., Mitchell, S. E., Jack, B. W., Paasche-Orlow, M. K., Pfeifer, L. M., & O'Donnell, J. (2010). Response to a relational agent by hospital patients with depressive symptoms. *Interacting with Computers, 22*(4), 289–298.

Bindoff, I., Stafford, A., Peterson, G., Kang, B. H., & Tenni, P. (2012). The potential for intelligent decision support systems to improve the quality and consistency of medication reviews. *Journal of Clinical Pharmacy and Therapeutics, 4*, 452–458. Available from: http://dx.doi.org/10.1111/j.1365-2710.2011.01327.x.

Bloom, D. E., Cafiero, E. T., Jané-Llopis, E., Abrahams-Gessel, S., Bloom, L. R., Fathima, S., et al. (2011). *The global economic burden of noncommunicable diseases*. Geneva: World Economic Forum. Available from: <http://www3.weforum.org/docs/WEF_Harvard_HE_GlobalEconomicBurdenNonCommunicableDiseases_2011.pdf>.

Boström, N. (2015). *Superintelligence: Paths, dangers, strategies*. Oxford, UK: Oxford University Press.

Bower, P., & Gilbody, S. (2005). Stepped care in psychological therapies: Access, effectiveness and efficiency: Narrative literature review. Available from: http://dx.doi.org/10.1192/bjp.186.1.11.

Brynjolfsson, E., & McAfee, A. (2011). *Race against the machine: How the digital revolution is accelerating innovation, driving productivity, and irreversibly transforming employment and the economy*. Cambridge, MA: MIT Sloan School of Management. Retrieved from: <http://ebusiness.mit.edu/research/Briefs/Brynjolfsson_McAfee_Race_Against_the_Machine.pdf>.

Caudell, T. P., Mizell, D. W. (1992). Augmented reality: An application of heads-up display technology to manual manufacturing processes. In *System Sciences, 1992: Proceedings of the twenty-fifth Hawaii international conference on system sciences* (Vol. 2, pp. 659–669). New York, NY: IEEE. Available from: http://dx.doi.org/10.1109/HICSS.1992.183317.

Chicchi Giglioli, I. A., Pallavicini, F., Pedroli, E., Serino, S., & Riva, G. (2015). Augmented reality: A brand new challenge for the assessment and treatment of psychological disorders. *Computational and Mathematical Methods in Medicine*. Available at: <http://www.hindawi.com/journals/cmmm/aa/862942/>.

Copeland, B. J. (2000). *What is artificial intelligence?* Available from: <http://www.alanturing.net/turing_archive/pages/Reference%20Articles/what_is_AI/What%20is%20AI02.html>.

Craig, A. B. (2013). *Understanding augmented reality: Concepts and applications.* Amsterdam: Morgan Kaufmann.

Defense Applied Research Projects Agency. (2013). *Detection and computational analysis of psychological signals (DCAPS).* Retrieved from: <http://www.darpa.mil/Our Work/I2O/Programs/Detection and Computational Analysis of Psychological Signals-(DCAPS).aspx>.

Defense Applied Research Projects Agency. (2014). *Journey of Discovery starts toward understanding and treating networks of the brain.* Available from: <http://www.darpa.mil/newsevents/releases/2014/05/27a.aspx>.

Dennett, D. (1985). Can machines think? In M. Shafto (Ed.), *How we know* (pp. 121−145). San Francisco, CA: Harper & Row.

Finlay, P. N. (1994). *Introducing decision support systems.* Cambridge, MA: Blackwell Publishers.

Fitzpatrick, T. (2006). *Teenager moves video icons just by imagination.* Washington University, 9. Available from: <http://news.wustl.edu/news/Pages/7800.aspx>.

Frey, C. B., & Osborne, M. A. (2013). The future of employment: How susceptible are jobs to computerization? Available at: <http://www.oxfordmartin.ox.ac.uk/downloads/academic/The_Future_of_Employment.pdf>.

Gorrindo, T., & Groves, J. E. (2009). Computer simulation and virtual reality in the diagnosis and treatment of psychiatric disorders. *Academic Psychiatry, 33,* 413−417.

Gratch, J., Wang, N., Gerten, J., Fast, E., & Duffy, R. (2007). Creating rapport with virtual agents. In C. Pelachaud, et al. (Eds.), *Intelligent virtual agents* (pp. 125−138). Springer: Berlin, Heidelberg.

Güzeldere, G., & Franchi, S. (1995). Dialogues with colorful "personalities" of early AI. *Stanford Humanities Review, 4,* 161−169.

Haykin, S., & Network, N. (2004). *Neural networks: A comprehensive foundation.* Prentice Hall, NJ.

Hebb, D. O. (1949). *The organization of behavior.* New York, NY: Wiley & Sons.

Hoffman, R. E., Grasemann, U., Gueorguieva, R., Quinlan, D., Lane, D., & Miikkulainen, R. (2011). Using computational patients to evaluate illness mechanisms in schizophrenia. *Biological Psychiatry, 69*(10), 997−1005. Available from: http://dx.doi.org/10.1016/j.biopsych.2010.12.036.

IBM. (2015). *IBM Watson.* Retrieved from: <http://www.ibm.com/smarterplanet/us/en/ibmwatson/>. Accessed on February 6, 2015.

Imel, Z. E., Steyvers, M., & Atkins, D. C. (2015). Computational psychotherapy research: Scaling up the evaluation of patient−provider interactions. *Psychotherapy, 52*(1), 19−30. Available from: http://dx.doi.org/10.1037/a0036841.

InTouch Health. (2012). *RP-VITA robot.* Retrieved from: <http://www.intouchhealth.com/products-and-services/products/rp-vita-robot/>. Accessed 02.11.14.

Jagielska, I., Matthews, C., & Whitfort, T. (1999). An investigation into the application of neural networks, fuzzy logic, genetic algorithms, and rough sets to automated knowledge acquisition for classification problems. *Neurocomputing, 24,* 37−54. Available from: http://dx.doi.org/10.1016/S0925-2312(98)00090-3.

Jain, A. K., Mao, J., & Mohiuddin, K. M. (1996). Artificial neural networks: A tutorial. *IEEE Computer Society Press, 29*(3), 31−44.

Kandalaft, M. R., Didehbani, N., Krawczyk, D. C., Allen, T., & Chapman, S. B. (2013). Virtual reality social skills training for young adults with high-functioning Autism. *Journal of Autism and Developmental Disorders, 43,* 34−44.

Krijn, M., Emmelkamp, P. M., Olafsson, R. P., & Biemond, R. (2004). Virtual reality expo-sure therapy of anxiety disorders: A review. *Clinical Psychology Review, 24*(3), 259–281.

Kurzweil, R. (2005). *The singularity is near: When humans transcend biology.* New York: Viking Penguin.

Lingley, R., Ali, M., Liao, Y., Mirjalili, R., Klonner, M., Sopanen, M., et al. (2011). A single-pixel wireless contact lens display. *Journal of Micromechanics and Microengineering, 21*, 125014. Available from: http://dx.doi.org/10.1088/0960-1317/21/12/125014.

Lowell, W. E., & Davis, G. E. (1994). Predicting length of stay for psychiatric diagnosis-related groups using neural networks. *Journal of the American Medical Informatics Association: JAMIA, 1*, 459–466.

Lucas, G. M., Gratch, J., King, A., & Morency, L. P. (2014). It's only a computer: Virtual humans increase willingness to disclose. *Computers in Human Behavior, 37*, 94–100.

Luxton, D. D. (2014a). Artificial intelligence in psychological practice: Current and future applications and implications. *Professional Psychology: Research & Practice, 45*(5), 332–339. Available from: http://dx.doi.org/10.1037/a0034559.

Luxton, D. D. (2014b). Recommendations for the ethical use and design of artificial intel-ligent care providers. *Artificial Intelligence in Medicine, 62*(1), 1–10. Available from: http://dx.doi.org/10.1016/j.artmed.2014.06.004.

Manning, C., & Schütze, H. (1999). *Foundations of statistical natural language processing.* Cambridge, MA: MIT Press.

Markoff, J. (2011). *Armies of expensive lawyers, replaced by cheaper software.* The New York Times. Retrieved from: <http://www.nytimes.com/2011/03/05/science/05legal.html>.

Markoff, J. (2013, February 18). Obama seeking to boost study of human brain. The New York Times. Retrieved from: <http://www.nytimes.com/ 2013/02/18/ science/project-seeks-to-build-map-of-human-brain.html? >.

McCarthy, J., Minsky, M., Rochester, N., Shannon, C. (1955). *A proposal for the dartmouth summer research project on artificial intelligence.* Available from: <http://www-formal.stanford.edu/jmc/history/dartmouth/dartmouth.html>. Retrieved 16.10.14.

McDuff, D., Kaliouby, R., Kodra, E., & Picard, R. W. (2013). Measuring voter's candi-date preference based on affective responses to election debates. In *Proceedings of the 5th biannual humaine association conference on affective computing and intelligent interaction* (ACII 2013), pp. 2–5.

McFowland, E., III, Speakman, S., & Neill, D. B. (2013). Fast generalized subset scan for anomalous pattern detection. *Journal of Machine Learning Research, 14*, 1533–1561.

McShane, M., Beale, S., Nirenburg, S., Jarrell, B., & Fantry, G. (2012). Inconsistency as a diagnostic tool in a society of intelligent agents. *Artificial Intelligence in Medicine, 55*, 137–148. Available from: http://dx.doi.org/10.1016/j.artmed.2012.04.005.

Merikangas, K. R., He, J. P., Burstein, M., Swendsen, J., Avenevoli, S., Case, B., et al. (2011). Service utilization for lifetime mental disorders in U.S. adolescents: Results of the National Comorbidity SurveyAdolescent Supplement (NCS-A). *Journal of the American Academy of Child & Adolescent Psychiatry, 50*(1), 32.

Microsoft. (2015). XBOX. <http://www.xbox.com/>.

Mirabzadeh, A., Bakhshi, E., Khodae, M. R., Kooshesh, M. R., Mahabadi, B. R., Mirabzadeh, H., et al. (2013). Cost prediction of antipsychotic medication of psychi-atric disorder using artificial neural network model. *Journal of Research in Medical Sciences, 18*(9), 782–785.

Mitchell, T. M. (1997). *Machine learning.* Burr Ridge, IL: McGraw Hill. p. 45.

Modha, D. S. (2015). *Introducing a Brain-inspired computer: TrueNorth's neurons to revolutionize system architecture.* Available from: <http://www.research.ibm.com/articles/brain-chip.shtml>.

Moore, G. E. (1965). Cramming more components onto integrated circuits. *Electronics*, *38*, 114−116. Available from: http://dx.doi.org/10.1109/N-SSC.2006.4785860.

Moravec, H. (1988). *Mind Children: The future of robot and human intelligence*. Cambridge, MA: Harvard University Press.

Naam, R. (2010). *More than human: Embracing the promise of biological enhancement*. New York, NY: Broadway Books.

National Institutes of Health. (2014). *BRAIN 2025: A scientific vision*. Retrieved from: <http://www.braininitiative.nih.gov/2025/BRAIN2025.pdf>.

Naumann, J. (2012). *Search for paradise: A patient's account of the artificial vision experiment*. Xlibris Corporation.

Neild, B. (2012, October 12). Scientists to simulate human brain inside a supercomputer. CNN Labs. Retrieved from: <http://www.cnn.com/2012/10/12/tech/human-brain-computer>.

Neill, D. B. (2012). Fast subset scan for spatial pattern detection. *Journal of the Royal Statistical Society (Series B: Statistical Methodology)*, *74*(2), 337−360.

Newell, S., & Simon, H. A. (1956). *The logic theory machine: A complex information processing system*. Santa Monica, CA: The Rand Corporation.

Parsons, S., & Mitchell, P. (2002). The potential of virtual reality in social skills training for people with autistic spectrum disorders. *Journal of Intellectual Disability Research: JIDR*, *46*(Pt 5), 430−443.

Picard, R. (1997). *Affective computing*. Cambridge, MA: MIT Press.

Powers, M. B., & Emmelkamp, P. M. (2008). Virtual reality exposure therapy for anxiety disorders: A meta-analysis. *Journal of Anxiety Disorders*, *22*(3), 561−569.

Rawlinson, K. (2015). *Microsoft's Bill Gates insists AI is a threat*. BBC News. Available from: <http://www.bbc.com/news/31047780>.

Riva, G. (2005). Virtual reality in psychotherapy: Review. *CyberPsychology & Behavior*, *8*(3), 220−230.

Rizzo, A. A., Buckwalter, J. G., & Neumann, U. (1997). Virtual reality and cognitive rehabilitation: A brief review of the future. *The Journal of Head Trauma Rehabilitation*, *12*(6), 1−15.

Rizzo, A. A., Lange, B., Buckwalter, J. G., Forbell, E., Kim, J., Sagae, K., et al. (2011). An intelligent virtual human system for providing healthcare information and support. *Studies in Health Technology and Informatics*, *163*, 503−509.

Rogers, C. (1959) A theory of therapy, personality and interpersonal relationships as developed in the client-centered framework. In S. Koch (Ed.), *Psychology: A study of a science. Vol. 3, formulations of the person and the social context* (pp. 184−256). New York, NY: McGraw Hill.

Salomoni, G., Grassi, M., Mosini, P., Riva, P., Cavedini, P., & Bellodi, L. (2009). Artificial neural network model for the prediction of obsessive-compulsive disorder treatment response. *Journal of clinical psychopharmacology*, *29*(4), 343−349.

Samuel, A. L. (2000). Some studies in machine learning using the game of checkers. *IBM Journal of Research and Development*, *44*(1.2.), 206−226.

Saxena, A., Jain, A., Sener, O., Jami, A., Misra, D. K., & Koppula, H. S. (2014). RoboBrain: Large-scale knowledge engine for robots. *arXiv preprint arXiv:1412.0691*.

Saygin, A. P., Cicekli, I., & Akman, V. (2000). Turing test: 50 years later. *Minds and Machines*, *10*, 463−518.

Schultheis, M. T., & Rizzo, A. A. (2001). The application of virtual reality technology in rehabilitation. *Rehabilitation Psychology*, *46*(3), 296.

Searle, J. (1980). Minds, brains and programs. *Behavioral and Brain Sciences*, *3*(3), 417−457. Available from: http://dx.doi.org/10.1017/S0140525X00005756.

Shibata, T., & Wada, K. (2011). Robot therapy: A new approach for mental healthcare of the elderly − a mini-review. *Gerontology*, *57*(4), 378−386.

Shieber, S. M. (2006). Does the turing test demonstrate intelligence or not? In *Proceedings of the twenty-first national conference on artificial intelligence (AAAI-06)*, Boston, MA, 16−20 July.

Shuhaiber, J. H. (2004). Augmented reality in surgery. *Archives of Surgery, 139*(2), 170−174.

Substance Abuse and Mental Health Services Administration. (2013). *Behavioral health, United States, 2012*. HHS Publication No. (SMA) 13-4797. Rockville, MD: Substance Abuse and Mental Health Services Administration. Available at: <http://www.in.gov/cji/files/G_US_Behavioral_Health_2012.pdf>.

Substance Abuse and Mental Health Services Administration. (2014). Use of behavioral health services is expected to increase under the Affordable Care Act. *The CBHSQ Report*. Retrieved from: <http://www.samhsa.gov/data/sites/default/files/spot139-ACA-behavioral-health-2014.pdf>.

Teuscher, C., & Hofstadter, D. R. (2006). *Alan Turing: Life and legacy of a great thinker*. New York, NY: Springer.

Turing, A. M. (1950). Computing machinery and intelligence. *Mind*, 433−460.

Velik, R. (2012). AI reloaded: Objectives, potentials, and challenges of the novel field of brain-like artificial intelligence. *BRAIN. Broad Research in Artificial Intelligence and Neuroscience, 3*(3), 25−54.

Viirre, E., Pryor, H., Nagata, S., & Furness, T. A., 3rd (1998). The virtual retinal display: A new technology for virtual reality and augmented vision in medicine. *Studies in Health Technology and Informatics, 50*, 252−257.

Vinge, V. (1993). *The coming technological singularity: How to survive in the post-human era*. Retrieved from: <http://www-rohan.sdsu.edu/faculty/vinge/misc/singularity.html>.

von Neumann, J. (2012). *The computer and the brain (The Silliman Memorial Lectures Series)*. New Haven, CT: Yale University Press.

Warwick, K. (2012). *Artificial intelligence: The basics*. New York: Routledge.

Weizenbaum, J. (1976). *Computer power and human reason: From judgment to calculation*. San Francisco, CA: W. H. Freeman.

Williams, N. R., & Okun, M. S. (2013). Deep brain stimulation (DBS) at the interface of neurology and psychiatry. *Journal of Clinical Investigation, 123*(11), 4546−4556. Available from: http://dx.doi.org/10.1172/JCI68341.

Wolpaw, J. R., Birbaumer, N., McFarland, D. J., Pfurtscheller, G., & Vaughan, T. M. (2002). Brain-computer interfaces for communication and control. *Clinical Neurophysiology, 113*, 767−791. Available from: http://dx.doi.org/10.1016/S1388-2457(02)00057-3.

World Health Organization (2008). *The global burden of disease: 2004 update*. Geneva: WHO.

World Health Organization (2011). *Global status report on non-communicable diseases 2010*. Geneva: WHO.

Zadeh, L. A. (1965). Fuzzy sets. *Information and Control, 8*(3), 338−353. Available from: http://dx.doi.org/10.1016/S0019-9958(65)90241-X.

Zhu, E., Hadadgar, A., Masiello, I., & Zary, N. (2014). Augmented reality in healthcare education: An integrative review. *Peer Journal, 2*, e469. Available from: http://dx.doi.org/10.7717/peerj.469.

ADDITIONAL RESOURCES

Affective Computing: Theory, Methods, and Applications by Eva Hudlicka, published by Chapman and Hall (2013).

Artificial Intelligence: A Modern Approach (3rd Edition) by Stuart Russell and Peter Norvig, published by Pearson Education Limited, Essex.

Artificial Intelligence: The Basics by Kevin Warwick published by Routledge (2011).

Brain-Computer-Interfaces in Their Ethical, Social and Cultural Contexts by Gerd Grübler & Elisabeth Hildt, published by Springer (2014).

Foundations of Statistical Natural Language Processing. Chris Manning and Hinrich Schütze, Cambridge, MA: MIT Press (1999).

Intelligence: A Very Short Introduction by Ian J. Deary, published by Oxford Paperbacks (2001).

Machine Ethics by Michael Anderson & Susan Leigh Anderson, published by Cambridge University Press (2011).

Machine Learning by Thomas M. Mitchell, published by McGraw Hill (1997).

Neural Networks and Learning Machines by S. Haykin, published by Pearson Education (2008).

The Oxford Handbook of Affective Computing edited by Rafael A. Calvo, Sidney D'Mello, Jonathan Gratch, and Arvid Kappas, published by Oxford Library of Psychology − Oxford University Press (2015).

CHAPTER 2

Expert Systems in Mental Health Care: AI Applications in Decision-Making and Consultation

Casey C. Bennett[1,2] and Thomas W. Doub[2]
[1]School of Informatics and Computing, Indiana University, Bloomington, IN, USA
[2]Department of Informatics, Centerstone Research Institute, Nashville, TN, USA

INTRODUCTION

Across real-world scenarios — clinical ones included — perceptions (e.g., observations) and actions (e.g., treatments) are structured in a circular fashion (Merleau-Ponty, 1945). The actions we take change what we perceive in the future, and in turn those perceptions may alter the future actions we take (isomorphic to changes in the human visual system due to movement in the world (Gibson, 1979)). There is *information* inherent in this dynamical process. As humans we leverage this fact every day to act "intelligently" in our environment. We think about problems in a temporally extended fashion, whether it be during treatment of a patient or making a left turn in our car. For instance, when driving a car we don't simply decide to make a left turn and then do it. Rather, there is constant perceptual feedback (e.g., if a pedestrian suddenly appears in the crosswalk, we adjust our actions). This alters further perceptions; we may alter our turning radius to avoid said pedestrian, which results in finding a fire hydrant directly in our path. Given the probability of such a sequence (e.g., how busy the pedestrian traffic is at the crosswalk), we may choose not to turn at the intersection at all, or find an alternate route. The point is that our actions lead to certain perceptions that we use to make decisions. The same is true for clinical decision-making. We are not merely passive observers of "data" — data is a process of interaction. Should not our clinical computing tools approximate the same process? If we want tools to enhance our cognition and/or improve our decision-making, those tools need to fit the way we think about the world. In other words, they should provide a sort of *cognitive scaffolding* that enables people to do what they do better (Clark, 2004, 2013; Sterelny, 2007).

Artificial Intelligence in Behavioral and Mental Health Care.
DOI: http://dx.doi.org/10.1016/B978-0-12-420248-1.00002-7

In this chapter, we describe emerging approaches for doing exactly that, i.e., temporal modeling. Such approaches are ripe for application to health care, where treatment decisions must be made over time, and where continually reevaluating ongoing treatment is critical to optimizing clinical care for individual patients. This is especially true for chronic health conditions, such as mental illness, which forms the bulk of healthcare expenditures in the United States (Orszag & Ellis, 2007). Clinicians do not just make decisions and move forward — rather they are constantly reevaluating those decisions, titrating medications, adjusting treatments, making new observations. It is a very dynamic process, both in terms of the treatment being delivered as well as the cognitive processes of the clinician and patient (e.g., how they integrate information into their decision-making over time (Patel, Kaufman, & Arocha, 2002)). This represents a major obstacle, because currently much of the focus of AI and clinical decision support systems (CDSS) in healthcare is on making a single recommendation at a single timepoint. But that is not how health care really works.

This chapter is laid out as follows. "The History — Expert Systems and Clinical Artificial Intelligence in Health Care" provides a brief history of AI, expert systems, and CDSS in physical and mental healthcare. The successes and failures of such efforts lead into "The Present — Dynamical Approaches to Clinical AI and Expert Systems," where we discuss current research around artificial intelligence in healthcare, including dynamical approaches that explicitly incorporate time. In "The Future," we expand upon this current work to detail future directions around how such approaches can integrate into the broader healthcare space, for example, cognitive computing, smart homes, cyborg clinicians, and robotics. We conclude with a discussion of what this all may mean for the future of health care, mental health, and clinicians and patients alike. AI is a term often loosely applied, with "intelligence" being more of a romantic notion than a precise descriptor (Brooks, 1991). But all is not lost. The aim of this chapter is to help readers understand where we have been, where we are, and where we are going in our ongoing quest to put "intelligence" into AI, for clinical applications and beyond.

THE HISTORY — EXPERT SYSTEMS AND CLINICAL ARTIFICIAL INTELLIGENCE IN HEALTH CARE

Efforts to develop AI, both within and outside of health care, have a long history. Some of the earliest successful applications of AI in health care were *expert systems* (Jackson, 1998; Luxton, 2014). An expert system is a

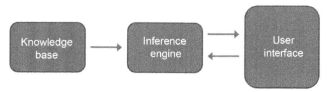

Figure 2.1 Basic outline of an expert system.

computer system that is designed to emulate the decision-making capabilities and performance of human experts. Traditionally, this was done by eliciting a knowledge base of rules from experts (*knowledge base*), from which inference about the present state or future could be performed (*inference engine*) by an end-user (via a *user interface*), as shown in Figure 2.1. The rules often took the form of "if-then", where the "then" component typically comprised a probability. For instance, *if* the patient has symptom *x*, *then* the probability of disease *y* is, say, 0.6. A multitude of such rules could then be used to calculate probabilistic recommendations.

One well-known early example of an expert system in health care was MYCIN, developed in the 1970s at Stanford University. The system was designed to identify bacterial infections and recommend appropriate antibiotic treatment (Shortliffe, 1976). Similar developments were also underway at the same time on the mental health side. For instance, DIAGNO was an early tool for computer-assisted psychiatric diagnosis that was developed at Columbia University in the 1960s and 1970s. It used as input 39 clinical-observation scores processed through a decision tree, resulting in a differential diagnosis. The system achieved comparable performance as human clinicians across a variety of mental disorders (Spitzer & Endicott, 1974), though it was never put to use in real-world practice.

Subsequent years saw the inclusion of expert systems into many CDSS. Decision support, as the name implies, refers to providing information to clinicians, typically at the point of decision-making (Osheroff et al., 2007). However, we should be careful to point out that not all CDSS tools are necessarily expert systems or AI — many are simply hard-coded rules that trigger alerts or messages, containing neither probabilistic rules nor inferential reasoning. Nonetheless, some CDSS tools do embody principles of expert systems. One recent example in mental health care is the TMAP project from UT-Southwestern Medical School for computer-assisted depression medication treatment (Shelton & Trivedi, 2011; Trivedi et al., 2009; Trivedi, Kern, Grannemann, Altshuler, & Sunderajan, 2004). The system used algorithms to suggest appropriate changes to medications and/or dosing via electronic health record systems. It worked well in research studies, though it faced various implementation challenges in practice (see "Ethics and Challenges" section below).

CDSS tools — both those based on expert system models and otherwise — have had a mixed history of success (Garg et al., 2005; Jaspers, Smeulers, Vermeulen, & Peute, 2011; Kawamoto, Houlihan, Balas, & Lobach, 2005). Many are based on evidence-based guidelines (typically derived from expert opinion or statistical averages) that prescribe a one-size-fits-all treatment regimen for every patient, or a standardized sequence of treatment options (Bauer, 2002; Bennett, Doub, & Selove, 2012; Green, 2008). However, real-world patients display individualized characteristics and symptoms that impact treatment effectiveness. As such, clinicians quickly learn to ignore recommendations that say the same or similar things for every patient. Practicing clinicians are also keenly aware that treatments that have been shown to be highly effective in clinical trial and research populations are not always directly transferable to individuals in real-world settings (Bennett et al., 2012; Green, 2008). Moreover, such evidence-based guidelines are often out-of-date by the time they reach the frontlines (Bauer, 2002).

Traditional expert systems and CDSS suffer from a *knowledge engineering* problem: the challenge of creating and maintaining a knowledge base of rules. Many of the issues raised in the preceding paragraphs are at least partially due to the need to simplify the creation/maintenance process. No matter how many rules you create, there are always some exceptions, leading to the necessity for more rules. The problem is one of infinite regress. How does one represent the *absolute* state of the world without infinite rules? This mirrors challenges in other application areas of AI (see below).

More recent attempts at using AI in health care have moved beyond the knowledge base of rules for probabilistic inference, incorporating sophisticated machine-learning algorithms — neural networks, random forests, support vector machines, natural language processing, and other techniques — often in combination to perform more *data-driven* probabilistic inference (Bellazzi & Zupan, 2008). IBM's Watson is an example of this and is currently being applied to certain healthcare problems like cancer, as well as being explored for utilization management purposes (Ferrucci, Levas, Bagchi, Gondek, & Mueller, 2013). These newer forms of AI encapsulate many of the principles of earlier expert systems, but do so in a more flexible and individualized way. For instance, these AI approaches can "learn" from the clinical data. Some of them can even evaluate the accuracy of their predictions/recommendations and further "learn" from their mistakes (Bennett & Doub, 2010; Bennett et al., 2011, 2012). Systems such as these can discover patterns that not even human experts may be aware of, and they can do so in an automated fashion. The turnaround time for new knowledge can shrink to a matter of days or weeks, rather than years. The approach is two-pronged — both developing new knowledge about effective clinical practices as well as modifying existing knowledge and evidence-based models to fit real-world settings (Bennett & Doub, 2010).

More broadly, AI has seen similar shifts in thinking — from the heydays of computationalist good-old fashioned AI (GOFAI), where the "mind = computer" and search algorithms predominated, through the emergence of systems-thinking in cybernetics, autopoiesis, and connectionism, to the modern methodological pluralism of embodied/situated/dynamical artificial intelligence, enaction, and machine-learning approaches (Beer, 2000; Brooks, 1991). Underlying these shifts were the continual shortcomings of algorithms and systems to exhibit the specificity and adaptivity seen in natural intelligence. In other words, artificially intelligent systems need to be both skillful (specificity) and flexible (adaptivity) in order to make sense of the world and interact with it intelligently (the same could be argued for evidence-based medicine protocols, see Green (2008)). For example, a well-performing chess AI based on traditional search and planning cannot cope if the rules of the game shift, i.e., what applies in one context may not apply in another (Brooks, 1991). Its utility is limited to an extremely narrow band of the world, and only a static world at that. It may be skillful, but lacks flexibility. Such flexibility comes from an understanding that the world changes over time — it is dynamic. More recent views of AI see this not as a problem, but as an opportunity. We can take advantage of those dynamics by learning the structure of them (Beer, 2000).

In similar fashion, the clinical process is a dynamical one that plays out over time. While moving away from traditional rules-based AI in health care has been a significant step forward, it still omits critical temporal aspects of clinical care. The decisions we make in a clinical setting, and the consequent actions (i.e., treatments), affect the future patient state (i.e., observations). The decisions *change* the world, and in doing so *constrain* future decisions we might make. There is information inherent in that dynamical process. But how do we leverage it?

THE PRESENT — DYNAMICAL APPROACHES TO CLINICAL AI AND EXPERT SYSTEMS

Temporal Modeling Overview

A multitude of computational approaches exist for determining optimal clinical decisions (e.g., most effective treatment) at a single timepoint, from traditional statistical methods to data-mining/machine-learning methods (Bellazzi & Zupan, 2008; Bennett & Doub, 2010; Boulesteix, Porzelius, & Daumer, 2008). We discussed some of these in the previous section. Leveraging dynamical information is simply an extension of these methods across multiple decision timepoints (i.e., sequential decision-making). In other words, *temporal modeling*. In fact, the predictions/probabilities of single-decision timepoint models can be utilized in tandem with multiple timepoint temporal models in order to provide individualized predictions, i.e., personalized medicine (see "Multi-Agent Models for Personalized Medicine" section).

Research has shown the potential for using temporal modeling, such as Markovian models (Alagoz, Hsu, Schaefer, & Roberts, 2010; Beck & Pauker, 1983), temporal data mining (Bellazzi, Larizza, Magni, & Bellazzi, 2005), and reinforcement learning (Shortreed et al., 2011; Zhao, Kosorok, & Zeng, 2009), as a tool for understanding patterns of clinical change in patients over time in the healthcare domain (Hauskrecht & Fraser, 2000; Shechter, Bailey, Schaefer, & Roberts, 2008). Such modeling can facilitate treatment planning and enhance clinical decision-making, which has potential implications for providing more sophisticated clinical decision support tools, both to patients and providers (Chakraborty & Murphy, 2014; Patel et al., 2009). The challenge is figuring out how that fits into the real-world clinical process.

Real-World Clinical Applications — Predicting in a Dynamic World

In previous work, we have shown empirically — using real-world clinical data — that combining particular temporal modeling techniques (Markov decision processes and dynamic decision networks, see below) can approximate human decision-making in a clinical realm (Bennett & Hauser, 2013). The result is a non-disease-specific computational *AI framework* that simulates the decision-making process in clinical care. This serves two potential functions: (i) a simulation environment for exploring various healthcare policies, payment methodologies, etc., and (ii) the basis for clinical AI — an AI that can "think like a doctor".

The framework was evaluated by using real patient data from the electronic health records of nearly 6000 patients. These patients were largely comprised of individuals with co-occurring mental and physical illness — primarily clinical depression and chronic physical disorders including hypertension, diabetes, chronic pain, and cardiovascular disease. Therefore, they were characteristic of the Medicaid/Medicare population in the United States (suffering from co-occurring chronic illnesses), though the actual payer mix was varied. Functioning outcomes, rather than specific symptomology outcomes, were utilized. Such outcomes track the patients' improvement/deterioration in functioning in daily life, a critical aspect in treatment of chronic illness where a "cure" is often not available. More importantly, outcomes were converted into a relative measure of cost-effectiveness (CPUC, cost per unit change) of treatment and then calculated as deltas (change over time) rather than absolute values. In other words, it is not the specific absolute values of some clinical observation or outcome (e.g., a patient's current OGTT glucose reading) that we are focused upon, but rather the *change over time* in these values. The use of such relative measures (CPUC) allows us to substitute any outcome or clinical measure for any disease, e.g., blood pressure, cancer metastasis stage, hospitalization days, quality-adjusted life years (QALYs). This enables the AI framework to be non-disease-specific (see Section 2.1 in Bennett & Hauser, 2013). The results showed that such an approach capable of producing a nearly 50% increase in outcomes for roughly half the costs over current treatment-as-usual approaches to health care (Figure 2.2).

We emphasize that Figure 2.2 is not necessarily an indictment of clinicians, who (at least in the United States) are incentivized for providing service volume, not necessarily for improving outcomes. Figure 2.2 is more of an indictment of the system — we can do better than our current fee-for-service or capacitation models of health care. Approaches, such as the one here, can help facilitate that.

As we mentioned above, the AI framework utilizes an approach combining partially observable Markov decision processes (POMDPs) and dynamic decision networks (DDNs) into a multiagent system (MAS) that simulates alternative possible future trajectories and reasons over beliefs, functioning as an online agent that continually reevaluates its choices and plans given new information (Bennett & Hauser, 2013). The critical point is that perceptions (observations) and actions (treatments) in the clinical scenario are structured in a linked, circular fashion over time, which relates to outcomes and costs at any given time (Figure 2.3). The

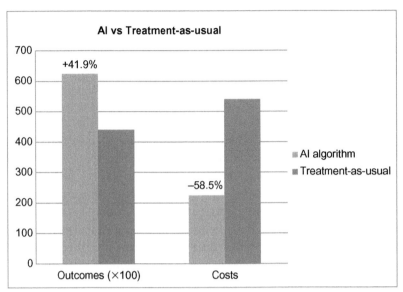

Figure 2.2 AI vs treatment-as-usual (Bennett & Hauser, 2013).

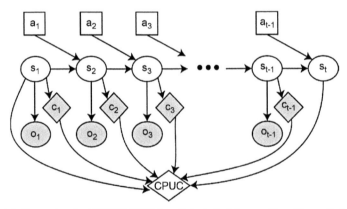

Figure 2.3 Example of a POMDP/DDN for clinical decision-making (Bennett & Hauser, 2013). a = action (treatment), s = state (patient health status), o = observations (clinical observations), c = costs (of treatment), CPUC = cost per unit change (of some outcome measure, i.e., a measure of cost-effectiveness of treatment). Subscripts are timepoints.

actions we take change what we perceive in the future, in the same way that perceptions may change the actions we take (isomorphic to changes in the human visual system due to movement in the world (Gibson, 1979)). In other words, *perceptual feedback*. There is information in that structure — information in the *relative* difference (i.e., deltas) between timepoints in Figure 2.3, whether discrete or continuous, that we can leverage to simplify the problem of operating optimally in the world, without necessarily having an *absolute* representation of the problem.

An obvious example of such deltas is clinical outcome measures, which change over time, particularly for chronic illnesses, both physical and mental. These can be symptomology measures (e.g., blood glucose reading, depression scales) or functional measures of the patient's ability to engage in normal daily activities (e.g., quality-of-life). The point is that it is the *change* in these values between timepoints, not their absolute values, that are of fundamental importance.

The deltas can be taken as representative of a *relative* state, as opposed to an *absolute* state (Bennett & Hauser, 2013). The relative states form the basis of recognizing the current situation as well as prediction of the future. As such (and in contrast to absolute states), there is a recursive nature inherent to their structure. Each prediction (e.g., $time_2$) is based on some delta (e.g., $time_1 - time_0$), which in turn generates behavior that leads to new deltas, both on the original single time-step timescale ($time_2 - time_1$) and recursive timescales ($time_2 - time_0$), similar to predictive state representations (Wingate, 2012). In other words, inherent in the process of prediction in this manner is the construction of relationships between the deltas on multiple timescales, deltas which represent the effects of actions and sequences of actions (on, e.g., patient outcomes and treatment costs) (Keijzer, 1998; Warren, 2006). In fact, it becomes a generative process. The "meaning" of one delta (e.g., change in some outcome variable) is emergent in the process of both *acting* and *predicting* in the world (Barsalou, Breazeal, & Smith, 2007; De Jaegher & Di Paolo, 2007).

The goal here is to build clinical AI tools that derive meaning from the data in a fashion similar to humans, rather than try to "program" solutions through brute force. Meaning is bound up in the relativity — a relativity based on the differences between things (or timepoints, see "Cognitive Computing" section below).

This has a number of implications both from a clinical standpoint and/or for creating CDSS tools. First, to reiterate from previous sections, one issue here is that providing data in the form of, say, a line graph, is limited in its helpfulness. A line graph informs you about trends, but it doesn't necessarily tell you *what to do*. In contrast, the human cognitive process is an interactive one over time, a dynamic intertwining of perception (i.e., data) and action. Our clinical computing tools should mirror that. Second, approaches like the one described here operate in the space of *belief states*. The patient's "state" (e.g., health status) in Figure 2.3 does not have to be definite. It is okay if an exact diagnosis is difficult to pin down, or if some clinical observations are missing or uncertain. Operating in the space of belief states affords us the possibility to deal with a world that is not black-and-white. Third, the approach described here is an *online* AI, which means that it is continually planning and re-planning as actions are performed and new observations are obtained. It is not simply making a treatment recommendation at a single point in time (e.g., intake), but rather constantly adjusting predictions of optimal treatment plans as evidence/data change. Moreover, it can learn from clinical data as it goes — the success/failure of its predictions — in order to make better predictions in the future (Bennett et al., 2012; Bennett & Hauser, 2013).

We emphasize here that it is *not* our specific framework, implementation, or technology that is key. What is fundamental are the *principles* that it encompasses: an ability to reason over time, to deal with uncertainty, and to learn. The goal is to develop technology that approximates our cognitive processes, so that we can do what we do better and/or focus on other tasks such as providing clinical care (rather than calculating probabilities of treatment success in our head). More broadly, such technology holds potential be a boon for understanding/simulating clinical treatment decisions, e.g., health policy research and comparative effectiveness research (Bennett & Doub, 2014; Rogers, 2013).

Multi-Agent Models for Personalized Medicine

In actual implementation, the framework described in the previous section operates as a MAS (Bennett & Hauser, 2013). This can be seen in Figure 2.4. The agents (e.g., Doctor, Patient) can be seen on the left. These can be thought of as *digital avatars* of their real-world counterparts in a sense, taking on the various characteristics of real individual patients and clinicians (shown within each box). There might exist hundreds or thousands of instances of each type of agent, one for each real-world individual it represents. Various other aspects and processes of the model can be seen to the right of the agents, which can be loosely grouped into three stages of the AI framework that occur at every timepoint. These reflect particular stages of the clinical process, e.g., evidence-gathering and decision-making.

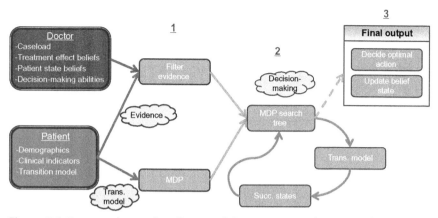

Figure 2.4 Framework overview (Bennett & Hauser, 2013). The types of agents are shown in double-line borders. The other boxes represent various aspects of the model. The general flow is: (1) create patient-specific MDPs/physician agent filters evidence into existing beliefs, (2) recurse through MDP search tree to determine optimal action, and (3) perform treatment action and update belief states.

What we emphasize here is that — in actual implementation (as a MAS) — the treatment recommendations for each patient are individualized, based on their characteristics. Moreover, variable clinician characteristics and preferences can also be captured. Every patient is different, every clinician as well. It is not a matter of simply relying on one-size-fits-all statistical averages. The key here is building *personalized transition models* for each patient, which capture likely changes over time from *sequences* of actions. This can be accomplished by constructing the probabilities of the transition model from patient-specific output probabilities of single timepoint data-mining models — e.g., neural network or support vector machine trained to classify, say, a group of patients into "likely-to-respond-to-treatment-X" and "likely-to-respond-to-treatment-Y", based on their probability of response (Bennett & Doub, 2014). In other words, we can base the probabilities of how we expect each patient to change over time on their unique genetic, clinical, and/or sociodemographic characteristics. Such an approach holds potential to provide a technical infrastructure for delivering *personalized medicine* in practice.

TECHNOLOGY-ENHANCED CLINICIANS

We should stress at this point that the overarching goal of research along these lines is not necessarily to replace human clinicians, but rather to help make them more effective. In his most recent book, Eric Topol argues for such *technology-enhanced clinicians*, the next-generation doctors of the future who function as information arbiters in the digital age of health care, a consequence of the ongoing "creative destruction of medicine" (Topol, 2012). The challenge of the future will likely be one of information overload, as data arrive from a multitude of sources (including potentially from sensors embedded within our own bodies, see "The Intersection Between Other Emerging Technologies and Clinical AI" section of this chapter). The question will be what to pay attention to, what to ignore, and how to make sense of it all. Clinicians of the future will likely fill that void. In some sense, it is not that different from what they do already. The point here is that one of the primary goals of research into clinical AI is to enable clinicians to do what they do better. By building tools that do what they do — that think the way they think — we allow them to offload those cognitive tasks so that they can focus on other things, such as delivering actual patient care. In that sense, one could envision clinicians of the future as sort of "clinician cyborgs." In fact, one could argue that they already sort of are (Clark, 2004). We return to this point in the "Conclusion" section.

SUMMARY OF DYNAMICAL APPROACHES FOR CLINICAL AI

The main point of this section is that temporal modeling and/or dynamical approaches to clinical AI better fit with the way we think about the world, and the challenges we face in decision-making. They leverage the information inherent in the dynamical process of perception (observation) and action (treatment). Recent research has shown empirically that such approaches can outperform current models of health care, providing a nearly 50% increase in outcomes for roughly half the costs (Bennett & Hauser, 2013). More broadly, temporal modeling can build upon existing single-decision time-point models. Research over the last couple of decades has shown that single-decision timepoint modeling (e.g., data mining) can be effective in variety of healthcare settings — from cancer to mental health — both our own work (Bennett & Doub, 2010; Bennett et al., 2011) and that of others (Bellazzi & Zupan, 2008; Boulesteix et al., 2008). Temporal modeling can be seen as a natural extension to these tremendous advances in data-mining over the last 20 years, and provide a practical method and technical infrastructure for delivering personalized medicine.

The academic literature is rife with arguments debating the comparative performance of particular methods in various clinical domains (e.g., debating whether neural networks or random forests or statistical relational learning are the "best"), and certainly producing better algorithms is a worthwhile goal (Demšar, 2006). However, such arguments miss the point from a practical front, and obfuscate an important discussion. If we can make predictions (regardless of the algorithm we choose) about the future, then those predicted probabilities can form the basis of our understanding of how the world changes over time. *And understanding how the world changes over time is the key to performing optimally in it.* Without doubt, the overarching goal here is not necessarily to replace the clinician, but to maximize the potential of both human and machine.

THE FUTURE

Cognitive Computing in Health Care

An exciting front in healthcare technology and clinical decision-making is that of *cognitive computing*. In its simplest form, it resembles many of the ideas that we have discussed throughout this chapter — re-conceptualizing our computing tools as a form of cognitive scaffolding to provide better synergy with the way our brains already interact with the environment (Bennett & Doub, 2014; Modha et al., 2011), both in terms of hardware and how we program it (Esser et al., 2013). At a basic level, this is what notepads and calculators already do, but in a limited way. They have little to no capacity to derive "meaning" or learn from what they do. They are thus limited in their roles as sidekicks in our quest for better understanding of our world, its mysteries, and their solutions. However, AI and temporal modeling approaches hold promise to extend this.

Temporal dynamics focus on the change of things over time. A legitimate question to more traditional viewpoints of cognition is that — if we can define everything we perceive in terms of deltas (i.e., change over time) — then what is it that "we know"? Is it relevant to describe absolute knowledge, or is all knowledge relative? A contrast of things, rather than an absolute definition. This certainly aligns with neuroscience research revealing that people use polar opposites to identify faces or determine emotions in others (Anastasi & Rhodes, 2005). Or lateral inhibition in the human visual system (Blakemore, Carpenter, & Georgeson, 1970). Perhaps it is not that we necessarily "know" anything, but that we know the difference between things. In fact, one could argue that such a view links basic sensorimotor coordination and/or embodied cognition with higher cognition and abstract thought (Clark, 2013). If our movements/actions in the world are guided by perceptual feedback that makes use of predictions about how the perceived world will change over time based on the actions we perform, then what matters principally is the relative difference (i.e., deltas) between the two timepoints. If we extend this notion to two objects in the world, abstract or concrete, then is it not the same principle at some fundamental level (Botvinick, 2012)? Things are defined as much by what they *are not*, as by what they *are*.

A more concrete example might help illustrate this point. For example, in population genetics, a group or population is defined as a subset of a species within the same geographical area that have a greater probability of interbreeding with each other than individuals from other populations. This *population structure* underlies group selection and serves as an important cog in the evolutionary machinery (Wade & McCauley, 1988). The fundamental principle here is that an individual is defined not just by its closeness to other members of a group, but also by its distance from individuals outside the group. Without both components, there is no population structure, even though there may be some pattern in the distribution of the individuals. The trajectory of evolution is affected by this *relative* difference between things. Coalescing to some adaptive state for a given environment at a given point in time leverages those differences, for example, balancing them out through gene flow (migration) or emphasizing them when necessary (genetic drift/selection). Focusing solely on "what things are", for example, some absolute features that identify group membership, misses fundamental aspects of what is occurring.

In the same way, a dynamical view argues that cognition utilizes the same principle to coalesce to some cognitive state, whether it be predictive (two timepoints) or categorical (two objects) (Beer, 2000). In a healthcare setting, we face these exact challenges everyday, whether it be distinguishing between possible diagnoses for a particular patient or trying to predict the course of a chronic illness.

This view has significant implications for the design of clinical AI and expert systems moving forward. Traditionally, AI in medicine has been seen as a way to elicit clinical rules from data — culling certain "truths", certain "knowledge", about the world, that can then be applied to act (e.g., make better clinical decisions). However, *such approaches are divorced from the world in which they operate*. Part of the prowess of natural organisms is that they are embedded in their environment, allowing a close alignment of their sensorimotor processes with the problems they are trying to solve (e.g., finding food) (Brooks, 1991). No doubt natural organisms have some sort of embodiment, inhabiting a 3-D world full of particular physical phenomena, such as light and sound waves, that demand certain forms of interaction. The clinical "environment" is one of different perceptual phenomena, but no less rich in sensory information — radiographic images, electrocardiogram (ECG) monitor data, blood glucose readings, depression outcome measures, etc. Similar to natural organisms, if we design a clinical AI to operate in a way such that its actions (treatment decisions) effect changes in future perceptions (clinical observations) — i.e., *perceptual feedback* (see "Real-World Clinical Applications" section) — then its environmental interaction becomes entangled with its own "being" in the world. Its success (existence and survival) becomes isomorphic to the healthcare problem we are trying to solve. Indeed, if we embed a clinical AI into the clinical decision-making process in the right way, making the clinical process its environment, its world, then the treatments and observations represent the same dynamical problem as, say, an agent trying to navigate obstacles or find food in any noisy, partially observable, probabilistic environment.

In short, we want to align our AI and CDSS tools with the clinical environment in a similar way that natural organisms are aligned with their environment. Such alignment in a clinical domain comes not in a physical realm of affordances, but in a computational one. The goal is to simplify the design of future clinical AI and expert systems, taking advantage of principles observed in nature and evolution to build smarter systems in a smarter way. This is the real promise of cognitive computing in health care.

The Intersection Between Other Emerging Technologies and Clinical Artificial Intelligence

A number of other emerging technologies hold potential to significantly enhance CDSS, AI/expert systems, and clinical decision-making in the future. This is principally by allowing us to collect data in new ways or new settings (e.g., outside the clinic), which in the past have been difficult to impossible to collect. Several other chapters in this volume provide excellent overviews of some of these technologies in detail, for example, virtual agents for in-home clinical care (Chapter 4) and robotics (Chapter 5). Here, we briefly touch on some of the implications of those technologies for informing AI and CDSS tools in the future.

One of the great challenges in providing clinical care (especially for mental health) is that patients are typically only seen in the clinic once a week or month, or sometimes just a few times a year. The impact of their illness on their day-to-day life occurs beyond the boundaries of those clinical walls, beyond direct clinical observation, and as such we have only a small window with which to peer through and try to understand the patient and their illness. At best, we can ask the patient for verbal reports of the time in between clinical visits, or perhaps try to infer it from clinical observations taken during the clinical visit. The emergence of ubiquitous in-home sensor technologies and/or smart homes, however, may open this window wider (Skubic, Alexander, Popescu, Rantz, & Keller, 2009; Zhou et al., 2009). For instance, sensors deployed in the home can monitor activity levels in individuals with clinical depression (Van Kasteren, Noulas, Englebienne, & Kröse, 2008; Wilson & Atkeson, 2005). Similar technology can monitor nutrition, eating habits, medication adherence, and physiological signals, which allows us to track a patient's day-to-day status in a more holistic way (Ko et al., 2010). Such technology can also facilitate aging-in-place for the elderly (in their own homes), rather than resorting to more expensive nursing home care. These approaches reflect the shift in health care in recent years towards a focus on improving health, rather than solely treating disease (e.g., the recovery-oriented practice in mental health (Davidson, Rowe, Tondora, O'Connell, & Lawless, 2008)).

From a CDSS and/or clinical AI perspective, such in-home sensor technology could provide a boon in terms of relevant temporal data (collected directly, rather than based on patient recall) about the patient, their illness, and the relationship to their functioning in day-to-day life. In chronic illness — where a "cure" is often not available — understanding functioning in daily life is critical to effective treatment (Bennett & Doub, 2014). Data that allow a portal into that aspect *outside* the clinic are thus critical to building better predictive models or CDSS tools, which can then be leveraged *inside* the clinic.

An exciting development towards further developing in-home sensor technologies is the development of in-home robotic technologies. This includes task-oriented service robots (e.g., Roomba) and socially interactive companion robots (e.g., PARO). These robots typically already have an array of sensors in order to perform particular tasks, and those sensors can be leveraged to provide data for clinical decision-making in the same way as smart homes described above. One example of this is PARO (Figure 2.5), an interactive robotic seal intended as a socially assistive

Figure 2.5 PARO — socially assistive robot.

robot (SAR) (Shibata & Wada, 2011). In a number of studies, PARO has been shown to have beneficial therapeutic and social effects in elderly dementia patients in nursing home settings (Šabanović, Bennett, Chang, & Huber, 2013; Wada & Shibata, 2006), including improvements in psychological functioning and stress levels measured through EEG (Wada, Shibata, Musha, & Kimura, 2005) and urine hormone levels (Wada & Shibata, 2006). Currently, we are working on a collaborative project evaluating the potential therapeutic and social effects of PARO in in-home settings, with elderly patients suffering from chronic clinical depression. Chronic depression is an important challenge for independently living older adults, which can lead to a steady decline in the person's mental and physical health followed by institutionalization (i.e., nursing homes). Part of the project is exploring the use of on-board robotic sensors to provide data for improved clinical decision-making and treatment (e.g., via AI/expert systems), and how we might utilize them to sustain independent living among elderly persons.

More directly, robotic technologies are being developed to help understand and potentially treat a number of healthcare issues, particularly cognitive disorders, through interaction with people. One of the predominant examples of this is autism (Scassellati, Admoni, & Matarić, 2012), where various studies have utilized interactive robots to explore aspects such as sensory overload (Dautenhahn et al., 2009) and social engagement deficits (Pioggia et al., 2007). More broadly, robots are being used to assist patients with movement disabilities (Riek & Robinson, 2011) and Alzheimer's (Tapus, Tapus, & Mataric, 2009). These various robots are equipped with an array of sensors, and — similar to above — can potentially deliver a rich

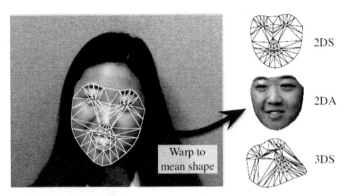

Figure 2.6 Facial expression recognition (Lucey et al., 2006).

source of data back to clinical environments simply through their process of interacting with the patient, allowing us to collect relevant clinical data in a more naturalistic and less intrusive manner (see Chapter 8).

The capacities of these kinds of smart home and robotic technologies are also entailed by the new generation of wearable devices coming to market (Pantelopoulos & Bourbakis, 2010), as well as mobile devices, smartphones, and apps (Luxton, McCann, Bush, Mishkind, & Reger, 2011; see Chapter 6). In the future, such devices may even be embedded inside our bodies, perhaps opening a new frontier in the "quantified self" movement (Topol, 2012).

Finally, there is exciting work in the area of automated facial expression recognition (Cohn, 2010; Pantic, 2009). Researchers have been able to build computer systems that can automatically recognize pain (Littlewort, Bartlett, & Lee, 2007) as well distinguish between patients with and without clinical depression (Cohn et al., 2009), all based on automated evaluation of images of the patient's face (Figure 2.6). These tools could potentially be used in the clinic (e.g., at a check-in kiosk), providing a less onerous way to measure a patient's current status — and thus provide data for clinical AI and/or CDSS — rather than a lengthy outcome measure to fill out.

The point here — from a clinical AI and CDSS standpoint — is that all of these technologies allow us to collect potentially clinically relevant data about a patient's day-to-day health and functioning, much of which was previously unobtainable, and to do so in a more naturalistic, *in situ* manner. Such data allow us a richer view into the temporal dynamics of health and disease, enabling us to construct better clinical computing tools along the lines described in "The Present" section, and — ultimately — to make better clinical decisions.

Ethics and Challenges

There are a number of ethical considerations and challenges with implementing much of the technology we have been addressing throughout this chapter into real-world clinical practice. One important consideration is the embedding of established clinical standards. In essence, this inserts hard-coded rules into the system, holding constant those treatment variables while varying other treatment recommendations around them. For instance, a patient diagnosed with schizophrenia should always be prescribed a certain class of medication, even though other aspects of treatment may vary. Such embedding of clinical standards is a necessity for clinical adoption, as well as ensuring compliance with ethical clinical practices. Fortunately, it is fairly straight-forward to do, by programming hard-coded rules into the system that supersede learned ones if certain conditions are met (Bennett et al., 2012). It is also of critical importance that these clinical computing tools be presented as decision assistants, rather than decision-makers. This is largely a matter of presentation, but also demands certain methodological approaches (e.g., implementation science, participatory design) (Bennett et al., 2011; Šabanović et al., 2014). Similar concerns are related to the design of system interfaces that deliver information from the AI to clinicians and/or patients (Bennett, 2012), including the need for the incorporation of human factor principles and mental workload approaches in order to understand how people actually interact with the system and how it can be best designed to integrate into existing clinical workflows. In summary, an engaging user interface that can incorporate clinical standards, provide appropriate decision-related information in a constructive format, and accommodate known human factor issues is key (Bennett et al., 2012; Saleem et al., 2009).

Another challenging issue with the technology and approaches laid out in this chapter is that they require a fairly significant population (i.e., sample size) and reliable data in order to produce validated models for production systems (i.e., systems used in real-world clinical practice). Smaller provider organizations may need to consider data aggregation (e.g., health information exchanges (HIE)) in order to leverage such technology (predictive modeling, analytics, AI) that can be fed back into their local Electronic Health Record (EHR). Of course, data aggregation and sharing raise their own ethical concerns. Privacy and security of health information will be paramount, so as to strike the optimal balance between protecting individual privacy and the collective benefit of data aggregation toward potential, meaningful advances in care (Bennett et al., 2012).

CONCLUSION

The history of human progress has been the story of inventing tools that allow us to offload certain tasks into artifacts in our environment. Cognitive tasks are no different — the first chiseling of writing into stone by humans was an act of cognitive offload. This has continued through time, with notepads and pens and calculators and abacuses and computers and so forth. In that sense, AI is not really new. It is a continuation of a story that humankind has been part of for thousands of years. The question is how that story moves forward.

The advantage of tools that enable us to offload cognitive tasks into our environment is that they allow our minds to focus on more complex issues, the bigger picture. This is certainly of utility in the modern health-care environment. The nuances of providing clinical care only grow more complicated with every passing year, with every new medication and treatment, every new piece of information (Bauer, 2002; Jackson & Tarpley, 2009; Orszag & Ellis, 2007). In the provision of chronic care, such as mental healthcare, that complexity compounds due to the numerous decisions that must be made over time, not to mention the idiosyncrasies of each individual patient's health state/disorder. We spend a lot of time debating the classification of disease (Cuthbert & Insel, 2013), but things like cancer and clinical depression are highly variable in their presentation, even their etiology, from patient to patient.

Of course, if we want our clinical computing tools to best assist our clinicians, then they need to "think like a doctor" (Bennett & Hauser, 2013). We are not merely passive observers of "data". Rather, people think about problems over time — it is a dynamic process. Our actions lead to certain perceptions — a fact we use to make intelligent decisions. Throughout this chapter, we present practical computing methods for doing exactly that, as well as how those methods can integrate into the broader healthcare space, e.g., clinical decision support systems, smart homes, cyborg clinicians, and robotics. We would be remiss, however, not to note how all of this feeds into the larger debate about the role of prediction and predictive modeling in health care — the delicate tension between the "art" and the "science" of clinical care. As Paul Meehl argued nearly half a century ago "When you are pushing [scores of] investigations [140 in 1991], predicting everything from the outcomes of football games to the diagnosis of liver disease and when you can hardly come up with a half dozen studies showing even a weak tendency in favor of the clinician, it is time to draw a practical conclusion" (Meehl, 1986, pp. 372−373). Certainly, the expanding reach of pattern recognition and predictive capabilities will continue to spur futurists to re-envision the world as it might be (Kurzweil, 2012).

However, the point we would like to focus on (and the point we have argued previously), is that the most effective long-term path in a domain such as health care is likely to be the combination of autonomous AI and human clinicians. Let humans do what they do well, and let machines do what they do well. In the end, we may maximize the potential of both (Bennett & Hauser, 2013). As we mention above, these tools that can think similarly to us enable a larger degree of cognitive offload (Clark, 2004). In a healthcare setting, this would allow clinicians to focus on the bigger picture, e.g., delivering actual patient care. But, more importantly, it extends the reach of human capability, without necessitating a change in the capabilities themselves. There is only so much information one person can process in a given space of time, and thus we are limited in how much we can do, learn, and understand. What makes the human brain incredible is not purely its information-processing throughput, but what it does with the patterns it finds in that information, and how it responds so flexibly and adaptively. The gift of higher intellect is that responsiveness. It is what differentiates a human from a sea slug, for instance. Freeing ourselves from some of the cognitive tasks is about enhancing our responsiveness, providing a vaster array of patterns for us to immerse into. AI is not just about creating cars that drive themselves or robot doctors that diagnose autonomously − it is about *empowering* people. If we can see more, know more, beyond the constraints with which we are born, then we can do more. Gain deeper insights. Better understand what lies upon the horizon. Mental health care is no exception.

The most hopelessly stupid man is he who is not aware that he is wise.

Isaac Asimov, Second Foundation (1953)

REFERENCES

Alagoz, O., Hsu, H., Schaefer, A. J., & Roberts, M. S. (2010). Markov decision processes: A tool for sequential decision making under uncertainty. *Medical Decision Making, 30* (4), 474−483.

Anastasi, J. S., & Rhodes, M. G. (2005). An own-age bias in face recognition for children and older adults. *Psychonomic Bulletin & Review, 12*(6), 1043−1047.

Barsalou, L. W., Breazeal, C., & Smith, L. B. (2007). Cognition as coordinated non-cognition. *Cognitive Processing, 8*(2), 79−91.

Bauer, M. S. (2002). A review of quantitative studies of adherence to mental health clinical practice guidelines. *Harvard Review of Psychiatry, 10*(3), 138–153.

Beck, J. R., & Pauker, S. G. (1983). The Markov process in medical prognosis. *Medical Decision Making, 3*(4), 419–458.

Beer, R. D. (2000). Dynamical approaches to cognitive science. *Trends in Cognitive Sciences, 4*(3), 91–99.

Bellazzi, R., Larizza, C., Magni, P., & Bellazzi, R. (2005). Temporal data mining for the quality assessment of hemodialysis services. *Artificial Intelligence in Medicine, 34*(1), 25–39.

Bellazzi, R., & Zupan, B. (2008). Predictive data mining in clinical medicine: Current issues and guidelines. *International Journal of Medical Informatics, 77*(2), 81–97.

Bennett, C. C. (2012). Utilizing RxNorm to support practical computing applications: Capturing medication history in live electronic health records. *Journal of Biomedical Informatics, 45*(4), 634–641.

Bennett, C. C., & Doub, T. W. (2010). Data mining and electronic health records: Selecting optimal clinical treatments in practice. In *International conference on data mining (DMIN)* (pp. 313–318).

Bennett, C. C., & Doub, T. W. (2014). Temporal modeling in clinical artificial intelligence, decision-making, and cognitive computing: Empirical exploration of practical challenges. *Proceedings of the 3rd SIAM Workshop on Data Mining for Medicine and Healthcare (DMMH)*. Philadelphia, PA, USA.

Bennett, C. C., Doub, T. W., Bragg, A., Luellen, J., Van Regenmorter, C., & Lockman, J., et al. (2011). Data mining session-based patient reported outcomes (PROs) in a mental health setting: Toward data-driven clinical decision support and personalized treatment. In *IEEE health informatics and systems biology conference (HISB)* (pp. 229–236).

Bennett, C. C., Doub, T. W., & Selove, R. (2012). EHRs connect research and practice: Where predictive modeling, artificial intelligence, and clinical decision support intersect. *Health Policy and Technology, 1*(2), 105–114.

Bennett, C. C., & Hauser, K. (2013). Artificial intelligence framework for simulating clinical decision-making: A Markov decision process approach. *Artificial Intelligence in Medicine, 57*(1), 9–19.

Blakemore, C., Carpenter, R. H., & Georgeson, M. A. (1970). Lateral inhibition between orientation detectors in the human visual system. *Nature, 228*(5266), 37–39.

Botvinick, M. M. (2012). Hierarchical reinforcement learning and decision making. *Current Opinion in Neurobiology, 22*(6), 956–962.

Boulesteix, A. L., Porzelius, C., & Daumer, M. (2008). Microarray-based classification and clinical predictors: On combined classifiers and additional predictive value. *Bioinformatics, 24*(15), 1698–1706.

Brooks, R. A. (1991). Intelligence without reason. *Robotics and Autonomous Systems, 20* (2–4), 291–304.

Chakraborty, B., & Murphy, S. A. (2014). Dynamic treatment regimes. *Annual Review of Statistics and Its Application, 1*(1).

Clark, A. (2004). *Natural-born cyborgs: Minds, technologies, and the future of human intelligence.* Oxford: Oxford University Press.

Clark, A. (2013). Whatever next? Predictive brains, situated agents, and the future of cognitive science. *Behavioral and Brain Sciences, 36*(3), 181–204.

Cohn, J. F. (2010). Advances in behavioral science using automated facial image analysis and synthesis. *IEEE Signal Processing Magazine, 27*(6), 128–133.

Cohn, J. F., Kruez, T. S., Matthews, I., Yang, Y., Nguyen, M. H., & Padilla, M. T., et al. (2009). Detecting depression from facial actions and vocal prosody. In *Third international conference on affective computing and intelligent interaction (ACII)* (pp. 1–7).

Cuthbert, B. N., & Insel, T. R. (2013). Toward the future of psychiatric diagnosis: The seven pillars of RDoC. *BMC Medicine, 11*(1), 126.

Dautenhahn, K., Nehaniv, C. L., Walters, M. L., Robins, B., Kose-Bagci, H., Mirza, N. A., et al. (2009). KASPAR — a minimally expressive humanoid robot for human—robot interaction research. *Applied Bionics and Biomechanics, 6*(3—4), 369—397.

Davidson, L., Rowe, M., Tondora, J., O'Connell, M. J., & Lawless, M. S. (2008). *A practical guide to recovery-oriented practice: Tools for transforming mental health care.* Oxford: Oxford University Press.

De Jaegher, H., & Di Paolo, E. (2007). Participatory sense-making. *Phenomenology and the Cognitive Sciences, 6*(4), 485—507.

Demšar, J. (2006). Statistical comparisons of classifiers over multiple data sets. *The Journal of Machine Learning Research, 7*, 1—30.

Esser, S. K., Andreopoulos, A., Appuswamy, R., Datta, P., Barch, D., & Amir, A., et al. (2013). Cognitive computing systems: Algorithms and applications for networks of neurosynaptic cores. In *IEEE international joint conference on neural networks (IJCNN)* (pp. 1—10).

Ferrucci, D., Levas, A., Bagchi, S., Gondek, D., & Mueller, E. T. (2013). Watson: Beyond Jeopardy!. *Artificial Intelligence, 199*, 93—105.

Garg, A. X., Adhikari, N. K., McDonald, H., Rosas-Arellano, M. P., Devereaux, P. J., Beyene, J., et al. (2005). Effects of computerized clinical decision support systems on practitioner performance and patient outcomes: A systematic review. *The Journal of the American Medical Association, 293*(10), 1223—1238.

Gibson, J. J. (1979). *The ecological approach to visual perception.* Boston, MA: Houghton, Mifflin and Company.

Green, L. W. (2008). Making research relevant: If it is an evidence-based practice, where's the practice-based evidence?. *Family Practice, 25*(Suppl. 1), i20—i24.

Hauskrecht, M., & Fraser, H. (2000). Planning treatment of ischemic heart disease with partially observable Markov decision processes. *Artificial Intelligence in Medicine, 18*(3), 221—244.

Jackson, G. P., & Tarpley, J. L. (2009). How long does it take to train a surgeon? *British Medical Journal, 339*, b4260—b4260.

Jackson, P. (1998). *Introduction to expert systems.* (3rd ed.). Harlow, England: Addison-Wesley.

Jaspers, M. W., Smeulers, M., Vermeulen, H., & Peute, L. W. (2011). Effects of clinical decision-support systems on practitioner performance and patient outcomes: A synthesis of high-quality systematic review findings. *Journal of the American Medical Informatics Association, 18*(3), 327—334.

Kawamoto, K., Houlihan, C. A., Balas, E. A., & Lobach, D. F. (2005). Improving clinical practice using clinical decision support systems: A systematic review of trials to identify features critical to success. *British Medical Journal, 330*(7494), 765—765.

Keijzer, F. A. (1998). Doing without representations which specify what to do. *Philosophical Psychology, 11*(3), 269—302.

Ko, J., Lu, C., Srivastava, M. B., Stankovic, J. A., Terzis, A., & Welsh, M. (2010). Wireless sensor networks for healthcare. *Proceedings of the IEEE, 98*(11), 1947—1960.

Kurzweil, R. (2012). *How to create a mind: The secret of human thought revealed.* New York, NY: Penguin Group.

Littlewort, G. C., Bartlett, M. S., & Lee, K. (2007). Faces of pain: Automated measurement of spontaneous facial expressions of genuine and posed pain. In *Proceedings of the ninth international conference on multimodal interfaces* (pp. 15—21).

Lucey, S., Matthews, I., Hu, C., Ambadar, Z., De la Torre, F., & Cohn, J. (2006). AAM derived face representations for robust facial action recognition. In *IEEE international conference on automatic face and gesture recognition (FGR)* (pp. 155–160).

Luxton, D. D. (2014). Artificial intelligence in psychological practice: Current and future applications and implications. *Professional Psychology: Research and Practice, 45*(5), 332–339.

Luxton, D. D., McCann, R. A., Bush, N. E., Mishkind, M. C., & Reger, G. M. (2011). mHealth for mental health: Integrating smartphone technology in behavioral healthcare. *Professional Psychology: Research and Practice, 42*(6), 505–512.

Meehl, P. (1986). Causes and effects of my disturbing little book. *Journal of Personality Assessment, 50*(3), 370–375.

Merleau-Ponty, M. (1945). *Phénoménologie de la Perception*. Paris: Gallimard.

Modha, D. S., Ananthanarayanan, R., Esser, S. K., Ndirango, A., Sherbondy, A. J., & Singh, R. (2011). Cognitive computing. *Communications of the ACM, 54*(8), 62–71.

Orszag, P. R., & Ellis, P. (2007). The challenge of rising health care costs—a view from the Congressional Budget Office. *The New England Journal of Medicine, 357*(18), 1793–1795.

Osheroff, J. A., Teich, J. M., Middleton, B., Steen, E. B., Wright, A., & Detmer, D. E. (2007). A roadmap for national action on clinical decision support. *Journal of the American Medical Informatics Association, 14*(2), 141–145.

Pantelopoulos, A., & Bourbakis, N. G. (2010). A survey on wearable sensor-based systems for health monitoring and prognosis. *IEEE Transactions on Systems, Man, and Cybernetics, Part C: Applications and Reviews, 40*(1), 1–12.

Pantic, M. (2009). Machine analysis of facial behaviour: Naturalistic and dynamic behaviour. *Philosophical Transactions of the Royal Society B: Biological Sciences, 364*(1535), 3505–3513.

Patel, V. L., Kaufman, D. R., & Arocha, J. F. (2002). Emerging paradigms of cognition in medical decision-making. *Journal of Biomedical Informatics, 35*(1), 52–75.

Patel, V. L., Shortliffe, E. H., Stefanelli, M., Szolovits, P., Berthold, M. R., Bellazzi, R., et al. (2009). The coming of age of artificial intelligence in medicine. *Artificial Intelligence in Medicine, 46*(1), 5–17.

Pioggia, G., Sica, M. L., Ferro, M., Igliozzi, R., Muratori, F., & Ahluwalia, A., et al. (2007). Human-robot interaction in autism: FACE, an android-based social therapy. In *16th IEEE international symposium on robot and human interactive communication, (RO-MAN)* (pp. 605–612).

Riek, L. D., & Robinson, P. (2011). Using robots to help people habituate to visible disabilities. In *IEEE international conference on rehabilitation robotics (ICORR)* (pp. 1–8).

Rogers, M. A. M. (2013). *Comparative effectiveness research*. Oxford: Oxford University Press.

Šabanović, S., Bennett, C. C., Chang, W.-L., & Huber, L. (2013). PARO robot affects diverse interaction modalities in group sensory therapy for older adults with dementia. In *IEEE international conference on rehabilitation robotics (ICORR)* (pp. 1–6).

Šabanović, S., Bennett, C. C., Piatt, J. A., Chang, W.-L., Hakken, D., & Kang, S., et al. (2014). Participatory design of socially assistive robots for preventive patient-centered healthcare. In *IEEE/RSJ IROS workshop on assistive robotics for individuals with disabilities*.

Saleem, J. J., Russ, A. L., Sanderson, P., Johnson, T. R., Zhang, J., & Sittig, D. F. (2009). Current challenges and opportunities for better integration of human factors research with development of clinical information systems. *Yearbook of Medical Informatics*, 48–58.

Scassellati, B., Admoni, H., & Matarić, M. (2012). Robots for use in autism research. *Annual Review of Biomedical Engineering, 14*, 275–294.

Shechter, S. M., Bailey, M. D., Schaefer, A. J., & Roberts, M. S. (2008). The optimal time to initiate HIV therapy under ordered health states. *Operations Research*, *56*(1), 20−33.

Shelton, R. C., & Trivedi, M. H. (2011). Using algorithms and computerized decision support systems to treat major depression. *The Journal of Clinical Psychiatry*, *72*(12), e36.

Shibata, T., & Wada, K. (2011). Robot therapy: A new approach for mental healthcare of the elderly − a mini-review. *Gerontology*, *57*(4), 378−386.

Shortliffe, E. (1976). *Computer-based medical consultations: MYCIN*. New York: Elsevier.

Shortreed, S. M., Laber, E., Lizotte, D. J., Stroup, T. S., Pineau, J., & Murphy, S. A. (2011). Informing sequential clinical decision-making through reinforcement learning: An empirical study. *Machine Learning*, *84*(1−2), 109−136.

Skubic, M., Alexander, G., Popescu, M., Rantz, M., & Keller, J. (2009). A smart home application to eldercare: Current status and lessons learned. *Technology and Health Care*, *17*(3), 183−201.

Spitzer, R. L., & Endicott, J. (1974). Can the computer assist clinicians in psychiatric diagnosis? *The American Journal of Psychiatry*, *131*(5), 522−530.

Sterelny, K. (2007). Social intelligence, human intelligence and niche construction. *Philosophical Transactions of the Royal Society B: Biological Sciences*, *362*(1480), 719−730.

Tapus, A., Tapus, C., & Mataric, M. J. (2009). The use of socially assistive robots in the design of intelligent cognitive therapies for people with dementia. In *IEEE international conference on rehabilitation robotics (ICORR)* (pp. 924−929).

Topol, E. J. (2012). *The creative destruction of medicine: How the digital revolution will create better health care*. New York: Basic Books.

Trivedi, M. H., Daly, E. J., Kern, J. K., Grannemann, B. D., Sunderajan, P., & Claassen, C. A. (2009). Barriers to implementation of a computerized decision support system for depression: An observational report on lessons learned in. *BMC Medical Informatics and Decision Making*, *9*(1), 6.

Trivedi, M. H., Kern, J. K., Grannemann, B. D., Altshuler, K. Z., & Sunderajan, P. (2004). A computerized clinical decision support system as a means of implementing depression guidelines. *Psychiatric Services*, *55*(8), 879−885.

Van Kasteren, T., Noulas, A., Englebienne, G., & Kröse, B. (2008). Accurate activity recognition in a home setting. In *Proceedings of the tenth ACM international conference on ubiquitous computing* (pp. 1−9).

Wada, K., & Shibata, T. (2006). Robot therapy in a care house − its sociopsychological and physiological effects on the residents. In *IEEE international conference on robotics and automation (ICRA)* (pp. 3966−3971).

Wada, K., Shibata, T., Musha, T., & Kimura, S. (2005). Effects of robot therapy for demented patients evaluated by EEG. In *IEEE/RSJ international conference on intelligent robots and systems, 2005. (IROS)* (pp. 1552−1557).

Wade, M. J., & McCauley, D. E. (1988). Extinction and recolonization: Their effects on the genetic differentiation of local populations. *Evolution*, *42*(5), 995−1005.

Warren, W. H. (2006). The dynamics of perception and action. *Psychological Review*, *113*(2), 358−389.

Wilson, D. H., & Atkeson, C. (2005). Simultaneous tracking and activity recognition (STAR) using many anonymous, binary sensors. In H.-W. Gellersen, R. Want, & A. Schmidt (Eds.), *Pervasive computing* (pp. 62−79). Berlin: Springer.

Wingate, D. (2012). Predictively defined representations of state. In M. Wiering, & M. van Otterlo (Eds.), *Reinforcement learning* (pp. 415−439). Berlin: Springer.

Zhao, Y., Kosorok, M. R., & Zeng, D. (2009). Reinforcement learning design for cancer clinical trials. *Statistics in Medicine*, *28*(26), 3294−3315.

Zhou, Z., Dai, W., Eggert, J., Giger, J. T., Keller, J., & Rantz, M., et al. (2009). A real-time system for in-home activity monitoring of elders. In *International conference of the IEEE engineering in medicine and biology society (EMBC)* (pp. 6115−6118).

CHAPTER 3

Autonomous Virtual Human Agents for Healthcare Information Support and Clinical Interviewing

Albert Rizzo, Russell Shilling, Eric Forbell, Stefan Scherer, Jonathan Gratch and Louis-Philippe Morency
University of Southern California Institute for Creative Technologies, Los Angeles, CA, USA

INTRODUCTION

A virtual revolution is ongoing in the use of simulation technology for clinical purposes. When discussion of the potential use of virtual reality (VR) applications for human research and clinical intervention first emerged in the early 1990s, the technology needed to deliver on this "vision" was not in place. Consequently, during these early years VR suffered from a somewhat imbalanced "expectation-to-delivery" ratio, as most users trying systems during that time will attest. Yet it was during the "computer revolution" in the 1990s that emerging technologically driven innovations in behavioral health care had begun to be considered and prototyped. Primordial efforts from this period can be seen in early research and development (R&D) that aimed to use computer technology to enhance productivity in patient documentation and record-keeping, to deliver cognitive training and rehabilitation, to improve access to clinical care via Internet-based teletherapy, and in the use of VR simulations to deliver exposure therapy for treating specific phobias. Over the last 20 years the technology required to deliver behavioral health applications has significantly matured. This has been especially so for the core technologies needed to create VR systems where advances in the underlying enabling technologies (e.g., computational speed, 3D graphics rendering, audio/visual/haptic displays, user interfaces/tracking, voice recognition, artificial intelligence, and authoring software) have supported the creation of low-cost, yet sophisticated VR systems capable of running on commodity-level personal computers and mobile devices. In part driven by digital gaming and

Artificial Intelligence in Behavioral and Mental Health Care.
DOI: http://dx.doi.org/10.1016/B978-0-12-420248-1.00003-9
53

entertainment sectors, and a near insatiable global demand for mobile and networked consumer products, such advances in technological "prowess" and accessibility have provided the hardware and software platforms needed to produce more usable, hi-fidelity VR scenarios for the conduct of human research and clinical intervention. Thus, evolving behavioral health applications can now usefully leverage the interactive and immersive assets that VR affords as the technology continues to get faster, better, and cheaper moving into the twenty-first century.

While such advances have now allowed for the creation of ever more believable context-relevant "structural" VR environments (e.g., combat scenes, homes, classrooms, offices, markets), the next stage in the evolution of clinical VR will involve creating virtual human (VH) representations that can engage real human users in believable and useful interactions. This emerging technological capability has now set the stage for the next major movement in the use of VR for clinical purposes with the "birth" of intelligent VH agents that can serve the role of virtual interactors for a variety of clinical purposes. VHs can be used to populate fully immersive virtual reality environments or be delivered on a standard nonimmersive display for user interaction. Such VH conversational agents, whether located within a virtual reality context or simply as a pop up on a computer monitor, provide new opportunities in the area of healthcare support and advice. Imagine a user going online and interacting with a VH "coach" who can answer questions about clinical issues, discuss treatment options, help you to locate a treatment center suited to your needs, guide you through self-assessment questionnaires, and generally provide a face-to-face human-like interaction to support healthcare awareness and access. Moreover, a VH could be waiting for you to appear at a clinic and, within the space of a private kiosk, be able to conduct an initial clinical interview with you to gather information that may useful to start the early steps for creating a treatment plan that would be followed on by a live clinician. At the same time, this kiosk-based VH agent can leverage advances in sensing technology (e.g., cameras and microphones) to "observe" your facial/body gestures and vocal features and use those sensed signals to infer your psychological state from these observable behaviors to enhance the interaction or document mental status over time. These types of VH interaction possibilities are not visions anticipated to occur in a far-away time later in the twenty-first century — they in fact exist today either as early production prototypes or are on the verge of escaping the laboratory following an appropriate course of research to determine their value and to better understand the ethical boundaries for their use.

The emphasis of this chapter is on the use of such autonomous VH conversational agents to support client interaction within a healthcare context. These forms of VH agents, armed with various levels of artificial intelligence, can play a role in healthcare support in a fashion that does not aim to replace well-trained care providers. Rather, they can be designed to fill in the gaps where the economics are such that there is not now or ever likely to be a real human available to fill these roles. After a brief discussion of the history of VHs in the clinical VR domain, this chapter will detail our applications in this area where a VH can provide private online healthcare information and support (i.e., *SimCoach*) and where a VH can serve the role as a clinical interviewer (i.e., *SimSensei*). Our work using intelligent VH agents in the role of virtual patients for clinical training and for other purposes can be found elsewhere (Rizzo et al., 2011; Swartout et al., 2013; Talbot, Sagae, John, & Rizzo, 2012).

THE RATIONALE AND BRIEF HISTORY OF THE CLINICAL USE OF VHS

Recent shifts in the social and scientific landscape have now set the stage for the next major movement in clinical VR with the "birth" of intelligent VHs. It is now technically feasible to create VH representations that are capable of fostering believable interaction with *real* VR users. This capability has been around since the 1990s, but the previous limitations in graphic rendering, natural language processing, voice recognition, and face and gesture animation made the creation of credible VHs for interaction a costly and labor-intensive process. Thus, until recently VHs existed primarily in the domain of high-end special effect studios/labs that catered to the film or game industry, far from the reach of those who thought to employ them in clinical health applications.

This is not to say that representations of human forms have not usefully appeared in clinical VR scenarios. In fact, since the mid-1990s, VR applications have routinely employed "primitive" VHs (e.g., low-fidelity graphics, nonlanguage interactive, limited face and gesture expression) to serve as stimulus elements to enhance the realism of a virtual world simply by their static presence. For example, VR exposure therapy applications for the treatment of specific phobias (e.g., fear of public speaking, social phobia) were successfully deployed using immersive simulations that were inhabited by "still-life" graphics-based characters or 2D photographic sprites (i.e., static full-body green-screen-captured photo images of a person) (Anderson, Zimand, Hodges, & Rothbaum, 2005; Klinger, 2005; Pertaub, Slater, & Barker, 2002). By simply adjusting the number and location of these VH representations, the intensity of these anxiety-provoking VR contexts could be modulated systematically with the aim of gradually habituating phobic patients to what they feared, leading to improved functioning in the real world with real people. In spite of the primitive nature of these VHs, phobic clients appeared to be especially primed to react to such representations and thus, they provided the necessary stimulus elements to be effective in this type of exposure-based cognitive behavioral treatment.

Other clinical applications have also used animated graphic VHs as stimulus entities to support and train social and safety skills in persons with high-functioning autism (Padgett, Strickland, & Coles, 2006; Parsons et al., 2012; Rutten et al., 2003) and as distracter stimuli for attention assessments conducted in a virtual classroom (Parsons, Bowerly, Buckwalter, & Rizzo, 2007; Rizzo et al., 2006). Additionally, VHs have been used effectively for the conduct of social psychology experiments, essentially replicating and extending findings from studies conducted with real humans on social influence, conformity, racial bias, and social proxemics (Bailenson & Beall, 2006; Blascovich et al., 2002; McCall, Blascovich, Young, & Persky, 2009).

In an effort to further increase the visual realism of such VHs for phobia treatment, Virtually Better Inc. (www.virtuallybetter.com), began incorporating whole video clips of crowds into graphic VR scenarios for therapeutic exposure with clients suffering from fear of public speaking. They later advanced the technique by using green-screen-captured dynamic video sprites of individual humans inserted into graphics-based VR social settings for social phobia and for cue-exposure substance abuse treatment and research applications (Bordnick, Traylor, Carter, & Graap, 2012). A large library of green-screen-captured video sprites of actors behaving or speaking with varying degrees of provocation could then be strategically inserted into the scenario with the aim of modulating the emotional state of the client by fostering encounters with these 2D video VH representations.

The continued quest for even more realistic simulated human interaction contexts led other researchers to use panoramic video capture (Macedonio, Parsons, Wiederhold, & Rizzo, 2007; Rizzo, Ghahremani, Pryor, & Gardner, 2003) of a real-world office space inhabited by hostile co-workers and supervisors to produce VR scenarios for anger management research. With this approach, VR scenarios were created using a 360-degree panoramic camera that was placed in the position of a worker at a desk. Actors then walked into the staged workspace, addressed the camera (as if it was the targeted user at work) and proceeded to verbally threaten and abuse the camera, vis-à-vis, the worker. Within such photorealistic scenarios, VH video stimuli could deliver intense emotional expressions and challenges and psychophysiological measures of users in these immersive video scenarios indicated increased arousal (i.e., skin conductance and heart rate) indicative of an emotional reaction (Macedonio et al., 2007). However, the number of clips available was limited and while the initial work demonstrated the capacity of such stimuli to activate nonclinical users, the system was never tested with actual anger management clients to determine their value in supporting the role-playing practice of more appropriate coping responses.

While others have similarly employed video-captured human content, particularly for commercial clinical training systems (cf. Simmersion, 2015), the use of such fixed video content to foster some level of *faux* interaction or exposure has significant limitations. For example, a video capture method requires the creation of a large catalog of all the possible relevant verbal and behavioral clips to support their tactical presentation to users to meet the requirements of a given therapeutic or training approach. This can be costly and time-consuming and requires significant forethought as to what needs to be captured in order to provide the necessary coverage of a specific domain (e.g., all possible settings where a user might avoid a social interaction or be engaged in a hostile conversation). This requires that a developer capture many clips, test with users, and determine what is actually needed to round out the application after initial testing with relevant users. Since this fixed content cannot be readily updated in a dynamic fashion, new clips need to be captured with the same actors in the same setting with the same clothes under the same lighting conditions. This method, while providing high-fidelity realism, is ultimately limited by its lack of flexibility in terms of upgrading or evolving the application as new information becomes available. Moreover, this process is more suited to clinical applications where the only requirement is for the VH character to deliver an open-ended statement or question that the user can react to with a response, but is lacking in allowing for any truly fluid and believable interchange following a response by the user. Consequently, the absence of dynamic bidirectional interaction with these video representations without a live person behind the "screen" actuating new clips in response to the user's behavior is a significant limiting factor for this approach. This has led some researchers to consider the use of artificially intelligent autonomous VH agents as entities for simulating human-to-human interaction.

Clinical interest in artificially intelligent VH agents designed for interaction with humans can trace its roots to the work of MIT AI researcher, Joseph Weizenbaum. In 1966, he wrote a language analysis program called ELIZA that was designed to imitate a Rogerian therapist. The system allowed a computer user to interact with a virtual therapist by typing simple sentence responses to the computerized therapist's questions. Weizenbaum reasoned that simulating a nondirectional psychotherapist was one of the easiest ways of simulating human verbal interactions and it was a compelling simulation that worked well on teletype computers (and is even instantiated on the Internet today; http://www-ai.ijs.si/eliza-cgi-bin/eliza_script). In spite of the fact that the illusion of ELIZA's intelligence soon disappears due to its inability to handle complexity or nuance, Weizenbaum was reportedly shocked upon learning how seriously people took the ELIZA program (Howell & Muller, 2000). This led him to conclude that it would be immoral to substitute a computer for a human function that "... involves interpersonal respect, understanding, and love" (Weizenbaum, 1976). While Weizenbaum's sentiment is understandable coming from the era that he worked on this, modern approaches to foster an interaction with a VH for a useful purpose but where no human is available, does not fit with the "substitute" concept that he specified.

More recently, seminal research and development has appeared in the creation of highly interactive, artificially intelligent and natural language capable VH agents. No longer at the level of a prop to add context or minimal faux interaction in a virtual world, these agents are designed to perceive and act in a 3D virtual world, engage in face-to-face spoken dialogues with real users (and other VHs) and in some cases, they are capable of exhibiting human-like emotional reactions. Previous classic work on VHs in the computer graphics community focused on perception and action in 3D worlds, but largely ignored dialogue and emotions. This has now changed. Intelligent VH agents are now being created that control computer-generated bodies and can interact with users through speech and gesture in virtual environments (Gratch et al., 2002, 2013). Advanced VHs can engage in rich conversations (Traum et al., 2008), recognize nonverbal cues (Morency, de Kok, & Gratch, 2008; Rizzo et al., 2014; Scherer et al., 2014), reason about social and emotional factors (Gratch & Marsella, 2004), and synthesize human communication and nonverbal expressions (Thiebaux et al., 2008).

Such fully embodied conversational characters have been around since the early 1990s (Bickmore & Cassell, 2005) and there has been much work on full systems that have been designed and used for training (Kenny, Rizzo, Parsons, Gratch, & Swartout, 2007; Prendinger & Ishizuka, 2004; Rickel, Gratch, Hill, Marsella, & Swartout, 2001; Talbot et al., 2012), intelligent kiosks (McCauley & D'Mello, 2006), and virtual receptionists (Babu et al., 2006). Both in appearance and behavior, VHs have now passed through "infancy" and are ready for service in a variety of clinical and research applications.

These advances in VH technology have now supported our research and development for clinical VR applications in two key domains: (i) VH healthcare support agents (i.e., SimCoach) that serve as online guides for promoting anonymous access to psychological healthcare information and self-help activities. (ii) VH agents that can serve the role as a clinical interviewer while sensing behavioral signals (e.g., face, body, and vocal parameters) that can be used by the agent to infer user state, update their behavior in real time, and quantify these behaviors over the course of a 20-min interview (i.e., SimSensei). These areas are detailed below.

USE CASES: SIMCOACH AND SIMSENSEI

SimCoach: A VH Agent to Support Healthcare Information Access

The inspiration for the development of the SimCoach project came from research suggesting that there was an urgent need to reduce the stigma of seeking mental health treatment in military service member (SM) and veteran populations. One of the more foreboding findings in an early report by Hoge et al. (2004) was the observation that among Iraq/Afghanistan War veterans, "... *those whose responses were positive for a mental disorder, only 23 to 40 percent sought mental health care. Those whose responses were positive for a mental disorder were twice as likely as those whose responses were negative to report concern about possible stigmatization and other barriers to seeking mental health care*" (p. 13). While US military training methodology has better prepared soldiers for combat in recent years, such hesitancy to seek treatment for difficulties that emerge upon return from combat, especially by those who may need it most, suggests an area of military mental health care that is in need of attention. Moreover, the dissemination of healthcare information to military SMs, veterans, and their significant others is a persistent and growing challenge. Although medical information is increasingly available over the web, users can find the process of accessing it to be overwhelming, contradictory, and impersonal.

In spite of a Herculean effort on the part of the US Department of Defense (DOD) to produce and disseminate behavioral health programs for military personnel and their families, the complexity of the issues involved continues to challenge the best efforts of military mental healthcare experts, administrators, and providers. Since 2004, numerous blue ribbon panels of experts have attempted to assess the current DOD and Veterans Affairs (VA) healthcare delivery system and provide recommendations for improvement (DOD Mental Health Task Force (DOD, 2007), National Academies of Science Institute of Medicine (IOM, 2007, 2012), Dole-Shalala Commission Report (Dole et al., 2007), the Rand Report (Tanielian et al., 2008), American Psychological Association (APA, 2007)).

For example, the American Psychological Association Presidential Task Force on Military Deployment Services for Youth, Families and Service Members (APA, 2007) presented their preliminary report that poignantly stated that they were, "... not able to find any evidence of a well-coordinated or well-disseminated approach to providing behavioral health care to service members and their families." The APA report also went on to describe three primary barriers to military mental health treatment: *availability, acceptability, and accessibility.* More specifically:

1. Well-trained mental health specialists are not in adequate supply (*availability*)
2. The military culture needs to be modified such that mental health services are more *accepted* and less stigmatized
3. Moreover, even if providers were available and seeking treatment was deemed acceptable, appropriate mental health services are often not readily *accessible* due to a variety of factors (e.g., long waiting lists, limited clinic hours, a poor referral process and geographical location).

In addition to problems with well-trained provider *availability, access* to care from distant locations and the *acceptance* of treatment as a viable solution by a segment of the population who have traditionally viewed asking for help as a sign of weakness, barriers with regard to the awareness of and anticipated benefit from treatment options complicate optimal care provision. In essence, new methods are needed to reduce such barriers to care.

The SimCoach project was designed to address this challenge by supporting users in their efforts to anonymously seek healthcare information and advice by way of online interaction with an intelligent, interactive, embodied VH healthcare guide. The primary goal of the SimCoach project is to break down barriers to care by providing military SMs, veterans, and their significant others with confidential help in exploring

Figure 3.1 Sample SimCoach Archetypes.

and accessing healthcare content and, if needed, for encouraging and supporting the initiation of care with a live provider. Rather than being a traditional web portal, SimCoach allows users to initiate and engage in a dialog about their healthcare concerns with an interactive VH. Generally, these intelligent graphical characters are designed to use speech, gesture, and emotion to introduce the capabilities of the system, solicit basic anonymous background information about the user's history and clinical/psychosocial concerns, provide advice and support, present the user with relevant online content and potentially facilitate the process of seeking appropriate care with a live clinical provider. An implicit motive of the SimCoach project is that of supporting users who are determined to be in need, to make the decision to take the first step toward initiating psychological or medical care with a live provider.

However, it is not the goal of SimCoach to breakdown all barriers to care or to provide diagnostic or therapeutic services that are best delivered by a live clinical provider. Rather, SimCoach was designed to foster comfort and confidence by promoting users' private and anonymous efforts to understand their situations better, to explore available options, and initiate treatment when appropriate. Coordinating this experience is a VH SimCoach, selected by the user from a variety of archetypical character options (see Figure 3.1), who can answer direct questions and/or guide the user through a sequence of user-specific questions, exercises, and assessments. Also, interspersed within the program are options that allow the user to respond to simple screening instruments, such as the PCL-M (PTSD symptom checklist) that are delivered in a conversational format with results fed back to the user in a supportive fashion. These screening results serve to inform the SimCoach's creation of a model of the user to enhance the reliability and accuracy of the SimCoach output to the user, to support user self-awareness via feedback, and to better guide the delivery of relevant information based on this self-report data. Moreover, an enhancement in user engagement with a SimCoach was thought to occur if a more accurate assessment of the user's needs is derived from this process to inform the relevancy of the interaction. This interaction between the VH and the user provides the system with the information needed to guide users to the appropriate next step of engagement with the system or with encouragement to initiate contact with a live provider. Again, the SimCoach project was not conceived as a replacement for human clinical providers and experts. Instead, SimCoach was designed to start the process of engaging the user by providing support and encouragement, increasing awareness of their situation and treatment options, and in assisting individuals who may otherwise be initially uncomfortable talking to a live care provider.

Users can flexibly interact with a SimCoach character by typing text and clicking on character-generated menu options. Since SimCoach was designed to be an easily accessible web-based application that requires no downloadable software, it was felt that voice recognition was not at a state where it could be reliably used at the start of the project in 2010. The feasibility of providing the option for full spoken natural language dialog interaction is currently being explored to determine whether off-the-shelf voice recognition programs are sufficiently accurate to maintain an engaged interaction between a SimCoach and a user. The options for a SimCoach's appearance, behavior, and dialog have been designed to maximize user comfort and satisfaction, but also to facilitate fluid and truthful disclosure of clinically relevant information. Focus groups, "Wizard of OZ" studies, and iterative formative tests of the system were employed with a diverse cross section of our targeted user group to create options for SimCoach interaction that would be both engaging and useful for this population's needs. Results from these user tests indicated some key areas that were determined to be important including user-choice of character archetypes across gender and age ranges, informal dialog interaction, and interestingly, a preference for characters that were not in uniform.

Engagement is also supported by insuring that the specific healthcare content that a SimCoach can deliver to users is relevant to persons with a military background (and, of course, their significant others). This was addressed by leveraging content assets that were originally created for established DOD and VA websites specifically designed to address the needs of this user group (e.g., Afterdeployment, Military OneSource, National Center for PTSD). Our early research with this user group indicated a hesitancy to directly access these sites when users sought behavioral health information, with a common complaint being that there was a fear that their use of those sites may be monitored and might jeopardize advancement in their military careers or later applications for disability benefits (Rizzo et al., 2011). In spite of significant efforts by the DOD and VA to dispel the idea that user tracking was employed on these sites, the prevailing suspicion led many of the users in our samples to conduct such healthcare queries using Google, Yahoo, and Medscape. To address this user concern, supplemental content presented by the SimCoach (e.g., video, self-assessment questionnaires, resource links) is typically "pulled" into the site, rather than directing users away "to" those sites. Users also have the option to print out a PDF summary of the SimCoach session. This is important for later personal review and for the access to links to relevant web content that the SimCoach provided during the session. The summary may also be useful when seeking clinical care to enhance their comfort level, armed with knowledge from the SimCoach interaction, when dealing with human clinical care providers and experts.

As the system evolves, it is our view that engagement would be enhanced if the user was able to interact with the SimCoach repeatedly over time. Ideally, users could progress at their own pace over days or even weeks as they perhaps develop a "relationship" with a SimCoach character as a "go-to" source of healthcare information and feedback. However, this option for evolving the SimCoach comfort zone with users over time would require significant database resources to render the SimCoach capable of "remembering" the information acquired from previous visits and to build on that information in similar fashion to that of a growing human relationship. Moreover, the persistence of a SimCoach memory for previous sessions would also require the user to sign into the system with a username and password. This would necessitate the SimCoach system to "reside" on a high-security server, such that content from previous visits could be stored and accessed with subsequent visits. Such functionality might be a double-edged sword as anonymity is a hallmark feature to draw in users who may be hesitant to know that their interactions are being stored, even if it resulted in a more relevant, less redundant and perhaps more meaningful interaction with a SimCoach over time. Likely, this would necessarily have to be a clearly stated "opt-in" function, as the technology may support this in the future. Recent developments with the SimCoach platform now allow for database access in a separate SimCoach-based project. This will allow for a SimCoach to support "opted-in" users to access their Electronic Medical

Records in applications where the SimCoach serves as a front-end interface for VA or other medical clinic-related uses. In essence, the SimCoach architecture has evolved for application beyond the original intent and, in fact, an online SimCoach authoring tool has recently been created. This allows other clinical professionals to create SimCoach content to enhance and evolve delivery of other care perspectives with this platform (cf. https://authoring.simcoach.org/sceditor/landing.html).

Although this project represents an early (and ongoing iterative) effort in this area, it is our view that the initial clinical aims of breaking down barriers to care can be usefully addressed even with this initial version of the system. The current version of SimCoach is available online (http://www.simcoach.org/) and unidentified user interaction is regularly mined to continue to advance the development of the system by examining the spectrum of interactions that take place with actual users. We expect that SimCoach will continue to evolve over time based on data collected from these ongoing user interactions with the system and with advances in technology, particularly with improved voice recognition. Along the way, this work will afford many research opportunities for investigating the functional and ethical issues involved in the process of creating and interacting with VHs in a clinical or healthcare support context.

For more information, see a SimCoach Video at: https://www.youtube.com/watch?v = PGYUqTvE6Jo/.

SimSensei: A VH Interviewing Agent for Detection and Computational Analysis of Psychological Signals

SimSensei is a VH interaction platform that is able to sense and interpret real-time audiovisual behavioral signals from users interacting with the system. The system was specifically designed for clinical interviewing and healthcare support by providing a face-to-face interaction between a user and a VH that can automatically react to the inferred state of the user through analysis of behavioral signals gleaned from the user's facial expressions, body gestures, and vocal parameters. User behavior is captured and quantified using a range of off-the-shelf sensors (i.e., webcams, Microsoft Kinect, and a microphone). Akin to how nonverbal behavioral signals have an impact on human-to-human interaction and communication, SimSensei aims to capture and infer from the user nonverbal communication to improve the engagement between a VH and a user. The system can also quantify and interpret sensed behavioral signals longitudinally to inform diagnostic assessment within a clinical context.

The development of SimSensei required a thorough awareness of the literature on emotional expression and communication. It has long been recognized that facial expressions and body gestures play an important role in human communicative signaling (Ekman & Rosenberg, 1997; Russell & Fernandez-Dols, 1997). Also, vocal characteristics (e.g., prosody, pitch variation, etc.) have also been reported to provide additive information regarding the "state" of the speaker beyond the actual language content of the speech (Pentland, Lazer, Brewer, & Heibeck, 2009). While some researchers postulate that the universal expression and decoding of face/body gestures and vocal patterns are indicative of genetic "hardwired" mammalian neural circuitry as Darwin proposed over a hundred years ago (Darwin, 2002), others have placed less emphasis on investigating underlying mechanisms and instead have focused on the empirical analysis of such implicit communication signals and what can be meaningfully derived from them. In the latter category, Pentland's MIT research group has characterized these elements of behavioral expression as "Honest Signals" (Pentland, 2008). Based on his research with groups of people interacting, he suggests: "... *this second channel of communication, revolving not around words but around social relations, profoundly influences major decisions in our lives—even though we are largely unaware of it.*" Pentland posits that the physical properties of this signaling behavior are constantly activated, not simply as a back channel or complement to our conscious language, but rather as a separate communication network. It is conjectured that these signaling behaviors, perhaps evolved from ancient primate nonverbal communication mechanisms, provide a useful window into our intentions, goals, values, and emotional state. Based on this perspective, an intriguing case can be made for the development of a computer-based sensing system that can capture and quantify such behavior, and from that activity data make inferences as to a user's cognitive and emotional state. Inferences from these sensed signals could then be used to supplement information that is garnered exclusively from the literal content of speech for a variety of purposes.

Recent progress in low-cost sensing technologies and computer vision methods has now driven this vision to reality. Indeed, recent widespread availability of low-cost sensors (webcams, Microsoft Kinect, microphones) combined with software advances for facial feature tracking, articulated body tracking, and voice analytics (Baltrusaitis, Robinson, & Morency, 2012; Morency, Whitehill, & Movellan, 2008; Whitehill, Littlewort, Fasel, Bartlett, & Movellan, 2009) has opened the door to new

Figure 3.2 User with SimSensei virtual clinical interviewer.

applications for automatic nonverbal behavior analysis. This sensing, quantification, and inference from nonverbal behavioral cues can serve to provide input to an interactive VH interviewer that can respond with follow-up questions that leverage inferred indicators of user distress or anxiety during a short interview. This is the primary concept that underlies the "SimSensei" interviewing agent (see Figure 3.2).

SimSensei is one application component developed from the DARPA-funded "Detection and Computational Analysis of Psychological Signals (DCAPS)" project. This DCAPS application has aimed to explore the feasibility of creating "empathic" VH health agents for use as clinical interviewers and to aid in mental health screening. The system seeks to combine the advantages of traditional web-based self-administered screening (Weisband & Kiesler, 1996), which allows for anonymity, with anthropomorphic interfaces which may foster some of the beneficial social effects of face-to-face interactions (Kang & Gratch, 2012). When the SimSensei system is administered in a private kiosk-based setting, it is envisioned to conduct a clinical interview with a patient who may be initially hesitant or resistant to interacting with a live mental healthcare provider. In this regard, SimSensei evolves the earlier web-based screening tool, SimCoach, to engage users in a private structured interview using natural language. What SimSensei adds to the mix is real-time sensing of user behavior that aims to identify behaviors associated with anxiety, depression, or PTSD. Such behavioral signals are sensed (with cameras and a microphone), from which inferences are made to quantify user state across an interview; that information is also used in real time to update the style and content of the SimSensei follow-up questions.

The SimSensei capability to accomplish this is supported by the "MultiSense" perception system (Morency, 2010; http://multicomp.ict. usc.edu/?p=1799; Devault, Rizzo, & Morency, 2014), a multimodal system that allows for synchronized capture of different modalities such as audio and video and provides a flexible platform for real-time tracking and multimodal fusion. MultiSense enables fusion of modality "markers" to support the development of more complex multimodal indicators of user state. MultiSense fuses information from a web camera, Microsoft Kinect, and audio capture and processing hardware to identify the presence of predetermined nonverbal indicators of psychological distress. This allows for the dynamic capture and quantification of behavioral signals such as 3D head position and orientation, type, intensity, and frequency of facial expressions of emotion (e.g., fear, anger, disgust, and joy), fidgeting, slumped body posture, along with a variety of speech parameters (e.g., speaking fraction, speech dynamics, latency to respond). These informative behavioral signals serve two purposes. First, they produce the capability to analyze the occurrence and quantity of behaviors to inform detection of psychological state. Second, they are broadcast to other software components of the SimSensei Kiosk to inform the VH interviewer of the state and actions of the participant. This information is then used by the VH to assist with turn taking, rapport building (e.g., utterances, acknowledging gestures/facial expressions), and to drive and deliver follow-on questions. In-depth technical details of the MultiSense software as well as the SimSensei dialog management, natural language system, and agent face and body gesture generation methods are beyond the scope of this chapter and can be found elsewhere (Devault et al., 2014; Scherer et al., 2014).

Nonverbal Behavior and Clinical Conditions

To begin to develop a corpus of automatic nonverbal behavior descriptors that MultiSense could track for the SimSensei application, we searched the large body of research that had examined the relationship between nonverbal behavior and clinical conditions. Most of this research resided in the clinical and social psychology literature and until very recently the vast majority relied on manual annotation of gestures and facial expressions. Despite at least 40 years of intensive research, there has still been surprisingly little progress on identifying clear relationships between clinical disorders and expressed behavior. In part, this is due to the difficulty in manually annotating data, inconsistencies in how both clinical states and expressed behaviors are defined across studies, and the wide range of social contexts in which behavior is elicited and observed. However, in spite of these complexities, there is general consensus on the relationship between some clinical conditions (especially depression and anxiety) and associated nonverbal cues. These findings informed our initial search for automatic nonverbal behavior descriptors.

For example, gaze and mutual attention are critical behaviors for regulating conversations, so it is not surprising that a number of clinical conditions are associated with atypical patterns of gaze. Depressed patients have a tendency to maintain significantly less mutual gaze (Waxer, 1974), show nonspecific gaze, such as staring off into space (Schelde, 1998), and avert their gaze, often together with a downward angling of the head (Perez & Riggio, 2003). The pattern for depression and PTSD is similar, with patients often avoiding direct eye contact with the clinician. Emotional expressivity, such as the frequency or duration of smiles, is also diagnostic of clinical state. For example, depressed patients frequently display flattened or negative affect including less emotional expressivity (Bylsam et al., 2008; Perez & Riggio, 2003), fewer mouth movements (Fairbanks, McGuire, & Harris, 1982; Schelde, 1998), more frowns (Fairbanks et al., 1982; Perez & Riggio, 2003), and fewer gestures (Hall, Harrigan, & Rosenthal, 1995; Perez & Riggio, 2003). Some findings suggest it is not the total quantity of expressions that is important, but their dynamics. For example, depressed patients may frequently smile, but these are often shorter in duration and perceived as less genuine (Kirsch & Brunnhuber, 2007) than what is found in nonclinical populations. Social anxiety and PTSD, while sharing some of the features of depression, also have a tendency for heightened emotional sensitivity and more energetic responses, including hypersensitivity to stimuli (e.g., more startle responses, and greater tendency to display anger) (Kirsch & Brunnhuber, 2007), or shame (Menke, 2011). Fidgeting is often reported with greater frequency in clinical populations. This includes gestures such as tapping or rhythmically shaking hands or feet and has been reported in both anxiety and depression (Fairbanks et al., 1982). Depressed patients also often engage in "self-adaptors" (Ekman & Friesen, 1969), such as rhythmically touching, hugging, or stroking parts of the body or self-grooming, such as repeatedly stroking the hair (Fairbanks et al., 1982). Examples of observed differences in verbal behavior in depressed individuals include increased speaker-switch durations and diminished variability in vocal fundamental frequency (Cohn et al., 2009), decreased speech output, slow speech, delays in delivery, and long silent pauses (Hall et al., 1995). Differences in certain lexical frequencies have been reported, including use of first-person pronouns and negatively valenced words (Rude, Gortner, & Pennebaker, 2004).

Thus, the key challenge when building such nonverbal perception technology is to develop and validate robust descriptors of human behaviors that are correlated with psychological distress. These descriptors should be designed to probabilistically inform diagnostic assessment or quantify treatment outcomes. However, no descriptor is completely diagnostic by itself, but rather may reveal "tendencies" in users' nonverbal behaviors that are informational to enhance clinical hypothesis testing and/or decision-making. As an initial step in this process, we examined a variety sources of information to identify such behaviors: (i) a review of the literature on nonverbal behaviors that are indicative of psychological conditions as reported by clinical observations; (ii) existing work on automatic analysis; (iii) qualitative analysis based on observations from the videos and consultation with experts (including trained clinicians) who looked at the videos and identified the communicative behaviors that they would use to inform a diagnosis. Once a road map of candidate behaviors was created, the next step required dual videotaping of face-to-face interviews with individuals who were likely to be in a state of psychological distress (i.e., a veteran sample that had high scores on self-report tests of anxiety, depression, and PTSD) versus those not deemed to be in distress from the same psychometric tests. This face-to-face corpus of videos was scored via manual annotation.

Following the analysis of face-to-face human interactions to identify potential emotional indicators, dialog policies, and commonality of human gestures, the development and analysis of a Wizard-of-Oz (WoZ) prototype system was required. The WoZ interaction allowed human operators to choose the spoken and gestural responses of a VH character (similar to digital puppetry) that interacted with a live research participant. The final step involved the development of a fully automatic SimSensei virtual interviewer that is able to engage users in 15−25 min interactions. A full detailing of this research methodology and results from this work can be found in Scherer et al. (2014). A brief discussion of comparisons between the face-to-face, WoZ-driven, and Automatic VH agent are presented in the next section.

COMPARATIVE EVALUATION ACROSS INTERVIEWS: FACE-TO-FACE, WOZ, AND AUTOMATIC INTERACTION WITH THE SIMSENSEI VH AGENT

After a large number of users were psychometrically characterized and behaviorally evaluated in both live interviews and WoZ systems, the next step involved programing the sensing of candidate behavior marker for integration into an autonomous SimSensei interview. More specifically, the perception system's functionality was tuned to automatically track and recognize candidate nonverbal behaviors deemed as important for the assessment of psychological distress, as reported from the previous steps, but in the context of an interview with an Automatic Interaction (AI) VH agent (essentially, all software-driven, no human in the loop), now named as "Ellie." The key sensed behaviors associated with depression, anxiety, and PTSD were extracted live during the interview, were used to guide Ellie's interactive behavior, and the summary statistics were available automatically at the end of the interview. At this stage the focus was on the capture and analysis of such behavioral signals in the real-time system and the validation of the previous analysis of face-to-face and WoZ data on the new corpus of fully automated interactions.

Across all three interview formats, 351 participants were recruited through Craigslist, posted flyers, and from access to a sample of veterans receiving services from the US Vets program (http://www.usvetsinc.org/). Of the 120 face-to-face participants, 86 were male and 34 were female. These participants had a mean age of 45.56 (SD = 12.26). Of the 140 WoZ participants, 76 were male, 63 were female, and one did not report their gender. The mean age of this group of participants was 39.34 (SD = 12.52). Of the 91 AI participants, 55 were male, 35 were female, and one did not report their gender. They had a mean age of 43.07 (SD = 12.84).

All participants were given a series of self-report assessment instruments to index their clinical state (i.e., Patient Health Questionnaire, Posttraumatic Stress Disorder Checklist, and the State/Trait Anxiety Questionnaire). Postexperience, all participants completed a validated measure of rapport (Kang & Gratch, 2012). Additionally, participants in WoZ and AI completed nine questions designed to evaluate and compare user impressions of both VH formats to test our success in meeting specific VH design goals (see Table 3.1). Examples include questions about disclosure ("I was willing to share information with Ellie"), the

Table 3.1 Means, standard errors, *t*-values, and effect sizes on user impression questions

Design goals	Method		*t*-value	*d*
	WoZ	**AI**		
I was willing to share information with Ellie	4.03 (0.83)	4.07 (0.73)	−0.33	0.05
I felt comfortable sharing information with Ellie	3.92 (0.98)	3.80 (1.07)	0.75	0.12
I shared a lot of personal information with Ellie	3.97 (1.04)	3.73 (1.14)	1.47	0.23
It felt good to talk about things with Ellie	3.69 (1.02)	3.60 (0.95)	0.55	0.08
There were important things I chose not to tell Ellie	2.93 (1.19)	2.66 (1.19)	1.48	0.23
Ellie was a good listener	4.10 (0.77)	3.56 (0.98)	3.94*	0.61
Ellie has appropriate body language	3.85 (0.85)	3.84 (0.86)	0.05	0.01
Ellie was sensitive to my body language	3.36 (0.72)	3.13 (0.86)	1.87	0.29
I would recommend Ellie to a friend	3.72 (1.10)	3.47 (1.03)	1.52	0.24
System usability	74.37 (13.63)	68.68 (12.05)	3.24*	0.44
Rapport	80.71 (12.10)	75.43 (11.71)	3.28*	0.44

* = <0.05

mechanics of the interaction ("Ellie was sensitive to my body language"), and willingness to recommend the system to others. All were rated on a scale from 1 (strongly disagree) to 5 (strongly agree). Note that in the WoZ condition, participants were told that the agent was autonomous and not puppeted by two people.

With regard to the design goals, most participants agreed or strongly agreed that they were achieved, whether they interacted with the Wizard-operated or AI system. For example, most people agreed or strongly agreed that they were willing to share information with Ellie (84.2% WoZ; 87.9% AI), were comfortable sharing (80.5% WoZ; 75.8% AI), and did share intimate information (79.3% WoZ; 68.2% AI). Both systems performed less well with regard to their perceived ability to sense and generate appropriate nonverbal behavior. For example, a minority of participants agreed or strongly agreed that Ellie could sense their nonverbal behavior (40.3% WoZ; 27.5% AI). However, this did not seem to

Table 3.2 Rapport scores in the three conditions

Face-to-face	WoZ	AI
74.42 (4.89)	80.71 (12.10)	75.43 (11.71)

seriously detract from the overall experience and the majority agreed or strongly agreed they would recommend the system to a friend (69.8% WoZ; 56.1% AI).

We next examined the relative impressions of the AI system when compared with the WoZ. Although this initial AI version was in no way expected to reach human-level performance, this comparison gives an insight into areas that need improvement. Surprisingly, design and usability rating results yielded only three significant differences in favor of the human-driven system (WoZ). WoZ participants reported feeling that the interviewer was a better listener than the AI participants ($t(166) = 3.94$, $P < 0.001$, $d = 0.61$), rated the system as higher in usability than AI participants ($t(229) = 3.24$, $P = 0.001$, $d = 0.44$), and felt more rapport ($t(229) = 3.28$, $P = 0.001$, $d = 0.44$).

We then examined how the WoZ and AI systems compared with the original face-to-face interviews (see Table 3.2). We conducted an ANOVA to compare ratings of rapport for the three methods. Results revealed a significant effect of method on rapport ($F(2, 345) = 14.16$, $P < 0.001$, $d = 0.52$). Interestingly, this effect was driven by the WoZ. WoZ participants felt greater rapport than AI participants ($t(345) = 3.87$, $P < 0.001$, $d = 0.42$) and compared to face-to-face participants ($t(345) = -4.95$, $P < 0.001$, $d = 0.53$). Surprisingly, AI and face-to-face participants' ratings of rapport did not differ ($t(345) = -0.77$, $P = 0.44$, $d = 0.07$).

The results of this first evaluation are promising. In terms of subjective experience, participants reported willingness to disclose, willingness to recommend and general satisfaction with both the WoZ and AI versions of the system. In terms of rapport, participants reported feelings comparable to a face-to-face interview. Unexpectedly, participants felt more rapport when interacting with the WoZ system than they did in face-to-face interviews. One possible explanation for this effect is that people are more comfortable revealing sensitive information to computers than face-to-face interviewers (Lucas, Gratch, King, & Morency, 2014; Weisband & Kiesler, 1996), though this will require further study. As expected, the initial version of SimSensei did not perform as well as human "wizards." This is reflected in significantly lower ratings of rapport and system usability. Participants also felt that the AI-controlled Ellie was less sensitive to their own body language and often produced inappropriate nonverbal behaviors. Such analyses are a central focus of current work to inform the design of the next iteration of the SimSensei system and the overall results are promising and suggest that the first pass on this system elicited positive use-intentions.

Initial results from the analysis of face, gesture, and voice in the AI condition indicated clear differences across known groups (high vs low distress) in the presence of behavioral signals that were hypothesized to represent psychological distress (Scherer et al., 2014). Automatic detection of behaviors found to reflect distress included smile dynamics, averted head and gaze, fidgeting, and self-adaptors, and at least three vocal parameters which showed strong concordance with the self-report psychometric evaluations of psychological distress (i.e., anxiety, depression, and PTSD) and significant differences across groups in the expected direction were found. Note that the detailed presentation of these data is beyond the space limits of this chapter and interested readers are referred to Scherer et al. (2014).

The SimSensei system is now in the process of being iteratively refined in validation trials within two clinical projects. In one ongoing project, US military service members prior to a combat deployment in Afghanistan, were given a full battery of psychological tests and interviewed by the automatic SimSensei (AI) interviewer. This unit returned from deployment in December 2014 and participated in a post-deployment round of SimSensei testing with follow-up psychological evaluations planned at 6 months and at 1 year post-deployment. At the time of this writing, the post-deployment data are being analyzed for comparison with the pre-deployment findings with psychometric measures of mental health. The aim of this project is to determine whether automatic behavior markers captured during a SimSensei interview at pre- and post-deployment can predict mental health status change across the deployment compared to the self-report of SMs on our measures and on the Post Deployment Health Assessment (PDHA). In line with this, one study compared the standard administration of the PDHA (computerized and directly documented in the SMs military health record) with an anonymous PDHA administration and the findings indicated that depression, PTS, suicidal ideation, and interest in receiving care were twofold to fourfold higher on the anonymous survey compared with the standard administration of the PDHA (Warner et al., 2011). Thus, it becomes important to determine whether we can get a more "honest" characterization of psychological distress from a SimSensei interview that will support better-informed recommendations for care to SMs who are struggling with mental health conditions, but who "fake-good" on standard self-report assessments to avoid stigma or negative career implications. Further validation testing of a SimSensei-conducted clinical interview is also being used as part of the assessment package within an ongoing clinical trial testing VR exposure therapy for the treatment of PTSD due to military sexual trauma. The SimSensei interview is being conducted at pre-, mid-, and post-treatment in order to compare results with a sample whose mental health status is expected to improve over the course of treatment. Results from these types of known group tests are expected to continue to inform the iterative evolution of the SimSensei VH agent. A video of a user interacting with the AI version of SimSensei is available at: http://youtu.be/Yw1c5h_p6Dc.

CONCLUSIONS

The systematic integration of autonomous VH agents into clinical applications is still clearly in its infancy. However, the days of limited use of VHs as simple props or static elements to add realism or context to a clinical VR application are clearly in the past. Work over the last 15 years in particular has produced a wealth of scientific and practical knowledge to advance both VH technology as well as the actual application of VHs. As advances in computing power, graphics and animation, artificial intelligence, speech recognition, and natural language processing continue at current rates, we expect that the creation and use of highly interactive, intelligent VHs for such clinical purposes will grow exponentially. This chapter presents the rationale and underlying structure of two clinically oriented autonomous VH applications: SimCoach and SimSensei. Each system was created with the idea of adding value to a process by providing users access to interaction with an autonomous VH agent. Neither of these applications are intended to replace an actual person in the conduct of clinical activities, but rather to fill a gap where a real person is unlikely to be available for the intended purpose. With SimCoach, the primary aim is to provide an activity that might encourage someone who is hesitant to seek care with a live provider, to seek or at least explore treatment options with a real clinician. SimSensei takes the SimCoach concept of providing a platform for a private interaction with a VH and attempts to add value by providing a novel format for clinical interviewing that supports a concurrent automated behavioral analysis designed to detect signals of psychological distress in the user. A similar case has been made across the general field of VR simulation, an advantage for a SimSensei Kiosk framework over a human interviewer is in the implicit replicability and consistency of the spoken questions and accompanying gestures. This standardization of the stimuli allows for a more detailed analysis of user responses to precisely delivered interview questions. Another advantage is that recent results suggest that VHs can reduce stress and fear associated with the perception of being judged and thereby lower emotional barriers to disclosing information (Hart, Gratch, & Marsella, 2013, Ch. 21; Lucas et al., 2014). Advancing these concepts will require iterative, research-driven VH development and future success may no longer be rate-limited by the pace of technology, but instead by the creativity and innovation of scientists and practitioners who can envision their useful application.

REFERENCES

American Psychological Association. (2007). Presidential task force on military deployment services for youth, families and service members. The psychological needs of U.S. military service members and their families: A preliminary report. Retrieved from: <http://www.apa.org/releases/MilitaryDeploymentTaskForceReport.pdf> Accessed 18.04.07.

Anderson, P. L., Zimand, E., Hodges, L. F., & Rothbaum, B. O. (2005). Cognitive behavioral therapy for public-speaking anxiety using virtual reality for exposure. *Depression and Anxiety, 22*(3), 156–158.

Babu, S., Schmugge, S., Barnes, T., & Hodges, L. (2006). What would you like to talk about? An evaluation of social conversations with a virtual receptionist. In J. Gratch, et al. (Eds.), *IVA 2006, LNAI 4133* (pp. 169–180). Berlin, Germany: Springer-Verlag.

Bailenson, J. N., & Beall, A. C. (2006). Transformed social interaction: Exploring the digital plasticity of avatars. In R. Schroeder, & A.-S. Axelsson (Eds.), *Avatars at work and play: Collaboration and interaction in shared virtual environments* (pp. 1–16). Berlin, Germany: Springer-Verlag.

Baltrusaitis, T., Robinson, P., & Morency, L.-P., (2012). 3D constrained local model for rigid and non-rigid facial tracking. In *Proceedings of the IEEE computer vision and pattern recognition*. Providence, RI.

Blascovich, J., Loomis, J., Beall, A., Swinth, K., Hoyt, C., & Bailenson, J. (2002). Immersive virtual environment technology: Not just another research tool for social psychology. *Psychological Inquiry, 13*, 103–124.

Bickmore, T., & Cassell, J. (2005). Social dialogue with embodied conversational agents. In J. van Kuppevelt, L. Dybkjaer, & N. Bernsen (Eds.), *Advances in natural, multimodal dialogue systems*. New York, NY: Kluwer Academic.

Bordnick, P. S., Traylor, A. C., Carter, B. L., & Graap, K. M. (2012). A feasibility study of virtual reality-based coping skills training for nicotine dependence. *Research on Social Work Practice, 22*(3), 293–300.

Bylsam, L. M., Morris, B. H., & Rottenberg, J. (2008). A meta-analysis of emotional reactivity in major depressive disorder. *Clinical Psychology Review, 28*, 676–691.

Cohn, J. F., Kruez, T. S., Matthews, I., Yang, Y., Nguyen, M. H., Padilla, M. T., et al. (2009). Detecting depression from facial actions and vocal prosody. In *Affective computing and intelligent interaction (ACII)*, September, 2009.

Darwin, C. (2002). *The expression of the emotions in man and animals* (3rd ed.) London: Oxford University Press.

Devault, D., Rizzo, A. A., & Morency, L.-P. (2014). SimSensei: A virtual human interviewer for healthcare decision support. In *The proceedings of the thirteenth international conference on autonomous agents and multiagent systems* (AAMAS).

DOD Mental Health Task Force Report. (2007). Available from: <http://www.health.mil/dhb/mhtf/MHTF-Report-Final.pdf> Accessed 15.06.07.

Dole-Shalala Commission. (2007). *Serve, support, simplify: Report of the president's commission on care for America's returning wounded warriors.* Available from: <http://www.nyshealthfoundation.org/content/document/detail/1782/> Accessed 21.11.11.

Ekman, P., & Friesen, W. V. (1969). The repertoire of nonverbal behavior: Categories, origins, usage, and coding. *Semiotica, 1*, 49−98.

Ekman, P., & Rosenberg, E. L. (1997). *What the face reveals: Basic and applied studies of spontaneous expressions using the Facial Action Coding System (FACS).* New York, NY: Oxford University Press.

Fairbanks, L. A., McGuire, M. T., & Harris, C. J. (1982). Nonverbal interaction of patients and therapists during psychiatric interviews. *Journal of Abnormal Psychology, 91* (2), 109−119.

Gratch, J., & Marsella, S. (2004). A domain independent framework for modeling emotion. *Journal of Cognitive Systems Research, 5*(4), 269−306.

Gratch, J., Morency, L. P., Scherer, S., Stratou, G., Boberg, J., Koenig, S., et al. (2013). User-state sensing for virtual health agents and telehealth applications. In *Proceedings of the 20th annual medicine meets virtual reality conference.*

Gratch, J., Rickel, J., Andre, E., Cassell, J., Petajan, E., Badler, N. (2002). Creating interactive virtual humans: Some assembly required. In *IEEE intelligent systems.* July/August. pp. 54−61.

Hall, J. A., Harrigan, J. A., & Rosenthal, R. (1995). Nonverbal behavior in clinician-patient interaction. *Applied and Preventive Psychology, 4*(1), 21−37.

Hart, J., Gratch, J., & Marsella, S. (2013). How virtual reality training can win friends and influence people. *Fundamental Issues in Defense Training and Simulation (Human Factors in Defence)*, pp. 235−249. Surrey: Ashgate.

Hoge, C. W., Castro, C. A., Messer, S. C., McGurk, D., Cotting, D. I., & Koffman, R. L. (2004). Combat duty in Iraq and Afghanistan, mental health problems, and barriers to care. *New England Journal of Medicine, 351*(1), 13−22.

Howell, S. R., & Muller, R. (2000). *Computers in psychotherapy: A new prescription.* Available from: <http://www.psychology.mcmaster.ca/beckerlab/showell/ComputerTherapy.PDF> Accessed 23.04.11.

IOM (Institute of Medicine). (2007). *Treatment of posttraumatic stress disorder: An assessment of the evidence.* Washington, DC: The National Academies Press. Available from: <http://www.nap.edu/catalog/11955.html> Accessed 24.10.07.

IOM (Institute of Medicine). (2012). *Treatment for posttraumatic stress disorder in military and veteran populations: Initial assessment.* Washington, DC: The National Academies Press. Available from: <http://www.iom.edu/Reports/2012/Treatment-for-Posttraumatic-Stress-Disorder-in-Military-and-Veteran-Populations-Initial-Assessment.aspx> Accessed 15.07.12.

Kang, S.-H., & Gratch, J. (2012). Socially anxious people reveal more personal information with virtual counselors that talk about themselves using intimate human back stories. In B. Weiderhold, & G. Riva (Eds.), *The annual review of cybertherapy and telemedicine* (pp. 202−207). Amsterdam, The Netherlands: IOS Press.

Kenny, P., Rizzo, A. A., Parsons, T., Gratch, J., & Swartout, W. (2007). A virtual human agent for training clinical interviewing skills to novice therapists. *Annual Review of Cybertherapy and Telemedicine, 2007, 5,* 81–89.

Kirsch, A., & Brunnhuber, S. (2007). Facial expression and experience of emotions in psychodynamic interviews with patients with PTSD in comparison to healthy subjects. *Psychopathology, 40*(5), 296–302.

Klinger, E. (2005). Virtual reality therapy for social phobia: Its efficacy through a control study. Paper presented at: *Cybertherapy 2005.* Basal, Switzerland.

Lucas, G. M., Gratch, J., King, A., & Morency, L.-P. (2014). It's only a computer: Virtual humans increase willingness to disclose. *Computers in Human Behavior, 37,* 94–100.

Macedonio, M. F., Parsons, T., Wiederhold, B., & Rizzo, A. A. (2007). Immersiveness and physiological arousal within panoramic video-based virtual reality. *CyberPsychology and Behavior, 10*(4), 508–515.

McCall, C., Blascovich, J., Young, A., & Persky, S. (2009). Proxemic behaviors as predictors of aggression towards Black (but not White) males in an immersive virtual environment. *Social Influence,* 1–17.

McCauley, L., & D'Mello, S. (2006). A speech enabled intelligent kiosk. In J. Gratch, et al. (Eds.), *IVA 2006, LNAI 4133* (pp. 132–144). Berlin, Germany: Springer-Verlag.

Menke, R. (2011). *Examining nonverbal shame markers among post-pregnancy women with maltreatment histories* (Ph.D. thesis). Wayne State University.

Morency, L.-P. (2010). Modeling human communication dynamics. *IEEE Signal Processing Magazine, 27*(6), 112–116.

Morency, L.-P., de Kok, I., & Gratch, J. (2008). Context-based recognition during human interactions: Automatic feature selection and encoding dictionary. In *10th International conference on multimodal interfaces,* Chania, Greece, IEEE.

Morency, L.-P., Whitehill, J., & Movellan, J. (2008). Generalized adaptive view-based appearance model: Integrated framework for monocular head pose estimation. In *Proceedings of the 8th IEEE international conference on automatic face gesture recognition* (FG08). pp. 1–8.

Padgett, L., Strickland, D., & Coles, C. (2006). Case study: Using a virtual reality computer game to teach fire safety skills to children diagnosed with Fetal Alcohol Syndrome (FAS). *Journal of Pediatric Psychology, 31*(1), 65–70.

Parsons, S., Bauminger, N., Cobb, S., Gal, E., Glover, T., Weiss, P.L., et al. (2012). Collaborative technologies for supporting social conversation and collaboration in the classroom: Overview and findings of the COSPATIAL project. In *1st international conference on innovative technologies for autism spectrum disorders. ASD: Tools, trends and testimonials.*Valencia, Spain, July 6–8, 2012.

Parsons, T., Bowerly, T., Buckwalter, J. G., & Rizzo, A. A. (2007). A controlled clinical comparison of attention performance in children with ADHD in a virtual reality classroom compared to standard neuropsychological methods. *Child Neuropsychology, 13,* 363–381.

Pentland, A. (2008). *Honest signals: How they shape our world.* Cambridge, MA: MIT Press.

Pentland, A., Lazer, D., Brewer, D., & Heibeck, T. (2009). Using reality mining to improve public health and medicine. *Studies in Health Technology and Informatics, 149,* 93–102.

Perez, J. E., & Riggio, R. E. (2003). Nonverbal social skills and psychopathology. In P. Philpot, R. S. Feldman, & E. J. Coats (Eds.), *Nonverbal behavior in clinical settings* (pp. 17–44). London: Oxford University Press.

Pertaub, D.-P., Slater, M., & Barker, C. (2002). An experiment on public speaking anxiety in response to three different types of virtual audience. *Presence, 11*(1), 68–78.

Prendinger, H., & Ishizuka, M. (2004). *Life-like characters — Tools, affective functions, and applications.* New York, NY: Springer.

Rickel, J., Gratch, J., Hill, R., Marsella, S., & Swartout, W. (2001). Steve goes to Bosnia: Towards a new generation of virtual humans for interactive experiences. In *The proceedings of the AAAI spring symposium on AI and interactive entertainment*, Stanford University, CA.

Rizzo, A. A., Bowerly, T., Buckwater, J. G., Klimchuk, D., Mitura, R., & Parsons, R. D. (2006). A virtual reality scenario for all seasons: The virtual classroom. *CNS Spectums*, *11*(1), 35−44.

Rizzo, A. A., Ghahremani, K., Pryor, L., & Gardner, S. (2003). Immersive 360-degree panoramic video environments. In J. Jacko, & C. Stephanidis (Eds.), *Human-computer interaction: Theory and practice* (Vol. 1, pp. 1233−1237). New York, NY: L.A. Erlbaum.

Rizzo, A. A., Sagae, K., Forbell, E., Kim, E., Lange, B., Buckwalter, J. G., et al. (2011). SimCoach: An intelligent virtual human system for providing healthcare information and support. In *Proceedings of the interservice/industry training, simulation and education conference*.

Rizzo, A. A., Scherer, S., DeVault, D., Gratch, J., Artstein, R., Hartholt, A., et al. (2014). Detection and computational analysis of psychological signals using a virtual human interviewing agent. In *The 2014 proceedings of the international conference on disability, virtual reality and associated technologies*.

Rude, S., Gortner, E.-M., & Pennebaker, J. (2004). Language use of depressed and depression-vulnerable college students. *Cognition & Emotion*, *18*(8), 1121−1133.

Russell, J. A., & Fernandez-Dols, J. M. (1997). What does a facial expression mean? In J. A. Russell, & J. M. Fernandez-Dols (Eds.), *The psychology of facial expression* (pp. 3−30). New York, NY: Cambridge University Press.

Rutten, A., Cobb, S., Neale, H., Kerr, S., Leonard, A., Parsons, S., et al. (2003). The AS interactive project: Single-user and collaborative virtual environments for people with high-functioning autistic spectrum disorders. *Journal of Visualization and Computer Animation*, *14*(5), 233−241.

Schelde, J. T. M. (1998). Major depression: Behavioral markers of depression and recovery. *The Journal of Nervous and Mental Disease*, *186*(3), 33−140.

Scherer, S., Stratou, G., Lucas, G., Mahmoud, M., Boberg, J., Gratch, J., et al. (2014). Automatic audiovisual behavior descriptors for psychological disorder analysis. *Image and Vision Computing*, *32*(10), 648−658.

Simmersion, Inc. Available from: <www.simmersion.com> Accessed 15.04.15.

Swartout, B., Artstein, R., Forbell, E., Foutz, S., Lane, H. C., Lange, B., et al. (2013). Virtual humans for learning. *Artificial Intelligence Magazine*, *34*(4), 13−30.

Talbot, T. B., Sagae, K., John, B., & Rizzo, A. A. (2012). Sorting out the virtual patient: How to exploit artificial intelligence, game technology and sound educational practices to create engaging role-playing simulations. *International Journal of Gaming and Computer-Mediated Simulations*, *4*(3), 1−19.

Tanielian, T., Jaycox, L. H., Schell, T. L., Marshall, G. N., Burnam, M. A., Eibner, C., et al. (2008). *Invisible wounds of war: Summary and recommendations for addressing psychological and cognitive injuries*. Rand Report. Retrieved from: <http://veterans.rand.org/>.

Thiebaux, M., Marshall, A., Marsella, S., Fast, E., Hill, A., Kallmann, M., et al. (2008). SmartBody: Behavior realization for embodied conversational agents. In *Proceedings of the international conference on autonomous agents and multi-agent systems (AAMAS)*. Portugal.

Traum, D., Marsella, S., Gratch, J., Lee, J., & Hartholt, A. (2008). Multi-party, multi-issue, multi-strategy negotiation for multi-modal virtual agents. In *8th International Conference on Intelligent Virtual Agents*. Tokyo, Japan, Springer.

Virtually Better Inc. Available from: <www.virtuallybetter.com> Accessed 15.04.15.

Warner, C. H., Appenzeller, G. N., Grieger, T., Belenkiy, S., Breitbach, J., Parker, J., et al. (2011). Importance of anonymity to encourage honest reporting in mental health screening after combat deployment. *Archives of General Psychiatry, 68*(10), 1065−1071.

Waxer, P. (1974). Nonverbal cues for depression. *Journal of Abnormal Psychology, 83*(3), 319−322.

Weisband, S., & Kiesler, S. (1996). Self-disclosure on computer forms: Meta-analysis and implications. In *Proceedings of CHI1996*, Vol. 96, pp. 3−10.

Weizenbaum, J. (1976). *Computer power and human reason* San Francisco, CA: W. H. Freeman.

Whitehill, J., Littlewort, G., Fasel, I., Bartlett, M., & Movellan, J. (2009). Toward practical smile detection. *IEEE Transactions on Pattern Analysis and Machine Intelligence, 31,* 2106−2111.

CHAPTER 4

Virtual Affective Agents and Therapeutic Games

Eva Hudlicka
Psychometrix Associates, Inc. and School of Computer Science, University of Massachusetts, Amherst, MA, USA

INTRODUCTION

The past decade has witnessed tremendous progress in the development of affective intelligent virtual agents and serious games (games used for training, coaching, therapy, and other non-entertainment purposes). These developments, in conjunction with an expanding interest in telemental health, have led to a growing recognition that these technologies can significantly enhance clinical practice and improve patient outcomes. This chapter provides a brief history of intelligent virtual affective agents and serious gaming technologies. The state-of-the-art in these areas and recent applications in health care, specifically behavioral health, are presented. Ethical and privacy considerations, as well as future prospects, are also discussed.

Intelligent virtual agents (IVAs) are synthetic virtual, computer-controlled characters that can interact with humans (Prendinger & Ishizuka, 2004). Virtual affective agents are IVAs capable of affective interaction, often emphasizing nonverbal interaction; that is, recognition of human emotions, and expression of "emotions" by the agent (Hudlicka et al., 2008; Hudlicka et al., 2009). Affective agents may also include affective user modeling and may explicitly model synthetic emotions within their architectures. These capabilities enable the agents to display degrees of emotional and social intelligence (e.g., awareness of social cues and user goals), to have some ability to form and manage relationships, and to adapt in real-time to the changing states and needs of the human user.

Both the visual appearance and the multi-modal interaction capabilities of these agents vary greatly, and can be customized to match the human user's preferences and needs. The embodiments range from cartoonish, animated characters or faces, to fully articulated full bodies, again, customizable to the user's preferences and needs. The interaction capabilities range from text-based, multiple-choice user input and

Artificial Intelligence in Behavioral and Mental Health Care.
DOI: http://dx.doi.org/10.1016/B978-0-12-420248-1.00004-0

Figure 4.1 Examples of virtual agents illustrating varying degrees of visual realism and a variety of embodiment types. From left to right: Woggles; coach Chris (top), coach Harmony (bottom); character from FearNot!; coach Laura; ECA Greta; agent Max.

text-based character output, to speech recognition and synthetic speech. The virtual agents also vary in the degree to which they can adapt to the user's knowledge, affective and motivational states, and their display of affective and social realism. Figure 4.1 shows examples of several virtual agents, illustrating the range of embodiments and degrees of visual realism. Increasingly, affective IVAs are being integrated in computer games, both in games for entertainment and in serious games.

Serious games are computer games developed for training and learning purposes, in contrast to games developed solely for entertainment. Games have a unique ability to engage the players, and to provide highly immersive learning, training and therapeutic environments that can be customized to the user's specific learning needs or therapeutic goals. Their potential in education and training, coaching, rehabilitation, and even psychotherapy has been increasingly recognized, and in spite of their relatively recent emergence within the past 2 decades, serious games represent the fastest-growing segment of the gaming market.

As is the case with games for entertainment, serious games typically provide a game "storyline", which evolves across distinct physical contexts within the simulated gameworld, and typically involves multiple non-playing characters (NPCs) and distinct tasks which the player aims to achieve as s/he progresses through the game levels. The skills to be learned or practiced are embedded within the game tasks, and the game levels provide progressively more challenging tasks. Depending on the type of task to be learned or the type of training or coaching, as well as on the age and abilities of the players, the gameplay may focus strictly on the "serious" task, or it may interleave these tasks with segments of gameplay designed only for entertainment. The latter is more typical for games aimed at children and younger users. Games have the potential to create highly customized learning, training and therapeutic environments and protocols. The gameplay levels, the reward structure, the NPCs, as well as the overall game storyline, can all be customized to provide an optimal learning and training experience for the user. As is the case with IVAs, the NPCs' appearance and behavior can be defined to match players' individual and cultural preferences as well as specific learning and training needs.

Both of these aforementioned technologies take advantage of two innate human needs and capabilities: the desire and ability to emotionally "connect" (i.e., to attach), and the desire and need to "play." To illustrate the potential of these technologies, consider the following questions. What if . . .

- a patient recovering from a major depressive episode could practice cognitive restructuring skills with the help of a virtual intelligent affective character or in the context of a customized serious game?
- a child on the autism spectrum could play with a virtual affective agent to learn social skills or interact with multiple such agents, in a customized learning environment embedded within a serious game?
- a patient with social phobia could attend "virtual parties" and practice approaching strangers and initiating and maintaining conversations?

These scenarios are rapidly approaching reality. Researchers are exploring the effectiveness of IVAs and social robots in helping children on the autism spectrum learn affective and social skills (Dautenhahn, 2007). Serious games are being used to help children and teens on the autism spectrum learn social skills and manage anxiety (Beaumont & Sofronoff, 2008), and games exist to help treat obsessive-compulsive disorder (OCD) (Brezinka, 2008; Brezinka & Hovestadt, 2007).

It must be emphasized that the discussion in this chapter in no way means to imply that virtual affective agents or serious games should be replacing human therapists or face-to-face therapy. These technologies cannot function at the level of an experienced, empathic human therapist, and likely never will. Rather, they have a unique role in the delivery of behavioral health care, both supportive of, and distinct from, the roles of human therapists. These include the following capabilities:

- Enhance dissemination of evidence-based treatment
- Make treatment more accessible (anytime/anywhere availability)
- Support treatment between sessions (facilitate homework and skills practice)
- Adapt to individual needs and cultural preferences
- Promote engagement and support motivation.

In some cases, technology may even be the preferred method of delivering services (e.g., for children on the autism spectrum or patients with social anxiety or agoraphobia). In addition, these technologies can also support enhanced diagnosis and assessment and play a role in research, where they can contribute to more mechanism-based diagnosis and treatment planning (e.g., Hudlicka, 2008a).

There are a number of unique benefits of both virtual affective agents and serious games, which make these technologies particularly well-suited for applications in health care in general, and behavioral health care in particular — both in the delivery of behavioral interventions and in training. This chapter introduces these technologies and discusses their applications in behavioral health.

BRIEF HISTORY OF VIRTUAL AFFECTIVE AGENTS AND SERIOUS GAMES

Both virtual affective agents and serious games are highly sophisticated technologies, which represent a culmination of decades of research and development across a number of sub-disciplines of computer science, engineering, and psychology. The two sections below provide a brief overview of the development of some of the core enabling technologies.

Virtual Affective Agents

Implementing believable and engaging virtual agents requires a broad range of computational resources and capabilities, including: natural language processing (understanding and generation), speech processing (speech understanding and speech synthesis), dialog management, fundamental artificial intelligence (knowledge representation, automated reasoning, machine learning), affective computing (emotion recognition, expression of emotions by virtual characters, affective user modeling, emotion modeling, and cognitive-affective architectures), human—computer interaction, and computer graphics (3D modeling and animation). Clearly, it is beyond the scope of this chapter to discuss the numerous developments and achievements in these sub-disciplines over the past 50 years that have made the development of contemporary virtual agents possible. The brief historical overview below therefore highlights only a subset of these areas: embodiment, agent architectures, and affective computing.

Embodiment, in the context of virtual characters, refers to the type of visible appearance of an agent, depicted graphically on a display device (display devices range from small screens on mobile devices, to larger screens on iPads and laptops, large external displays, and finally to wall-sized virtual reality displays). Note that while most contemporary virtual agents are anthropomorphic, that is, they aim to resemble humans, this is not a necessary "feature." A number of engaging virtual agents have non-human, and even non-animal, form. In fact, one of the very first attempts at embodiment were the simple, non-anthropomorphic "Woggles" (see Figure 4.1).

Woggles were developed in the context of the OZ interactive drama project at Carnegie Mellon University (CMU) (Bates, Loyall, & Reilly, 1992). Woggles' agents were represented by oval shapes with eyes, and were capable of several simple movements (jumping, turning, sliding), squashing, puffing up, changing color, as well as eye movement, including tracking a moving object (Loyall & Bates, 1993). Woggles had some perceptual capabilities and could sense each other's presence, whether or not another Woggle was "looking" at them, and the presence of a human via a "sonar" sensor. In spite of their simplicity, and no attempt at visual, anthropomorphic realism, Woggles were able to convey some degree of affective realism and the users experienced a high-degree of engagement. Woggles' behavior was controlled by a relatively sophisticated agent architecture (the Tok architecture) (Reilly & Bates, 1992), that included both reactive and goal-directed behavior control, as well as an emotion modeling component that was based on the Ortony Clore Collins (OCC) model (discussed later) (Ortony, Clore & Collins, 1988).

As interest in anthropomorphic user interface agents grew, researchers began to explore various forms of agent appearance, ranging from highly simplified, cartoonish agents to fully articulated, fully embodied (head, upper torso, lower torso) 3D agents, aiming for a high-degree of visual realism (refer to Figures 4.1–4.3). Examples of the former include nutrition and exercise coach Harmony (Hayes-Roth, 2009; Hayes-Roth & Saker, 2010), virtual mindfulness coach Chris (Hudlicka, 2013), information presenter agent PPP persona (André, Rist, & Muller, 1998), medical education tutor Adele (Rickel & Johnson, 1999), and cartoonish characters in a system developed to help children cope with bullying (see character from FearNot! in Figure 4.1). Examples of more visually realistic agents include information presenter agent Jack (Norman & Badler, 1997) and instructional agent Steve, that was designed to provide naval personnel with system diagnostics training (Rickel & Johnson, 1999). An example of an agent aiming for a high degree of visual realism is the fully embodied agent Max (Becker, Nakasone, Prendinger, Ishizuka, & Wachsmuth, 2005), which has been evaluated in multiple contexts and roles, including a museum guide and a gaming partner (see Figure 4.1).

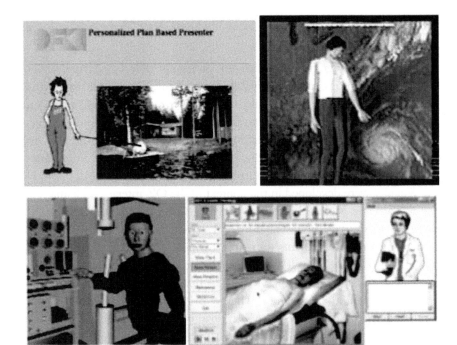

Figure 4.2 Examples of virtual agents illustrating different degrees of embodiment complexity (cartoonish vs full-body; simple vs anatomically based animation) and different interaction contexts: Presenter agents PPP Persona (upper left; André et al., 1998) and Jack (upper right; Norman & Badler, 1997); instructional agents Steve (lower left) and Adele (lower right).

Figure 4.3 Examples of anthropomorphic, fully embodied virtual agents aiming for a high degree of visual realism. From left to right — virtual patients Justina and Justin (Rizzo et al., 2012) and counselor Amy (Lisetti et al., 2013).

These early agents laid the foundations for contemporary *embodied conversational agents* (ECAs) (Cassell, Sullivan, Prevost, & Churchill, 2000), with increasingly complex and often highly visually realistic, anthropomorphic embodiments, multi-modal interaction capabilities including conversational capabilities, complex dialog management and nonverbal expressions (e.g., facial expressions, head movement and gaze, gestures, body language), and competence in a specific domain. Examples of ECAs are agents Greta (De Rosis, Pelachaud, Poggi, Carofiglio, & De Carolis, 2003) and Laura (Bickmore & Picard, 2005) (refer to Figure 4.1). Interaction with ECAs requires minimal or no training, due to their ability to engage in naturalistic interactions with humans through dialog and nonverbal expression. The ability to interact with human users without prior training is especially critical for populations such as the elderly, children, and individuals with disabilities, and therefore significantly extends their usefulness.

These complex, and increasingly visually and socially realistic, agents are also being integrated into both serious and entertainment games as NPCs and player avatars.

Serious Games

Serious games have been developed across diverse contexts and cover a wide range of domains, including: language and cultural skills, most academic subjects, sports and motor skills ("exergaming"), a variety of corporate and business skills, policy planning, and military and law enforcement training (Hudlicka, 2011a). In healthcare, serious games are used both for training and education purposes for healthcare professionals (e.g., emergency room triage, dental surgery, nursing care), and for therapeutic and educational purposes for patients and clients (e.g., education about diet and exercise, coaching to increase physical activity, pain management, social skills training) (Horne-Moyer, Moyer, Messer, & Messer, 2014).

It is beyond the scope of this chapter to review the rapid development of computer gaming technologies, which have progressed from simple 2D games such as Pong, PacMan, and Tetris to today's highly realistic and engaging, often multi-player, games. The realistic graphics, depicting complex, 3-D environments, visually and increasingly even affectively realistic NPCs, and real-time, multi-modal interaction contribute to levels of user engagement which are closer to immersive virtual reality and participatory film experiences than simple gameplays. The visual realism and dynamic interaction are supported by a range of enabling technologies that include

3D modeling and animation, simulation, artificial intelligence, and affective computing. Player engagement is further enhanced by real-time performance and complex gameplays and storylines, facilitated by advances in the underlying hardware, including minimally intrusive input devices (e.g., Microsoft Kinect), and networking technologies that support multiplayer games. Game engines have been developed to facilitate rapid and systematic game development (e.g., Unity) and specialized engines supporting the development of affective games are being explored (Popescu, Broekens, & van Someren, 2014; Hudlicka, 2009). Increasingly, adaptive gaming is being implemented, where the gameplay is modified in response to the players' changing state and goals. These adaptations include game level difficulty as well as actual game content. This development is particularly critical for serious games and is facilitated by user modeling technologies.

The agent technologies discussed above further contribute to the games' realism and users' engagement, as both the NPCs and player avatars can increasingly behave in an autonomous manner, and display socially and affectively realistic expressions and behavior. The former facilitated by a variety of artificial intelligence knowledge-based systems and planning techniques, the latter by affective computing technologies. Affective computing (Picard, 1997) is a sub-discipline of computer science addressing four core areas: emotion recognition by machines, emotion expression by agents and robots, affective user modeling, and emotion modeling and cognitive-affective agent architectures (Hudlicka, 2008b).

In fact, probably the most significant advances in gaming that are especially relevant for serious games in health care, particularly therapeutic games, are techniques from affective computing that facilitate the development of affective games and affect-adaptive games (Gilleade, Dix, & Allanson, 2005; Hudlicka, 2008a; Yannakakis & Paiva, 2014). This topic is discussed in more detail in the following section.

STATE OF THE ART

To the users, the most apparent aspects of virtual affective agents are their interactional capabilities and their appearance. Interactional capabilities include both verbal and nonverbal interaction. Appearance is defined by the agent's embodiment, which of course also determines the types of nonverbal interaction possible. To be effective, affective agents must also be believable. This global characteristic can be further deconstructed into several distinct capabilities, including verbal and nonverbal interaction and conversational abilities, affective and social realism, and the ability to adapt and personalize the interaction to the human user's needs (Ortony, 2001). This section discusses the state-of-the-art of these capabilities in more detail.

Nonverbal Interaction: Emotion Recognition, Emotion Expression, and Agent Embodiment

Nonverbal interaction is of course critical in any human relationship, and may be even more important than verbal interaction in "helping relationships" (e.g., coaching, teaching, support, therapy), as it is an essential component of conveying emotional understanding and empathy. It is also important for managing conversation flow and dialog, since many critical conversational cues are nonverbal, such as showing understanding or confusion, agreement or disagreement. Nonverbal interaction in humans is mediated via a number of expressive channels associated with the human body; primarily the face and the myriad of facial expressions that convey emotional and other mental states, but also eye gaze and head movement, hand gestures, body posture, and body movement. In human–agent interaction, nonverbal interaction requires monitoring and sensing of the user's nonverbal expressions and recognizing these in terms of states that are relevant for the interaction, primarily emotional states.

On the output side, nonverbal interaction is closely linked to agent embodiment, since some type of a physical form is necessary to convey nonverbal information (with the exception of speech, which allows nonverbal information to be conveyed via prosody). Again, the ability to express emotions by the agent is critical here, or, more precisely, to display visible manifestations that would be interpreted as emotions by the human user. (No claim is made that virtual agents can or should experience emotions.) Nonverbal interaction, emotion recognition and expression, and agent embodiment are therefore discussed together below.

Emotion Recognition and Expression

Recognition of human emotions by computers, and expression of "emotions" by agents and robots, represent two of the core areas of affective computing. The two processes can be viewed as inverses of each other. Both rely on the identification of semantic primitives (features) associated with each expressive channel, to facilitate the data analysis, the recognition process, and the rendering of the expressions (Hudlicka,

2005). Detailed discussion of these topics is beyond the scope of this chapter and the reader is referred to a number of recent reviews of emotion recognition and expression technologies (Gunes, Piccardi, & Pantic, 2008; Zeng, Pantic, Roisman, & Huang, 2009). A brief summary of the state-of-the-art is provided below.

In *emotion recognition*, human user data, typically from multiple channels (face, speech prosody, head movement, body movement, physiology) are analyzed to identify the user's emotional state. The computational task consists of mapping the filtered data onto a set of emotional states, via some pattern recognition classification algorithms. Currently, the recognized emotions are typically limited to the basic emotions (e.g., joy, sadness, anger, fear), but progress is being made in recognizing more complex, typically social emotions, such as shame, guilt, and pride. Success rates in forced-choice conditions for the basic emotions are beginning to approach those of humans (Zeng et al., 2009). Recognition of naturalistic emotions, that is, emotions displayed in non-laboratory settings and unconstrained interactions, is more difficult, and represents one of the major challenges in emotion recognition research.

Recognition rates thus depend greatly on the modality and channels used, on the quality of the sensed data, the feature sets used as input to the classification algorithm, and the classification algorithms themselves. Increasingly, multi-modal approaches are being used, combining primarily the visual (facial expression) and audio (speech content and prosody) channels. Physiological signals are also being incorporated to increase recognition accuracy, primarily signals reflecting the activity of the autonomic nervous systems (arousal). Contextual variables (e.g., recent history of the interaction, the tasks the user is attempting to accomplish) can also help increase recognition rates (e.g., Kapoor, Burleson, & Picard, 2007). In health care, recognition of user states ("smart sensing") is particularly important, and can augment and even replace often unreliable self-report data.

In *emotion expression*, the agent's available expressive channels are used to convey an "emotional state" to the human user, to promote engagement. These channels are similar to the human expressive channels, with the exception of the physiological channel. The computational task consists of mapping the emotion the agent should express onto the set of expressive channels available in the agent's embodiment.

The *expression of emotions* in agents requires two distinct components. The agent must not only depict the emotion in an appropriate manner, along its available expressive channels (e.g., face, speech, movement), appropriately synchronized, and depicting realistic affective dynamics, but it must also display an appropriate emotion for the specific context. Achieving these goals involves very different sets of methods and technologies, with the former closely linked to computer graphics (rendering and animation technologies), and the latter involving emotion models and agent architectures (discussed later).

Whereas in emotion recognition multiple channels provide a redundant source of data and enhance recognition accuracy, in emotion expression multiple channels present a challenge, by requiring that expression be coordinated and synchronized across the channels, to ensure character realism. For example, expressions of anger must involve consistent signals in speech, movement and gesture quality, facial expression, body posture, and specific action selection, with the manifestations evolving and decaying at appropriate rates across the distinct channels.

A number of markup languages have been developed to facilitate emotion expression, by providing vocabularies of channel-specific semantic primitives (e.g., the Facial Action Coding System (Ekman & Friesen, 1978)) and an intermediate, implementation-independent representation of the expressions, and by facilitating coordination among multiple expressive channels. While no standard language has yet emerged, the EmotionML markup language represents a good candidate (Schröder et al., 2011).

Embodiment

As outlined above, virtual affective agents take on a wide variety of embodiments, ranging from a "talking head", through upper torso and arms, to fully articulated 3D bodies. Agent developers must make careful choices regarding the agent's embodiment, to balance the need for expressiveness, and the complexity of the associated processing, with the needs of the users within the given interaction context.

In terms of their appearance, most affective agents are rendered to resemble humans, and take on anthropomorphic, often highly visually realistic, embodiments. It is important to point out that while increasingly visually realistic anthropomorphic agents are being developed, visual realism is not necessary for affective realism, and may in fact interfere with affective realism and believability, as evidenced by the phenomenon of uncanny valley (MacDorman, 2005; Mori, 1970). Uncanny valley refers to a drop in perceived believability as the agent's visual realism increases and its appearance increasingly resembles a human. The reason for this apparently counterintuitive finding is that the unconscious criteria used to evaluate believability and affective realism shift as the appearance of the agent becomes more human-like. In effect, for more cartoonish characters, our expectations are lower. Once the synthetic agent begins to resemble human appearance, our evaluation criteria become more stringent, we begin to expect human-like realism and effectiveness in verbal and nonverbal interaction, and when these expectations are not met, we feel that the character is not believable, or, worse, even disturbing.

To address this problem, researchers are exploring agent embodiments that are anthropomorphic but not aiming to be visually realistic, and several studies suggest that simpler, 2D, often cartoonish characters can be very effective in conveying nonverbal information and promoting engagement, particularly with children (Dautenhahn & Werry, 2004; Paiva et al., 2005). Finding the optimal balance between expressiveness afforded by highly visually realistic embodiments and the risk of reaching the uncanny valley represents one of the core challenges in emotion expression research.

In summary, significant progress has been made in nonverbal interaction capabilities of IVAs. Facilitated by developments in affective computing, virtual affective agents are increasingly able to recognize basic human emotions and display affective expressions (again, typically limited to a few of the basic emotions) to their human users, to enhance engagement and effectiveness. Agent researchers are exploring the specific elements of nonverbal interaction that contribute to more realistic, engaging interaction. This research is not only contributing to more effective agents, but also contributing to our understanding of complex phenomena such as empathy. For example, Kang et al. (2012) found that specific nonverbal behavior correlates with disclosure of intimate information in humans (more head tilts (vs nods), less eye contact and more gaze aversion, and more pauses) and that similar behavior in a virtual agent is perceived by a human as indicating the disclosure of intimate information, which can enhance a sense of intimacy and improve the therapeutic alliance.

Believability, Affective Realism, and Emotional Intelligence

The notion of believability comes from the narrative and dramatic arts (film and animation, drama, and literature), and is related to two other notions: "illusion of life" and "suspension of disbelief." The term *believability* was first used in agent research by Bates, who introduced the notion of a "believable software agent" (Bates, 1994). Believability includes a number of agent attributes, including domain competence, appearance, and affective and social realism. Two of the most critical components of believability are *affective realism* and *emotional intelligence*. *Affective realism* refers to the agent's ability to generate and display emotions that are appropriate for the interaction context, and significantly contributes to the effectiveness of user–agent relationships, particularly coaching relationships (Bickmore, Gruber, & Picard, 2005; Hayes-Roth, 2009). As discussed above, this requires that the agent react affectively in real-time, and display affective expression along all available expressive channels, in a coordinated fashion (e.g., speech content and prosody matches facial expression and gestures), and display realistic affective dynamics over time (i.e., onset and decay rates of emotions, or transitions between emotional states, should be consistent with the agent's personality).

Emotional intelligence refers to a broader set of affective skills that includes perceiving and recognizing emotions in self and others, understanding the causes and consequences of emotions (in self and others), regulating emotions in the self, and managing emotions in others (Mayer & Salovey, 1995). Emotionally intelligent agents are expected to not only recognize the users' emotions, but understand their meaning within the given context and determine the best response, affective and nonaffective, that will help the users achieve their goals. Emotional intelligence is of course particularly critical for agents used in behavioral care, where the user's emotional state is often the focus of the interaction.

Personalization and Adaptation Capabilities

Much as we become more effective and engaging communicators as our knowledge of our interaction partner increases, so can affective agents become more effective as they "get to know" the user's preferences and idiosyncratic characteristics. To be engaging, an affective agent's interaction should be personalized to the user's preferences, needs, and goals, and adapt to his/her changing cognitive, emotional, and possibly physical state (e.g., fatigue, disability). A key benefit of virtual agents is that both their appearance (ethnicity, gender, age, style of dress) and their behavior (personality, emotional expressiveness, manner of addressing the user, small talk topics, degree of self-disclosure) can be personalized. For example, an agent interacting with a teen might address the user informally ("Hey, are you ok?"), whereas an agent interacting with an elderly user would be more formal ("How are you doing today, Mrs. Smith?").

Personalization and adaptation (user-adapted interaction) refer both to the ability to customize the agent's appearance and behavior to the user's preferences, and to the agent's ability to adapt its behavior to the user's long-term goals and needs, and the user's changing state and short-term goals. User-adapted interaction is mediated by knowledge about the user stored in an *affective user model*, which is dynamically constructed and updated during the interaction. Affective user models contain information about the types of emotions the user is likely to experience in a given context, an affective user profile (Hudlicka, 2011a) and how those emotions are manifested by the user, within the modalities the agent is able to sense (Hudlicka & McNeese, 2002). Since affective behavior can be highly idiosyncratic, affective models typically involve a learning component, which enables the identification of characteristic affective patterns by tracking the user's behavior over time. For example, frustration may be manifested in User A by agitated speech, but in User B by increasingly long delays between utterances. Significant existing research in intelligent tutoring systems provides the knowledge and methods supporting affective user modeling (e.g., D'Mello, Craig, Witherspoon, Mcdaniel, & Graesser, 2008; Forbes-Riley, Rotaru, & Litman, 2008; Mcquiggan, Mott, & Lester, 2008; Yannakakis, Hallam, & Lund, 2008).

Alternatively, affective user models can attempt to reconstruct the user's mental apparatus, including internal constructs such as beliefs, expectations, goals, and plans, and attempt to simulate the user's actual cognitive-affective processing, within the context of the specific gameplay. Such models then provide a "deeper" representation of the user's mental architecture. In other words, the affective user model may try to simulate the user's own appraisal of the on-going situation, and infer his/her goals and beliefs. These models then begin to resemble cognitive-affective architectures, and may be capable of simulating some of the user's own cognitive/affective processing; e.g., the cognitive appraisal processes resulting in a particular emotion. Clearly, the construction of these types of models is much more challenging than simple recognition of patterns in user behavior and research in this area represents one of the current challenges in affective computing and affect-adaptive interaction.

Putting It All Together: Agent Architectures

The broad range of capabilities outlined above requires a number of distinct functionalities and their coordination, as well as a significant amount of domain knowledge and user-specific data. Agents therefore require an associated system architecture, referred to as *cognitive agent architecture* or,

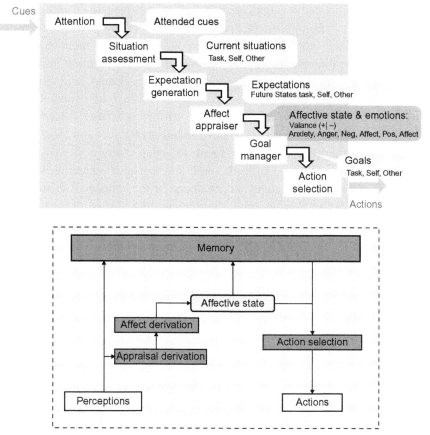

Figure 4.4 Examples of cognitive-affective agent architectures (top) MAMID architecture, implementing a see—think/feel—do sequence and focusing on modeling of emotion effects on cognition and personality-induced affective variability (Hudlicka, 2002, 2003); (bottom) FaTIMA architecture (Paiva et al., 2005).

when including affective processing, *cognitive-affective agent architecture*. An agent architecture consists of several modules, each responsible for a particular aspect of the agent's processing or behavior. Figure 4.4 shows two examples of agent architectures, illustrating the types of modules typically included and their interconnections.

At an abstract level, an agent architecture performs a "see—think—do" sequence: it senses and processes external data ("see"), engages in situation assessment, problem-solving, decision-making, and planning ("think"), and executes its plans to accomplish its goals, including verbal and nonverbal interaction goals and behavior in a simulated environment ("do"). In affective agents, this sequence is augmented to "see—think/feel—do", and affective agents therefore also implement a subset of a range of emotion-specific functions, as outlined above: sensing and recognition of the user's emotional states, affective user modeling, generation of the agent's emotion in response to particular interactions or situations (emotion modeling), and expressing this emotion to the user. Emotion recognition, affective user modeling, and emotion expression were outlined above. Below is a brief description of emotion modeling in cognitive-affective architectures.

Emotion modeling enables the agents to generate emotions dynamically, in response to evolving situations, both interpersonal situations (e.g., an affective reaction by the user) and situations in the simulated environment the agent may be sharing with the human user. Once an emotion is generated within the agent, it can be expressed to the human user, and it can influence both internal processing within the agent architecture, much as human emotions influence cognitive processes, and exert an effect on behavior and action selection. Most agent emotion models represent a subset of the basic emotions (e.g., joy, fear, anger, sadness), but increasingly researchers are attempting to develop models of more complex, social emotions (e.g. Becker, Tausch, & Wagner, 2011). These are, of course, particularly important for affectively realistic agents in behavioral health applications.

From a computational perspective, emotion modeling requires two categories of processes: those mediating emotion generation, and those mediating emotion effects (Hudlicka, 2008b, 2011b). The former is required to dynamically generate affectively and socially realistic agent behavior. The latter is necessary for translating particular emotions into the associated patterns of expression, in terms of the multiple channels available (e.g., speech, facial expression, gestures), and, possibly, to implement the effects of emotions on internal processing (attention, perception, memory, and reasoning).

In the majority of existing agent architectures, the emphasis is on emotion generation, and the subsequent relatively simple mapping of the emotion into the available expressive channels (e.g., agent's facial expression, hand gestures) and the agent's behavior. Emotion generation is typically implemented via models of cognitive appraisal (André, Klesen, Gebhard, Allen & Rist, 2000; Bates et al., 1992; Broekens, DeGroot, & Kosters, 2008; Reilly, 2006). Most of these appraisal models are based on either the OCC model (Ortony, 2002), or the explicit appraisal dimension theories developed by the componential emotion theorists (Smith and Kirby, 2000; Scherer, Schorr, & Johnstone, 2001) (e.g., *novelty, valence, goal relevance and congruence, responsible agent, coping potential*).

Typically, symbolic AI methods are used to implement the stimulus-to-emotion mapping, whether this is done via an intervening set of appraisal dimensions, or directly from the domain stimuli to the emotions. In general, the complexity of this process lies in analyzing the domain stimuli (e.g., features of a game situation, behavior of game characters, player behavior) and extracting the appraisal dimension values. This may require representation of complex mental structures, including the game characters' and players' goals, plans, beliefs, and values, their current assessment of the evolving game situation, and expectations of future developments, as well as complex causal representation of the gameplay dynamics. Rules, semantic nets, and Bayesian belief nets are some of the frequently used formalisms implementing this mapping.

Much less frequently, emotion effects on cognition are included in agent architectures, and modeled via parametric representations of distinct emotion states and their effects on the processing within the architecture modules (Hudlicka, 1998, 2002, 2003, 2008c). Models of emotion effects on expressive behavior and action selection are typically implemented via direct mapping of a particular emotion onto specific behavior, or patterns of expression along one or more modalities; e.g., if "happy" then "jump" and "smile." Some models implement mappings onto components of expressive behaviors, rather than fully formed expressions; mapping values of individual appraisal dimensions onto elements of facial expressions, e.g., eyebrow position (Scherer, 1992).

It is beyond the scope of this chapter to discuss the extensive work in emotion modeling that supports increasingly sophisticated affective modeling in agent architectures, including models of emotion effects on cognitive processing, to implement affective biases (Hudlicka, 2008c), and models of emotion regulation and emotion contagion (Bosse, Broekens, Dias, & van der Zwaan, 2014). For a recent review of existing work in emotion modeling see Hudlicka (2011b, 2014a) and affective agent architectures see Hudlicka (2014b).

Nonplaying Characters and Player Avatars

Not every game has or needs characters. For example, the popular game Tetris does not have any characters, and a number of serious games focusing on skills training do not include NPCs. However, most entertainment games, and many serious games, require or benefit from the presence of game characters. Characters in games fall into two categories: NPCs and player avatars. NPCs are characters controlled by the game software, which interact with the player and play various roles within the gameplay, as determined by the game plot and narrative. NPCs vary in their degree of autonomy and sophistication, increasingly take advantage of the technologies developed in intelligent agents and affective computing research, and are becoming more autonomous and believable, thereby contributing to a more engaging player experience. Player avatar characters represent the player within the context of the game.

Affective and Affect-Adaptive Gaming

Recognizing the key role that emotion plays in learning, in the training of new cognitive and affective skills, and in the acquisition of new behavioral skills, and the elimination of undesirable behaviors (e.g., addictions), developers of serious games are increasingly recognizing the importance of affective gaming (Sykes, 2004; Gilleade et al., 2005). Gilleade and colleagues (2005) captured the objectives of affective gaming in a succinct statement, describing a progression of functionalities an affective game should support: "Assist me, Challenge me, Emote me."

Affective gaming focuses on the integration of emotion into game design and development, and includes the following areas: recognition of player emotions, adaptations of the gameplay to the players' affective states, and modeling and expression of emotions by NPCs (Hudlicka, 2008b). Affective gaming thus emphasizes the use of virtual affective agents as NPCs and the use of affective player modeling and affect-adaptive gameplay.

Within the broad area of affective gaming, Hudlicka has previously suggested that a distinction be made between affect-sensitive games and affect-centered games. The former being games that recognize and adapt to the player's emotional state, whereas the latter are games where emotions play a central role, and whose explicit purpose is to train affective and social skills, or to aid in psychotherapy (Hudlicka, 2011a). Continued progress in the development of affective game engines will facilitate the development of affect-centered therapeutic games.

Overview of Recent Applications in Health Care

Serious games are being explored in health care across a number of contexts, including patient education and psycho-education, medical decision-making, support for behavior change (e.g., in exercise, nutrition, and specific health behaviors such as dental health), rehabilitation and physical therapy, pain reduction, and psychotherapy. Games are also increasingly used in the training of healthcare professionals. A recent review of serious games in health care identified over 20 serious games used in training of medical professionals, and some intended for use by patients; e.g., for pain management, decision-making, patient education, and health behavior coaching (Ricciardi & De Paolis, 2014). Examples of games developed for patients and clients include "Escape from Diab" (archimage.com) and "Squire's Quest" (http://www.squiresquest.com), health behavior coaching games to help children adopt healthy eating and exercise habits, and a game for motor rehabilitation following stroke or brain trauma (Burke et al., 2009).

While the majority of existing serious games in health care, whether for professional training or for patients, focus on physical health (e.g., surgery, emergency medicine, pain management), games focusing on behavioral care are beginning to emerge (Brezinka & Hovestadt, 2007). These include social skills training (Beaumont & Sofronoff, 2008); support for children experiencing divorce, based on family therapy (www.ziplandinteractive.com); cognitive-behavioral treatment of OCD (Brezinka, 2008); game to help veterans overcome posttraumatic stress disorder (PTSD) (Rizzo et al., 2010); and a game designed to motivate adolescents for solution-focused therapy ("Personal Motivator" (Coyle, Matthews, Sharry, Nisbet, & Doherty, 2005)).

An important distinction must be made here between games designed for entertainment only that are used in health care and behavioral care contexts as adjuncts to traditional therapy vs serious games developed expressly for the purpose of direct administration of healthcare interventions and education, including interventions for support, symptom reduction, and behavior change in psychotherapy.

Examples of the former are any entertainment games where the gameplay is incorporated into traditional treatment. For example, games developed solely for entertainment purposes (e.g., Tetris) can be used to help train children with ADHD in attention focusing strategies and first-person shooter (FPS) games have been used to help patients visualize their immune system attacking tumors (Sajjad, Hanan Abdullah, Sharif, & Mohsin, 2014). A number of entertainment games are also used for physical rehabilitation purposes (e.g., WiiFit, Dance Dance Revolution). (The effectiveness of these rehabilitation games is greatly enhanced by input devices, which facilitate gross motor movement exercise and tuning (e.g., Dance Dance Revolution dance mat, WiiMote, and Microsoft Xbox Kinect).)

Examples of the latter are games designed to address a particular symptom (e.g., obsessive-compulsive behavior) or teach a particular emotional or social skill (e.g., emotion regulation, handling difficult social situations such as bullying). These are the games that are emphasized in the discussion below.

The majority of these games are in the exploratory stages, with only a few pilot studies having been conducted to date to evaluate the games' effectiveness. This is especially the case for psychotherapeutic games, which represent both the most challenging applications of the serious gaming technologies (vs psycho-education, training), and also the most promising. Ricciardi and De Paolis (2014) report that only nine of the reviewed games were subjected to an evaluation study, with six of the studies reporting improved training results with game-based training compared with traditional training. Examples of serious games in behavioral care are discussed below.

Pediatric Pain Management — "Free Dive"

Free Dive is a game designed to help children control pain during medical procedures (http://www.breakawaygames.com/serious-games/solutions/healthcare/; Figure 4.5). Free Dive presents a visually rich, underwater environment to the player, whose objective is to swim around with the fish and sea turtles in search of a hidden treasure. The game concept is based on the underlying assumption that distracting attention away from painful stimuli reduces the subjective experience of pain. Data from a pilot study suggest that children are able to tolerate painful procedures more easily

BreakAway Games' *Free Dive* uses game environments to distract.

Figure 4.5 Examples of serious games for children: "Free Dive" (game to control pain by serving as a distraction activity during medical procedures) (left) and "Ricky and the Spider" (game to treat OCD) (right).

while playing the game. Another pain management game was developed for adults, based on EEG technologies and biofeedback principles (Sourina, Wang, & Nguyen, 2011).

OCD in Children — "Ricky and the Spider"

Ricky and the Spider is a game designed to treat OCD in children (Brezinka, 2008; Figure 4.5). The game is based on a cognitive-behavioral approach to OCD treatment. The players are provided psycho-education about the condition, and are supported in creating a hierarchy of symptoms and provided with opportunities for simulated exposure and response prevention: these are established, evidence-based approaches to treating OCD. The players are also taught techniques for externalizing their symptoms, as a means of reducing anxiety. The game characters include "Dr. Owl", who provides advice and guidance (a stand-in for a therapist), "Spider", who represents the OCD condition and issues commands for the other game characters to engage in OCD behavior, and two characters with OCD symptons: "Ricky the grasshopper", who must hop in a specific pattern, and "Lisa the Ladybug", who must count her polka dots before falling asleep. The Spider threatens Ricky and Lisa with terrible consequences if they do not follow his orders. The game is played by a child under the supervision of a therapist.

The game is being used by several thousand users across more than 40 countries. Data from an initial evaluation (Brezinka, 2013), conducted with 18 children and 13 therapists, were positive, with the children reporting satisfaction with use of the game during treatment, and the therapist reporting that the children enjoyed playing the game and experienced increased motivation for treatment. The symptoms of OCD were significantly reduced in 15 children, and unchanged in one child.

PTSD in War Veterans — "Virtual Iraq"

Virtual Iraq is, strictly speaking, a virtual reality (VR) environment, rather than a game. However, due to the increasing overlap between these two types of technologies, and the influential role that Rizzo's work has played in computerized technologies for behavioral health, Virtual Iraq is included here.

Virtual Iraq implements a VR-mediated exposure therapy approach to the treatment of PTSD in veterans returning from the Iraq and Afghanistan wars. Exposure therapy is a behavioral therapy treatment of

PTSD, based on systematic desensitization and habituation. PTSD patients are provided with head-mounted displays and exposed to realistic wartime scenarios in Iraq. Sound and motion are included, to simulate explosions and shaking vehicles. Some scenarios include smells. The scenarios include multiple locations (desert, city), and ranges of stimuli intensity and potential (simulated) danger. The patients are exposed to increasingly intense scenes, under the supervision of a therapist. An early evaluation study showed promising results, with 16 out of 20 patients not meeting the criteria for PTSD following treatment (Rizzo et al., 2010).

These initial results are promising and some existing reviews suggest that VR-based exposure therapy is as effective as traditional exposure therapy (Goncalves, Pedrozo, Coutinho, Figueira, & Ventura, 2012) and may be even more effective in some situations (Malbos, Boyer, & Lançon, 2013). This is a significant finding, since computer-delivered therapy has a number of advantages, most importantly cost and accessibility, and may even be a preferred mode of treatment for some patients. However, as is the case with most of the technologies reviewed in this chapter, systematic, randomized controlled trials are still lacking in this area and there is need for more standardization in the therapeutic environments and treatment manuals (Motraghi, Seim, Meyer, & Morissette, 2014).

Social and Emotion Regulation Skills for Children on the Autism Spectrum — "Secret Agent Society"

Secret Agent Society is a game designed to teach children and adolescents on the autism spectrum social skills and emotion regulation skills (Beaumont & Sofronoff, 2008; Figure 4.6). The specific skills include the fundamental emotion intelligence skills (recognition of emotions in self and others) and emotion regulation strategies, as well as a variety of social problem-solving skills (e.g., how to deal with teasing, bullying, losing a game).

The game was developed as a component of an integrated social skills training program for children with Asperger syndrome: the "Junior Detective Training Program." (The other components of the program include group training in social skills and parent and teacher training.) Within the game, the child acts as a junior detective, whose task is to recognize the suspects' emotions. The game progresses through several levels of difficulty, with the lower levels involving recognition of emotions in game characters from their facial expressions, body posture, and speech prosody. In higher levels, the children are taught how to recognize more complex social emotions (guilt, embarrassment). In the

Figure 4.6 Secret Agent Society — game designed to teach children on the autism spectrum social and emotion regulation skills.

highest level of the game, children are asked to complete missions where they learn and practice strategies for dealing with bullying and appropriately playing with others. For example, the player might feel frustrated at losing a game and must identify the emotion (frustration) and then select a strategy for dealing with the emotion in a socially acceptable manner. The player is provided with multiple-choice options and asked to select the best response for the situation; e.g., congratulate other player, yell at other player, talk to a mentor agent in the game, jump on a trampoline, or punch a wall. The children are also taught how to recognize their own emotions via physiological self-assessment scales. To help children learn emotion regulation skills, the game presents a series of anxiety-inducing situations (e.g., flying an airplane) and possible coping strategies for anxiety control. The player chooses a coping strategy and is provided with feedback regarding its appropriateness for the situation.

An earlier version of the game was evaluated via a randomized controlled trial ($N = 49$; 7.5–11-year-olds) over a 2-month period, and yielded positive results: 76% of the children not only improved their social functioning and reached the level of neurotypical children, but these gains were maintained over a 5-month period (Beaumont & Sofronoff, 2008). Maintaining social skills gains following training, and generalizing to non-training contexts, is a major challenge for children on the autism spectrum.

The data regarding the maintenance of gains following game-based training are therefore particularly encouraging, and reflect the promise that gaming technologies provide for this population.

APPLICABLE ETHICAL AND PRIVACY CONSIDERATIONS

Any technology that has the potential to track human behavior, and collect personal data, must address privacy and data security considerations. These considerations have been codified into the legal system via the HIPAA regulations, which are actively enforced. Of course, there is the very serious issue of unwarranted and potentially illegal government spying, which makes any HIPAA regulations meaningless. In this regard, it is quite surprising that no professional organization in behavioral health has yet raised this issue, as it has a direct impact on health care, and particularly on telemedicine and telemental health.

However, the issues of data privacy, data sharing, and security are addressed elsewhere in this book, and are not specific to virtual affective agents and therapeutic games. This section therefore focuses on ethical and privacy considerations that are specific to these technologies. These contexts, in conjunction with the significant emphasis on the user's emotion, raise an entirely new set of ethical considerations: *affective privacy, the ethics of affect induction in users, and the ethics of virtual relationships*, that is, relationships with virtual affective agents.

Affective Privacy

Our emotions, perhaps even more so than our thoughts, are likely the most personal and private aspects of our lives. The development and use of applications that sense, infer, or track our emotions therefore presents considerable and as yet unexplored ethical challenges. This is especially the case in any applications in behavioral health, where the users may be addressing a particularly painful experience, or reveal emotions and thoughts that could have negative repercussions on their lives if they were made public, or revealed to other parties (e.g., employers, insurance companies). User modeling, and especially affective user modeling, thus presents an ethical challenge since these models may contain the most guarded personal information about the users: the emotions they feel, including "undesirable" emotions; the events that trigger those emotions, including triggers that may be considered inappropriate, etc.

Technological advances are increasingly facilitating the collection of affective data, often without our knowledge: facial expressions can be recognized from data collected by the ubiquitous video cameras that watch most of our activities in public spaces and in the workplace; our posts on social networks can be, and are being, analyzed, to "mine" affective data; our telephone conversations are recorded. We have no control over these activities and no option to opt out. Even in situations where we willingly agree to have our data collected, there are privacy concerns: data are lost, compromised, stolen. A number of technologists are predicting an end to privacy. However, we interpret this based on historical possibilities, and thus our worst privacy breach nightmare might be that our financial data will be compromised. We do not generally expect that data about our most intimate mental and affective states are being collected, analyzed, stored, and perhaps used. And yet these are precisely the types of data that will be collected as behavioral healthcare applications begin to proliferate.

The existing concerns about data security and privacy protection are thus multiplied when we consider the personal nature of data now being collected. As remote sensing and emotion recognition technologies continue to advance, it will be increasingly possible to intrude into our private lives. It is therefore essential that healthcare professionals actively address the ethical challenges associated with the privacy of affective data, and become active and proactive, both within their specific professional organizations and more broadly at the political level, as government surveillance increases.

Emotion Induction

Both virtual affective agents and serious games not only have the potential to induce strong emotions, but may often be designed with the express purpose of inducing specific emotions, including negative emotions. Virtual agents acting as coaches may be designed to induce affection, so that they are viewed as empathic, that their message is trusted, and they can be more persuasive (e.g., induce behavior change such as more exercise, less smoking, better nutrition). In some behavioral healthcare applications, agents and games may be designed to induce a negative or unpleasant emotion; for example, when the technology aims to implement exposure-based treatments that require some degree of anxiety to be effective, such as PTSD or OCD treatments based on exposure.

Of course, computers already induce a range of negative emotions on a daily basis, without explicitly attempting to, and computer games designed for entertainment also induce a range of emotions, including frustration, disappointment, even rage. However, the use of these technologies in behavioral health, where emotion manipulation may be desirable and necessary to achieve the therapeutic goals, presents a unique set of ethical concerns.

How can we ensure that the induced emotions will not overwhelm the user, or have a deleterious effect in the future? What if systematic desensitization occurs to the wrong stimulus (e.g., simulated violence or abusive behavior)? What emotions can ethically be induced in the user? In therapeutic contexts, it is generally accepted that the induction of some negative emotions is not only acceptable or unavoidable, but even necessary for treatment (e.g., anxiety induction during exposure therapies; shame experience in a safe, supportive setting to help individuals reorganize some trauma-induced cognitive-affective schema).

Most existing active therapeutic systems are designed to be used under the supervision of a clinician (e.g., "Ricky and the Spider" OCD treatment game, The "Secret Agent Society" social skills and emotion regulation game, "Virtual Iraq" PTSD treatment environment). However, it is conceivable that users could gain access to these technologies without the supervision of a clinician, or that the supervising clinician might not be aware that a negative emotion of undesirable intensity was being induced.

One can go even further, and consider situations where an increasingly autonomous and sophisticated virtual affective agent, with a detailed affective model of the user, can misapply a therapeutic technique and induce an emotion in the user that will be traumatizing, or will undo previous gains made in treatment.

There are no easy answers to these ethical dilemmas and carefully monitored application of these technologies, along with extensive education of both the end-users and the professionals administering the technologies regarding the possible risks, will be essential.

Virtual Relationships

As stated earlier in this chapter, humans are "wired to relate", and one of the most powerful features of the affective agent technologies is precisely their ability to induce the "relational instinct" and attachment behavior in the human users (Reeves & Nass, 1996). Through the ensuing connection, and associated trust, agents can then provide support and coaching, even social companionship. By inducing attachment and trust, virtual affective agents have the potential to mimic aspects of human relationships and humans can thus, at least theoretically, enter into relationships with agents. These virtual relationships present yet another ethical challenge.

How does a human user know when to trust a virtual agent? If the agent appears "confident" (e.g., an eldercare companion agent telling the human to take a particular medication), is this an indication that it should be trusted? What about the risk of virtual relationships replacing actual human relationships? What if an elderly person finds their synthetic companion more compelling, and empathic, than his/her family members, and reduces contact with family, eventually investing emotions into a relationship with an entity not capable of experiencing real emotions, engaging in a emotionally responsible relationship, or, for that matter, bringing the elderly food or medicine? What if the agent uses its persuasive capabilities to induce beliefs or behavior which are not in the human user's best interests? One may think that these are outlandish possibilities, given the state-of-the-art of agent technologies. However, one has only to consider the fact that DSM-5 has identified both "Internet Addiction" and "Internet Gaming Disorder" as possible new Axis I diagnostic categories to realize that as the virtual agent technologies advance we may soon be facing a variety of new potential disorders to consider, including, perhaps, a "Virtual relationship addiction disorder."

Some of these issues have begun to be raised by several agent and affective computing researchers (Castellano et al., 2010; Bickmore, 2005) but the research community has a long way to go in adequately understanding and addressing the ethics of virtual relationships. However, attention is increasingly being focused on the issue of ethics in human−agent interactions, as evidenced, for example, by the 2015 workshop on "The Emerging Policy and Ethics of Human−Robot Interaction" held at the HRI conference in Portland Oregon, USA (http://www.openroboethics.org/hri15/).

FUTURE PROSPECTS

It is difficult, one might say even irresponsible, to make predictions in technological developments, and prognosticians in artificial intelligence, a core technology mediating both virtual affective agents and serious games, have a particularly dismal track record. It is also difficult not to be influenced by one's wishes (or concerns) when making predictions. With these caveats in mind, a discussion of near-term anticipated developments in virtual affective agent and serious gaming technologies is offered below.

Proliferation

Given the recent growth in both of these technologies, coupled with the recognition of their potential in behavioral health and the increasing need and acceptance of technologies in behavioral health, it is safe to assume that both affective agents and serious therapeutic games will continue to expand beyond research contexts and beyond the currently typical applications in coaching of health behavior. A good example of this trend is the increasing popularity of the Secret Agent Society game for children on the autism spectrum, which is integrated into a formal training program offered to clinicians worldwide. Use of therapeutic games will become more commonplace, particularly for children and adolescents, and gaming elements will be integrated into training, learning, and rehabilitation environments.

Formal Evaluations

Increasing emphasis will be placed on formal evaluations of therapeutic games and affective agents within these games. As these technologies mature, it will no longer be sufficient to demonstrate feasibility and user acceptance, and increasingly emphasis will be placed on formal, randomized controlled trials demonstrating effectiveness. These studies will in turn help determine the populations, disorders, and contexts within which these technologies are helpful. For example, while we may wish it to be the case that loneliness among the elderly can be reduced through the use of social robots, it is likely that these technologies will not be readily accepted by the current generation of elders.

Improved Understanding of Suitable Applications and Contexts for Agents and Games

As agents and games proliferate, and are increasingly subjected to more formal evaluations with end-users (clients, patients, trainees, students), we will begin to develop a better understanding of the benefits and the limits of these technologies, including:
- types of roles agents can effectively play in different contexts and for different skills; e.g., trainer, mentor, coach, virtual therapist;
- types of therapies for which virtual agents and games are most suitable; e.g., highly structured, protocol-based therapies that emphasize the acquisition of specific skills and do not rely on free-form natural language interaction, and the associated nuanced understanding and interpretation of complex constructs and mental and emotional states;

- types of conditions and symptoms amenable to agent- and game-mediated treatment; e.g., in psychotherapy, Axis I disorders, such as anxiety, depression, PTSD, and substance use for which evidence-based treatment protocols exist; e.g., dialectical behavior therapy (DBT), exposure and systematic desensitization, possibly motivational interviewing. In contrast, therapeutic approaches focusing on Axis II disorders, requiring gradual transformations of cognitive-affective schemas, and the context of a strong therapeutic alliance created over the long term, are unlikely to be facilitated by these technologies (although they may be useful as adjuncts to face-to-face therapy to facilitate particular skill training, such as emotion regulation).

Agents: Empathy and Personality

Much recent work in affective agents has focused on the development of empathic agents, capable of establishing an affective loop between the agent and a human user (e.g., Paiva et al., 2004). While short-term pseudo-empathic behavior may be feasible, the establishment of true empathy between agents and humans will remain a challenge. It is unlikely that the near future will see virtual affective agents with either the degree of affective realism, or the degree of cognitive competence, required to convey empathy to a human user during long-term interactions.

However, creating agents with distinct personalities will be increasingly possible, and research in this area is yielding promising results (e.g., Hudlicka, 1998, 2003). These types of agents will make it possible to create customized social environments within therapeutic games, tailored to the specific needs of the user; for example, create feared social situations to support cognitive-behavioral treatments for social anxiety.

Improved User State Recognition, Affective User Modeling and Personalization

One of the most rapidly advancing areas in affective computing is emotion recognition. Advances in both nonintrusive sensing hardware, and classification algorithms capable of automatic feature extraction and unsupervised learning, contribute to increasing accuracy. This, in turn, increases the accuracy of affective user modeling and facilitates affect-adaptive interactions between the user and the gaming environment, including any affective agents within the game. Increasingly, emphasis will be placed not only on single-frame *emotion recognition* (e.g., "player is feeling frustrated") but on longer-term *emotion understanding* (e.g., "player is feeling frustrated because the last three game tasks were too anxiety-provoking and s/he needs some encouragement to improve her sense of social competence"). These developments will contribute to increasingly personalized therapeutic games, targeted for specific symptoms, emotions, or skills, which will, hopefully, enhance their effectiveness and patient outcomes.

Natural Language Understanding

Although progress will be made in statistically based natural language understanding, and agents' ability to converse in restricted gameplay contexts will be much improved; these systems will remain "brittle": they will not be able to carry on the types of wide-ranging conversations that humans engage in. This will continue to limit agent interactions to narrow contexts, within which they may be quite effective, but will not enable more complex natural-language interactions, such as those required for psychotherapy. Clinicians worried about agents and robots taking over the world, and their jobs, can relax.

New Types of Relationships and Improved Understanding of Relationships

Virtual affective agents, whether stand-alone or used in the context of games, will create opportunities for humans to create unique types of relationships: human—agent relationships. Researchers are attempting to develop relational agents (e.g., Bickmore, 2003), capable of long-term relationships, and are using research in psychology and sociology to determine the types of functionalities relational agents need to be engaging. Human—agent interactions will provide valuable test beds for exploring the nature of both human—human relationships, and also the unique nature of human—agent relationships. New types of relationships may be identified, and we may be surprised to find that particular attributes we value in humans may not be valued in agents. The assumption that effective human—agent relationships need to emulate human—human relationships may therefore need to be questioned, including, perhaps such deep-seated assumptions that effective and engaging virtual agents need to be empathic. While for certain applications this will likely be the case, and preliminary research suggests that empathic agents are often more effective, it is also possible that we will see entirely different directions of development. As humans begin to coexist with virtual agents, new sets of expectations for human—agent interactions are likely to develop, and different expectations will develop for different contexts. We should not assume that empathic and affective agents will always be more desirable and effective, and researchers are beginning to identify contexts where nonempathic agents may be more effective.

CONCLUSIONS

Therapeutic games have a unique ability to engage the user by providing an immersive environment, directly engaging the user in a pleasurable activity, and by providing immediate positive feedback via a well-defined reward structure. The often-quoted "no pain, no gain" assumption about skill acquisition does not apply to games, where the players can acquire and practice skills effortlessly, often without the exertion associated with conscious effort.

Whether used as stand-alone tools to provide coaching, training, and support behavior change, or playing supportive roles in psychotherapy, these technologies can perform many functions and significantly enhance both the delivery and the training of behavioral healthcare interventions. Taking advantage of the innate human capabilities and desires to connect and to play, virtual affective agents and serious games provide immersive affective experiences, where skill acquisition happens naturally and effortlessly, through a series of engaging interactions.

A number of challenges exist, of course, both technological (e.g., development of affectively realistic agents) and ethical (ensuring privacy of affective data and understanding the benefits and potential undesirable side effects of virtual relationships). However, existing technological developments, the recognized need and desire by the research community to conduct formal evaluation studies, and, most importantly, the recognized need and promise of these technologies in behavioral health, suggest that both affective virtual agents and serious therapeutic games will represent a major growth area in the next few decades.

REFERENCES

André, E., Klesen, M., Gebhard, P., Allen, S., & Rist, T. (2000). *Integrating models of personality and emotions into lifelike characters* (pp. 150—165). *Affective interactions* Berlin: Springer.

André, E., Rist, T., & Müller, J. (1998). Integrating reactive and scripted behaviors in a life-like presentation agent. In K. P. Sycara, & M. Wooldridge (Eds.), *Proceedings of the second international conference on autonomous agents* (pp. 261—268). Minneapolis, MN: ACM Press.

Bates, J. (1994). The role of emotion in believable agents. *Communications of the ACM, 37*(7), 122–125.

Bates, J., Loyall, A., & Reilly, W. (1992). Integrating reactivity, goals, and emotion in a broad agent. In *Proceedings of the 14th meeting of the cognitive science society.*

Beaumont, R., & Sofronoff, K. (2008). A multi-component social skills intervention for children with Asperger syndome: The Junior Detective Training Program. *Journal of Child Psychology and Psychiatry, 49,* 743–753.

Becker, C., Nakasone, A., Prendinger, H., Ishizuka, M., & Wachsmuth, I. (2005). Physiologically interactive gaming with the 3D agent Max. In *Paper presented at the international workshop on conversational informatics at JSAI-05,* Kitakyushu, Japan.

Becker, J. C., Tausch, N., & Wagner, U. (2011). Emotional consequences of collective action participation differentiating self-directed and outgroup-directed emotions. *Personality and Social Psychology Bulletin, 37*(12), 1587–1598.

Bickmore, T. (2003). *Relational agents: Effecting change through human-computer relationships* Cambridge, MA: MIT Press.

Bickmore, T. (2005). Ethical issues in using relational agents for older adults. In *Proceedings of the AAAI fall symposium.*

Bickmore, T., Gruber, A., & Picard, R. (2005). Establishing alliance in automated health behavior change interventions. *Patient Education and Counseling, 59,* 21–30.

Bickmore, T., & Picard, R. W. (2005). Establishing and maintaining long-term human–computer relationships. *ACM Transactions on Computer–Human Interaction (TOCHI), 12*(2), 293–327.

Bosse, T., Broekens, J., Dias, J., & van der Zwaan, J. (2014). *Emotion modeling: Towards pragmatic computational models of affective processes* Berlin: Springer.

Brezinka, V. (2013). Rick and the spider—A video game to support cognitive behavioral treatment of children with obsessive-compulsive disorder. *Clinical Neuropsychiatry, 10*(3 Suppl. 1), 6–12 . Retrieved from: <http://www.clinicalneuropsychiatry.org/pdf/01Brezinka.pdf> .

Brezinka, V. (2008). Treasure hunt—a serious game to support psychotherapeutic treatment of children. *Studies in Health Technology and Informatics, 136,* 71.

Brezinka, V., & Hovestadt, L. (2007). *Serious games can support psychotherapy of children and adolescents* (pp. 357–364). Berlin: Springer.

Broekens, J., DeGroot, D., & Kosters, W. A. (2008). Formal models of appraisal: Theory, specification, and computational model. *Cognitive Systems Research, 9*(3), 173–197.

Burke, J. W., McNeill, M. D. J., Charles, D. K., Morrow, P. J., Crosbie, J. H., & McDonough, S. M. (2009). Optimising engagement for stroke rehabilitation using serious games. *The Visual Computer, 25*(12), 1085–1099.

Castellano, G., Leite, I., Pereira, A., Martinho, C., Paiva, A., & McOwan, P. W. (2010). Affect recognition for interactive companions: Challenges and design in real world scenarios. *Journal of Multimodal User Interfaces, 3*(1–2), 89–98.

Cassell, J., Sullivan, J., Prevost, S., & Churchill, E. (2000). *Embodied conversational agents* Cambridge, MA: MIT Press.

Coyle, D., Matthews, M., Sharry, J., Nisbet, A., & Doherty, G. (2005). Personal investigator: A therapeutic 3D game for adolecscent psychotherapy. *Interactive Technology and Smart Education, 2*(2), 73–88.

Dautenhahn, K. (2007). Socially intelligent robots: Dimensions of human–robot interaction. *Philosophical Transactions of the Royal Society B: Biological Sciences, 362*(1480), 679–704.

Dautenhahn, K., & Werry, I. (2004). Towards interactive robots in autism therapy: Background, motivation and challenges. *Pragmatics & Cognition, 12*(1), 1–35.

D'Mello, S. K., Craig, S. D., Witherspoon, A., Mcdaniel, B., & Graesser, A. (2008). Automatic detection of learner's affect from conversational cues. *User Modeling and User-Adapted Interaction, 18*(1–2), 45–80.

Ekman, P., & Friesen, W. V. (1978). *Facial action coding system* Palo Alto, CA: Consulting Psychologists Press.

Forbes-Riley, K., Rotaru, M., & Litman, D. J. (2008). The relative impact of student affect on performance models in a spoken dialogue tutoring system. *User Modeling and User-Adapted Interaction, 18*(1−2), 11−43.

Gilleade, K., Dix, A., & Allanson, J. (2005). Affective videogames and modes of affective gaming: Assist me, challenge me, emote me. Retrieved from: <http://comp.eprints. lancs.ac.uk/1057/1/Gilleade_Affective_Gaming_DIGRA_2005.pdf>.

Goncalves, R., Pedrozo, A. L., Coutinho, E. S. F., Figueira, I., & Ventura, P. (2012). Efficacy of virtual reality exposure therapy in the treatment of PTSD: A systematic review. *PLoS One, 7*(12), e48469.

Gunes, H., Piccardi, M., & Pantic, M. (2008). *From the lab to the real world: Affect recognition using multiple cues and modalities* (pp. 185−218). Aarhus, Denmark: InTech Education and Publishing.

Hayes-Roth, B. (2009). Putting intelligent characters to work. *AI Magazine, 29*(2), 43.

Hayes-Roth, B., & Saker, R. (2010). Automating individualized coaching and authentic role-play practice for brief intervention training. *Methods of Information in Medicine, 49*(4), 406−411.

Horne-Moyer, H. L., Moyer, B. H., Messer, D. C., & Messer, E. S. (2014). The use of electronic games in therapy: A review with clinical implications. *Current Psychiatry Reports, 16*(12), 520. Available from http://dx.doi.org/10.1007/s11920-014-0520-6.

Hudlicka, E. (1998). Modeling emotion in symbolic cognitive architectures. In *Proceedings of the AAAI fall symposium: Emotional and intelligent I*, Orlando, FL, AAAI Press.

Hudlicka, E. (2002). Increasing socially-intelligent architecture realism by modeling and adapting to affect and personality. In K. Dautenhahn, A. H. Bond, L. Canamero, & B. Edmonds (Eds.), *Multiagent systems, artificial societies, and simulated organizations*. Dordrecht, The Netherlands: Kluwer Academic Publishers.

Hudlicka, E. (2003). *Modeling effects of behavior moderators on performance: Evaluation of the MAMID methodology and architecture* Phoenix, AZ: BRIMS-12.

Hudlicka, E. (2005). Affect sensing, recognition and expression: State-of-the-art overview. In *Proceedings of the first international conference on augmented cognition*, Las Vegas, NV.

Hudlicka, E. (2008a). Affective computing for game design. In *Proceedings of the 4th international North American conference on intelligent games and simulation (GAMEON-NA)*, Montreal, Canada.

Hudlicka, E. (2008b). What are we modeling when we model emotion? In *AAAI spring symposium: Emotion, personality, and social behavior*. Stanford University, CA; Menlo Park, CA: AAAI Press. Technical Report SS-08-04, pp. 52−59.

Hudlicka, E. (2008c). Modeling the Mechanisms of Emotion Effects on Cognition. In *AAAI fall symposium: Biologically inspired cognitive architectures*. Arlington, VA: Menlo Park, CA: AAAI Press. TR FS-08-04, pp. 82−86.

Hudlicka, E. (2009). Affective game engines: Motivation and requirements. In *4th international conference on foundations of digital games*. Orlando, FL: ACM Press.

Hudlicka, E. (2011a). Affective gaming in education, training and therapy: Motivation, requirements, techniques. In P. Felicia (Ed.), *Handbook of research on improving learning and motivation through educational games: Multidisciplinary approaches*. Hershey, PA: IGI Global.

Hudlicka, E. (2011b). Guidelines for developing computational models of emotions. *International Journal of Synthetic Emotions, 2*(1), 26−79.

Hudlicka, E. (2013). Virtual training and coaching of health behavior: Example from mindfulness meditation training. *Patient Education and Counseling, 92*(2), 160−166.

Hudlicka, E. (2014a). From habits to standards: Towards systematic design of emotion models and affective architectures. In Tibor Bosse, Joost Broekens, Joao Dias, & Janneke van der Zwaan (Eds.), *Towards pragmatic computational models of affective processes*. Berlin: Springer LNAI 8750, pp. 1−21.

Hudlicka, E. (2014b). Affective BICA: Challenges and open questions. *Biologically Inspired Agent Architectures, 14*, 98−125.

Hudlicka, E., Lisetti, C., Hodge, D., Paiva, A., Rizzo, A., & Wagner, E. (2008). Artificial agents for psychotherapy. In *Proceedings of the AAAI spring symposium on emotion, personality and social behavior*. Menlo Park, CA: AAAI. TR SS-08-04, pp. 60—64.

Hudlicka, E., & McNeese, M. (2002). User's affective & belief state: Assessment and GUI adaptation. *International Journal of User Modeling and User Adapted Interaction*, *12*, 1—47.

Hudlicka, E., Payr, S., Ventura, R., Becker-Asano, C., Fischer, K., Leite, I., et al. (2009). Social interaction with robots and agents: Where do we stand, where do we go? In *Proceedings of the 3rd international conference on affective computing and intelligent interaction*, Amsterdam, Holland.

Kang, S., Gratch, J., Sidner, C., Artstein, R., Huang, L., & Morency, L.-P. (2012, June 4—8). Towards building a virtual counselor: Modeling nonverbal behavior during intimate self-disclosure. In Conitzer, Winikoff, Padgham, & van der Hoek (Eds.), *Proceedings of the 11th International Conference on Autonomous Agents and Multiagent Systems (AAMAS 2012)*, Valencia, Spain.

Kapoor, A., Burleson, W., & Picard, R. W. (2007). Automatic prediction of frustration. *International Journal of Human-Computer Studies*, *65*(8), 724—736.

Lisetti, C., Amini, R., Yasavur, U., & Rishe, N. (2013). I Can Help You Change! An empathic virtual agent delivers behavior change health interventions. *ACM Transactions on Management Information Systems*, *4*(4) Article 19.

Loyall, A. B., & Bates, J. (1993). Real-time control of animated broad agents. In *Proceedings of the fifteenth annual conference of the cognitive science society* (pp. 664—669).

MacDorman, K. F. (2005). Androids as an experimental apparatus: Why is there an uncanny valley and can we exploit it. In *CogSci-2005 workshop: Toward social mechanisms of android science* (pp. 106—118).

Malbos, E., Boyer, L., & Lançon, C. (2013). Virtual reality in the treatment of mental disorders. *Presse Medicale (Paris, France: 1983)*, *42*(11), 1442—1452.

Mayer, J. D., & Salovey, P. (1995). Emotional intelligence and the construction and regulation of feelings. *Applied and Preventive Psychology*, *4*(3), 197—208.

Mcquiggan, S. W., Mott, B. W., & Lester, J. C. (2008). Modeling self-efficacy in intelligent tutoring systems: An inductive approach. *User Modeling and User-Adapted Interaction*, *18*(1-2), 81—123.

Mori, M. (1970). Bukimi no tani. *Energy*, *7*, 33—35.

Motraghi, T. E., Seim, R. W., Meyer, E. C., & Morissette, S. B. (2014). Virtual reality exposure therapy for the treatment of posttraumatic stress disorder: A methodological review using CONSORT guidelines. *Journal of Clinical Psychology*, *70*(3), 197—208.

Norman, T., & Badler, N. (1997). A virtual human presenter. In *IJCAI'97 Workshop on Animated Interface Agents*.

Ortony, A., Clore, G., & Collins, A. (1988). *The cognitive structure of emotions* New York: Cambridge University Press.

Ortony, A. (2001). On making believable emotional agents believable. In R. Trappl, & P. Petta (Eds.), *Emotions in humans and artifacts*. Cambridge, MA: MIT Press.

Ortony, A. (2002). On making believable emotional agents believable. In R. Trappl, P. Petta, & S. Payr (Eds.), *Emotions in humans and artifacts* (pp. 189—211).

Paiva, A., Dias, J., Sobral, D., Aylett, R., Sobreperez, P., Woods, S., et al. (2004). Caring for agents and agents that care: Building empathic relations with synthetic agents. In *Proceedings of the third international joint conference on autonomous agents and multiagent systems* (pp. 194—201). New York, NY.

Paiva, A., Dias, J., Sobral, D., Aylett, R., Woods, S., Hall, L., et al. (2005). Learning by feeling: Evoking empathy with synthetic characters. *Applied Artificial Intelligence*, *19*(3—4), 235—266.

Picard, R. (1997). *Affective computing* Cambridge, MA: MIT Press.

Popescu, A., Broekens, J., & van Someren, M. (2014). GAMYGDALA: An emotion engine for games. *IEEE Transactions on Affective Computing*, *5*(1), 32—44.

Prendinger, H., & Ishizuka, M. (2004). *Life-like characters* (Heidelberg: *Springer* pp. 1−4).

Reeves, B., & Nass, C. (1996). The media equation: How people treat computers, television, and new media like real people and places. *Computers & Mathematics with Applications, 33*(5) 128−128.

Reilly, W. S. & Bates, J. (1992). Building emotional agents. Pittsburgh, PA: School of Computer Science, Carnegie Mellon University.

Reilly, W. S. N. (2006). Modeling what happens between emotional antecedents and emotional consequents. In *Paper presented at ACE 2006*, Vienna, Austria.

Ricciardi, F., & De Paolis, L. T. D. (2014). A comprehensive review of serious games in health professions. *International Journal of Computer Games Technology, 2014*, 9.

Rickel, J., & Johnson, W. L. (1999). Animated agents for procedural training in virtual reality: Perception, cognition, and motor control. *Applied Artificial Intelligence, 13*, 343−382.

Rizzo, A., Difede, J., Rothbaum, B. O., Reger, G., Spitalnick, J., Cukor, J., et al. (2010). Development and early evaluation of the Virtual Iraq/Afghanistan exposure therapy system for combat-related PTSD. *Annals of the New York Academy of Sciences, 1208*(1), 114−125.

Rizzo, A., Forbell, E., Lange, B., Buckwalter, J. G., Williams, J., Sagae, K., et al. (2012). *SimCoach: An online intelligent virtual agent system for breaking down barriers to care for service members and veterans. Healing War Trauma: A Handbook of Creative Approaches* New York: Routledge.

De Rosis, F., Pelachaud, C., Poggi, I., Carofiglio, V., & De Carolis, B. (2003). From Greta's mind to her face: Modelling the dynamics of affective states in a conversational embodied agent. *International Journal of Human-Computer Studies, 59*(1), 81−118.

Sajjad, S., Hanan Abdullah, A., Sharif, M., & Mohsin, S. (2014). Psychotherapy through video game to target illness related problematic behaviors of children with brain tumor. *Current Medical Imaging Reviews, 10*(1), 62−72.

Scherer, K. R. (1992). Emotions are biologically and socially constituted: A response to Greenwood. *New Ideas in Psychology, 10*(1), 19−22.

Scherer, K., Schorr, A., & Johnstone, T. (2001). *Appraisal processes in emotion: Theory, methods, research* NY: Oxford University Press.

Schröder, M., Baggia, P., Burkhardt, F., Pelachaud, C., Peter, C., & Zovato, E. (2011). EmotionML − An upcoming standard for representing emotions and related states. In S. D'Mello, A. Graesser, B. Schuller, & J.-C. Martin (Eds.), *Affective computing and intelligent interaction* (pp. 316−325). Berlin: Springer.

Sourina, O., Wang, Q., & Nguyen, M. K. (2011). EEG-based "serious" games and monitoring tools for pain management. *Studies in Health Technology and Informatics, 163*, 606−610.

Smith, C. A., & Kirby, L. (2000). Consequences require antecedents: Toward a process model of emotion elicitation. In J. P. Forgas (Ed.), *Feeling and thinking: The role of affect in social cognition*. NY: Cambridge University Press.

Sykes, J. (2004). Affective gaming. Retrieved May 2008, from: <http://www.jonsykes. com/Ivory.htm>.

Yannakakis, G. N., & Paiva, A. (2014). Emotion in games. In R. A. Calvo, S. D'Mello, J. Gratch, & A. Kappas (Eds.), *Handbook of affective computing* (pp. 459−471). NY: Oxford University Press.

Yannakakis, G. N., Hallam, J., & Lund, H. H. (2008). Entertainment capture through heart rate activity in physical interactive playgrounds. *User Modeling and User-Adapted Interaction, 18*(1−2), 207−243.

Zeng, Z., Pantic, M., Roisman, G. I., & Huang, T. S. (2009). A survey of affect recognition methods: Audio, visual, and spontaneous expressions. *Pattern Analysis and Machine Intelligence, IEEE Transactions On, 31*(1), 39−58.

CHAPTER 5

Automated Mental State Detection for Mental Health Care

Sidney K. D'Mello

Departments of Psychology and Computer Science, University of Notre Dame, Notre Dame, IN, USA

INTRODUCTION

Jackson, a 30-year-old male, was recently diagnosed with depression and is receiving weekly cognitive-behavioral therapy (CBT) sessions. He wears a device that records his physiological activity (e.g., electrodermal activity, heart rate variability) as he goes about his everyday routine. At the onset of each CBT session, his therapist inputs his physiological data for the week into a computer program. The program provides an aggregate of Jackson's levels of positive and negative affect as well as pinpoints moments where these responses peaked. The therapist uses this information to monitor Jackson's progress and to dynamically tailor the therapy, for example, by asking Jackson to recall events corresponding to some of the peaks in affect.

Olivia is a 3-year-old girl who recently dislocated her right shoulder. She feels some pain, but has difficulty precisely expressing the intensity of the felt pain to her physician. The physician asks her to hold still for 5 s and then to rotate her arm using standard range of motion tests (e.g., abduction, flexion). This makes her wince and she utters a small cry. The physician records a video of her face both when her arm was still and during the tests. An audio recording of her cry is also synchronized with the video. A computer program provides an estimate of Olivia's pain intensity by analyzing the change in her facial expressions and sound patterns during the range of motion tests compared to when her arm was held still. In addition to the X-ray taken earlier, and his physical exam, he uses the computer-provided estimate of Olivia's pain intensity to select a course of treatment.

Luis was recently diagnosed with attention deficit hyperactivity disorder (ADHD). He simply cannot concentrate on his schoolwork and his grades are beginning to suffer. This causes him to feel depressed

Artificial Intelligence in Behavioral and Mental Health Care.
DOI: http://dx.doi.org/10.1016/B978-0-12-420248-1.00005-2

because he thinks he is not "smart enough" to succeed in college. Luis's psychiatrist prescribes him with a standard amphetamine stimulant. He also gives Luis a small device that can be affixed to his laptop. The device monitors Luis's eye gaze when he uses his laptop to complete homework assignments, do assigned readings, or to study for a test. A computer program automatically analyzes his eye gaze and provides estimates of Luis's levels of attention during various phases in the study session. For example, it estimates when Luis is concentrating, when he is distracted, and even when he zones out despite trying to focus. The software provides Luis with feedback on his levels of attention aligned with the various study activities. Luis uses this information to replan his study strategy and to restudy certain topics. In addition, a new software program he downloaded can actually use this information in real-time to suggest topics for restudy. Luis's grades start to improve and he feels empowered.

These hypothetical scenarios illustrate how machines (devices and computer programs) that can automatically detect a person's mental state can provide actionable information to improve mental health care. These machine-provided mental state estimates can complement self- or observer-reports of the same constructs as in the cases of Jackson and Olivia. They can also afford reflection and dynamic action as with Luis. These machines can detect a variety of affective and cognitive states, such as physiological arousal, feelings (e.g., pain), affective dimensions (e.g., valence and arousal), cognitive states (e.g., attention and mental workload), emotional states (e.g., sad, happy, angry), and even complex cognitive-affective blends (e.g., confusion, frustration). They can target both momentary episodes (e.g., specific attentional lapses), intermediate mood states (e.g., a bad day), and prolonged mental phenomena (e.g., stress and depression). Some are best suited for use in controlled settings (e.g., a physician's office), others are best suited for home and office use, while some can be deployed in the wild for long-term ambulatory monitoring of mental states.

The "AI" in automated mental state detection comes from the overall goal of developing machines with the capability of sensing complex mental phenomena, which was previously a uniquely human ability, and from the different subfields of AI involved in the development of such machines (e.g., computer vision, machine learning). The purpose of this chapter is to demystify these seemingly magical machines that can "read-out" a person's mental state. This is done by first providing the theoretical and technical foundation of the highly interdisciplinary field of "automatic mental state detection." This is followed by an exposition of a few illustrative examples of recent mental state detection systems. The chapter concludes with a discussion of open issues in the field and provides some speculative comments on its future.

THEORETICAL AND TECHNICAL FOUNDATION

Automated detection of mental states is an active area of research within the broader umbrella of *human—computer interaction* and its sister field of *human factors and cognitive ergonomics*. It is composed of different subfields, such as social signal processing (Mehu & Scherer, 2012; Vinciarelli, Pantic, & Bourlard, 2009), affective computing (Cowie et al., 2001; Douglas-Cowie et al., 2007; Marsella, Gratch, & Petta, 2010; McKeown, Valstar, Cowie, Pantic, & Schroder, 2012; Picard, 1997, 2010), attention-aware computing (D'Mello, Cobian, & Hunter, 2013; Roda & Thomas, 2006), and augmented cognition (Marshall, 2005; St. John, Kobus, Morrison, & Schmorrow, 2004), each focusing on different mental states in different contexts. Automated mental state detection is truly an interdisciplinary field. Its psychological roots are in cognitive psychology, affective sciences, social psychology, study of nonverbal behavior, and psychophysiology. Its technical roots lie in engineering and computer science, specifically sensors and wearable devices, digital signal processing (e.g., computer vision, acoustic modeling), and machine learning.

The psychological arm of automated mental state detection is grounded in theories that highlight the embodied nature of mental processes. Embodied theories of cognition and affect posit that mental states are not restricted to the confines of the mind but are manifested in the body (Barsalou, 2008; deVega, Glenberg, & Graesser, 2008; Ekman, 1992; Niedenthal, 2007; Russell, Bachorowski, & Fernandez-Dols, 2003). One of the most direct examples of a mind—body link is the increased activation of the sympathetic nervous system during fight-or-flight responses (Larsen, Berntson, Poehlmann, Ito, & Cacioppo, 2008). There are also well-known relationships between facial expressions and affective states (Coan, 2010; Ekman, 1984), for example, the furrowed brow during experiences of confusion (Darwin, 1872; D'Mello & Graesser, 2014). There is also a long history of using bodily/physiological responses to investigate cognitive processes like attention and cognitive load. For example, the study of eye movements (oculesics) has emerged as an invaluable tool to investigate visual attention (Deubel & Schneider, 1996; Hoffman & Subramaniam, 1995; Rayner, 1998), while

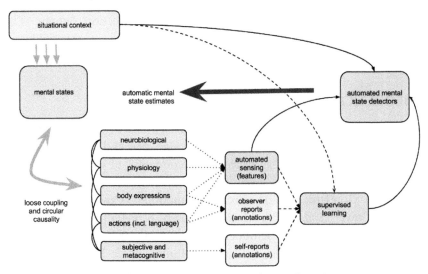

Figure 5.1 Processes and steps in automatic mental state detection.

electroencephalography has long been used as an index into mental workload (Berka et al., 2007). This close mind—body relationship is unsurprising once one realizes that cognition and affect are in the service of action. Simply put, we think and we feel in order to act. Bodies are the agents of action, hence, monitoring observable bodily changes can provide critical insights into unobservable mental states. This key idea underlies the automated detection approach which attempts to infer mental states from bodily responses.

Figure 5.1 provides a summary of the foundational ideas of automated mental state detection. The general idea is that a person's interactions with the world (situational context) give rise to latent (or hidden) mental states that cannot be directly measured. The mental states are associated with changes at multiple levels (neurobiological, physiological, bodily expressions, overt actions, and subjective/metacognitive feelings/reflections), which in turn influence the mental states themselves — this is referred to as circular causality (Lewis, 2005). Some of these changes are implicit (e.g., neurobiological, some physiological changes) in that they occur outside of conscious awareness, while others are more explicit (e.g., overt actions, metacognitive reflections). A subset of these implicit and explicit changes is readable by machine sensors and human observers, while others are only accessible to the self (dotted lines in Figure 5.1).

The computational problem is to infer (or estimate) the latent mental states from the machine-readable signals recorded by the sensors.

Solving the aforementioned inference problem requires solving two interrelated computational challenges. The first challenge is to extract diagnostic information (called features) from the signals recorded by the sensors. This is a sensor-specific component of mental state detection because the method used varies based on the sensor and corresponding signal. For example, if the sensor is a webcam, then the signal is a video (presumably of the face). In this case, the features might be the activation of specific facial muscles or Action Units (AUs) (Ekman & Friesen, 1978), such as the inner brow raise (AU 1) or the lip pucker (AU 18). Computer vision-based techniques are needed to automatically compute these facial features from video (Pantic & Patras, 2006; Valstar, Mehu, Jiang, Pantic, & Scherer, 2012). Similarly, pitch and amplitude are common paralinguistic (acoustic-prosodic) features extracted from an audio signal recorded with a microphone (the sensor). Here, digital signal processing methods applied to the speech domain are needed (Eyben, Wöllmer, & Schuller, 2010). If the content of the spoken signal is to be analyzed, then this requires automatic speech recognition followed by natural language processing techniques to identify pertinent features (Pang & Lee, 2008).

The second challenge involves making inferences of a person's mental state from the features extracted from the signals. This falls under the purview of machine learning and is somewhat, but not entirely, signal-independent. Most (but not all) researchers adopt supervised learning methods to solve this problem. In its simplest form, supervised learning attempts to automatically learn a program from training data (Domingos, 2012). Supervised learning generally proceeds as follows. Annotated training data in the form of features (extracted from signals recorded by sensors as noted above) with temporally synchronized annotations of mental states (annotations are usually provided by humans) is collected as (ideally) a large number of people are in the midst of experiencing the mental states. Supervised learning methods are then applied to automatically *model* (learn) the relationship between the features and corresponding annotations (dashed lines in Figure 5.1). Aspects of the situational context are sometimes used as additional input to provide contextual information to the learning process. The resulting *model*, created during supervised learning, is then used to produce computer-generated estimates of mental states when presented with new data without corresponding annotations (e.g., collected at some later time and/or from a person not in the training data — solid lines in Figure 5.1). Accuracy and generalizability are the two immediate metrics of performance. Accuracy is measured as the extent to which automated mental state estimates align with some objective standard, typically self- or observer-reports of the mental states. Generalizability is concerned with the robustness of the detectors when applied to data beyond what was used to train the supervised classifiers.

It should be noted that the aforementioned discussion intentionally glosses over several of the complexities involved in the various stages of building an automated mental state detector. Data collection and annotation has subtle nuances that need to be mastered. Computing diagnostic features requires solving all sorts of open problems in respective fields (e.g., computer vision, acoustic signal processing, digital signal processing, time series modeling, natural language understanding). Then there is the issue of selecting a subset of diagnostic features, modeling relationships among features, and reducing dimensionality of the feature subspace. The training data usually need to be sampled and manipulated in numerous ways before supervised learning can proceed. Then comes the choice of supervised learning method from the multiple available possibilities (e.g., neural networks, Bayesian classifiers, decision trees, and support vector machines), followed by methods to parameterize the model. If multiple modalities (e.g., audio + visual) are used, then this brings about the additional challenge of deciding how to combine modalities. Finally, appropriate validation methods and metrics need to be selected, which is a nontrivial issue as well. Taken together, these challenges have supported rich and productive interdisciplinary research agendas and will continue to do so for years to come.

EXAMPLE SYSTEMS

This section turns to a discussion of a few exemplary case studies depicting the measurement of the variety of mental states of relevance to mental health care. The exposition is far from comprehensive, nor does it intend to be, since an in-depth discussion of the relevant work in this area would be more in line with an edited volume devoted solely to the subject of mental state detection. The idea is to highlight a few recent systems that have had some success in detecting mental states of particular relevance to mental health care.

Affective States

Affect is implicated in a number of mental disorders (e.g., depression, stress), so automated affect detection might be a promising way to obtain an indirect estimate of a person's underlying mental health. Affect is used as a general term to encompass both moods and emotions, which can be differentiated along a number of dimensions (Rosenberg, 1998). Moods are considered to be more transitory and have a background influence on consciousness, while emotions are brief, intense states that occupy the forefront of consciousness, have significant physiological and behavioral manifestations, and rapidly prepare the bodily systems for action. Most of the work on affect detection has focused on detecting emotions rather than moods, and an overwhelming majority of this work has emphasized the so-called "basic emotions," which typically include anger, surprise, happiness, disgust, sadness, and fear (Ekman, 1992). Nonbasic emotions, such as boredom, confusion, frustration, engagement, and curiosity, share a subset of the features commonly attributed to basic emotions (Ekman, 1992) and have received far less attention (D'Mello & Calvo, 2013). Some researchers eschew discrete affect representations (e.g., sad vs angry) by focusing on identifying levels of intensity on one or more core affect dimensions (Fontaine, Scherer, Roesch, & Ellsworth, 2007), with a specific emphasis on valence (unpleasant to pleasant) and arousal (sleepy to active).

Affect detection is one of the most widely studied mental state detection problems, evidenced by numerous recent reviews (Calvo & D'Mello, 2010; Calvo, D'Mello, Gratch, & Kappas, 2014; D'Mello & Kory, 2015; Zeng, Pantic, Roisman, & Huang, 2009). Affect detection systems greatly differ in terms of sensors/signals used, the affect representation (i.e., discrete vs dimensional), the specific affective states detected, whether the states naturally occur or are experimentally induced, and the contexts in which affect detection is situated. To give a sense of the work in this area, three affect detection efforts are reviewed, each emphasizing a different combination of sensor/signal, affect representation, affect state, and situational context.

Basic Emotions

The first study reviewed is a lab study that focused on detection of basic emotions elicited through an affect elicitation procedure. Janssen et al. (2013) compared automatic detection versus human perception of three basic emotions (happy, sad, angry), relaxed, and neutral induced via an autobiographical recall procedure (Baker & Guttfreund, 1993). According to this procedure, 17 participants were asked to write about two events in their life associated with experiences of happiness, anger, sadness, and neutral. Participants were then asked to recall a subset of those events in a way that made them relive the emotions experienced and to verbally describe each event (in Dutch). Audio, video, and physiological signals (electrodermal activity, skin temperature, respiration, and electrocardiography) were recorded while participants recalled and described the events. Each recording was associated with the label of the corresponding emotion that the participant was asked to recall.

A variety of standard features, such as specific facial landmarks, head position, fundamental frequency of speech, and overall level and variance in each physiological signal, were automatically computed. A support vector machine classifier (supervised learning method) produced the best result when it only focused on facial and physiological features. It obtained an accuracy of 82% in correctly identifying the emotion label of each recording. In addition, the authors directly compared computer detection to human detection of emotion. This was done by asking a set of human judges (both US and Dutch) to identify the participants' emotions based on various stimuli combinations (audio-only, video-only, audio-video). The Dutch judges were the most accurate (63%) when only provided with the audio (which was also in Dutch) while the US judges were the most accurate (31%) when they had access to both audio and video. However, accuracy of the humans (63% and 31%) was considerably lower than accuracy of the automated detector (82%), a finding with profound implications.

Nonbasic Emotions

The second study (Bosch et al., 2015) adopted a markedly different approach from Janssen et al. (2013), which focused on multimodal detection of (mostly) basic emotions experimentally elicited in controlled laboratory environments. Bosch et al. (2015) studied unimodal detection of nonbasic emotions that naturally occurred in a noisy real-world setting of a computer-enabled classroom. In this study, 137 middle and high school students played a conceptual physics educational game in small groups for 2.5 h across 3 days as part of their regular physics/physical science classes. Trained observers performed live affect annotations by observing students one at a time using a round-robin technique (observing one student until visible affect was detected or 20 s had elapsed and then moving on to the next student in a preplanned order — see Ocumpaugh, Baker, and Rodrigo (2012)). The emotions of interest were boredom, confusion, delight, engagement, and frustration. Videos of students' faces and upper bodies were recorded during game-play and synchronized with the affect annotations. The videos were processed using the FACET computer-vision program (Emotient, 2014), which provides estimates of the likelihood of 19 facial AUs (Ekman & Friesen, 1978) (e.g., raised brow, tightened lips), head pose (orientation), and position. Body movement was also estimated from the videos using motion-filtering algorithms (Kory, D'Mello, & Olney, in press). A machine learning approach was adopted to automatically discriminate each affective state from all the others and was validated in a manner that generalizes to new students. Person-independent automatic detection accuracies ranged from 62% (frustrated vs. other states) to 83% (delighted vs. other states), which is notable given the noisy nature of the environment with students incessantly fidgeting, talking with one another, asking questions, leaving to go to the bathroom, and even occasionally using their cellphones (against classroom policy).

Affect Dimensions

The third study reviewed is not exactly a study, but a collection of different efforts aimed at solving a particular affect detection problem. The idea is that it is difficult to ascertain progress in any given research area (affect detection in this case) when individual researchers apply their own methods to their own data sets and use their own selected metrics to evaluate performance. Direct comparisons of results from different research groups are confounded as any observable difference can be attributed to the method, the data, or the performance metric. Challenge competitions, a common theme in computer science and AI research, offer one answer to this problem. Here, researchers are asked to apply their methods to a fixed dataset and the results are evaluated with a fixed metric(s), thereby affording direct comparisons across methods developed by different research groups.

The Audio-Video Emotion Recognition Challenge (AVEC) is an annual affect detection challenge that was first organized as part of the 2011 Affective Computing and Intelligent Interaction (ACII) conference series (D'Mello, Graesser, Schuller, & Martin, 2011). The focus here is on the 2012 AVEC challenge (Schuller, Valster, Eyben, Cowie, & Pantic, 2012), which considered automatic detection of affect dimensions during human—computer interactions. The AVEC 2012 challenge used data from the SEMAINE corpus (McKeown et al., 2012), which was designed to collect naturalistic data of humans interacting with artificial agents. The artificial agents take on different emotionally stereotyped roles (e.g., Spike is angry and confrontational while Prudence is even-tempered and sensible), thereby biasing the affective tone of the conversation. Videos of participants' faces and audio of their speech recorded during these somewhat affectively charged interactions were provided to researchers. Two to six human raters annotated each video along four affect dimensions: valence (negative to positive), arousal (sleepy to active), power (low control to high control), and expectation (unexpected to expected). The affect annotations were continuously scaled and ranged from -1 to 1, so the task was to predict the intensity of each affect dimension via automated audio-visual affect detection methods. This emphasis on dimensional representations of affect (e.g., valence, arousal, power, expectation) is a more important discriminating factor than the categorical or discrete representations (e.g., anger, fear) adopted in the previous two studies reviewed.

Researchers were given two subsets of the annotated data to develop their models (training and development subset), which were then applied on a separate subset for which the annotations were not available to the researchers (test subset). Each research group submitted affect predictions for each dimension independently by applying their methods on the test subset. Results were available from 10 research groups. The winning team achieved a correlation of 0.45 when averaged across the four dimensions (Nicolle, Rapp, Bailly, Prevost, & Chetouani, 2012), a notable performance given the complexity of the task.

Attentional Lapses (Mind Wandering)

Mindfulness, or the ability to devote one's attentional resources to the present task and surroundings, is considered to be an important component of mental health (Brown & Ryan, 2003). However, mind wandering, defined as involuntary lapses in attention from the task at hand to internal task-unrelated thoughts (Smallwood & Schooler, 2015), is all too frequent. For example, in a large-scale study, mind wandering was tracked in 5,000 people from 83 countries working in 86 occupations with an iPhone app that prompted people to report off-task thoughts at random intervals (Killingsworth & Gilbert, 2010). The main finding was that people reported mind wandering for 46.9% of the prompts, and a time-lagged analysis provided some evidence that mind wandering could potentially cause feelings of unhappiness. Furthermore, research has indicated that individuals with dysphoria (i.e., symptoms of depression) and ADHD have elevated levels of mind wandering across a variety of tasks (Shaw & Giambra, 1993; Smallwood et al., 2004; Smallwood, O'Connor, Sudbery, & Obonsawin, 2007). Thus, automated detectors of mind wandering as people go about their daily routines have the potential to provide valuable information into the attentional processes implicated in mental health.

Automated detectors of mind wandering are just beginning to emerge. As is typical for early stages of research, initial efforts are concentrated on one or more restricted task domains. In the case of mind wandering, the focus has been on reading comprehension tasks (Bixler & D'Mello, 2014; Blanchard, Bixler, & D'Mello, 2014; Drummond & Litman, 2010; Franklin, Smallwood, & Schooler, 2011). As an illustrative example, Bixler and D'Mello (2014) investigated whether eye gaze could be used to develop an automated mind wandering detector during reading. Their focus on eye gaze was motivated by decades of research highlighting the tight coupling between visual attention and eye movements (Deubel & Schneider, 1996; Hoffman & Subramaniam, 1995; Rayner, 1998). In their study, training data were collected from 178 undergraduate students from two US universities in a lab study. Tobii T60 and TX 300 eye trackers (one at each university) were used to record gaze patterns of the students over the course of a 30-min text-comprehension activity. Mind wandering was measured via auditory thought probes, which is a standard technique used for online tracking of mind wandering (Smallwood et al., 2004). Eye gaze features were computed from gaze fixations in windows of variable length (3, 5 s, etc.) that immediately preceded a mind wandering probe. Example features include fixation durations, number of words skipped, fixations on different types of words, and saccade lengths. Supervised learning methods, applied to detect mind wandering, yielded an average recognition rate of 66% and in a manner that generalized to new people. Though preliminary, these results are promising since they denote the possibility of automatically measuring a highly internal mental state like mind wandering. The increased availability of cost-effective consumer-grade eye trackers (some retail for as low as $99) also suggests that this line of work can soon be taken out of the lab and into the wild.

Pain

Pain has been associated with numerous mental disorders. A large-scale study of 85,088 people from 17 countries indicated that chronic back/neck pain in a 12-month period was a positive predictor of mood disorders, anxiety disorders, and alcohol abuse/dependence after covarying age and sex (Demyttenaere et al., 2007). Measurement of pain, which primarily relies on self-report questionnaires (Hjermstad et al., 2011), is subject to well-known limitations of subjectivity, interpretability, and feasibility of administration in some populations (Stinson, Kavanagh, Yamada, Gill, & Stevens, 2006).

Automatic pain detectors can alleviate several of these challenges by offering reliable monitoring of pain. The numbers of automated pain detection systems are few and far between (Hammal & Cohn, 2012; Lai, Levinger, Begg, Gilleard, & Palaniswami, 2009; Littlewort, Bartlett, & Lee, 2007), presumably due to the complexities in obtaining suitable datasets for detector building. However, the recent release of the UNBC-McMaster shoulder pain expression archive database is expected to catalyze research in this area. The database includes 129 participants who self-identified as experiencing shoulder pain. The data consist of videos of participants performing eight range of motion tests (e.g., abduction, internal and external arm rotation) along with self-reports of pain intensity following each test. A subset of the data (200 video sequences from 25 participants) has been made available to the research community for the purpose of building automatic pain detection systems (Lucey, Cohn, Prkachin, Solomon, & Matthews, 2011).

Hammal and Cohn (2012) provide an illustrative example of one such automated pain detection system utilizing the UNBC-McMaster database. Their approach consisted of extracting appearance-based features from each frame in the video and filtering them via a set of log-normal filters. A support vector machine classifier was used to build detectors of four levels of pain (no pain, trace pain, weak pain, strong pain). They achieved an average classification accuracy of 0.56 (F1 metric) when the validation method ensured generalizability to new participants, a promising result given the complexity of the problem and the early stages of research in this area.

Depression

Depression is perhaps one of the most common and serious mental health conditions. Automatic depression detection systems have considerable potential to combat its negative effects by providing early warning indicators of depression as well as serving as an objective measure of the effectiveness of depression treatments. Research in depression detection has recently accelerated, presumably due to the introduction of the Depression Recognition Sub-challenge (DSC) as part of the 2013 and 2014 AVEC series (Valstar et al., 2013, 2014). The challenge requires researchers to develop and evaluate their own depression detectors on the same dataset, thereby affording meaningful comparisons of each method since data and evaluation metrics are held constant.

The dataset used in the DSC challenge consisted of 240 h of videos (with audio) of 84 participants who completed simple tasks guided by a computer interface across multiple sessions. The number of tasks, sessions, and session length varied across participants. Participants' levels of depression were obtained via the Beck Depression Inventory-II (Beck, Steer, & Brown, 1996). The data were also annotated for basic affect dimensions, but these are not discussed here. A subset of these data was used for the 2013 and 2014 challenges. In the most recent 2014 challenge, this included 300 videos of participants reading aloud in German excerpts from a German fable (northwind task) and responding to simple questions in German (e.g., "what is your favorite dish" — freeform task). Videos of participants' faces and audio of their speech were recorded during these tasks. A subset of these data along with depression levels of each participant were made available to researchers (training and development partitions). A different subset, called the test partition, was used to evaluate results and the depression levels for these participants were withheld.

Researchers adopted a wide variety of approaches in response to this challenge. The results were quantified via root mean square error (RMSE) between predicted and actual depression levels for participants in the test partition and ranged from 8 to 12. The winning system emphasized modeling the timing and coordination between speech production and facial expression and achieved an RMSE of 8.12 (Williamson, Quatieri, Helfer, Ciccarelli, & Mehta, 2014). This result represented a small improvement over the best result of the 2013 challenge (RMSE of 8.50), which was won by the same research team (Williamson et al., 2013) on a related but different dataset.

Stress

Both episodic and chronic stress have long been associated with numerous physical and mental health outcomes (see review by Lupien, McEwen,

Gunnar, & Heim, 2009). Automatic detection of stress has important applications for stress diagnosis, treatment, and monitoring. Consequently, considerable research has been devoted toward the design of automatic stress detection systems. Computational researchers use the term stress somewhat broadly to include cognitive stress (e.g., induced by taxing working memory), emotional stress (e.g., induced via negative activating emotions), and social stress (e.g., induced by social stressors). The focus of this chapter is on automatic detection of clinical stress as measured via the widely used Perceived Stress Scale (PSS) (Cohen, Kamarck, & Mermelstein, 1983).

The study by Sano and Picard (2013) is unique from the other studies reviewed in this chapter because it adopts a multimodal approach for ambulatory stress monitoring of stress across a period of 5 days. Eighteen participants were asked to complete the PSS along with other pertinent self-report questionnaires (sleep habits, alcoholic consumption, moods). Participants were then affixed with an Affectiva Q-sensor, a wearable wristband with an electrodermal activity sensor and an accelerometer. An Android application installed on their phones was used to record various aspects of their daily routine including phone usage (e.g., number of calls made, texts received, screen on times) as well as location using GPS (e.g., distance traveled). Participants also completed a short morning survey and an evening survey on their phones (e.g., sleep time, alertness on waking up, cups of coffee consumed in the day). The physiological, activity, and survey data were collected for a period of 5 days as participants went about their everyday activities. Participants were then assigned to a low-versus high-stress group based on their scores on the PSS. Supervised learning methods were then used to discriminate among the low- and high-stress groups using various combinations of features. As a baseline, the authors reported a classification accuracy of 87.5%, obtained via the use of the self-report surveys. However, accuracies of approximately 75% were obtained using solely objective information gleaned from the activity logs based on cell phone usage and location data. Surprisingly, the physiological features did not make a substantial contribution to stress detection on these data. Nevertheless, the fact that stress could be predicted with reasonable accuracy from activity logs and location data is a significant finding because it highlights the potential for ambulatory stress monitoring using an everyday device (a smart phone) and without requiring any additional sensors.

CONCLUDING REMARKS

Measurement is a precursor to meaningful change. The science and practice of mental health care has much to gain from fully automated systems that provide fine-grained assessments of a person's mental state over extended periods of time and in a variety of contexts. These mental state detection systems can be integrated within the overall mental healthcare system at multiple levels, for example clinical decision-making, ambulatory monitoring, and technology-supported therapies. This chapter discussed some of the theoretical and technical issues underlying such systems and grounded the key issues in the context of a few case studies focused on automatically detecting mental states of relevance to mental health care (i.e., affect, attention (or lack thereof), pain, depression, and stress). The highly selective nature of this review regrettably precluded a discussion of many other excellent systems developed by dedicated groups of international researchers in many different fields who are continually making theoretical, technical, and practical innovations to crack the challenge of automatic mental state detection.

Automatic mental state detection is a tough nut to crack. The current systems are not yet ready for practical use although there has been much progress over the years. Many of the earlier years in the field were focused on demonstrating research prototypes as proof-of-concepts of the possibility of automatic mental state detection. This was necessary to convince the initial skeptics and naysayers who ridiculed the early pioneers of the field (as discussed in Picard, 2010). These early (generation 1) systems focused on a small subset of mental states that were acted (or induced) by a small number of people in the confines of the laboratory. Generation 1 was also marked by the use of expensive and obtrusive sensing devices that were inherently nonscalable and with the use of less technically sophisticated computational techniques and less stringent validation methods. We are now in generation 2, where the emphasis is on detecting naturalistic experiences of a larger variety of mental states in more real-world contexts using more scalable, wearable, and unobtrusive sensing and with more sophisticated techniques and more stringent validation methods. Much progress is anticipated for these generation 2 systems, but they may still fall short in some respects. In particular, there needs to be an eye for improving detection accuracies, for demonstrating applicability across a range of real-world contexts, for realizing generalizability across different populations, and for satisfactorily addressing thorny ethical issues. It is not a matter of "will" but "when" these challenges will be addressed, upon which automatic mental state detection systems will make a meaningful and measurable impact on peoples' lives by improving their mental health.

ACKNOWLEDGMENTS

This research was supported by the National Science Foundation (NSF) (DRL 1108845) and the Bill & Melinda Gates Foundation. Any opinions, findings and conclusions, or recommendations expressed in this chapter are those of the authors and do not necessarily reflect the views of the funding agencies.

REFERENCES

Baker, R. C., & Guttfreund, D. O. (1993). The effects of written autobiographical recollection induction procedures on mood. *Journal of Clinical Psychology*, *49*(4), 563–568.

Barsalou, L. W. (2008). Grounded cognition. *Annual Review of Psychology*, *59*(1), 617–645.

Beck, A. T., Steer, R. A., & Brown, G. K. (1996). *Manual for the Beck depression inventory-II*. San Antonio, TX: Psychological Corporation.

Berka, C., Levendowski, D. J., Lumicao, M. N., Yau, A., Davis, G., Zivkovic, V. T., et al. (2007). EEG correlates of task engagement and mental workload in vigilance, learning, and memory tasks. *Aviation, Space, and Environmental Medicine*, *78*(Suppl. 1), B231–B244.

Bixler, R., & D'Mello, S. (2014). Toward fully automated person-independent detection of mind wandering. In V. Dimitrova, T. Kuflik, D. Chin, F. Ricci, P. Dolog, & G.-J. Houben (Eds.), *Proceedings of the 22nd international conference on user modeling, adaptation, and personalization* (pp. 37–48). Switzerland: Springer International Publishing.

Blanchard, N., Bixler, R., & D'Mello, S. K. (2014). Automated physiological-based detection of mind wandering during learning. In S. Trausan-Matu, K. Boyer, M. Crosby, & K. Panourgia (Eds.), *Proceedings of the 12th international conference on Intelligent Tutoring Systems (ITS 2014)* (pp. 55–60). Switzerland: Springer International Publishing.

Bosch, N., D'Mello, S. K., Baker, R., Ocumpaugh, J., Shute, V., Ventura, M., et al. (2015). Automatic detection of learning-centered affective states in the wild. In *Proceedings of the 2015 international conference on Intelligent User Interfaces (IUI 2015)* (pp. 379–388). New York, NY: ACM.

Brown, K. W., & Ryan, R. M. (2003). The benefits of being present: Mindfulness and its role in psychological well-being. *Journal of Personality and Social Psychology*, *84*(4), 822.

Calvo, R. A., & D'Mello, S. K. (2010). Affect detection: An interdisciplinary review of models, methods, and their applications. *IEEE Transactions on Affective Computing*, *1*(1), 18–37. Available from: http://dx.doi.org/10.1109/T-AFFC.2010.1.

Calvo, R. A., D'Mello, S. K., Gratch, J., & Kappas, A. (Eds.), (2014). *The Oxford handbook of affective computing*. New York, NY: Oxford University Press.

Coan, J. A. (2010). Emergent ghosts of the emotion machine. *Emotion Review*, *2*(3), 274–285.

Cohen, S., Kamarck, T., & Mermelstein, R. (1983). A global measure of perceived stress. *Journal of Health and Social Behavior, 24*(4), 385–396.

Cowie, R., Douglas-Cowie, E., Tsapatsoulis, N., Votsis, G., Kollias, S., Fellenz, W., et al. (2001). Emotion recognition in human-computer interaction. *IEEE Signal Processing Magazine, 18*(1), 32–80.

Darwin, C. (1872). *The expression of the emotions in man and animals.* London: John Murray.

Demyttenaere, K., Bruffaerts, R., Lee, S., Posada-Villa, J., Kovess, V., Angermeyer, M. C., et al. (2007). Mental disorders among persons with chronic back or neck pain: Results from the World Mental Health Surveys. *Pain, 129*(3), 332–342.

Deubel, H., & Schneider, W. X. (1996). Saccade target selection and object recognition: Evidence for a common attentional mechanism. *Vision Research, 36*(12), 1827–1837.

deVega, M., Glenberg, A., & Graesser, A. (Eds.), (2008). *Symbols, embodiment, and meaning.* Oxford: Oxford University Press.

D'Mello, S., & Calvo, R. (2013). Beyond the basic emotions: What should affective computing compute? In S. Brewster, S. Bødker, & W. Mackay (Eds.), *Extended abstracts of the ACM SIGCHI conference on human factors in computing systems (CHI 2013)* (Vols. (2287–2294)New York, NY: ACM.

D'Mello, S., Cobian, J., & Hunter, M. (2013). Automatic gaze-based detection of mind wandering during reading. In S. K. D'Mello, R. A. Calvo, & A. Olney (Eds.), *Proceedings of the 6th international conference on Educational Data Mining (EDM 2013)* (pp. 364–365). International Educational Data Mining Society.

D'Mello, S., Graesser, A., Schuller, B., & Martin, J. (Eds.), (2011). *Proceedings of the 4th international conference on Affective Computing and Intelligent Interaction (ACII 2011).* Berlin Heidelberg: Springer.

D'Mello, S. K., & Graesser, A. C. (2014). Confusion. In R. Pekrun, & L. Linnenbrink-Garcia (Eds.), *International handbook of emotions in education* (pp. 289–310). New York, NY: Routledge.

D'Mello, S. K., & Kory, J. (2015). A review and meta-analysis of multimodal affect detection systems. *ACM Computing Surveys, 47*(3), 43:1–43:46.

Domingos, P. (2012). A few useful things to know about machine learning. *Communications of the ACM, 55*(10), 78–87.

Douglas-Cowie, E., Cowie, R., Sneddon, I., Cox, C., Lowry, O., Mcrorie, M., et al. (2007). The HUMAINE database: Addressing the collection and annotation of naturalistic and induced emotional data. *Proceedings of the 2nd international conference on affective computing and intelligent interaction* (pp. 488–500). Berlin/Heidelberg: Springer.

Drummond, J., & Litman, D. (2010). In the zone: Towards detecting student zoning out using supervised machine learning. In V. Aleven, J. Kay, & J. Mostow (Eds.), *Intelligent tutoring systems* (Vol. 6095, pp. 306–308). Berlin/Heidelberg: Springer-Verlag.

Ekman, P. (1984). Expression and the nature of emotion. In K. Scherer, & P. Ekman (Eds.), *Approaches to emotion* (pp. 319–344). Hillsdale, NJ: Erlbaum.

Ekman, P. (1992). An argument for basic emotions. *Cognition & Emotion, 6*(3–4), 169–200.

Ekman, P., & Friesen, W. (1978). *The facial action coding system: A technique for the measurement of facial movement* Palo Alto, CA: Consulting Psychologists Press.

Emotient. (2014). FACET — Facial Expression Recognition Software.

Eyben, F., Wöllmer, M., & Schuller, B. (2010). Opensmile: The munich versatile and fast open-source audio feature extractor. *Proceedings of the international conference on multimedia* (pp. 1459–1462). New York, NY: ACM.

Fontaine, J., Scherer, K., Roesch, E., & Ellsworth, P. (2007). The world of emotions is not two-dimensional. *Psychological Science, 18*, 12.

Franklin, M. S., Smallwood, J., & Schooler, J. W. (2011). Catching the mind in flight: Using behavioral indices to detect mindless reading in real time. *Psychonomic Bulletin & Review, 18*(5), 992–997.

Hammal, Z., & Cohn, J. F. (2012). Automatic detection of pain intensity. *Proceedings of the 14th ACM international conference on multimodal interaction* (pp. 47–52). New York, NY: ACM.

Hjermstad, M. J., Fayers, P. M., Haugen, D. F., Caraceni, A., Hanks, G. W., Loge, J. H., Collaborative, EPCR, et al. (2011). Studies comparing numerical rating scales, verbal rating scales, and visual analogue scales for assessment of pain intensity in adults: A systematic literature review. *Journal of Pain and Symptom Management, 41*(6), 1073–1093.

Hoffman, J. E., & Subramaniam, B. (1995). The role of visual attention in saccadic eye movements. *Attention, Perception, & Psychophysics, 57*(6), 787–795.

Janssen, J. H., Tacken, P., de Vries, J., van den Broek, E. L., Westerink, J. H., Haselager, P., et al. (2013). Machines outperform laypersons in recognizing emotions elicited by autobiographical recollection. *Human–Computer Interaction, 28*(6), 479–517.

Killingsworth, M. A., & Gilbert, D. T. (2010). A wandering mind is an unhappy mind. *Science, 330*(6006), 932.

Kory, J., D'Mello, S., & Olney, A. Motion tracker: Cost-effective, non-intrusive, fully-automated monitoring of bodily movements using motion silhouettes. *PLoS ONE*, in press.

Lai, D. T., Levinger, P., Begg, R. K., Gilleard, W. L., & Palaniswami, M. (2009). Automatic recognition of gait patterns exhibiting patellofemoral pain syndrome using a support vector machine approach. *IEEE Transactions on Information Technology in Biomedicine, 13*(5), 810–817.

Larsen, J., Berntson, G., Poehlmann, K., Ito, T., & Cacioppo, J. (2008). The psychophysiology of emotion. In M. Lewis, J. Haviland-Jones, & L. Barrett (Eds.), *Handbook of emotions* (3rd ed., pp. 180–195). New York, NY: Guilford.

Lewis, M. D. (2005). Bridging emotion theory and neurobiology through dynamic systems modeling. *Behavioral and Brain Sciences, 28*(2), 169–245.

Littlewort, G. C., Bartlett, M. S., & Lee, K. (2007). Faces of pain: Automated measurement of spontaneous facial expressions of genuine and posed pain. *Proceedings of the 9th international conference on multimodal interfaces* (pp. 15–21). New York, NY: ACM.

Lucey, P., Cohn, J. F., Prkachin, K. M., Solomon, P. E., & Matthews, I. (2011). Painful data: The UNBC-McMaster shoulder pain expression archive database. *IEEE international conference on automatic face & gesture recognition and workshops (FG 2011)* (pp. 57–64). Washington, DC: IEEE.

Lupien, S. J., McEwen, B. S., Gunnar, M. R., & Heim, C. (2009). Effects of stress throughout the lifespan on the brain, behaviour and cognition. *Nature Reviews Neuroscience, 10*(6), 434–445.

Marsella, M., Gratch, J., & Petta, P. (2010). Computational models of emotion. In K. R. Scherer, T. Bänziger, & E. Roesch (Eds.), *A blueprint for a affective computing: A sourcebook and manual* (pp. 21–46). Oxford: Oxford University Press.

Marshall, S. P. (2005). Assessing cognitive engagement and cognitive state from eye metrics. In D. D. Schmorrow (Ed.), *Foundations of augmented cognition* (Vol. 11, pp. 312–320). Mahwah: Lawrence Erlbaum Assoc Publ.

McKeown, G., Valstar, M., Cowie, R., Pantic, M., & Schroder, M. (2012). The SEMAINE database: Annotated multimodal records of emotionally coloured conversations between a person and a limited agent. *IEEE Transactions on Affective Computing, 3*(1), 5–17.

Mehu, M., & Scherer, K. (2012). A psycho-ethological approach to social signal processing. *Cognitive Processing, 13*(2), 397–414.

Nicolle, J., Rapp, V., Bailly, K., Prevost, L., & Chetouani, M. (2012). Robust continuous prediction of human emotions using multiscale dynamic cues. *Proceedings of the 14th ACM international conference on multimodal interaction* (pp. 501–508). New York, NY: ACM.

Niedenthal, P. M. (2007). Embodying emotion. [Review]. *Science, 316*(5827), 1002–1005. Available from: http://dx.doi.org/10.1126/science.1136930.

Ocumpaugh, J., Baker, R. S., & Rodrigo, M. M. T. (2012). *Baker-Rodrigo Observation Method Protocol (BROMP) 1.0. Training Manual version 1.0.* New York, NY: EdLab.

Pang, B., & Lee, L. (2008). Opinion mining and sentiment analysis. *Foundations and Trends in Information Retrieval, 2*(1–2), 1–135.

Pantic, M., & Patras, I. (2006). Dynamics of facial expression: Recognition of facial actions and their temporal segments from face profile image sequences. *IEEE Transactions on Systems, Man, and Cybernetics, Part B., 36*(2), 433–449. Available from: http://dx.doi.org/10.1109/tsmcb.2005.859075.

Picard, R. (1997). *Affective computing.* Cambridge, MA: MIT Press.

Picard, R. (2010). Affective computing: From Laughter to IEEE. *IEEE Transactions on Affective Computing, 1*(1), 11–17.

Rayner, K. (1998). Eye movements in reading and information processing: 20 years of research. *Psychological Bulletin, 124*(3), 372–422.

Roda, C., & Thomas, J. (2006). Attention aware systems: Theories, applications, and research agenda. *Computers in Human Behavior, 22*(4), 557–587. Available from: http://dx.doi.org/10.1016/j.chb.2005.12.005.

Rosenberg, E. (1998). Levels of analysis and the organization of affect. *Review of General Psychology, 2*(3), 247–270. Available from: http://dx.doi.org/10.1037//1089-2680.2.3.247.

Russell, J. A., Bachorowski, J. A., & Fernandez-Dols, J. M. (2003). Facial and vocal expressions of emotion. *Annual Review of Psychology, 54,* 329–349.

Sano, A., & Picard, R. W. (2013). *Stress recognition using wearable sensors and mobile phones.* Washington, DC: IEEE.

Schuller, B., Valster, M., Eyben, F., Cowie, R., & Pantic, M. (2012). Avec 2012: The continuous audio/visual emotion challenge. *Proceedings of the 14th ACM international conference on Multimodal interaction* (pp. 449–456). New York, NY: ACM.

Shaw, G., & Giambra, L. (1993). Task unrelated thoughts of college students diagnosed as hyperactive in childhood. *Developmental Neuropsychology, 9*(1), 17–30.

Smallwood, J., Davies, J. B., Heim, D., Finnigan, F., Sudberry, M., O'Connor, R., et al. (2004). Subjective experience and the attentional lapse: Task engagement and disengagement during sustained attention. *Consciousness and Cognition, 13*(4), 657–690.

Smallwood, J., O'Connor, R. C., Sudbery, M. V., & Obonsawin, M. (2007). Mind-wandering and dysphoria. *Cognition and Emotion, 21*(4), 816–842.

Smallwood, J., & Schooler, J. W. (2015). The science of mind wandering: Empirically navigating the stream of consciousness. *Annual Review of Psychology, 66,* 487–518.

Stinson, J. N., Kavanagh, T., Yamada, J., Gill, N., & Stevens, B. (2006). Systematic review of the psychometric properties, interpretability and feasibility of self-report pain intensity measures for use in clinical trials in children and adolescents. *Pain, 125*(1), 143–157.

St. John, M., Kobus, D. A., Morrison, J. G., & Schmorrow, D. (2004). Overview of the DARPA augmented cognition technical integration experiment. *International Journal of Human-Computer Interaction, 17*(2), 131–149.

Valstar, M., Mehu, M., Jiang, B., Pantic, M., & Scherer, K. (2012). Meta-analysis of the first facial expression recognition challenge. *IEEE Transactions on Systems, Man, and Cybernetics, Part B: Cybernetics, 42*(4), 966–979.

Valstar, M., Schuller, B., Smith, K., Almaev, T., Eyben, F., & Krajewski, J. (Eds.), (2014). *AVEC 2014: 3D dimensional affect and depression recognition challenge.* New York, NY: ACM.

Valstar, M., Schuller, B., Smith, K., Eyben, F., Jiang, B., & Bilakhia, S. (Eds.), (2013). *AVEC 2013: The continuous audio/visual emotion and depression recognition challenge.* New York, NY: ACM.

Vinciarelli, A., Pantic, M., & Bourlard, H. (2009). Social signal processing: Survey of an emerging domain. *Image and Vision Computing, 27*(12), 1743—1759.

Williamson, J. R., Quatieri, T. F., Helfer, B. S., Ciccarelli, G., & Mehta, D. D. (2014). Vocal and facial biomarkers of depression based on motor incoordination and timing. *Proceedings of the 4th international workshop on Audio/visual emotion challenge* (pp. 65—72). New York, NY: ACM.

Williamson, J. R., Quatieri, T. F., Helfer, B. S., Horwitz, R., Yu, B., & Mehta, D. D. (2013). Vocal biomarkers of depression based on motor incoordination. *Proceedings of the 3rd ACM international workshop on Audio/visual emotion challenge* (pp. 41—48). New York, NY: ACM.

Zeng, Z., Pantic, M., Roisman, G., & Huang, T. (2009). A survey of affect recognition methods: Audio, visual, and spontaneous expressions. *IEEE Transactions on Pattern Analysis and Machine Intelligence, 31*(1), 39—58.

CHAPTER 6

Intelligent Mobile, Wearable, and Ambient Technologies for Behavioral Health Care

David D. Luxton[1,2], Jennifer D. June[3,4], Akane Sano[5] and
Timothy Bickmore[6]
[1]Naval Health Research Center, San Diego, CA, USA
[2]Department of Psychiatry and Behavioral Sciences, University of Washington School of Medicine,
Seattle, WA, USA
[3]National Center for Telehealth & Technology, WA, USA
[4]Department of Human Centered Design and Engineering, University of Washington, Seattle, WA, USA
[5]MIT Media Lab, Massachusetts Institute of Technology, Cambridge, MA, USA
[6]College of Computer and Information Science, Northeastern University, Boston, MA, USA

INTRODUCTION

Advancements in computing power, sensing technologies, and wireless communication are enabling the creation of useful tools for behavioral health purposes that can be carried by people or unobtrusively installed in households or other locations. Mobile devices, such as smartphones and tablet computers, provide multiuse platforms for collecting behavioral data, monitoring symptoms, accessing information, and providing treatments. Smart wearable technologies, such as intelligent eyeglasses and smart watches, provide powerful methods to measure and assess physiological and behavioral data in real time. Sensing and computing technologies that are embedded within an environment, such as in a home, create new ways to provide interactive behavioral interventions and treatments. The incorporation of artificial intelligence (AI) methods, such as machine learning (ML), natural language processing (NLP), and integrated computer sensing technologies are examples of what make these tools "smart."

In this chapter, we present AI applications in smart mobile, wearable, and ambient technologies for use in behavioral and mental health care. For our purposes, we use the term *mHealth* (mobile health) *devices* to refer to both wearable devices and those that are carried by hand (e.g., phones and tablet computers). mHealth software applications or *apps*, are the software programs that operate on mobile devices to accomplish a particular purpose. We use the term *ambient intelligence* (AmI) to refer to smart technologies that

Artificial Intelligence in Behavioral and Mental Health Care.
DOI: http://dx.doi.org/10.1016/B978-0-12-420248-1.00006-4
137

are embedded within a space, such as in a home, hospital room, or a public area that interact with persons within the environment. The term *user* refers to a person who interacts with any of these technologies.

We begin by providing a brief overview of mHealth and its benefits. We then follow with descriptions of key AI methods for mHealth and examples of their application in behavioral and mental health care. Next, we focus on AmI and discuss its use for behavioral health care. We also provide design recommendations and discuss relevant privacy, regulatory, and ethical considerations specific to the use of these technologies. We conclude with discussion of emerging technologies and opportunities.

Overview of Intelligent Mobile Health

According to the Global Mobile Health Market Report 2010—2015 (research2guidance, 2013), there are an estimated 500 million smartphone users worldwide (including healthcare professionals, consumers, and patients) who are using healthcare-related apps. By 2018, it is estimated that 50% of the more than 3.4 billion smartphone and tablet users will have downloaded mHealth apps. Medical apps are available for all types of useful functions such as electronic prescribing, assessment, clinical decision support, treatment practice management, coding and billing, self-care, and e-learning (Martínez-Pérez et al., 2014; Terry, 2010). There are also a growing number of mobile apps for specific behavioral and mental health purposes. For example, apps are available to help with the management of health-related behaviors such as diet, exercise, sleep, smoking cessation, relaxation, and medication adherence. Apps are also available to directly assist with the treatment of mental health conditions, such as anxiety disorders, depression, eating disorders, psychosis, and for suicide prevention (Donker et al., 2013; Luxton, McCann, Bush, Mishkind, & Reger, 2011).

mHealth devices (i.e., smartphones and tablet computers) give care providers the benefit of increased access to point-of-care tools, which has been shown to improve clinical decision-making and patient outcomes (Martínez-Pérez et al., 2014; Ventola, 2014). For care seekers, they provide a convenient and cost-effective platform for accessing self-care information and tools, such as self-assessments and treatments that are available 24/7 (Luxton et al., 2011; Luxton, Hansen, & Stanfill, 2014). They also provide a platform for live chatting with healthcare professionals, SMS texting interventions, scheduling and appointment reminders, and the capability for synchronous video telehealth services (Luxton et al., 2011; Luxton, Mishkind, Crumpton, Ayers, & Mysliwiec, 2012).

The development and deployment of intelligent wearables is also on the rise. Highly popular consumer wearables include fitness trackers, or other types of smart wearable devices, from companies such as Apple, Fitbit, Nike, or Jawbone. Data collected with wearables may include physiologic, behavioral, environmental (e.g., from ambient sensors), biological and self-reported assessments (Chan, Estève, Fourniols, Escriba, & Eric Campo, 2012). Data can be collected with multiple sensors at very high sampling rates and sent via a wireless connection to another mobile device, a stationary desktop computer, or to data systems at a medical center, where the data can be reviewed and monitored by healthcare professionals. Wearable technologies provide the added benefit of being in physical contact with users for an extended time and do not require the user to interact with a keyboard or touch screen while wearing them.

The expanding collection of smart devices also provides opportunities for users to share data to better understand health, wellness, and health-related behaviors. The *Quantified Self*, for example, is the popular movement whereby people acquire a wide range of data about themselves (e.g., physiological, mood states, behavioral patterns, environmental information) from wearable technologies and mobile self-tracking apps and compare them to the data of millions of other people (Lupton, 2013; Wolf, 2011). The intent of collecting these data is for self-monitoring and self-reflection in order to facilitate change or improvement. The data that are collected are quantified and can be made visible to others on the Internet.

INTELLIGENT CAPABILITIES FOR MOBILE HEALTH

AI provides powerful methods to enhance the functions and capabilities of mHealth devices. For example, AI techniques can make mobile devices more aware of the needs and preferences of users by leveraging real-time situational data, such as location and mood of the users, that is collected via sensors and other data inputs (e.g., survey apps). AI ML methods provide ways for a system to adapt to user preferences, to analyze collected data, and to predict behavior of users. Speech recognition and NLP improve how people may interface with the technology by providing a more natural and transparent interaction experience. Other capabilities that make use of AI, such as virtual reality and augmented reality (AR) applications, provide all new opportunities for accessing information and for delivering interactive treatments. In this section, we provide an overview of several AI technologies and techniques applied to mobile devices.

Mobile Sensors

Mobile sensors, whether built into the device or attached to it via external hardware, provide a natural starting place to discuss how smart devices make use of contextual, physiological, and other data about users and their environment. For further information about mobile sensors, see the review by Patel, Park, Bonato, Chan, and Rodgers (2012).

Motion and location. *Accelerometers* are commonly implemented in mobile and wearable devices to track movement, such as steps and overall activity levels and states (e.g., walking, sitting, climbing stairs, etc.). Actigraphy, for example, makes use of wrist-worn accelerometer devices to identify sleep vs. wake patterns, such as during sleep studies (Ancoli-Israel et al., 2003).

Global positioning systems (GPS), or location services functions on mobile devices that use cellular triangulation, can be used to locate the user in geographic space. The location services feature can be useful for behavioral health purposes when tracking the whereabouts of a user is important. For example, it may be important to locate patients with dementia if they wander away, tracking location of patients participating in exposure therapy (such as trips to busy locations), or also to locate proximity to medical resources (e.g., hospitals and clinics) (Luxton et al., 2011).

Environmental. Modern mobile devices, can also detect changes in environment conditions, such as sound or the amount of ambient light. Some mobile devices also have the capability to detect air temperature, air pressure, and humidity. The ambient light detection feature, for example, can be useful for detecting diurnal sleep patterns during sleep studies (Sano, 2014).

Physiological. A collection of mobile wearable physiological measurement systems is commercially available as either stand-alone equipment or as hardware affixed to smart mobile devices. These include electroencephalogram (EEG), electrocardiogram (ECG), photoplethysmogram (PPG), and ballistocardiogram (BCG) systems. Electrodermal activity (EDA) can be measured with sensors worn on the wrist or ankle. Blood pressure cuffs are now commercially available for use with smartphones and wearable devices can be used for the measurement of long-term respiration data. For

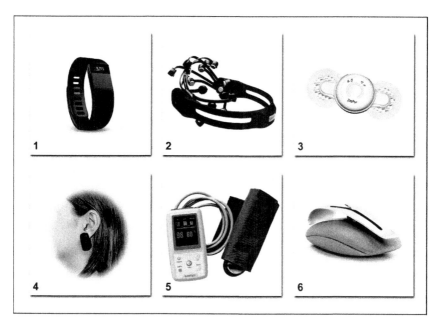

Figure 6.1 An assortment of commercially available wearable sensors for physiological assessment. (1) Activity monitor (Fitbit), (2) EEG sensor (Emotive), (3) EKG sensor, (4) PPG sensor, (5) blood pressure monitor, (6) Respiration sensor (Spire).

example, Spire uses a pressure sensor to track subtle movement around the waist (see Figure 6.1). Accelerometers, gyroscopes, and other sensors can also be used to measure respiration (Bates et al., 2010; Hernandez, Li, Rehg, & Picard, 2014).

All of these physiological measurement devices have practical uses in behavioral health care and research. For example, EEG is used in home sleep monitoring, biofeedback, and brain−computer interface (BCI) applications (Allison et al., 2013). Meditation apps, games, and toys that make use of EEG technology have also been developed and commercialized in the market (Vernon, Dempster, & Bazanova et al., 2009). ECG is also used to measure heart rate variability, which can have practical application for behavioral health research and in treatments (e.g., biofeedback) (Lehrer & Gevirtz, 2014). EDA has been widely used in psychophysiology research and in clinical applications to assess schizophrenia, emotional states, sleep, epilepsy, and stress (Boucsein, 2012). Mobile respiration measurement devices, such as Spire, can be used to monitor the breathing rate as part of biofeedback interventions.

Example Applications of Multi-Modal Sensor Technology in Smart Mobile Health

Mobile phone sensors can be leveraged to develop context-aware mHealth app systems that automatically detect when patients require assistance or intervention. For example, Burns et al. (2011) developed and evaluated the *Mobilyze!* app that is intended to help people manage depressive symptoms. The conceptual model of the app system is displayed in Figure 6.2. Mobile-device-sensed data (e.g., GPS, ambient light, recent calls) and user-entered data (e.g., patients' mood, emotions, cognitive/motivational states) are transmitted via encrypted, password-protected channels to several server-based software components. ML algorithms are used to generate a user-specific model to predict that state from sensed data in the future as well as discard irrelevant information that did not improve the predictive value of the model. The output can then be used to automatically assist the patient, such as by providing feedback, or by clinicians to help identify whether further intervention is needed.

Another example is The College Sleep Project (Sano et al., 2015) conducted at MIT. The project investigated how behavioral and physiological data from wearable devices and mobile phones can be used to identify associations among and develop predictors for sleep behaviors, stress, mental health, and academic performance. The project entailed the collection of multi-modal data (physiological, behavioral, environmental, and social data) from smartphones, laboratory data (e.g., biomarkers),

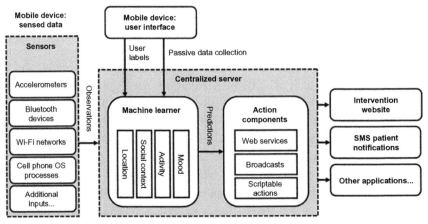

Figure 6.2 Conceptual diagram of *Mobilyze!* app system. *Adapted from Burns et al. (2011).*

and survey data collected from 66 undergraduate students over a 30-day period. Specifically, EDA (an index of stress), diurnal and sleep activity data, and light exposure were measured with wearable sensors. Data from mobile phones also included phone usage (calls, emails, and SMS history), location, screen on/off timing, and app usage. Feature extraction and ML techniques were then used to predict what behaviors were associated with perceived stress level (high/low stress levels), sleep quality, mental health symptom levels, and academic performance. The initial data from the project suggest that objective wearable and mobile data can be useful for making predictions about the impact of behavioral choices on mood, stress, GPA, and mental health.

Speech Recognition and NLP

Speech processing and NLP allow intelligent devices, such as smartphones, to interact with users via verbal language. Perhaps the most well-known example of speech recognition technology on a mobile device is Apple's voice-recognition service, *Siri*. Siri was the result of the Cognitive Assistant that Learns and Organizes (CALO) project within the Defense Advanced Research Projects Agency's (DARPA) Personalized Assistant that Learns (PAL) program — the largest AI project in United States history (SRI, 2015). The goal of the program was to design an AI personal assistant for use by the United States military (Bosker, 2013).

Siri uses onboard microphones to detect speech (e.g., commands, questions, or dictations) and Automatic Speech Recognition (ASR) to transcribe it into text. The software then translates the transcribed text into "parsed text" and then evaluates it locally on the device. If the request cannot be handled on the device, Siri communicates with servers in the Cloud (web services) to help process the request. Once the command is executed (such as to perform an Internet search or provide directions to a restaurant), Siri presents the information and/or provides a verbal response back to the user. Siri also makes use of ML methods to adapt to the user's individual language usage and individual searches (preferences) and returns personalized results.

Other examples of speech processing programs that operate on mobile devices include Dragon Dictation (http://www.nuance.com/dragonmobileapps/) and Microsoft's Catana (for Windows mobile OS). IBM has also supported development of mobile apps that make use of its NLP system *Watson* (Hamm, 2014).

Examples of Speech Recognition Technologies in Health Care

Speech recognition and NLP technologies, such as those used by Siri, Cortana, or Watson, makes interaction with technology much more natural and efficient and can enhance user engagement. For example, this technology allows virtual humans, such as those designed to interact with trainees or patients, to be able to interact with users in a more life-like manner. Another useful application of speech processing technology is to help mental health professionals enter notes into electronic health records (EHR). EpicCare®, for example, is EHR software that makes use of Dragon® Medical speech recognition technology (Nuance Communications, 2008). This use of NLP technology has the potential to enhance clinical documentation by assuring accurate and timely documentation that leads to optimal patient outcomes and that reduces costs.

Speech detection technology on mobile devices has also been proposed as part of an immediate crisis intervention tool. For example, Apple's Siri has the capability to connect people directly to support services. If they say certain phrases associated with self-harm, such as "I want to kill myself" or "how do you kill yourself," the user will be provided with the National Suicide Prevention Hotline number or locations of support services in their geographical area. While the ability of the system to quickly and accurately respond to users has been criticized in the past (e.g., a statement about "jumping off a bridge" may have inadvertently returned directions to a bridge), improvements in the system assure that lists to local suicide prevention centers are provided (Stern, 2013). In the future, advanced ambient intelligent systems may be able to listen to conversations, such as in smart home environments or in hospital rooms, to automatically call for help when a person is in need of immediate assistance.

It should be noted that any technology that relies on unconstrained text or speech input has the potential for misunderstanding the user's communicative intent. This is due to the inherent ambiguity in natural language, errors in speech recognition (amplified for users whose speech does not fit the standard models the systems were trained on), and the very large number of assumptions humans make in creating their utterances, spanning common sense knowledge about the world, linguistic knowledge about how conversation works, and pragmatic knowledge about context. Such errors may be tolerable for clinician-facing informational or training applications, but may result in serious negative consequences in patient-facing systems if they are making recommendations to patients based solely on natural language input.

Virtual Humans on Mobile Platforms

Virtual humans are animated computer characters that use simulated face-to-face conversation as a communication medium. Although these have been used as "standardized patients" to train health providers (Deladisma, Cohen, Stevens, & Wagner, 2007; Talbot, Sagae, Bruce, & Rizzo, 2012), they have also been extensively used as virtual coaches, counselors, and therapists to interact directly with patients to provide automated health education and health behavior change interventions. Virtual human coaches have been used on desktop computers, kiosks, and websites to provide a wide range of interventions, including patient education at the time of hospital discharge (Bickmore, Pfeifer, Byron, Forsythe, & Henault, 2010), medication adherence for individuals with schizophrenia (Bickmore, Puskar, Schlenk, Pfeifer, & Sereika, 2010), substance abuse screening in the outpatient setting (Checchi et al., 2013), genetic risk factor counseling (Wang, Bickmore, Bowen, Norkunas, & Campion, 2015), exercise promotion for individuals with Parkinson's disease (Ellis et al., 2013), and more. Importantly, none of these patient-facing virtual counselors relied on unconstrained natural language input. Instead, they all used highly constrained patient input modalities.

Mobile devices, such as smartphones, provide unique affordances for implementing virtual humans for health interventions. First, the virtual human is available to provide advice and motivation to users anytime and anywhere it is needed. Second, when coupled with real-time sensors that can identify user behavior, virtual humans can take the initiative in providing advice and help. Finally, close physical proximity and extended contact time with patients, along with the perception that the virtual human is sharing more of their personal experience, could contribute to the virtual human's ability to establish what the patient perceives to be a trusting, working alliance relationship with them.

At their core, virtual humans are comprised of a dialog engine that manages simulated conversations with patients, a graphical user interface that presents an animated character, either recorded or synthesized speech for the virtual human, input mechanisms for users to contribute their part of the conversation, persistent memory (for longitudinal interventions), a possible range of sensors for the virtual human to automatically identify contextual cues and user behavior, and possible interfaces with other information systems.

There are several frameworks for dialog systems, ranging from simple pattern-response rules, to sophisticated planning systems (Bickmore & Giorgino, 2006). The dialog planning problem can be simplified, and the overall reliability of the system can be greatly increased, if the user's contributions to the conversation are highly constrained.

Automatic generation of the virtual human's verbal and nonverbal conversational behavior represents another active area of research in the virtual agent's community. Virtual human utterance generation can range from invariant scripted responses, to "template-based" text generation, in which slots in agent utterances are filled at runtime, to full-blown AI-planner-based text generation in multiple stages (Reiter & Dale, 1995). The latter approaches require that speech be generated at runtime using a speech synthesizer/text-to-speech (TTS) engine; recorded speech sounds much better but affords only very limited flexibility and tailoring at runtime.

One study investigated the efficacy of using a virtual human on a mobile device compared to more conventional interfaces for health counseling applications (Bickmore & Mauer, 2006). In this study, four versions of a mobile device interface were developed (Figure 6.3): (FULL) an animated virtual human that used a text balloon for agent utterances

Figure 6.3 Example virtual human on mobile device (Bickmore & Mauer, 2006).

with some paraverbal audio; (ANIM) the same as FULL without audio; (IMAGE) the same as ANIM but showing only a static image of the character; and (TEXT) the interface without any character or audio. In a within-subjects experiment, subjects tried each version of the interface, with characters and health topic counterbalanced, as well as the interface modality. The FULL and ANIM conditions were significantly more effective at building a user-rated working alliance (evaluating using the Working Alliance Inventory (Horvath & Greenberg, 1989)) compared to the other two conditions.

Examples of Virtual Human Health Interventions on Mobile Platforms

Despite the recent explosion in mHealth technologies and interventions, there are still few examples of systems that use virtual human interfaces. One early system was DESIA, developed by Johnson, LaBore, and Chiu (2004). DESIA was a psychosocial intervention on a handheld computer that featured an animated conversational agent who uses balloon text and optional recorded speech output for the agent utterances. Outcome evaluations have not been reported.

Bickmore and Mauer (2009) developed a virtual exercise coach on a handheld device that used information from an integrated accelerometer to motivate sedentary users to walk more (Figure 6.3). A preliminary study investigated the effectiveness of the accelerometer, by comparing one version of the system in which the agent could sense whether the user was walking at moderate intensity or not and automatically and proactively provided feedback whenever they finished a walk, while in the other condition the user had to explicitly tell the agent when they were starting or ending a walk. Participants rated the automatic version more highly on its awareness of their behavior and on the closeness of their perceived relationship with the coach, however, they actually did less exercise in the automatic version (Bickmore & Mauer, 2009). A second study compared five versions of the system with users carrying the coach for 1 week per treatment. Results indicated that just-in-time motivational counseling by the virtual coach resulted in more steps/day walked compared to a version of the coach that simply reminded users it was time to walk (Bickmore, Gruber, Intille, & Mauer, 2006).

Several additional virtual human health interventions have been developed on tablets and "mini" tablets, including mindfulness meditation and yoga for patients with chronic pain (Gardiner, Hempstead, Ring,

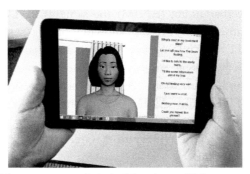

Figure 6.4 Virtual human cancer clinical trial assistant (Bickmore et al., 2013).

Bickmore, & Yinusa-Nyahkoon, 2013; Mccue, Gardiner, Crooks, Bickmore, & Barnett, 2015), and help for cancer patients in navigating oncology clinical trials (Bickmore, Utami, Barry, Henault, & Waite, 2013; Utami, Barry, Bickmore, & Paasche-Orlow, 2013) (Figure 6.4).

Augmented Reality on Mobile Devices

Augmented reality (AR) combines virtual reality with the real world by overlaying computer-generated graphics with live video imagery of the physical world (Caudell & Mizell, 1992; Craig, 2013). AR and other AI capabilities can be applied to mobile devices such as smartphones, tablet computers, and other wearable devices. Google's Glass (wearable intelligent glasses), for example, has been tested in the medical setting as a wearable AR platform (Kamphuis, Barson, Schijven, & Christoph, 2014). AR uses virtual elements to build upon the existing environment and it can also be used to inhibit the perception of physical objects in the real world by overlaying them with virtual representations (e.g., with virtual objects or even virtual empty spaces) (Azuma, 1997; Azuma et al., 2001). AR experiences can also be extended with the use of sound, smell, and touch (Azuma et al., 2001).

Example AR Applications in Behavioral Health Care

Augmented Reality Exposure Therapy (ARET) is used to create anxiety-provoking virtual stimuli in the patient's real-world environment during prolonged exposure therapy (Baus & Bouchard, 2014). It is especially suitable for exposure therapy because it enables displaying targeted virtual fear stimuli in the real world. AR has support as a cost-effective medium through which individuals with specific phobia can be exposed "safely" to the object(s) of their fear. A benefit of using a mobile AR system in exposure treatment is that it allows patients to use their own body to interact with the stimuli in a natural environment that can further enhance interactivity and realism (Baus & Bouchard, 2014).

Relatively few, but a growing number, of studies that have evaluated ARET have been published. One of the first was that of Botella et al. (2005) who evaluated the treatment of a specific phobia to small animals (cockroaches in this case) using ARET. The single-subject study demonstrated the ability of virtual cockroaches to activate a patient's anxiety, and effectively decrease scores on measures of fear, avoidance, and belief in catastrophic thought. In 2013, Wrzesien and colleagues published a pilot study ($n = 12$) that compared in vivo exposure therapy (IVET) with ARET in the treatment of specific phobia to small animals (spiders and cockroaches). The results of the pilot study showed that both ARET and IVET were clinically effective, although the ARET group showed better improvement in reductions of catastrophic thought and the IVET group showed higher improvement of avoidance scores. For an additional review of ARET studies, see Baus and Bouchard (2014).

Summary

In summary, mHealth technologies provide a powerful and cost-effective way to provide point-of-care tools that can improve health outcomes. They also provide a convenient way for end users to manage their own care. AI provides methods to enhance the capabilities and functions of mobile devices by making the technology more aware of the needs and preferences of users, improving the user interface with mobile devices, facilitating real-time monitoring, and by providing innovative ways to provide evidence-based treatments.

There remains a need for more research on the effectiveness of mHealth to improve health outcomes (Mohr, Burns, Schueller, et al., 2013). As noted by Kumar et al. (2013), whether mHealth leads to better overall health outcomes and reduced disease burden is still unknown and premature adoption of untested mHealth technologies may detract from, rather than contribute to, what is needed for overall health improvement. There is a specific need for randomized controlled trials that examine the use of mHealth interventions compared to traditional alternatives (e.g., in-office care). Research is also needed on the use of virtual humans on mobile devices in order to understand how users interact with artificial intelligence agents when they are carried and accessible 24/7.

OVERVIEW OF AmI

AmI refers to intelligent electronic environments that are sensitive and responsive to the presence of people inhabiting them (Aarts & de Ruyter, 2009; Aarts & Wichert, 2009; Vasilakos & Pedrycz, 2006). AmI entails the integration of sensors and processors into everyday objects (Cook, Augusto, & Jakkula, 2009). By relying on various AI techniques, AmI makes use of contextual information obtained from these sensors in order to adapt the environment to the user needs in an interactive, transparent, and anticipatory manner (Acampora, Cook, Rashidi, & Vasilakos, 2013).

Acampora et al. (2013) provide the following list and description of AmI characteristics:

- Context Aware: It exploits the contextual and situational information.
- Personalized: It is personalized and tailored to the needs of each individual.
- Anticipatory: It can anticipate the needs of an individual without the conscious mediation of the individual.
- Adaptive: It adapts to the changing needs of individuals.
- Ubiquity: It is embedded and is integrated into our everyday environments.
- Transparency: It recedes into the background of our daily life in an unobtrusive way.

By use of advances in AI such as activity recognition, reasoning, decision-making, and spatiotemporal logic, AmI systems become even more sensitive, responsive, adaptive, and ubiquitous. AmI can also make use of technological advances in other related fields including *sensor networks* to facilitate data collection, *robotics* to build actuators and assistive robots, and *human–computer interactions* to build more natural interfaces (Acampora et al., 2013; Pauwels, Salah, Albert, & Tavenard, 2007). ML and statistical techniques such as naïve Bayes classifiers, dynamic Bayes networks, and Markov models, can be implemented to mathematically combine and classify sensor data streams to recognize activities being performed by users, such as in smart homes (Liao, Fox, & Kautz, 2005; Philipose et al., 2004; Wren et al., 2006).

Example of AmI for Behavioral Health Applications

Ambient persuasive technologies (Kaptein, Markopoulos, Ruvter, & Aarts, 2010) refer to ubiquitous systems embedded within one's everyday environment that are intended to aid in behavior and lifestyle change

(Kaptein et al., 2010; Verbeek, 2009). Ambient persuasive technologies involve the convergence of the behavioral sciences and the field of information technology (Verbeek, 2009). An example of an ambient persuasive technology is the *Persuasive Mirror* (del Valle & Opalach, 2005; del Valle et al., 2006; Mattheij, Postma-Nilsenova, & Postma, 2015; Nakajima & Lehdonvirta, 2013; Nakajima, Lehdonvirta, Tokunaga, & Kimura, 2008).

del Valle and Opalach (2005, 2006) designed a persuasive mirror that has the appearance of a standard bathroom mirror but has advanced embedded technologies that allow users to peer into the mirror to see a simulated reflection or other images. To accomplish this, the mirror utilizes an AR component that makes use of two cameras placed on the sides of a flat-panel display and combines video streams from both cameras to create a realistic replication of a mirror reflection. Advanced facial tracking (both 2D and 3D face tracking) is utilized and image processing software is used to visually alter the person's reflection. Ubiquitous sensors placed throughout the home or worn on the user are intended to provide the system with data about the user's daily activities.

The overall intent of the system is to make use of psychological concepts such as reward and punishment, positive and negative preferences (using colors, shape, and structural features to the user likes or dislikes), and positive reinforcements (indicators to remind the user how good they are progressing toward personal goals). For example, the mirror system can be configured to provide representational feedback of the user's recent behaviors, such as showing a reflection of an obese person to a person who is trying to lose weight or a reflection of a slimmer person, depending on data of daily dietary and exercise habits. Another form of visualization can be provided to people during tobacco cessation interventions by showing a person aged and sickly from smoking tobacco products.

Some other examples of persuasive mirror technology for behavioral change include persuasive art systems that alter the image based on performance toward a desired goal (Nakajima and Lehdonvirta, 2011). For example, one version has the image of the Mona Lisa that will change from a younger face (reflecting the successful completion of walking 8,000 steps) or an older-looking Mona Lisa to indicate the failure to complete the walking exercise. Another version is the Virtual Aquarium that promotes dental hygiene (Nakajima et al., 2008). A sensor is attached to the user's toothbrush and measures the amount of brushing. When the user engages in tooth-brushing the simulated fish within the aquarium become lively, or they die off if the user fails to brush.

The Internet of Things

Up to this point in the chapter we have presented mHealth technologies and AmI as separate topics, however, integration of these technologies is the future. The *Internet of Things* (IoT) allows users to interconnect mobile and computerized devices (e.g., sensors) that can communicate with each other via the Internet (Huang & Li, 2010). Each device or "thing" is provided with unique identifiers to allow data to flow autonomously between devices without requiring human-to-human or human-to-computer interaction (Farooq, Waseem, Khairi, & Mazhar, 2015). Devices may include various types of sensors, mobile and wearables, and home appliances (e.g., washer/dryers that utilize Wi-Fi for remote monitoring) and automobiles with built-in sensors (Waterson, Carpaij, & Schild-Meerfield, 2015). There are estimated to be nearly 26 billion (Gartner, 2014) to more than 30 billion (ABI Research, 2013) devices on the IoT by 2020. Healthcare applications include monitoring and control of medical devices and other technologies such as blood pressure, body weight scales, and heart rate monitors to advanced applications of implants (e.g., pacemakers) or hearing aids (Jara, Zamora, & Skarmeta, 2012; Rohokale et al., 2011). Several versions of intelligent, networked pill boxes have also been developed to track patient medication-taking to support and promote medication adherence (Cressey, 2012).

DESIGN RECOMMENDATIONS

mHealth interventions and AmI environments will likely succeed if they are seamlessly integrated into the patterns of people's daily lives and make minimal external demands. It is therefore important for developers of mobile and ambient technologies to apply the best practices in user experience (UX) and user-centered design in order to assure optimal function and effectiveness of these technologies. It is also important for healthcare professionals and organizations that use these tools for patient care to be cognizant of the design and usability factors that may impact how their patients (and care providers) interact with these technologies. In this section we provide a brief overview of best practices for design and testing of these technologies with a focus on how AI methods can enhance the usability and UX of these technologies for use in behavioral and mental health care.

Mobile Health Design Considerations

UX is concerned with all the elements that together make up the interface, including layout, visual design, text, brand, sound, and interaction and coordinates these aspects to allow for the best possible interaction by users (Albert & Tullis, 2013). UX also considers a person's emotions about using a particular product, system, or service (Albert & Tullis, 2013; Desmet, Porcelijn, & Dijk, 2007; Hassenzahl, Diefenbach, & Göritz, 2010; Norman, 2004). For virtual human interfaces, some researchers have even used standardized measures of patient-rated therapeutic alliance to assess the emotional and relational dimensions of their attitudes about the application (Bickmore, Gruber, & Picard, 2005). Usability refers to the level of efficiency, effectiveness, and satisfaction of a given product or service determined within a specified context by the intended user group (ISO, 1998).

Zhang and Adipat (2005) point out that there are general design issues associated with mobile devices that impact usability, including the fact that users' attention may be distracted due to connectivity issues, small screen sizes and possible lower screen resolution, limited processing power, and difference in input devices (e.g., smaller buttons) that may cause errors. In the case of modern wearables, the user interface may be much smaller than on smartphones and also lack a display. While this may offer a more simple interaction with the device, it may also present design challenges as far as ease of use.

Based on a thorough review of the extant usability literature, Harrison, Flood, and Duce (2013) have proposed the PACMAD (People at the Centre of Mobile Application Development) usability model, which was designed to address the limitations of existing usability models when applied to mobile devices. The seven attributes of this model are:

- *Effectiveness:* the user's ability to complete the intended task within the established context.
- *Efficacy:* the user's ability to complete the intended task "with speed and accuracy."
- *Satisfaction:* the user's perception of "comfort and pleasantness" while engaging with the system.
- *Learnability:* how easily a user can gain proficiency with the given system.
- *Memorability:* the user's ability to retain how the system works even if the user has not used it frequently.

- *Errors:* the ability to complete any given task within the system without hitting into errors.
- *Cognitive load:* refers to a user's total amount of mental exertion required to use the specified system, such as a mobile application or website.

The PACMAD model is comprised of several of the key factors included in extant models (e.g., ISO, 1998; Nielsen, 1993), but also places emphasis on factors associated with cognitive load. Unlike traditional desktop computers, the use of mobile devices may be subject to more distraction from their environment, auditory, visual, and simply the fact that the user may be walking. These experiences can be a source of distraction requiring multi-tasking that places a cognitive load on mobile technology users. People tend to slow down while walking (or running) when they are preoccupied with looking at their devices. The use of vibration-based notifications to get the user's attention can be helpful, but such indicators could become confusing and overwhelming with frequent occurrences.

AI technologies and techniques can help to address each of the limitations and challenges of mHealth design by enhancing the UX. As we discussed previously, the use of speech detection and NLP is one example of how AI methods can improve user interaction with these devices. AI is also key to automatic control of the functions of these devices. For example, AI can evaluate the environmental context of the user (e.g., determine whether it is day or night, location based on proximity detection) and either include or prohibit some distracting functions, such as notifications, phone calls, reminders, etc. AI can also assist with other basic, but important, "behind the scenes" functions such as preserving battery life of mobile technologies, again by being aware of the environment (turning some functions off). Simple functions such as battery life may be critical, especially when considering the use of wearables in health contexts, such as patient monitoring.

AmI Design Considerations

With AmI, sensors are a key element "that link available computational power with physical applications" (Cook et al., 2009). The multitude of sensors, complexity of data input from the sensor network, other environmental inputs (e.g., ambient noise), and the many ways that users may interact within an environment can make the design of AmI quite challenging. Cook et al. (2009) emphasize two primary considerations when designing AmI: *context awareness* and *natural interfaces*.

Context awareness refers to how the technology infers the current activity state of the user and the characteristics of the environment to intelligently manage both the information content and the means of information distribution (Cook et al., 2009). As noted by Traynor, Xie, and Curran (2010), understanding of context is essential for creating truly intelligent environments for the future that can accommodate the rapidly changing and increasingly diverse contexts in which human—computer interactions occur.

Natural interfaces describes the goal of AmI to ultimately rid itself of direct human—computer interaction. There are, however, users who may prefer to have direct access to a user interface to communicate needs and preferences. As such, it is imperative for the user interface to be easy to use, navigable, and learnable, or the user may abandon the technology altogether. Aside from the old standard touch pad interface, AmI can incorporate "human-life communication capabilities" (Cook et al., 2009) such as motion tracking, facial and emotion recognition, speech and whistle processing (Esnaola & Smithers, 2006) to further human interactions with the intelligent systems.

User-centered methods such as focus groups, contextual inquiries, user testing, participatory design, and co-creation design (Olivier, Xu, Monk, & Hoey, 2009; Kohler, Fueller, Matzler, & Stieger, 2011; Strömberg, Pirttilä, & Ikonen, 2004) are vital to assure that users' experiences are incorporated throughout the design and development of these systems. Because ambient intelligent systems are intended to be experienced seamlessly and transparently by users, a deep understanding of how users interact with the system within the intended context is essential. It is also important to incorporate users into testing and evaluating these technologies so that researchers, technologists, and businesses can obtain an accurate understanding of how users want to use such technologies in their daily life. Ambient intelligent solutions that are easily personalizable, customizable, and that enhance daily living will likely be successfully integrated into people's lives (Coelho, 2012).

Privacy, Data Security, and Ethics Considerations

As with other electronic mediums used in health care, mHealth and AmI technologies present several privacy and data security challenges. If these technologies are to be used in the context of medical care, privacy and electronic data security requirements will need to be met, such as those imposed by the Health Insurance Portability and Accountability Act

(HIPAA) in the United States. Whenever a user is to transmit protected health information to a healthcare provider (if a covered entity), the provider must assure HIPAA compliance, which includes appropriate data encryption and other data security procedures. These technologies may also collect, store, and transmit physiological data, such as EEG, which could be used to identify a person. mHealth and AmI also create privacy issues associated with third parties (e.g., bystanders, family members). Examples of this include the use of mobile cameras or microphones, features that also collect images and sounds from nonparticipants. Smart homes also pose privacy risks given that data may be collected on residents and guests who are unaware of the data collection. The multitude and complexity of sensor inputs and wireless networks used for AmI and the IoT can also contribute to electronic data security vulnerabilities (Farooq et al., 2015).

All of these issues should be evaluated during the design process so that appropriate encryption and other data security features are built in. For more detailed information about data security methods for mHealth, see Luxton, Kayl, and Mishkind (2012) and for AmI, see Friedewald, Vildjiounaite, Punie, and Wright (2007).

Healthcare professionals that integrate these technologies into their services must be cognizant of the data security risks and requirements to assure that they do not inadvertently violate privacy laws by using these technologies. Consumers must also be careful about how their personal data collected via these technologies may be intentionally shared with third parties, such as for marketing purposes (Luxton et al., 2011). Moreover, manufacturers and healthcare providers should consider requirements, such as those of the Food and Drug Administration (FDA) in the United States, in regards to what constitutes a medical device and therefore falls under regulatory oversight. Healthcare providers must communicate expectations to their patients regarding privacy and data security, and discuss any potential safety risks involving use of these technologies.

CONCLUSION

The development of intelligent mobile and AmI technologies for behavioral health care is an expanding industry. AI is providing opportunities to make these systems more adaptive to the preferences and needs of users while also greatly enhancing the capabilities and functions of these systems. The implementation of best practices in UX and user-centered design can help optimize the performance of these systems.

We can expect ongoing technological advances to bring even more exciting capabilities and opportunities in the years ahead. Future mobile apps will include larger databases and more powerful integration with the ever-expanding capabilities of Cloud Computing. Improved sensing and affect detection technologies will allow for more adaptive mobile operating systems and applications. AI algorithms and ML software will continue to improve the accuracy and efficiency of mHealth apps and enable the creation of highly interactive apps beyond the capabilities of existing ones. As suggested by Acampora and colleagues (2013), Brain Computer Interface (BCI) systems represent a natural extension for AmI environments. BCI technology that leverages micro- and nanotechnologies for smart mobile and ambient applications, such as for monitoring, has the potential to make these technologies even more transparent to the user. With these exciting advances, we can expect mobile, wearable, and ambient intelligent technologies to only increase in their use as part of creative strategies to support behavior change and mental health care.

REFERENCES

Aarts, E., & de Ruyter, B. (2009). New research perspectives on ambient intelligence. *Journal of Ambient Intelligence and Smart Environments, 1*(1), 5−14.

Aarts, E., & Wichert, R. (2009). Ambient intelligence. *Technology Guide*, 244−249.

ABI Research. (2013). *More than 30 billion devices will wirelessly connect to the internet of everything in 2020*. Available from: <https://www.abiresearch.com/press/more-than-30-billion-devices-will-wirelessly-conne/>.

Acampora, G., Cook, D. J., Rashidi, P., & Vasilakos, A. V. (2013). A survey on ambient intelligence in health care. *Proceedings of the IEEE Institute of Electrical and Electronics Engineers, 101*(12), 2470−2494. Available from: http://dx.doi.org/10.1109/JPROC.2013.2262913.

Albert, W., & Tullis, T. (2013). *Measuring the user experience: Collecting, analyzing, and presenting usability metrics*. New York: Morgan Kaufmann.

Allison, B. Z., Dunne, S., Leeb, R., Del Millán, R. J., & Nijholt, A. (Eds.), (2013). *Towards Practical Brain−Computer Interfaces: Bridging the Gap from Research to Real-World Applications*. Berlin: Springer-Verlag.

Ancoli-Israel, S., Cole, R., Alessi, C., Chambers, M., Moorcroft, W., & Pollak, C. (2003). The role of actigraphy in the study of sleep and circadian rhythms. American Academy of Sleep Medicine Review Paper. *Sleep, 26*(3), 342−392.

Azuma, R., Baillot, Y., Behringer, R., Feiner, S., Julier, S., & MacIntyre, B. (2001). Recent advances in augmented reality. *Computer Graphics, 25*, 1−1510. Available from: http://dx.doi.org/10.1109/38.963459.

Azuma, R. T. (1997). A survey of augmented reality. *Presence: Teleoperators and Virtual Environments, 6*(4), 355−385.

Baus, O., & Bouchard, S. (2014). Moving from virtual reality exposure-based therapy to augmented reality exposure-based therapy: A review. *Frontiers in Human Neuroscience, 8*, 112. Available from: http://dx.doi.org/10.3389/fnhum.2014.00112.

Bickmore, T., & Giorgino, T. (2006). Health dialog systems for patients and consumers. *Journal of Biomedical Informatics, 39*(5), 556–571.

Bickmore, T., Gruber, A., Intille, S., & Mauer, D. (2006). A handheld animated advisor for physical activity promotion. In *American medical informatics association annual symposium*. Washington, DC.

Bickmore, T., Gruber, A., & Picard, R. (2005). Establishing the computer-patient working alliance in automated health behavior change interventions. *Patient Education and Counseling, 59*(1), 21–30.

Bickmore, T. & Mauer, D. (2006). Modalities for building relationships with handheld computer agents. In *ACM SIGCHI conference on human factors in computing systems (CHI)*. Montreal.

Bickmore, T., & Mauer, D. (2009). Context awareness in a handheld exercise agent. *Pervasive and Mobile Computing Special Issue on Pervasive Health and Wellness, 5*, 226–235.

Bickmore, T., Pfeifer, L., Byron, D., Forsythe, S., Henault, L., Jack, B., et al. (2010). Usability of conversational agents by patients with inadequate health literacy: Evidence from two clinical trials. *Journal of Health Communication, 15*(Suppl. 2), 197–210.

Bickmore, T., Puskar, K., Schlenk, E., Pfeifer, L., & Sereika, S. (2010). Maintaining reality: Relational agents for antipsychotic medication adherence. *Interacting with Computers, 22*, 276–288.

Bickmore, T., Utami, D., Barry, B., Henault, L., Waite, K., Matsuyama, R., et al. (2013). *Enabling web search for low health literacy individuals using conversational agents.* Washington, DC: Health Literacy Annual Research Conference (HARC).

Bates, A., Ling, M. J., Mann, J. & Arvind, D. K. (2010). Respiratory rate and flow waveform estimation from tri-axial accelerometer data. *International Conference on Body Sensor Networks*, Singapore. Available from: http://dx.doi.org/10.1109/BSN.2010.50.

Bosker, B. (2013). SIRI RISING: The inside story of Siri's origins – and why she could overshadow the iPhone. Available from: < http://www.huffingtonpost.com/2013/01/22/siri-do-engine-apple-iphone_n_2499165.html > .

Botella, C., Juan, M., Baños, R. M., Alcañiz, M., Guillen, V., & Rey, B. (2005). Mixing realities? An application of augmented reality for the treatment of cockroach phobia. *Cyberpsychology & Behavior, 8*, 161–171. Available from: http://dx.doi.org/10.1089/cpb.2005.8.162.

Boucsein, W. (2012). *Electrodermal activity.* (2nd ed.). New York: Springer.

Burns, M. N., Bengale, M., Duffecy, J., Gergle, D., Karr, C. J., Giangrande, E., et al. (2011). Harnessing context sensing to develop a mobile intervention for depression. *Journal of Medical Internet Research, 13*, 3. Available from: http://dx.doi.org/10.2196/jmir.1838.

Caudell, T. P. & Mizell, D. W. (1992). Augmented Reality: An application of heads-up Display Technology to Manual Manufacturing Processes. *Proceedings of 1992 IEEE Hawaii International Conference on Systems Sciences* (pp. 659–669).

Chan, M., Estève, D., Fourniols, J., Escriba, C., & Eric Campo, E. (2012). Smart wearable systems: Current status and future challenges. *Artificial Intelligence in Medicine, 56*, 137–156.

Checchi, K., McNair, S., Rubin, A., Marcello, T., Bickmore, T., & Simon, S. (2013). A pilot study of a computer-based relational agent to screen for substance-use problems in primary care. In *Society for General Internal Medicine (SGIM) annual meeting*.

Coelho, V. (2012). *Creating ambient intelligence: Applications and design guidelines for the home.* Retrieved from: <http://130.216.33.163/courses/compsci705s1c/exams/Seminar Reports/SeminarReport_vcoe002.pdf>.

Cook, D. J., Augusto, J. C., & Jakkula, V. R. (2009). Ambient intelligence: Technologies, applications, and opportunities. *Pervasive and Mobile Computing, 5*(4), 277–298.

Craig, A. B. (2013). *Understanding augmented reality: Concepts and applications.* Amsterdam: Morgan Kaufmann.

Cressey, D. (2012). Say hello to intelligent pills. Nature News. Available from: <http://www.nature.com/news/say-hello-to-intelligent-pills-1.9823>.

del Valle, A. C., & Opalach, A. (2005). The persuasive mirror: Computerized persuasion for healthy living. In *Proceedings of the 11th international conference on human-computer interaction*.

del Valle, A. C., Mesnage, A. C., & Opalach, A. (2006). Intelligent home services initiative. *Gerontechnology*, *5*(2), 118−120.

Deladisma, A., Cohen, M., Stevens, A., Wagner, P., Lok, B., Bernard, T., et al. (2007). Do medical students respond empathetically to a virtual patient? *American Journal of Surgery*, *193*(6), 756−760.

Desmet, P. M., Porcelijn, R., & Van Dijk, M. B. (2007). Emotional design; application of a research-based design approach. *Knowledge, Technology & Policy*, *20*(3), 141−155.

Donker, T., Petrie, K., Proudfoot, J., Clarke, J., Birch, M. R., & Christensen, H. (2013). Smartphones for smarter delivery of mental health programs: A systematic review. *Journal of Medical Internet Research*, *15*(11), e247. Available from: http://dx.doi.org/10.2196/jmir.2791.

Ellis, T., Latham, N., DeAngelis, T., Thomas, C., Saint-Hilaire, M., & Bickmore, T. (2013). Feasibility of a virtual exercise coach to promote walking in community-dwelling persons with Parkinson disease. *American Journal of Physical Medicine and Rehabilitation*, *92*(6), 472−485.

Esnaola, U., & Smithers, T. (2006). Whistling to machines. In Y. Cai, & J. Abascal (Eds.), *Ambient intelligence in everyday life* (pp. 198−226). Springer.

Farooq, M. U., Waseem, M., Khairi, A., & Mazhar, S. (2015). A critical analysis on the security concerns of internet of things (IoT). *International Journal of Computer Applications*, *11*(7), 1−6.

Friedewald, M., Vildjiounaite, E., Punie, Y., & Wright, D. (2007). Privacy, identity and security in ambient intelligence: A scenario analysis. *Telematics and Informatics*, *24*(1), 15−29.

Gardiner, P., Hempstead, M. B., Ring, L., Bickmore, T., Yinusa-Nyahkoon, L., Tran, H., et al. (2013). Reaching women through health information technology: The gabby preconception care system. *American Journal of Health Promotion*, *27*(3S), 11−20.

Gartner. (2014). *Gartner says the internet of things will transform the data center*. Available from: <http://www.gartner.com/newsroom/id/2684616>.

Hamm, S. (2014). *Expanding the watson ecosystem with the mobile developer challenge*. Available from: <http://asmarterplanet.com/blog/2014/06/expanding-watson-ecosystem-mobile-developer-challenge.html>.

Harrison, R., Flood, D., & Duce, D. (2013). Usability of mobile applications: Literature review and rationale for a new usability model. *Journal of Interaction Science*, *1*(1), 1−16.

Hassenzahl, M., Diefenbach, S., & Göritz, A. (2010). Needs, affect, and interactive products—Facets of user experience. *Interacting with Computers*, *22*(5), 353−362.

Hernandez, J., Li, Y., Rehg, J. M., & Picard, R. W. (2014). BioGlass: Physiological parameter estimation using a head-mounted wearable device. In *Wireless mobile communication and healthcare (Mobihealth), 2014 EAI 4th international conference on* (pp. 55−58). IEEE.

Horvath, A. O., & Greenberg, L. S. (1989). Development and validation of the working alliance inventory. *Journal of Counseling Psychology*, *36*(2), 223−233. Available from: http://dx.doi.org/10.1037/0022-0167.36.2.223.

Huang, Y., & Li, G. (2010). A semantic analysis for internet of things. In *624 IEEE 2010 international conference on intelligent computation 625 technology and automation* (pp. 336−339).

International Organization for Standardization. (1998). ISO 9241-11:1998. Available from: <http://www.iso.org/iso/catalogue_detail.htm?csnumber=16883>.

Jara, A. J., Zamora, M. A., & Skarmeta, A. F. (2012). Knowledge acquisition and 627 management architecture for mobile and personal Health environments 628 based on the Internet of Things. In *IEEE 2012 IEEE 11th international 29 629 conference on trust, security and privacy in computing and 630 communications* (pp. 1811–1818).

Johnson, W., LaBore, C., & Chiu, Y. (2004). A pedagogical agent for pyschosocial intervention on a handheld computer. In *AAAI fall symposium on dialogue systems for health communication*. Washington, DC.

Kamphuis, C., Barson, E., Schijven, M., & Christoph, N. (2014). Augmented reality in medical education? *Perspectives on Medical Information, 3*(4), 300–311. Available from: http://dx.doi.org/1010.1007%2Fs40037-013-0107-7.

Kaptein, M. C., Markopoulos, P., de Ruyter, B., & Aarts, E. (2010). Persuasion in ambient intelligence. *Journal of Ambient Intelligence and Humanized Computing, 1*(1), 43–56.

Kohler, T., Fueller, J., Matzler, K., & Stieger, D. (2011). Co-creation in virtual worlds: the design of the user experience. *MIS Quarterly, 35*(3), 773–788.

Kumar, S., Nilsen, W. J., Abernethy, A., Atienza, A., Patrick, K., Pavel, M., et al. (2013). Mobile health technology evaluation: The mHealth evidence workshop. *American Journal of Preventive Medicine, 45*(2), 228–236. Available from: http://dx.doi.org/10.1016/j.amepre.2013.03.017.

Lehrer, P. M., & Gevirtz, R. (2014). Heart rate variability biofeedback: How and why does it work? *Front Psychol, 5*, 756.

Liao, L., Fox, D., & Kautz, H. (2005). Location-based activity recognition using relational Markov networks. In *Proceedings of the international joint conferences on artificial intelligence* (pp. 773–778).

Lupton, D. (2013). Quantifying the body: Monitoring and measuring health in the age of mHealth technologies. *Critical Public Health, 23*(4), 393–403. Available from: http://dx.doi.org/10.1080/09581596.2013.794931.

Luxton, D. D., Hansen, R. N., & Stanfill, K. (2014). Mobile app self-care versus in-office care for stress reduction: A cost minimization evaluation. *Journal of Telemedicine and Telecare, 20*(8), 431–435. Available from: http://dx.doi.org/10.1177/1357633X14555616.

Luxton, D. D., Kayl, R. A., & Mishkind, M. C. (2012). mHealth data security: The need for HIPAA-compliant standardization. *Telemedicine Journal & e-Health, 18*, 284–288. Available from: http://dx.doi.org/10.1089/tmj.2011.0180.

Luxton, D. D., McCann, R. A., Bush, N. E., Mishkind, M. C., & Reger, G. M. (2011). mHealth for mental health: Integrating smartphone technology in behavioral healthcare. *Professional Psychology: Research & Practice, 42*, 505–567. Available from: http://dx.doi.org/10.1037/a0024485.

Luxton, D. D., Mishkind, M. C., Crumpton, R. M., Ayers, T. D., & Mysliwiec, V. (2012). Usability and feasibility of smartphone video capabilities for telehealth care in the U.S. military. *Telemedicine Journal & e-Health, 18*, 409–412. Available from: http://dx.doi.org/10.1089/tmj.2011.0219.

Martínez-Pérez, B., de la Torre-Díez, I., López-Coronado, M., Sainz-de-Abajo, B., Robles, M., & García-Gómez, J. M. (2014). Mobile clinical decision support systems and applications: A literature and commercial review. *Journal of Medical Systems, 38*(1), 4. Available from: http://dx.doi.org/10.1007/s10916-013-0004-y.

Mattheij, R., Postma-Nilsenová, M., & Postma, E. (2015). Mirror mirror on the wall: Is there mimicry in you all? *Journal of Ambient Intelligence and Smart Environments, 7*(2), 121–132.

Mccue, K., Gardiner, P., Crooks, D., Bickmore, T., Barnett, K., Shamekhi, A., et al. (2015). Integrative medicine group visits: A feasibility study to introduce digital tablets into a group medical visit American Public Health Association.

Mohr, D. C., Burns, M. N., Schueller, S. M., Clarke, G., & Klinkman, M. (2013). Behavioral intervention technologies: Evidence review and recommendations for future research in mental health. *General Hospital Psychiatry, 35*, 332–338.

Nakajima, T., & Lehdonvirta, V. (2011). Designing motivation using persuasive ambient mirrors. *Personal and Ubiquitous Computing, 17*(1), 1–20.

Nakajima, T., & Lehdonvirta, V. (2013). Designing motivation using persuasive ambient mirrors. *Personal and Ubiquitous Computing*, *17*(1), 107−126.

Nakajima, T., Lehdonvirta, V., Tokunaga, E., & Kimura, H. (2008). Reflecting human behavior to motivate desirable lifestyle. In *Proceedings of the 7th ACM conference on designing interactive systems* (pp. 405−414). ACM.

Nielsen, J. (1993). *Usability engineering*. Boston, MA: Academic Press.

Norman, D. A. (2004). *Emotional design: Why we love (or hate) everyday things*. New York: Basic Books.

Nuance Communications. (2008). *Speech recognition: Accelerating the adoption of electronic medical records*. Available from: <http://www.himss.org/files/HIMSSorg/content/files/EMR_WP1208.pdf>.

Olivier, P., Xu, G., Monk, A., & Hoey, J. (2009). Ambient kitchen: Designing situated services using a high fidelity prototyping environment. In *Proceedings of the 2nd international conference on pervasive technologies related to assistive environments* (p. 47). ACM.

Patel, S., Park, H., Bonato, P., Chan, L., & Rodgers, M. (2012). A review of wearable sensors and systems with application in rehabilitation. *Journal of NeuroEngineering and Rehabilitation*, *9*, 21.

Pauwels, E. J., Salah, A. A., Tavenard, R. (2007) Sensor networks for ambient intelligence, multimedia signal processing. MMSP 2007. IEEE 9th Workshop on, Vol. no., pp. 13, 16, Oct. 1−3, 2007 Available from: <http://dx.doi.org/10.1109/MMSP.2007.4412806>.

Philipose, M., Fishkin, K. P., Perkowitz, M., Patterson, D. J., Fox, D., Kautz, H., et al. (2004). Inferring activities from interactions with objects. *IEEE Pervasive Computing*, *3* (4), 50−57.

Reiter, E., & Dale, R. (1995). Building applied natural language generation systems. *Natural Language Engineering*, *1*(1), 1−31.

research2guidance. (2013). Mobile Health Market Report 2013−2017: The commercialization of mHealth applications (Vol. 3). Available from: <http://www.research2guidance.com/shop/index.php/mhealth-report-2>.

Rohokale, V. M., Prasad, N. R., & Prasad, R. (2011). A cooperative Internet of 655 Things (IoT) for rural healthcare monitoring and control 2011 2nd 656 international conference on wireless communication, Vehicular 657 Technology, Information Theory and Aerospace & Electronic Systems 658 Technology (Wireless VITAE) (pp. 1−6).

Sano, A. (2014). *Got sleep?: Mobile phone application to improve sleep*. Available from: < http://affect.media.mit.edu/pdfs/14.Sano-CHI.pdf >.

Sano, A., Phillips, A. J. K., Yu, A., McHill, A. W., Taylor, S., Jaques, N., et al. (2015). Classifying academic performance, sleep quality, stress level, and mental health using personality traits, wearable sensors and mobile phones. In *Proceedings of the 2015 IEEE international conference on body sensor networks*.

SRI International. (2015). Siri. <http://www.sri.com/work/timeline-innovation/timeline.php?timeline=computing-digital#!&innovation=siri>.

Stern, J. (2013). Apple's siri be first call for users thinking of suicide. ABC News. Retrieved from: <http://abcnews.go.com/Technology/apples-siri-now-prevent-suicides/story?id=19438495>.

Strömberg, H., Pirttilä, V., & Ikonen, V. (2004). Interactive scenarios − Building ubiquitous computing concepts in the spirit of participatory design. *Personal and Ubiquitous Computing*, *8*(3−4), 200−207.

Talbot, T. B., Sagae, K., John, B., & Rizzo, A. A. (2012). Sorting out the virtual patient: How to exploit artificial intelligence, game technology, and sound educational practices to create engaging role-playing simulations. *International Journal of Gaming and Computer-Mediated Simulations*, *4*(3), 1−19.

Terry, M. (2010). Medical apps for smartphones. *Telemedicine and e-Health*, *16*(1), 17−22. Available from: http://dx.doi.org/10.1089/tmj.2010.9999.

Traynor, D., Xie, E., & Curran, K. (2010). Context-awareness in ambient intelligence. *International Journal of Ambient Computing and Intelligence (IJACI)*, *2*(1), 13–23. Available from: http://dx.doi.org/10.4018/jaci.2010010102.

Utami, D., Barry, B., Bickmore, T., & Paasche-Orlow, M. (2013). A conversational agent-based clinical trial search engine. In *Proceedings of the annual symposium on human-computer interaction and information retrieval (HCIR)* (pp. 3–4). Vancouver, BC, Canada.

Vasilakos, A., & Pedrycz, W. (2006). *Ambient intelligence, wireless networking, and ubiquitous computing*. Norwood, MA: Artech House, Inc.

Ventola, C. L. (2014). Mobile devices and apps for health care professionals. *Uses and Benefits*, *39*(5), 356–364.

Verbeek, P. (2009). Ambient intelligence and persuasive technology: The blurring boundaries between human and technology. *Nanoethics*, *3*(3), 231–242.

Vernon, D., Dempster, T., Bazanova, O., Rutterford, N., Pasqualini, M., & Andersen, S. (2009). Alpha neurofeedback training for performance enhancement: Reviewing the methodology. *Journal of Neurotherapy*, *13*, 1–13.

Wang, C., Bickmore, T., Bowen, D., Norkunas, T., Campion, M., Cabral, H., et al. (2015). Acceptability and feasibility of a virtual counselor (VICKY) to collect family health histories. *Genetics in Medicine*. Available from: http://dx.doi.org/10.1038/gim.2014.198 [Epub ahead of print].

Waterson, J., Carpaij, J., & Schild-Meerfield, D. (2015). *Big data and the internet of medical things*. Available from: <www.arabhealthmagazine.com>.

Wolf, G. (2011). *What is the quantified self?* Available from: <http://quantifiedself.com/2011/03/what-is-the-quantified-self/>.

Wren, C. R., & Munguia-Tapia, E. (2006) Toward scalable activity recognition for sensor networks. In *Proc int workshop in location and context-awareness* (pp. 168–185).

Wrzesien, M., Alcañiz, M., Botella, C., Burkhardt, J.-M., Bretón-López, J., Ortega, M., et al. (2013). The therapeutic lamp: Treating small-animal phobias. *IEEE Computer Graphics and Applications*, *33*, 80–86. Available from: http://dx.doi.org/10.1109/MCG.2013.12.

Zhang, D., & Adipat, B. (2005). Challenges, methodologies, and issues in the usability testing of mobile applications. *International Journal of Human-Computer Interaction*, *18*(3), 293–308.

CHAPTER 7

Artificial Intelligence and Human Behavior Modeling and Simulation for Mental Health Conditions

Barry G. Silverman[1], Nancy Hanrahan[2], Lina Huang[1], Emilia Flores Rabinowitz[2] and Samuel Lim[1]
[1]Electrical and Systems Engineering, University of Pennsylvania, Philadelphia, PA, USA
[2]School of Nursing, University of Pennsylvania, Philadelphia, PA, USA

INTRODUCTION

Modeling the complexity of individuals with multimorbid physical and mental health problems within a social context is one of the greatest challenges for the post Affordable Care Act era. Stigma associated with mental illness promotes silos that prevent full integration of a person living within a dynamic and contextualized matrix. Traditional regression modeling strategies fail to embrace dynamic health patterns within systems. Synthesizing systems science, agent modeling and simulation, knowledge management architecture and domain theories, we explore the use of Agent-Based Modeling and Simulation (ABMS) for understanding individual, organizational, and societal levels of a hospitalization. In essence, we apply computational science to explore underlying mechanisms that explain medical/surgical hospital outcomes — readmissions — for individuals with comorbid physical and mental illness. In the first section of this chapter, ABMS is conceptualized. Then, a case study serves to demonstrate an ABMS application and gains from knowledge that is unique to this systems social science approach. We conclude with a discussion of strengths and limitations of the ABMS application.

BACKGROUND

Chronic illnesses are the leading cause of disability and death and, in the United States, affect almost half the adult population, or about 133 million Americans (Institute of Medicine, 2012). A recent study places chronic

Artificial Intelligence in Behavioral and Mental Health Care.
DOI: http://dx.doi.org/10.1016/B978-0-12-420248-1.00007-6

care at 78% of total US healthcare spending, and forecasts costs of over a trillion dollars per year by 2020 (Institute of Medicine, 2012). Among individuals with chronic illness who incur the highest costs are those with mental illness who have multiple layers of physical and/or mental health problems that interfere with their capacity to socialize, plan, organize, and function in their life (Kronick, Bella, & Gilmer, 2009). People with serious mental illness (SMI), approximately 15 million Americans, are in the top 5% of Medicaid beneficiaries for per capita costs and account for more than 50% of all Medicaid spending, with annual per person costs of $43,130−$80,374 (Coughlin, Waidmann, & Phadera, 2012). Despite this level of investment, the poor health of people with SMI is striking; they die 25 years earlier than the general population from preventable illnesses (Colton & Mandersheid, 2006). Compared with the general population, persons with SMI are 3.4 times more likely to die from heart disease or diabetes; 3.8 times more likely to die from accidents; 5 times more likely to die from respiratory ailments; 6.6 times more likely to die from pneumonia or influenza (Hardy & Thomas, 2012); and 3.8 times more likely to be HIV positive than the general population (Rothbard, Miller, Lee, & Blank, 2009).

The health delivery systems for mental health and medical care are extremely complex, operate independently, communicate with one another inefficiently, and often have different financing arrangements and policies for mental health care (Druss, von Esenwein, Compton, Zhao, & Leslie, 2011). These systems are virtual silos of care and a nightmare for consumers to negotiate (Institute of Medicine, 2006). For individuals with a SMI, an encounter with this fragmented healthcare system is not only burdensome, but can be perilous, and often results in exacerbation of symptoms and rehospitalizations (Institute of Medicine, 2006). Other consequences of ineffective health systems are devastating and costly − homelessness, victimization, incarceration, repeated hospitalization, and death (Druss et al., 2011). A new study suggests that people with SMI are three times more likely to be in jail or prison than in a psychiatric hospital (Bloom, 2010). These statistics speak volumes about the ineffectiveness of current health systems to care for some of the most vulnerable of populations, and the need for innovative solutions to their care.

The challenges associated with addressing the needs of the most vulnerable populations in our society are related to complex networks of interconnected social, economic, and political systems. One of the best tools for attempting to understand and better manage complex systems is computational modeling and simulation. In this chapter we will model the complexities of individuals with SMI and the environmental factors that influence their health using simulation and agent-based modeling technology. None of the current research methods or technology captures the quantity, quality, or breadth of individual and contextual factors used in the simulation and agent-based modeling that we will use in the proposed research. The virtual system we will use operationalizes complex patterns and mechanisms of health over the life course including physical environments, sociocultural context, peers and families, coping responses, behavior, biology, and genes, all of which determine the health of individuals within complex environments and social networks (Silverman, 2010).

In the field of health care, ABM is already used to analyze a variety of operations and personnel management issues. Examples of such issues are the performance of hospital emergency departments, various resource assignment strategies, and how the decision processes of doctors and nursing staff impact diagnostic and treatment efficacy (Cil & Mala, 2010; Sibbel & Urban, 2001; Stainsby, Taboada, & Luque, 2009). These models are quite prolific within academic circles but have yet to be included into widely available commercial software packages, which instead tend to rely on purely mathematical or stochastic models (Silverman, 2010). Furthermore, these models are also consistently focused on micro issues without addressing the organizational structure of the healthcare system and the different policy options available to those in the public sector, which is the focus of our project.

Health reform is ultimately concerned with social justice and social change. These goals require a sophisticated understanding of the contexts that give rise to social problems and the use of research methods and change strategies that attend to the complexities of social settings. Although researchers dedicate considerable attention to these concerns, the ability to understand the intricate and dynamic relationship at individual, organizational, and societal levels still lags behind the considerable need in our society for transformative change in healthcare delivery. The following section describes the conceptual underpinnings of Agent-Based Modeling and Simulation (ABMS), followed by an application of ABMS to explore the hospital trajectory and outcomes for patients with medical and surgical conditions. Our goal is to increase an understanding of ABMS's conceptual and methodological tools available to those involved in designing, implementing, and assessing social change.

Why ABMS and Challenges

Our approach to improving models of care is innovative, as agent-based simulation provides a systems approach that includes attention to the dynamic relationships between individual, social, and environmental factors. Over the last 30 years, minimal progress has been made on the discriminative ability of traditional risk prediction models, and they are little better than coin flipping at predicting readmissions (Calvillo-King et al., 2013). Most traditional risk models focus on *clinical determinants* of readmission (e.g., severity of illness, prior use of medical services and other comorbidities), while ignoring many higher-level *social and environmental factors* associated with overall health and functional status (e.g., income, insurance status, education, marital status, caregiver availability, access to care, discharge location, crime rates, walkability, and access to transportation services). Traditional risk models are statistical and largely rely on regression to extract cause and effect correlations from large datasets. This is "black box" modeling and it works best on predicting the average behavior, leaving the outliers to error terms. ABMS characterizes the high degree of complexity and uncertainty of healthcare systems and models underlying processes, sequences of mechanisms, and behavior theories of individual patients and how all these interact to produce emergent macro-effects. In this case, cause and effect are considered circular and dynamic; feedback/feedforward may exist, as can time delays, workflow sequences, and other complex interactions. A challenge is to integrate data from multiple national, community, and health system sources needed to develop such care models.

HISTORY OF ABMS IN MEDICINE/MENTAL HEALTH CARE

Brailsford, Harper, Patel, and Pitt (2009) taxonomized the literature on healthcare simulation models into three main groupings: the human body level, the healthcare unit level, and the system-wide level. Their survey showed numerous excellent models exist for each level separately. A review of ABMS in health care by Paranjape and Sadanand (2009) is consistent with this taxonomy. A noteworthy agent model by Schlessinger and Eddy (2012), Archemedes, makes use of both patient clinical factors and clinical cost. However, patient behavioral factors were not included. Our prototype model, further explained in the following sections, complements Archimedes by including mind—body, workflows, and societal factors.

To date, there are no models addressing all three levels as defined by Brailsford et al. (2009). System-wide models tend to be focused largely on the health system facilities alone, not embracing the larger societal issues. As described previously, to effectively model the healthcare ecosystem, the model framework must address all three levels (individuals, organizations, and societal) as important dynamics often lie in the social and behavioral determinants outside the scope of typical clinic services.

SYNERGIES WITH OTHER INDUSTRIES

Over the past decade, the lead author has created multi-tiered ABMSs for the United States Military, Central Intelligence Agency, and the Department of State (Silverman, 2010). These agent—society modeling tools have been applied to hundreds of political events, and these agencies are in various stages of fielding and using these deliverables to support training and decision support of command staffs, reconstruction teams, and country desk people seeking to help communities overseas. The basic approach is open architecture and follows the model driven architecture standard that uses a model factory where best practice models of a given component can be added into the suite (or removed) and run with data inputs and outputs going to a publish and subscribe style of data store. A model controller exists that allows one to design ABMS experiments, run Monte Carlo style, or explore sensitivities.

To our knowledge, the system science and artificial intelligence methods the investigators are using are unique. Their designs are highly scalable, portable, and can be embedded to drive the behaviors of agents in numerous third party simulators. The three levels of the ABMS framework will be further described in the next section.

SOCIOLOGICAL INPUTS INTO MULTI-TIERED ABMS

We used two key sociological theories and a comprehensive systematic review on the social factors impacting hospital readmissions to inform our multi-tier modeling approach.

Antonovksy's Salutogenesis Model

Antonovsky (1996) developed this model on the principle of a sense of coherence, in gauging how individuals respond to their surroundings and cope with stress. The model has been utilized in a broad array of settings to analyze coping mechanisms in the fields of health psychology, sociology, and preventative medicine in Europe. In addition, its close linkages with the field of decision science have also seen its transformation into a heuristic to guide decision-making on the fly, healthcare architecture, and psychiatry engagements. The model consists of three components: *Comprehensibility* — a belief that things happen in an orderly and predictable fashion and a sense that you can understand events in your life and reasonably predict what will happen in the future. *Manageability* — a belief that you have the skills or ability, the support, the help, or the resources necessary to take care of things, and that things are manageable and within your control. *Meaningfulness* — a belief that things in life are interesting and a source of satisfaction, that things are really worth it and that there is good reason or purpose to care about what happens. The Salutogenesis Model's efficacy in connecting psychological stimuli to physiological effects has made it an apt choice for the framework of our value trees, described in the next section. While goals are short-term concerns best described by Maslow's hierarchy, standards and preferences are more accurately linked to patient coping styles and perspectives on managing life.

Theory of Reasoned Action

The Theory of Reasoned Action (TRA) suggests that a person's behavior is determined by their intention to perform the behavior and that this intention is, in turn, a function of their attitude toward the behavior and subjective norms (Fishbein & Ajzen, 1975). The best predictor of behavior is intention or instrumentality (belief that the behavior will lead to the intended outcome). Instrumentality is determined by three things: their attitude toward the specific behavior, their subjective norms, and their perceived behavioral control. The more favorable the attitude and the subjective norms and the greater the perceived control, the stronger the person's intention to perform the behavior.

Social Factor Impact on Readmission or Mortality

The study by Calvillo-King et al. (2013) provided a comprehensive overview of the factors that affect patient readmissions and mortality, including economic and demographic parameters. Through conducting rigorous magnitude of association and statistical significance tests, factors were ranked according to the degree of correlation that they have with readmission or mortality. The majority of factors analyzed in the study indirectly impacted decision-making and were largely demographic in nature, which provided a useful context for identifying behavioral habits that were harmful to health and had a statistically significant correlation.

A TOOLBOX FOR MULTI-LAYER MODELING OF SOCIAL SYSTEMS

In terms of the history of this toolbox, we started by modeling individuals from the social psychological and mind—body perspective (deep—narrow) and then added more models that broadened the capability in the economic—political—sociologic dimensions. Specifically, we used two types of models — PMFserv and StateSim — to model the agent, organizational, and societal levels. For further discussion of these tools, see publications by Silverman, Sun, Bharathy, and Weyer (under review) and Silverman, Hanarahan, and Bharathy (2015). In 2011—2012 we applied these tools to model the community mental health of Philadelphia. In this section, we will illustrate the models with examples from this domain. The section below, Example Application, will then show results from running these models.

Agent Mind—Body Level: The PMFserv Architecture

The basic building block is a model of an agent's bodily needs (physiology, fatigue, hunger, injuries, belonging, etc.) and mind. Ortony, Clore, and Collins (1990) stated that the agent mind is where agents apply their moralistic value system, form relationships, appraise the world, and autonomously carry out courses of action. The value system oversees all of this and also regulates the level of attending to internal needs. These needs are governed by performance moderator functions (PMFs). A PMF is a micro-model covering how human performance (e.g., perception, memory, or decision-making) might vary as a function of a single factor (e.g., hunger, need for sleep, injury, event stress, time pressure, grievance, and so on). PMFserv culls from the literature dozens of the best available PMFs and synthesizes them within a unifying framework and thereby offers a family of models where micro-decisions lead to the emergence of macro-behaviors within an individual. PMFserv includes a plugin architecture that facilitates turning on and off different models and trying new ones. An intel agency, for instance, sponsored us (2000—2005) to implement part of their leader profiling methodology inside of PMFserv. There are too many models to review them all here, but we will sample a few of them.

As an example of just the cognitive appraisal loop, let us examine some agents representing different populations in a large urban setting. The primary components of this framework are Motives, State, and Actions as summarized in Figure 7.1 and explained in what follows.

Agent Motives

In cognitive appraisal, an agent's motives arise based on its value system (Ortony et al., 1990). In PMFserv, this is implemented as Goals, Standards, and Preferences (GSP) Trees, which specify a value system that is based on multi-attribute utility theory and Bayesian probability mathematics. In this context, utility refers to the nonmonetary measure of satisfaction one derives from various outcomes or situations. These utilities are multi-attribute, meaning that there are several attributes or values (hence, the use of a tree) that are considered when evaluating the utility of a certain outcome. In this case, we embellish the GSP trees with factors from Salutogenesis and TRA. Finally, the use of Bayesian mathematics allows a frequency distribution of the past choices of an agent to define the relative important of each branch of the value system to the agent. An example of a portion of such a value system for a cognitive agent is presented in Table 7.1. There we see that *goals* are the near-term events that an agent wants to happen, *standards* are the socially and morally imposed guidelines for behavior, and *preferences* are the ideals about the long term and the desired state of the world. In order to drive its own behavior, an agent evaluates these three dimensions to assess the utility of any potential action it could take as well as those taken by other agents. For instance, an agent with a "negative" patient archetype value system described by Table 7.1 is apathetic and short-term gratification-oriented. It also believes its choices have little impact on outcomes (perceived control) and it views itself as generally ineffective (low efficacy). In the future, we plan to research the branches more fully in terms of what defines a relevant range of patient behaviors, and then based on actual patient histories; we will try to derive important agent archetypes or personas in terms of specific values we assign to each node in a GSP Tree for that personality.

Agent State Properties

In the current prototype, the well-being of an agent is described along three dimensions: their physiological, mental, and socioeconomic state. Each of these three dimensions contains numerous metrics, called state

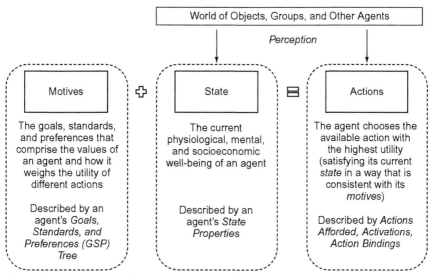

World of Objects, Groups, and Other Agents

Perception

Motives	State	Actions
The goals, standards, and preferences that comprise the values of an agent and how it weighs the utility of different actions	The current physiological, mental, and socioeconomic well-being of an agent	The agent chooses the available action with the highest utility (satisfying its current *state* in a way that is consistent with its *motives*)
Described by an agent's *Goals, Standards, and Preferences (GSP) Tree*	Described by an agent's *State Properties*	Described by *Actions Afforded, Activations, Action Bindings*

Figure 7.1 Framework of agent behavior in PMFserv.

Table 7.1 Example of Value System for a Cognitive Agent for a Negative Patient Archetype

Goals		Standards			Preferences		
Esteem	0.20	Compliance	0.30		Instrumentality	0.50	
Love and belonging	0.20	Gratification horizon	0.30		High efficacy		0.10
Physiology	0.30	Long term		0.10	Low efficacy		0.90
Safety	0.30	Short term		0.90	Satisfaction	0.50	
Total	1.00	Perceived control	0.40		Apathetic		0.90
		Irrelevant choices		0.90	Engaged		0.10
		Perceived control		0.10	**Total**	1.00	
		Total	1.00				

Source: Based on research by Samuel Lim with inputs from R. Trotta, M. Mikolajczyk.

properties, each of which describes a different aspect of the state of an agent. Table 7.2 shows the state properties of an agent representing a mental health patient in the current version. These states are variously computed by dynamical models in the agent (e.g., hunger, stress, mood), and models and rule sets external to an agent (e.g., employment opportunities, injuries, and social support). Some states are set as initial variables that might be changed stochastically over time (e.g., income, living conditions, psychotic intensity).

Table 7.2 Categories of State Properties in an Agent

State properties	Description
A. Physiologic state properties	
Fatigue	Level of physical exhaustion
Hunger	Level of hunger and malnutrition
Stress	Level of anxiety and social pressure
Bodily injury	Amount of personal injury sustained
B. Mental state properties	
Psychotic intensity	Intensity of paranoia and delusions
Mood	Level of depression or anger
Personality	Ability to deal with stress
Substances	Level of influence or withdrawal
C. Socioeconomic state properties	
Employment status	How an individual is employed (if at all) and how they support themselves economically
Living conditions	Where an individual lives and what kind of atmosphere it provides
Income (monthly)	Amount of income an individual is able to spend
Social support	Amount of support (emotionally or economically) an individual receives from friends and family

Organizational Level: StateSim

This toolset introduces a model of a state (or cross-state or sub-state) region including all the important organizations, the relevant portions of government and its institutional services, economic and security conditions, political processes, domestic practices, and external influences. StateSim adds plugins and models atop FactionSim, including a population model, economic services models, and the actual institutional agencies that allocate public goods and services (or not) to the factions in that region of interest. StateSim was originally built for three DARPA programs. To date, it has been applied in Afghanistan, Iraq, Palestine, Africa, Sri Lanka, Bangladesh, Thailand, and the Koreas (as well as for UK soccer hooligans and USA crowds) to model (forecast) emergence of state instabilities (insurgency, rebellion, domestic political violence, repression, etc.), which are macro-behaviors that emerge from the micro-decisions of all the participants, including the diverse leaders and followers. In tests run during 2010, DARPA indicated StateSim was better than 80% accurate in over 240 backcast trials they put it through. One can use this model to experiment on and study operations that might influence a region's instabilities and to assess the primary, secondary, and tertiary effects of different courses of action on the stakeholder groups and actors. In an extension for the Army in 2011−2012, we scaled up this capability so that StateSim now also includes a module that permits many 10,000s of less-cognitive, follower agents. These exist in networks that carry out the workflows of their daily lives. They also execute the cognitive leader agents' courses of action decisions in a spatial and temporally realistic fashion.

The goal of our analysis is to utilize StateSim to represent the behavioral healthcare services of a community in a large urban setting, though it also minimally portrays other governmental and non-governmental services (e.g., police, courts and justice system, private hospitals, social service agencies, places of employment, and so on) that might impact the lives of the individuals being modeled. Briefly, in terms of Medicaid healthcare services, *Pre-Admission* represents the periods when individuals do not interact with hospitals or psychiatric resources. Depending on the status of income level and mental stability, individuals will attend regular checkups or take prescribed medicine. *Admission* to a hospital requires physician approval and physicians are accessed in many different ways. Health providers attending patients, policemen, and family or significant others may present patients to a hospital for a physician evaluation. Individuals can also present themselves for a hospital admission. In some cases, individuals seek hospital admission for shelter and meals for the night, or "three hots and a cot," an inefficiency for hospitals. This leads to *Assessment*, or the different ways patients are redirected to receive the care they need. Inpatient *Treatment* or services can be divided into four general categories: ER/Intensive Care − immediate care is required; Acute Treatment − urgent, short-term treatment required; Sub-acute Treatment − in between acute and chronic treatment; slightly urgent, medium-term treatment required; 24-h Bed − patient is provided with food, bed and is released the following day. The *outpatient* stage is crucial in assessing relapse rates, which are, as noted above, very high in Philadelphia.

An important capability of this tool is that it captures, represents, and runs the workflow of individual agents in all of the groups and organizations one is interested in modeling. In the current prototype, we authored 43 workflows for the residents' daily life activities (e.g., sleep/wake up, get dressed, take medication, do errands) and for workers such as those in hospitals, homeless shelters, and jails. Each of these workflows involve steps that the agent must take, participant roles that must be filled and carried out for the workflow to succeed, various inputs/resources that get consumed (e.g., facilities, space, medicines, supplies, equipment, and so on), and specific outputs or outcome possibilities.

Societal Level: StateSim

This level of PMFserv adds in a model of the social and organizational roles that exist in a community of interest (e.g., multi-state, state, sub-state, or region/neighborhood) and that may be played by the PMFserv agents. Developed under a 3-year grant from AFOSR, FactionSim implements a number of recognized scientific theories from sociology (mobilization, leader–follower theories, motivational congruence, social norms, etc.) and political-economy (developmental economics). To apply it to a region, one adds neighborhood factors; activities of home, social, and work life; the role of added institutions; and public/private goods and services.

We use this technology in the ABMS to model neighborhood issues, living arrangements (housing quality, safety, support), income, payments, and so on.

In our urban community mental health case study, we organized the groups according to the widely used four-quadrant clinical integration model (Bartels, 2004). The groups categorize those who have low mental and physical health problems (Quadrant I), high mental health problems and low physical health problems (Quadrant II); low mental health and high physical health problems (Quadrant III); and, high mental and physical health problems (Quadrant IV). Thus, individuals in Quadrants I and II function well, with few medical and mental health problems; in contrast to those who have greater functional limitations from physical health problems with high mental health comorbidities − Quadrant III; or greater functional limitations from mental health problems with high medical comorbidities − Quadrant IV. Individuals categorized in Quadrants III and IV often have major social needs due to poverty, unemployment, and unstable housing. These people are often insured by Medicaid or Medicare or both. The population with SMI and comorbid medical problems represents one of the most complex social problems for public health administrators. Druss et al. (2012) show that two thirds of people with SMI do not access timely physical or mental health care and do not receive adequate treatment.

Causes and consequences of wellbeing are woven in a complex web of social—cultural—technological conditions and associated human decisions. For instance, belonging to a group (quadrant), sets up social norms such as what such a member is expected to be capable of performing. However, behavior is tempered by a number of other factors as well. For example, do they have family support and live in a safe area? Or are they living in dangerous neighborhoods where they might be preyed upon, resulting in loss of their payment checks and medications, or exposed to drug dealers and become dependent on substances? The agent state properties are also used to capture and represent further variability such as, among other factors: acuity and risks of disease levels in each quadrant, age, income, gender, race, migrant status, social support system, and social class.

DATA AND PRIVACY CONSTRAINTS FOR ABMS IN MENTAL HEALTH MODELING APPLICATIONS

This chapter has shown the data points needed for designing agent-based models. However, there are a number of challenges to obtaining data useful for such analyses. The federal Health Insurance Portability and Accountability Act (HIPAA) protects health information privacy and requires de-identification of data prior to release to researchers. The de-identification process involves removing 18 types of identifiers, including geographic information, such as city, county, and precinct, as well as date elements (except year), including admission and discharge dates. The strength of agent-based models comes from being able to simulate individuals in their local environments. Models utilizing de-identified data cannot be truly correlated with any geographic information system (GIS) data, thus limiting their value.

Data availability presents another challenge to agent-based modeling. In the case of our model, hospital readmission data were only available at the summary level, thus preventing us from conducting a regression analysis for comparison with the model results. Key risk factors associated with hospital readmissions, such as co-morbidity, ability to perform activities of daily living, socioeconomic status, and environment and support were also not available in publically available data sets.

In what follows, we review some ways that researchers might overcome some of these challenges and utilize data that are available from national and local sources.

National Data Sources

There are few national data sets dedicated for mental health. The following two data sets are the most comprehensive sources for mental health researchers.

National Survey on Drug Use and Health (NSDUH)

This survey, sponsored by the Substance Abuse and Mental Health Services Administration (SAMHSA) and US Department of Health and Human Services, constitutes the primary source of data on the use of illicit drugs, alcohol, and mental health. The target population for this survey is noninstitutionalized civilians, 12 years old or older. Homeless persons, active duty military personnel, residents of institutional group quarters, such as jails and hospitals, are excluded. For the 2013 survey, 160,325 addresses were screened and approximately 67,500 interviews were completed. All data have been de-identified (United States Department of Health and Human Services Substance Abuse and Mental Health Services Administration Center for Behavioral Health Statistics, and Quality, 2014). In our case study (detailed in the Example Application section) the NSDUH data set measures for SMI related to functional status and safety were derived from 2012 survey data.

Local Data Sources

National data sets do not contain all the data needed for constructing agent-based models, especially those that seek to model SMI. Other potential sources of data include local health systems databases. However, due to privacy and HIPAA constraints, the utility of these data for modeling is also limited. Consider the following examples.

Penn Data Warehouse

The University of Pennsylvania Health System hosts a data warehouse that contains clinical and encounter data. Data on patient demographics, encounter/visits, diagnosis and procedures, and medical history are available in de-identified form. A recent study by Hanrahan et al., utilized these data to examine the impact of SMI on all-cause hospital readmissions. The authors constructed a variable for SMI by using a 12-month look-back from index hospitalization and patients who had a comorbid psychiatric diagnosis. The final sample yielded 70,858 without SMI and 3,221 patients with SMI. This is useful for examining SMI versus non-SMI readmission differences, and this was the source of the statistics cited in the case. However, due to de-identification, there is no easy way to equate these patients to the further data available about SMI individuals in the national datasets above.

US Census and GIS Data

One can obtain US Census Bureau data for 2010. Geocoded data cannot be matched directly with de-identified data, so one must make inferences about the census tract and block group that a de-identified patient might live at. GeoLytics, a public provider and repackager of US Census Bureau data (10-year census, annual American Community Survey, ACS, etc.). The data that one could obtain from GeoLytics at the block-group level are the Census 2010, the American Community survey (ACS) 2010 and 2011 (and newer ones as they come out). With a lot of work and effort, one could possibly compute block averages for data elements, such as form of income, race/ethnicity, total population, poverty, age, sex, occupation, language isolation, immigration, labor force participation, home structure type, structure age, expenditures, educational attainment, ability to speak English, health insurance coverage, time leaving home to go to work, travel time to work, poverty status, school enrollment and type of school, social security income, journey to work, facilities, home-owner vacancy rates, mortgage status. These summary stats could then be linked with the local patient data in an effort to further understand the impact of living environment, SES status, and neighborhood on read-missions of SMI versus non-SMI individuals.

EXAMPLE APPLICATION

In this section, we present a prototype that illustrates both of these issues — construction and data. The goal of this example application was to explore factors affecting readmission rates of patients with SMI compared to patients without a SMI. In order to bridge disconnects between the national and local datasets, de-identified patient archetypes are identified. One patient archetype represents the population with SMI and the other archetype, no SMI. We used the University of Pennsylvania Hospital System dataset from 2011 to 2013 to extract patient demographic and clinical data from three urban hospitals. We used these data to study patterns of rehospitalization, comparing 74,079 patients with and without a SMI (no SMI, $n = 71,080$ and SMI, $n = 3,230$).

National datasets contribute to understanding behaviors and intentions of these archetypes. For the sake of illustration, we took just two variables from the NSDUH dataset for the prototype model: MHSUITRY (suicide attempt), a binary variable used to model safety; WHODASC2, which is the World Health Organization Disability Assessment Schedule (WHODAS) that covers six domains of functioning including cognition, mobility, self-care, getting along, life activities, and participation. We use these as proxies for safety and instrumentality, which represent the goals and preferences categories, respectively, in the agents' motivational structure (Table 7.1). The database provides different probability distributions for these two properties depending on the two sample populations (SMI or no SMI), each of size greater than 35,000.

The application of this input in each layer of the model is summarized in descriptions below at the individual, organizational, and population levels.

Agent/Individual Modeling

The model of the individual profiles lifestyle and compliance behaviors that lead to being at home, in the hospital, in the process of discharge, or "NoReadmit30," which in the simulation represents that the patient will not be readmitted within the next 30 days. According to the TRA an individual is at higher risk for return to the hospital if decisions about adherence to medication, diet, and exercise are poorly managed. For instance, a patient may have short-term goals and low adherence level under standards (Table 7.1), making the patient at higher risk for readmission. As already mentioned, based on the NSDUH, we were able to derive a probability distribution of safety and instrumentality and apply these to the two archetypes to inform this model.

Organization Modeling

The model on the organizational level is the workflow diagram presented earlier (Figure 7.2) of discrete event processes which include: (i) admittance to the hospital through the ER, General Admission, or Other Institutions, (ii) discharge to Home, Home with Health or home with care, a skilled nursing facility, hospice, or rehab, and extended care; and (iii), after being discharged to a center or staying at home for 30 days, an agent either leaves the system ("NoReadmit30") or may be readmitted. The time spent in each node and the likelihood of going to one of the others has been derived as frequencies or probability distributions corresponding to statistics taken from the data from

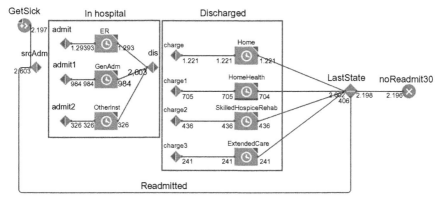

Figure 7.2 High-level view of patient daily life/health activities for the baseline scenario.

the three local hospitals. For example, admittance to the hospital through the ER, General Admission, or Other Institutions relies on randomization using these distributions. The emergency department is the top source of 61.52% of admissions for patients with SMI, while routine admits is the major source of 48.42% of patients without SMI. Likewise, length of stay in any of the hospital or other care facilities and discharge destination relies on similar distributions. In a future version, these could be informed by decision criteria that a model user inputs and rely on agent parameters like socioeconomic status, age, illness severity, comorbidities, functioning, and environment.

Population Modeling

Lastly, at the population level the prototype integrates the individual and organizational layers by illustrating important statistics about readmission. These include the percentage of the population susceptible for read-mission or in the hospital, 30-day readmission rates for agents with SMI or no SMI over time, and the average individual parameters for the read-mitted population. The left-most graph (Figure 7.3a) shows the ratio of patients who are at home at the time of the simulation and therefore at risk for readmission compared with the population percentage currently in the hospital. The model outcome for readmission rates for the agents with SMI or no SMI, shown in Figure 7.3b, reasonably reflects the read-mission averages for each group at approximately 17% and 11%, respec-tively. Given the appropriate individual data input for a population's distributions, the model predicts with general accuracy the type of

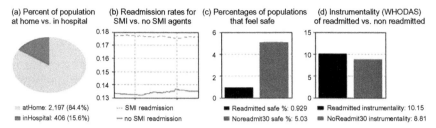

Figure 7.3 Population analysis graph.

individuals who are readmitted. This statement is explained by an example in the following paragraph.

The next two graphs (Figure 7.3c and d) show the parameter levels for safety and instrumentality, respectively, of the agent population that gets readmitted. For instance, data that compare patients with or without SMI, a simulation run of 2,608 patients processed (among those 412 patients readmitted) shows an average functionality (WHODAS score) of patients readmitted at 10.15 and an average functionality of patients not readmitted at 8.81, and this difference is significant with a P value of 0.03 (see Figure 7.3d). Thus, the model reveals how differences in patient parameters — functionality — correlate with distinctions in readmission probability. Furthermore, because certain characteristics like poverty (using Medicaid insurance status as a proxy) can be correlated with patients with SMI, the model predicts whether those characteristics are correlated with readmission. These live-feed graphs (Figure 7.3), captured during a simulation, provide insights into the hospitalization process and time-correlated statistics that previous statistical analysis do not.

An important limitation is that the data used in these models did not have a high level of specificity. Additionally, we provide only one example of how parameters are tested. As we develop the models and add more specific metrics at the individual, organization, and population levels, our ABMS becomes more sensitive and accurate.

FUTURE PROSPECTS

The multi-tiered framework we used readily supports fuller modeling of patient physiology, cognition, and socioeconomic determinants, as well as the workflows and caregiving of providers. Adding depth to these dimensions will allow for a fuller assessment of interventions and their impacts. Further research is thus warranted to add flesh to the component models. As one example, the underlying PMFserv agent framework allows one to replace the physiologic state properties with a model of physiologic dynamics. Also, we hope to extend agent cognition to the point where they use individualized value trees (goals, standards, and preferences, or GSPs) as described in the section describing model tools. Indeed, this is consistent with the TRA (Fishbein & Ajzen, 1975), which presumes that people's behavioral intentions are based on their attitudes about that particular behavior and the current subjective norms based on societal influence. PMFserv supports quantifying of attitudes via the GSP approach, though we are interested in adopting more formal instruments for profiling these in the future. As to the social norms, the current prototype clusters agents into heterogeneous categories based on disease type, severity quadrants, and social property levels (family support, neighborhood, lifestyle). The underlying agent models exist for dynamically modeling activities of daily life. Adding all these models to a future version would more fully inform the analysis and be more useful for assessing the impact of interventions.

CONCLUSION

This chapter presents a roadmap to using ABMS and three-level architecture to overcome the limitation of black box modeling (e.g., regression based). We have demonstrated the use of ABMS using three levels of models of the health of a community — the individual population members, the healthcare "system" including the various practices and services that comprise its "parts," and the overall "containing society." The first and last are critical since the decision-making of individuals in the population and societal determinants are the primary drivers of living well. ABMS supports decisions about and management of SMI facilities and care decisions. The section on tools for multi-tiered modeling (A Toolbox for Multi-layer Modeling of Social Systems) outlined the types of parameters that would help in the construction of such models, while the Data and Privacy Constraints section delineated a number of privacy-related obstacles to getting the data to parameterize those models.

ACKNOWLEDGMENTS

We thank the University of Pennsylvania Leonard Davis Institute of Health Economics, the Sr. Design Fund of the School of Engineering, and the Year of Games Fund of the School of Nursing for financial support. All claims, opinions, plus any errors, are the responsibility of the authors alone.

REFERENCES

Antonovsky, A. (1996). The salutogenic model as a theory to guide health promotion. *Health Promotion International, 11*(1), 11–18.

Bartels, S. J. (2004). Caring for the whole person: Integrated health care for older adults with severe mental illness and medical comorbidity. *Journal of the American Geriatrics Society, 52,* S249–S257. Available from: http://dx.doi.org/10.1111/j.1532-5415.2004.52601.x.

Bloom, J. D. (2010). The incarceration revolution 1: The abandonment of the seriously mentally ill to our jails and prisons. *The Journal of Law, Medicine & Ethics, 38*(4), 727–734. Available from: http://dx.doi.org/10.1111/j.1748-720X.2010.00526.x.

Brailsford, S., Harper, P., Patel, B., & Pitt, M. (2009). An analysis of the academic literature on simulation and modelling in health care. *Journal of Simulation, 3*(3), 130–140.

Calvillo-King, L., Arnold, D., Eubank, K. J., Lo, M., Yunyongying, P., Stieglitz, H., et al. (2013). Impact of social factors on risk of readmission or mortality in pneumonia and heart failure: Systematic review. *Journal of General Internal Medicine, 28*(2), 269–282.

Cil, I., & Mala, M. (2010). A multi-agent architecture for modelling and simulation of small military unit combat in asymmetric warfare. *Expert Systems with Applications, 37* (2), 1331–1343. Available from: http://dx.doi.org/10.1016/j.eswa.2009.06.024.

Colton, C. W., & Mandersheid, R. W. (2006). Congruencies in increased mortality rates, years of potential life lost, and causes of death among public mental health clients in eight states. *Prevention of Chronic Disease, 3*(2), 1–14.

Coughlin, T. A., Waidmann, T. A., & Phadera, L. (2012). Among dual eligibles, identifying the highest-cost individuals could help in crafting more targeted and effective responses. *Health Affairs (Project Hope), 31*(5), 1083–1091. Available from: http://dx.doi.org/10.1377/hlthaff.2011.0729.

Druss, B. G., von Esenwein, S. A., Compton, M. T., Zhao, L., & Leslie, D. L. (2011). Budget impact and sustainability of medical care management for persons with serious mental illnesses. *American Journal of Psychiatry, 168*(11), 1171–1178. Available from: http://dx.doi.org/10.1176/appi.ajp.2011.11010071.

Druss, B. G., Zhao, L., Cummings, J. R., Shim, R. S., Rust, G. S., & Marcus, S. C. (2012). Mental comorbidity and quality of diabetes care under medicaid: A 50-state analysis. *Medical Care, 50*(5), 428–433. Available from: http://dx.doi.org/10.1097/MLR.0b013e318245a528.

Fishbein, M., & Ajzen, I. (1975). *Belief, attitude, intention and behavior: An introduction to theory and research.* Reading, MA: Addison Wesley.

Hardy, S., & Thomas, B. (2012). Mental and physical health comordibity: Political imperatives and practice implications. *International Journal of Mental Health Nursing, 21*(3), 289–298. Available from: http://dx.doi.org/10.1111/j.1447-0349.2012.00823.x.

Institute of Medicine. (2006). *Improving the quality of health care for mental and substance-use conditions: Quality chasm series.* Washington, DC: National Academy Press.

Institute of Medicine. (2012). *Living well with chronic illness: A call for public health action.* Washington, DC: The National Academies Press.

Kronick, R. G., Bella, M., & Gilmer, T. P. (2009). *The faces of medicaid III: Refining the portrait of people with multiple chronic conditions.* Center for Health Care Strategies, Inc. <www.chcs.org/facesofmedicaid>.

Ortony, A., Clore, G. L., & Collins, A. (1990). *The cognitive structure of emotions.* Cambridge University Press.

Paranjape, R., & Sadanand, A. (2009). *Multi-agent systems for healthcare simulation and modeling: Applications for system improvement* (1st ed.). Hershey, PA: IGI Global.

Rothbard, A. B., Miller, K., Lee, S., & Blank, M. (2009). Revised cost estimates of medicaid recipients with serious mental illness and HIV-AIDS. *Psychiatric Services, 60*(7), 974–977. Available from: http://dx.doi.org/10.1176/ps.2009.60.7.974.

Schlessinger, L., & Eddy, D. M. (2012). Archimedes: A new model for simulating health care systems — The mathematical formulation. *Journal of Biomedical Informatics*, *35*(1), 37—50. Available from: http://dx.doi.org/10.1016/S1532-0464(02)00006-0.

Sibbel, R., & Urban, C. (2001). Agent-based modeling and simulation for hospital management. In *Cooperative agents*, (pp. 183—202). Amsterdam, the Netherlands: Springer.

Silverman, B. G. (2010). Systems social seience: A design inquiry approach for stabilization and reconstruction of social systems. *Intelligent Decision Technologies*, *4*(1), 51—74. Available from: http://dx.doi.org/10.3233/IDT-2010-0069.

Silverman, B. G., Hanarahan, N., & Bharathy, G. (2015). Systems approach to healthcare: Agent based modeling, community mental health, and population well-being. *Artificial Intelligence in Medicine*, *63*(2), 61—71.

Silverman, B. G., Sun, D., Bharathy, G., & Weyer, N. What is a good pattern of life (PoL): Guidance for simulations. (Available from the Author), Penn/ACASA Tech Report (Subm for publication).

Stainsby, H., Taboada, M., & Luque, E. (2009). Towards an agent-based simulation of hospital emergency departments. Services Computing, 2009. *SCC' 09. IEEE international conference on*, pp. 536—539. Available from: http://dx.doi.org/10.1109/SCC.2009.53.

United States Department of Health and Human Services Substance Abuse and Mental Health Services Administration Center for Behavioral Health Statistics, and Quality (2014). *Substance abuse and mental health services administration, results from the 2013 National Survey on drug use and health: Summary of national findings.* (No. NSDUH Series H-48) Rockville, MD: United States Department of Health and Human Services, Substance Abuse and Mental Health Services Administration.

CHAPTER 8

Robotics Technology in Mental Health Care

Laurel D. Riek
Department of Computer Science and Engineering, University of Notre Dame, Notre Dame, IN, USA

INTRODUCTION

This chapter discusses the existing use of and future potential use of robotics technology in mental health care. Robotics technology primarily refers to robots, which are physically embodied systems capable of enacting physical change in the world. Robots enact this change with effectors that either move the robot itself (locomotion), or move objects in the environment (manipulation), and often use data from sensors to make decisions.

Robots can have varying degrees of autonomy, ranging from fully teleoperated (the operator makes all decisions for the robot) to fully autonomous (the robot is entirely independent). The term robotics technology also broadly includes affiliated technology, such as accompanying sensor systems, algorithms for processing data, etc.

As a discipline, robotics has traditionally been defined as "the science which studies the intelligent connections between perception and actions," though in recent years this has shifted outward, becoming focused on problems related to interacting with real people in the real world (Siciliano & Khatib, 2008). This shift has been referred to in the literature as human-centered robotics, and an emerging area in the past decade focusing on problems in this space is known as human−robot interaction (HRI).

The use of robotics technology in mental health care is nascent, but represents a potentially useful tool in the professional's toolbox. Thus, the goal of this chapter is to provide a brief overview of the field, discuss the recent use of robotics technology in mental healthcare practice, explore some of the design issues and ethical issues of using robots in this space, and finally to explore the potential of emerging technology.

Artificial Intelligence in Behavioral and Mental Health Care.
DOI: http://dx.doi.org/10.1016/B978-0-12-420248-1.00008-8

Background

Human–Robot Interaction

Goodrich and Schultz (2007) describe the HRI problem as seeking "to understand and shape the interactions between one or more humans and one or more robots." They decompose the problem into five principle attributes: (i) the level and behavior of a robot's autonomy, (ii) the nature of information exchange between human and robot, (iii) the structure of the human–robot team, (iv) how people and robots adapt and learn from one another, and (v) how the task shapes interaction.

All of these factors play a role in how a mental healthcare professional might consider the use of robotics technology in their practice. However, there are two additional factors that may be of particular importance to practitioners. The first is the morphology, or form, of the robot itself. Robots can range in appearance from very mechanical-looking to very anthropomorphic in appearance (Riek, Rabinowitch, Chakrabarti, & Robinson, 2009). Morphology is a richly debated topic in the research community, with many studies showing people will anthropomorphize and form attachments to nearly anything conveying animacy. Some researchers worry this not only conveys inaccurate expectations to people about a robot's capabilities, but may also be unethical when treating vulnerable populations (Riek, Hartzog, Howard, Moon, & Calo, 2015; Riek & Howard, 2014). For example, individuals with cognitive impairments or children may be more susceptible to deception and manipulation by robots.

A second factor that can impact the HRI problem is individual differences between people. People have a wide range of existing cognitive and physical attributes which can greatly influence how they perceive, interact with, and accept robots (Hayes & Riek, 2014). These factors may be particularly important when considering the use of robotics technology for clients in mental healthcare settings, who may have further unique needs.

Robot Morphology

Figure 8.1 depicts several consumer and research robots used in mental healthcare applications, many of which will be discussed in next section. The robots in this figure are representative of the state-of the-art for socially interactive robots. Robots with more mechanistic appearances have been used in other applications, though very few in mental health care.

Figure 8.1 Robots currently used in mental healthcare vary greatly in their morphology, and include zoomorphic, mechanistic, cartoon-like, and humanoid representations. These robots have been used for helping treat people with dementia, autism, and cognitive impairments; have helped provide companionship for people who were lonely; have been used to help educate children with developmental disabilities; and have been used to help improve how people with visible disabilities are treated. (1) KeepOn (Kozima, Michalowski, & Nakagawa, 2009), (2) Paro (Shibata, 2012), (3) Kabochan (Tanaka et al., 2012), (4) Probo (Vanderborght et al., 2012), (5) Autom (Kidd & Breazeal, 2008), (6) NAO (Diehl et al., 2014), (7) Flobi (Damm et al., 2013), and (8) Charles (Riek & Robinson, 2011).

While zoomorphic, anthropomorphic, and cartoon-like morphologies are the most common, some robot designers have explored other unique representations. For example, actuating "everyday objects" like balls, drawers, and ottomans (Michaud, Duquette, & Nadeau, 2003; Sirikin & Ju, 2014). These robots are quite engaging, due to people's innate tendency to anthropomorphize anything with animacy (Heider & Simmel, 1944; Waytz, Cacioppo, & Epley, 2010). They may serve a useful role in therapeutic applications with clients who are less comfortable with anthropomorphic or zoomorphic representations, such as individuals on the autism spectrum (Diehl et al., 2014).

Often a robot's morphology is directly related to its functional capability requirements; for example, a robot that needs to manipulate objects is likely to have a grasper, and a robot that needs to climb stairs is likely to have legs. However, consumer robots often have appearances that reflect science fiction depictions in their color (grey) and shape (boxy). They also sometimes convey extreme feminine representations (i.e., fembots), which has raised ethical concerns in some research communities (Riek & Howard, 2014).

While consumers do not have much choice over the appearance of the robot they purchase, they frequently dress, name, and otherwise take steps to personalize it. For example, extensive, long-term, in-home studies of the Roomba vacuum cleaning robot reflect this consumer personalization (Forlizzi & DiSalvo, 2006; Sung, Guo, Grinter, & Christensen, 2007).

As will be discussed in the "Ethical Issues" section of this chapter, it is important that mental healthcare professionals are careful when selecting a robot morphology to use in treatment. Many people have a latent fear of robots due to 60 years of sordid science fiction depictions, and these fears could be exacerbated in a mental healthcare scenario. On the other hand, some morphologies may inhibit or delay transfer of learned skills from the therapy setting to everyday life. In general, when selecting a platform, mental healthcare professionals need to carefully weight the capabilities of the robot against the therapeutic needs for the patient.

Robot Capabilities

Current robots have an extensive range of physical capabilities, and as the service robotics industry continues to blossom these capabilities will only grow. In terms of physical capability, robots of various morphologies can exhibit limb-like motion, such as walking, running, climbing, turning, grabbing, shaking, gesturing; face-like motion, such as facial expressions, gaze, nodding; and other forms of biological motion, such as flipping, flying, and undulating.

However, the technology to enable these platforms to autonomously act safely and capably in the presence of humans is still very much nascent. While the research community has made significant strides in recent years, it still faces a number of challenges, particularly within domestic environments. Thus, the majority of present-day robots used in mental health care are either fully controlled by an operator (i.e., by a Wizard), or fully preprogrammed and thus somewhat limited in their abilities (Riek, 2012, 2013).

Robot Autonomy

Figure 8.2 depicts the types of autonomy a robot can employ in an HRI scenario. Many modern robotic systems have adjustable autonomy, where a person can change how they interact with a robot in real time (Dorais,

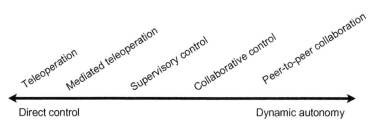

Figure 8.2 The scale of autonomy which a robot may employ during an HRI scenario. *Scale from Goodrich and Schultz (2007), used with permission.*

Bonasso, Kortenkamp, Pell, & Schreckenghost, 1999). This is particularly useful in mental healthcare scenarios, where a professional may wish to have certain robot behaviors directly controlled and others autonomous. For example, a therapist working with a child with autism might want to have the robot autonomously play a game, and based on the child's progress adjust how the robot administers rewards.

Recent Applications

Robotics technology has been applied in a variety of ways in mental healthcare scenarios. Such applications include interventions for conditions ranging from autism spectrum disorder to cognitive impairments, as well as ways to encourage physical activity and provide companionship to individuals living alone.

It is worth noting that due to the nascency of consumer robotics technology and its tendency to change rapidly, few randomized controlled clinical trials (RCTs) have been reported in the literature. Many published studies have small sample sizes, lack adequate controls, and are difficult to replicate due to variability in hardware and software. Thus, one should be cautious when interpreting the efficacy of these interventions. That being said, there is still value in learning from qualitative and case-based studies, therefore some of these findings are also reported here.

Autism Spectrum Disorders

One of the most common applications of robotics technology in mental health care is in the diagnosis and treatment of autism spectrum disorders (ASD). As Diehl et al. (2014) reported in a recent review article, robotics technology holds great potential for people with ASD, as they are very responsive to treatment involving robotics technology, possibly more so than treatment with human therapists. Thus, there are many recent studies in the literature reporting the use of robots in this fashion (cf. Damm et al., 2013; Feil-Seifer & Matarić, 2009; Goodrich et al., 2012; Kozima et al., 2009; Robins & Dautenhahn, 2014; Scassellati, Admoni, & Mataric, 2012; Vanderborght et al., 2012).

However, Diehl et al. (2014) advise caution in deploying this technology clinically, as few RCTs have been conducted, and the majority of reported research in the literature has been more technology-focused rather than client-focused. Thus, the authors argue that using robots clinically for ASD diagnosis and treatment should be considered as an experimental approach, and suggest "clinical innovation should parallel technological innovation" if robots are to be fully realized in the ASD clinical space.

Activity Engagement and Physical Exercise

Lancioni et al. describe several robot-based intervention studies intended to encourage activity engagement and ambulation among a small number of participants ($n = 6$) with severe physical and cognitive disabilities (Lancioni, Sigafoos, O'Reilly, & Singh, 2012). The mobile robots used in the studies helped participants' engagement with the physical world in a significant way, both increasing their independence as well as their "social image."

Numerous studies report the use of robotics technology in upper-limb therapy post-stroke (see Kwakkel, Kollen, and Krebs (2007) for a thorough review). However, more recently, a large-scale RCT ($n = 127$) conducted by Lo et al. (2010) showed no significant difference between the use of a robot vs. more conventional therapy. Furthermore, anecdotal evidence suggests that many of these upper-limb rehabilitative robots are so difficult for therapists to use that they remain dormant in closets after they are purchased.

In a different area of post-stroke rehabilitation, Matarić et al. introduce the concept of socially assistive robots (SAR), which provide social or cognitive assistance to people without physically interacting with them.[1] SAR "focuses on achieving specific convalescence, rehabilitation, training, or education goals." Across several small ($n = 2$), non-RCT pilot studies, the authors have found positive effects from the use of a

---

[1] In later work, the authors extend this definition to include "robots that assist people with special needs through social interactions" (Scassellati et al., 2012).

SAR for post-stroke activity encouragement (Matarić, Tapus, Winstein, & Eriksson, 2009).

Kidd and Breazeal report another application for using robots for encouraging activity engagement: weight loss. The authors designed a robotic weight loss coach, Autom, which after a controlled study ($n = 45$) was shown to be more effective at maintaining long-term weight loss (i.e., encouraging diet adherence and exercise) compared to a paper-based or computer-based system (Kidd & Breazeal, 2008).

Dementia and Age-Related Cognitive Decline

Mordoch et al. provide a detailed review of the literature on robot use in dementia care, and report details from approximately 21 studies involving patients with dementia from 2004−2011 (Mordoch, Osterreicher, Guse, Roger, & Thompson, 2013). It should be noted that none of these studies included a randomized controlled trial, most have small sample sizes, the majority lack adequate controls, and most will likely be difficult to replicate due to a lack of standardized hardware/sofware (Broekens, Heerink, & Rosendal, 2009; Mordoch et al., 2013).

Shibata et al. reported numerous studies of patients with cognitive impairments who received Paro as a therapeutic invention (Shibata, 2012; Shibata & Wada, 2011). Paro is a zoomorphic platform that resembles a seal (see Figures 8.1 and 8.2), and has been used worldwide in care homes as a substitute for physical animal therapy. Therapy using Paro typically involves patients holding, hugging, stroking, or talking to Paro, as they would an actual animal or baby. The dementia-related studies reported by Shibata include a mix of short-term and long-term studies, with both qualitative and quantitative data collected. Therefore, it is difficult to draw any conclusions as to Paro's overall effectiveness in therapy for people with dementia.

For age-related cognitive decline, there was one well-designed RCT reported in the literature suggesting the effectiveness of a robot intervention. Tanaka et al. (2012) report a trial on 34 ($n = 34$) healthy Japanese women living alone, aged between 66 and 84 years old. The study lasted for 8 weeks. Participants in the intervention group interacted with the Kabochan Nodding Communication ROBOT, a cartoon-like platform that would talk and nod at participants (see Figure 8.1); while participants in the control group received a robot that had an identical morphology, but did not talk or nod. At the end of the study, participants in the intervention group had lower cortisol levels (as measured by their saliva), improved judgment and verbal memory function (as measured by the Mini-Mental State Examination), and improved nocturnal sleep (self-report).

Companion Robots to Improve Psychosocial Outcomes

Several controlled studies have suggested companion-like robots may be an effective treatment to reducing loneliness and lowering blood pressure. For example, a recent randomized controlled trial was conducted in 2013 by Robinson et al. at a care home in New Zealand ($n = 40$). Over the course of 12 weeks, participants in the intervention group interacted with Paro, and participants in the control group participated in standard activities at the care home. Participants who interacted with Paro showed a significant decrease in loneliness over the trial period compared to the control group (Robinson, MacDonald, Kerse, & Broadbent, 2013).

This effect of loneliness reduction from a pet-like robot has also been observed in other RCTs with AIBO, a robotic dog, in the US ($n = 25$). This effect was also seen in Japan across several between-subject and within-group experiments ($n = 13$, $n = 5$, respectively) (Banks, Willoughby, & Banks, 2008; Tamura et al., 2004). Bemelmans et al. present a detailed systematic review of this literature (Bemelmans, Gelderblom, Jonker, & de Witte, 2012).

In 2014, Robinson et al. published a pilot study in both a rest home and hospital setting with people briefly interacting with Paro in a repeated measures design ($n = 21$). Participants' blood pressure was taken before, during, and after interacting with the robot. The researchers found a significant decrease in systolic and diastolic blood pressure when participants had Paro, and a significant increase in diastolic blood pressure after the robot was withdrawn (Robinson, MacDonald, & Broadbent, 2014).

Clinician Training for Interacting with People with Disabilities

We have been researching novel ways to use humanoid robots to train clinicians to better interact with patients during face-to-face interaction (Gonzales, Moosaei, & Riek, 2013; Moosaei, Gonzales, & Riek, 2014; Riek & Robinson, 2011). This work was motivated by the fact that clinicians have been shown to express bias against people with both visible and invisible disabilities, which is thus a pertinent topic for mental health care (Deegan, 1990; Mason & Scior, 2004).

We have pioneered the concept of naturalistic, patient-based facial expression synthesis for simulated patients, and have synthesized pathologies including cerebral palsy, dystonia, and pain (see Figure 8.3). Mental healthcare training already includes the use of medical simulation technology, including life-sized human-patient simulators, which are essentially humanoid robots. We plan to conduct an RCT with nurses that will explore the effectiveness of realistic facial expressions in critical care settings, and may explore psychiatric care settings as well (Moosaei et al., 2014; Riek & Robinson, 2011).

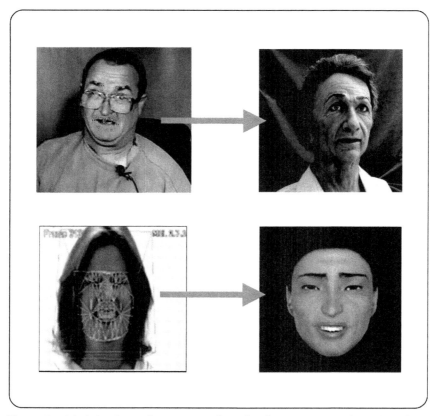

Figure 8.3 Work by the author on naturalistic facial expression synthesis, based on real patients, to be used to train clinicians to better interact with people with disabilities. On the top, facial movements tracked on a person with cerebral palsy is used to move the robot Charles. On the bottom, facial movement from a person with chronic shoulder pain is used to animate a virtual patient (the author is currently transitioning this technology to a physical robot) (Moosaei et al., 2014; Riek & Robinson, 2011).

Diagnosing and Studying Schizophrenia

Robotics technology has also been used in novel ways to study people with schizophrenia. Lavelle, Healey, and McCabe (2013, 2014) ran a series of experiments in which people with schizophrenia were placed in triads with matched control participants who were unaware of their diagnosis. Each group was tracked by a Vicon motion capture system, and their body motion was analyzed in terms of their social rapport and group participation. Interaction between 20 mixed triads was compared to 20 control triads (total $n = 120$). The results supported the hypothesis that people with schizophrenia truly do experience reduced rapport during first-time meetings when compared with controls.

The work by Lavelle et al. was the first to quantitatively explore the natural interaction between people with schizophrenia and matched controls on such a detailed level. Since this work has been published, new sensors have gone on the market that are a fraction of the cost of a Vicon motion capture system and provide even more detail. Thus, this technology offers researchers and practitioners an entirely novel way to study interpersonal interactions.

For example, our own recent work uses non-linear analysis techniques and motion modeling to explore how teams synchronize with one another during psychomotor entrainment tasks (Iqbal & Riek, 2014, 2015; Iqbal, Gonzales, and Riek, 2015; Rack, Iqbal, and Riek, 2015). As synchronizing with others is a key indicator of brain health and social development, the methods we are developing may be useful for therapists and researchers working with individuals with autism, post-traumatic stress disorder, and traumatic brain injury.

Design Issues

Potential Barriers to Provider Technology Adoption

Robot designers should be cognizant of the fact that mental healthcare professionals may be hesitant to embrace robotics technology in their practice for several reasons. First, it may interfere with, or be perceived by patients to interfere with, face-to-face communication between the provider and patient. This has been a growing problem in treatment and safety across other healthcare disciplines, and there is all the more reason to suspect this problem would be magnified for a profession centered on face-to-face interaction (cf. Levinson, Gorawara-Bhat, & Lamb, 2012; Meeks et al., 2014; Montague & Asan, 2014).

Second, providers may feel robotics technology could interfere with or hinder their practice, such as has been found in some studies with telepresence psychiatric treatment delivery systems (May et al., 2001). The mere presence of robotics technology itself could be perceived by providers as a threat to care delivery, and without long-term, thorough RCTs showing the effectiveness of the new technology, this effect may be worsened.

Finally, just as with any new technology introduced into a profession, many latent barriers to adoption exist. Several scholars have identified models for predicting technology adoption among various professionals, including mental health practitioners, which may be useful to employ (cf. Aarons, 2004; Chau & Hu, 2002). Robotics technology presents a unique adoption barrier, due to its sordid cultural history in science fiction (Riek, Adams, & Robinson, 2011). It is important that robots are well-designed to quickly convey their true capabilities to end-users, to alleviate any concerns.

Cultural Barriers to Technology Adoption

Mental healthcare professionals considering the use of robotics technology in their practice should also be sensitive to how clients from a given culture might accept a robot. Many of the studies reported in the literature were conducted with Japanese populations, who may have more positive attitudes toward some robot morphologies compared to other cultures (Bartneck, 2008; Hornyak, 2006). Wang et al. found in a cross-cultural study between Chinese and American participants, that robots that respect cultural norms are more likely to be accepted (Wang, Rau, Evers, Robinson, & Hinds, 2010). Lee et al. found similar findings when comparing Korean and American participants (Lee, Sung, Sabanovic, & Han, 2012).

Some cultures may be more accepting of robotics in healthcare practice than one might expect. For example, while traditionally Middle Eastern culture is opposed to iconic technology, such as humanoid robots, people are often willing to make exceptions when it comes to health care. Riek et al. conducted a large-scale study ($n = 131$) in the United Arab Emirates, and brought an interactive android robot that resembled Ibn Sina to a shopping mall (see Figure 8.4; Riek et al., 2010). The researchers surveyed participants from 21 different countries on their attitudes toward human-like robots, and found that generally participants were accepting of robots in domestic life (e.g., positive responses to discrete-visual analog scale questions such as "I wouldn't mind if a human-like robot treated me at a hospital," "I wouldn't mind if a

Figure 8.4 Participants at a shopping mall in the United Arab Emirates interact with a humanoid robot resembling the philosopher Ibn Sina. Despite being situated in a culture that is frequently associated with anti-iconography, such a robot was found to be well-accepted if used for hospital care, and for domestic tasks such as housework (Riek et al., 2010).

human-like robot cleaned my house," etc.). More work is needed to fully understand the potential effect of culture on robotics technology adoption for mental healthcare use, but the robot's morphology and behavior are key components to consider.

A Need for Evidence-Based Robotics Use in Mental Health Care

As discussed previously in this chapter, before robots can be effectively deployed in mental healthcare practice it is important that rigorous RCTs are conducted. These studies should study not only patient benefit and technology acceptance issues, but also explore the socio-technological needs of caregivers (Chang and Šabanović, 2015). While it is unlikely most robots would cause direct harm to clients or practitioners, adopting this technology before the evidence base is developed runs the risk of displacing proven interventions with less effective or ineffective treatments.

Thus, robot designers wishing to explore the use of robotics technology in mental health care should, from the outset, aim to run rigorous studies in concert with practitioners and researchers. This is particularly important for several reasons. First, it is important to ensure suitable controls are selected. For example, rather than the treatment group receiving the robot and the control group receiving an alternate therapy, the control group could instead receive a non–actuated analog.

This strategy was successful for the aforementioned Kobachan intervention for age-related cognitive decline (Tanaka et al., 2012), and thus may prove useful for other interventions.

Second, by partnering with practitioners, robot designers are more likely to have access to desired patient populations, and are more likely to be able to engage in long-term studies. For many mental healthcare applications, clinical effectiveness is related to treatment length, i.e., the dose–response relationship (Hansen, Lambert, & Forman, 2002). Thus, a single encounter with a robot is not as useful a metric, particularly given the high likelihood of novelty effects (Gockley et al., 2005; Leite, Martinho, Pereira, & Paiva, 2009).

Finally, both robot designers and mental healthcare professionals should be sensitive to the fact that people with disabilities and their families can be swept up in treatment fads and pseudoscience, some of which can be truly damaging (Jacobson, Foxx, & Mulick, 2005). Despite the allure of new technology, it is better to tread carefully and run thorough RCTs before embracing new treatment modalities.

Ethical Issues

Riek and Howard (2014) recently published a paper describing unique ethical challenges in HRI, and proposed a code of ethics for HRI practitioners. HRI practitioners include: robotics designers, engineers, researchers, designers, product managers, and marketers, and also may include mental healthcare professionals and other healthcare workers interested in exploring the use of robots in their practice. Riek and Howard (2014) specifically focus on ethical challenges to using robots with vulnerable populations, including socially and physically assistive robots.

The proposed code of ethics is recounted here verbatim (see Riek & Howard, 2014 for full details and examples of unique ethical challenges):

The Prime Directive

All HRI research, development, and marketing should heed the overall principle of respect for human persons, including respect for human autonomy, respect for human bodily and mental integrity, and the affordance of all rights and protections ordinarily assumed in human–human interactions. The robot actor is expected to behave in a manner at least as respectful of human personhood as human actors to the extent feasible.

Specific Principles
Human Dignity Considerations
- The emotional needs of humans are always to be respected.
- The human's right to privacy shall always be respected to the greatest extent consistent with reasonable design objectives.
- Human frailty is always to be respected, both physical and psychological.

Design Considerations
- Maximal, reasonable transparency in the programming of robotic systems is required.
- Predictability in robotic behavior is desirable.
- Trustworthy system design principles are required across all aspects of a robot's operation, for both hardware and software design, and for any data processing on or off the platform.
- Real-time status indicators should be provided to users to the greatest extent consistent with reasonable design objectives.
- Obvious opt-out mechanisms (kill switches) are required to the greatest extent consistent with reasonable design objectives.

Legal Considerations
- All relevant laws and regulations concerning individuals' rights and protections (e.g., FDA, HIPPA, and FTC) are to be respected.
- A robot's decision paths must be re-constructible for the purposes of litigation and dispute resolution.
- Human informed consent to HRI is to be facilitated to the greatest extent possible consistent with reasonable design objectives.

Social Considerations
- Wizard-of-Oz should be employed as judiciously and carefully as possible, and should aim to avoid Turing deceptions.
- The tendency for humans to form attachments to and anthropomorphize robots should be carefully considered during design.
- Humanoid morphology and functionality is permitted only to the extent necessary for the achievement of reasonable design objectives.
- Avoid racist, sexist, and ableist morphologies and behaviors in robot design.

Since this initial paper was published, we have run a workshop entitled "The Emerging Policy and Ethics of Human–Robot Interaction"

(Riek et al., 2015). The workshop has further expanded upon these issues, and we will shortly release a consensus document to the community.

CONCLUSION

The personal robotics sector is expanding rapidly, with new companies forming, products being developed, and applications appearing in the commercial space in ways unimaginable a decade ago. While it is impossible to form specific predictions, the current trend of research and development suggests a future where robots are able to assist us in a variety of daily tasks. For people with physical disabilities in particular, robots are uniquely poised to be a remarkably enabling technology, affording an improved quality of life and an increase in independent living.

Robots may also help individuals with invisible health conditions, such as mental health disorders, and they may also assist their caregivers. As one participant stated at our HRI Policy and Ethics Workshop (Riek et al., 2015), often people just want a "robot that can change the oil." In other words, a robot that can help with mundane chores around the house or daily living tasks. Simple things can prove hugely beneficial.

For care providers, robots may prove useful in training. For example, similar to how researchers in the virtual agent communities have employed both virtual patients and coaches to train clinical students (Lok et al., 2006; Rizzo, 2002), perhaps robots could also be used in this capacity. For example, to teach interaction, listening skills, and enable destigmatization (Arkin, 2014; Riek & Robinson, 2011).

However, providers are advised caution in using autonomous robots to directly provide therapy for individuals with mental health disorders. It is important that a strong evidence base is first established through the employment of rigorous RCTs. Despite the appeal of "Sigfrid von Shrink," the robotic psychologist in Fredrick Pohl's novel Gateway (Pohl, 1977), the actual realization of AI has nowhere near caught up to the remarkable physical capabilities of robots. That being said, this is indeed an exciting era for robotics technology. As computer processors and storage get faster and cheaper, and as new advances emerge in machine learning and multimodal processing, a world of possibility exists for robots ever more capable and agile in human social environments.

ACKNOWLEDGMENT

Some research reported in this article is based upon work supported by the National Science Foundation under Grant No. IIS-1253935.

REFERENCES

Aarons, G. A. (2004). Mental health provider attitudes toward adoption of evidence-based practice: The evidence-based practice attitude scale (ebpas). *Mental Health Services Research, 6*(2), 61−74.

Arkin, R. C. (2014). Ameliorating patient-caregiver stigma in early-stage Parkinson's disease using robot co-mediators. *Proceedings of the AISB 50 Symposium on Machine Ethics in the Context of Medical and Health Care Agents,* London, UK, April 2014.

Banks, M. R., Willoughby, L. M., & Banks, W. A. (2008). Animal-assisted therapy and loneliness in nursing homes: Use of robotic versus living dogs. *Journal of the American Medical Directors Association, 9*(3), 173−177.

Bartneck, C. (2008). Who like androids more: Japanese or US Americans? In *The 17th IEEE International Symposium on Robot and Human Interactive Communication (RO-MAN)* (pp. 553−557). IEEE.

Bemelmans, R., Gelderblom, G. J., Jonker, P., & de Witte, L. (2012). Socially assistive robots in elderly care: A systematic review into effects and effectiveness. *Journal of the American Medical Directors Association, 13*(2), 114−120.e1. Available from: http://dx. doi.org/10.1016/j.jamda.2010.10.002.

Broekens, J., Heerink, M., & Rosendal, H. (2009). Assistive social robots in elderly care: A review. *Gerontechnology, 8*(2), 94−103. Available from: http://dx.doi.org/10.4017/gt.2009.08.02.002.00.

Chang, W.-L., & Šabanović, S. (2015). Interaction expands function: Social shaping of the therapeutic robot paro in a nursing home. In *Proceedings of the Tenth Annual ACM/IEEE International Conference on Human-Robot Interaction* (pp. 343−350). ACM.

Chau, P. Y., & Hu, P. J.-H. (2002). Investigating healthcare professionals decisions to accept telemedicine technology: An empirical test of competing theories. *Information & Management, 39*(4), 297−311.

Damm, O., Malchus, K., Jaecks, P., Krach, S., Paulus, F., Naber, M., et al. (2013). Different gaze behavior in human-robot interaction in asperger's syndrome: An eye tracking study. In *IEEE International Symposium on Robot and Human Interactive Communication (RO-MAN)* (pp. 368−369). IEEE.

Deegan, P. E. (1990). Spirit breaking: When the helping professions hurt. *The Humanistic Psychologist, 18*(3), 301−313.

Diehl, J. J., Crowell, C. R., Villano, M., Wier, K., Tang, K., & Riek, L. D. (2014). Clinical applications of robots in autism spectrum disorder diagnosis and treatment. In *Comprehensive guide to autism* (pp. 411−422). Springer.

Dorais, G., Bonasso, R. P., Kortenkamp, D., Pell, B., & Schreckenghost, D. (1999). Adjustable autonomy for human-centered autonomous systems. In *Working Notes of the Sixteenth International Joint Conference on Artificial Intelligence Workshop on Adjustable Autonomy Systems* (pp. 16−35).

Feil-Seifer, D., & Matarić, M. J. (2009). Toward socially assistive robotics for augmenting interventions for children with autism spectrum disorders. In *Experimental robotics* (pp. 201−210). Springer.

Forlizzi, J., & DiSalvo, C. (2006). Service robots in the domestic environment: A study of the roomba vacuum in the home. In *Proceedings of the 1st ACM SIGCHI/SIGART Conference on Human-Robot Interaction* (pp. 258−265). ACM.

Gockley, R., Bruce, A., Forlizzi, J., Michalowski, M., Mundell, A., Rosenthal, S. et al. (2005). Designing robots for long-term social interaction. In *IEEE/RSJ International Conference on Intelligent Robots and Systems, (IROS)* (pp. 1338–1343). IEEE.

Gonzales, M., Moosaei, M., & Riek, L. (2013). A novel method for synthesizing naturalistic pain on virtual patients. *Simulation in Healthcare, 8*(6). Available from: http://dx.doi.org/10.1097/01.SIH.0000441715.40653.4e.

Goodrich, M. A., Colton, M., Brinton, B., Fujiki, M., Atherton, J. A., Robinson, L., et al. (2012). Incorporating a robot into an autism therapy team. *IEEE Intelligent Systems, 27* (2), 0052–60.

Goodrich, M. A., & Schultz, A. C. (2007). Human-robot interaction: A survey. *Foundations and Trends in Human-computer Interaction, 1*(3), 203–275.

Hansen, N. B., Lambert, M. J., & Forman, E. M. (2002). The psychotherapy dose-response effect and its implications for treatment delivery services. *Clinical Psychology: Science and Practice, 9*(3), 329–343.

Hayes, C., & Riek, L. D. (2014). Establishing human personality metrics for adaptable robots during learning tasks. In *AAAI Fall Symposium on Artificial Intelligence and Human Robot Interaction*. <https://www.aaai.org/ocs/index.php/FSS/FSS14/rt/captureCite/9213/0>.

Heider, F., & Simmel, M. (1944). An experimental study of apparent behavior. *The American Journal of Psychology*, 243–259.

Hornyak, T. N. (2006). *Loving the machine*. Tokyo, Japan: Kodansha International.

Iqbal, T., & Riek, L. (2014). Assessing group synchrony during a rhythmic social activity: A systemic approach. In *6th Conference of the International Society for Gesture Studies (ISGS)*. San Diego, CA, 74.

Iqbal, T., & Riek, L. D. (2015). A method for automatic detection of psychomotor entrainment. *IEEE Transactions on Affective Computing, 2015*, Available from: < http://dx.doi.org/10.1109/TAFFC.2015.2445335>.

Iqbal, T., Gonzales, M. J., & Riek, L. D. (2015). Joint action perception to enable fluent human-robot teamwork. In Proceedings of the 24th IEEE International Symposium on Robot and Human Interactive Communication. Kobe, Japan, Aug, 2015. IEEE.

Jacobson, J. W., Foxx, R. M., & Mulick, J. A. (2005). *Controversial therapies for developmental disabilities: Fad, fashion, and science in professional practice*. New Jersey, NY, USA: CRC Press.

Kidd, C. D., & Breazeal, C. (2008). Robots at home: Understanding long-term human-robot interaction. In *IEEE/RSJ International Conference on Intelligent Robots and Systems (IROS)* (pp. 3230–3235). IEEE.

Kozima, H., Michalowski, M. P., & Nakagawa, C. (2009). Keepon. *International Journal of Social Robotics, 1*(1), 3–18.

Kwakkel, G., Kollen, B. J., & Krebs, H. I. (2007). Effects of robot-assisted therapy on upper limb recovery after stroke: A systematic review. *Neurorehabilitation and Neural Repair*. http://www.ncbi.nlm.nih.gov/pubmed/17876068.

Lancioni, G., Sigafoos, J, O'Reilly, M., & Singh, N. (2012). *Assistive technology: Interventions for individuals with severe/profound and multiple disabilities*. New York, NY, USA: Springer.

Lavelle, M., Healey, P. G., & McCabe, R. (2013). Is nonverbal communication disrupted in interactions involving patients with schizophrenia? *Schizophrenia Bulletin, 39*(5).

Lavelle, M., Healey, P. G., & McCabe, R. (2014). Participation during first social encounters in schizophrenia. *PloS One, 9*(1), e77506.

Lee, H. R., Sung, J., Sabanovic, S., & Han, J. (2012). Cultural design of domestic robots: A study of user expectations in korea and the united states. In *IEEE International Symposium on Robot and Human Interactive Communication (RO-MAN)* (pp. 803–808). IEEE.

Leite, I., Martinho, C., Pereira, A., & Paiva, A. (2009). As time goes by: Long-term evaluation of social presence in robotic companions. In *IEEE International Symposium on Robot and Human Interactive Communication (RO-MAN)* (pp. 669–674). IEEE.

Levinson, W., Gorawara-Bhat, R., & Lamb, J. (2012). A study of patient clues and physician responses in primary care and surgical settings. *The Journal of the American Medical Association, 284*(8), 1021−1027.

Lo, A. C., Guarino, P. D., Richards, L. G., Haselkorn, J. K., Wittenberg, G. F., Federman, D. G., et al. (2010). Robot-assisted therapy for long-term upper-limb impairment after stroke. *New England Journal of Medicine, 362*(19), 1772−1783.

Lok, B., Ferdig, R. E., Raij, A., Johnsen, K., Dickerson, R., Coutts, J., et al. (2006). Applying virtual reality in medical communication education: Current findings and potential teaching and learning benefits of immersive virtual patients. *Virtual Reality, 10*(3−4), 185−195.

Mason, J., & Scior, K. (2004). Diagnostic overshadowingamongst clinicians working with people with intellectual disabilities in the UK. *Journal of Applied Research in Intellectual Disabilities, 17*(2), 85−90.

Matarić, M., Tapus, A., Winstein, C., & Eriksson, J. (2009). Socially assistive robotics for stroke and mild TBI rehabilitation. *Advanced Technologies in Rehabilitation, 145*, 249−262.

May, C., Gask, L., Atkinson, T., Ellis, N., Mair, F., & Esmail, A. (2001). Resisting and promoting new technologies in clinical practice: The case of telepsychiatry. *Social Science & Medicine, 52*(12), 1889−1901.

Meeks, D. W., Smith, M. W., Taylor, L., Sittig, D. F., Scott, J. M., & Singh, H. (2014). An analysis of electronic health record-related patient safety concerns. *Journal of the American Medical Informatics Association.* http://www.ncbi.nlm.nih.gov/pubmed/24951796.

Michaud, F., Duquette, A., & Nadeau, I. (2003). Characteristics of mobile robotic toys for children with pervasive developmental disorders. In *IEEE International Conference on Systems, Man and Cybernetics* (Vol. 3, pp. 2938−2943). IEEE.

Montague, E., & Asan, O. (2014). Dynamic modeling of patient and physician eye gaze to understand the effects of electronic health records on doctor−patient communication and attention. *International Journal of Medical Informatics, 83*(3), 225−234.

Moosaei, M., Gonzales, M., & Riek, L. (2014). Naturalistic pain synthesis for virtual patients. In *Proceedings of the 14th International Conference on Intelligent Virtual Agents* (pp. 1−14).

Mordoch, E., Osterreicher, A., Guse, L., Roger, K., & Thompson, G. (2013). Use of social commitment robots in the care of elderly people with dementia: A literature review. *Maturitas, 74*(1), 14−20.

Pohl, F. (1977). *Gateway.* New York: St. Martin's Press.

Rack, S., Iqbal, T., & Riek, L. D. (2015). Enabling Synchronous Joint Action in Human-Robot Teams. In Proceedings of the Tenth Annual ACM/IEEE International Conference on Human-Robot Interaction Extended Abstracts (HRI'15 Extended Abstracts). (pp. 153−154): ACM Press.

Riek, L. D. (2012). Wizard of oz studies in HRI: A systematic review and new reporting guidelines. *Journal of Human Robot Interaction, 1*, 119−136.

Riek, L. D. (2013). The social co-robotics problem space: Six key challenges. In *Proceedings of Robotics: Science, and Systems (RSS), Robotics Challenges and Visions.* Berlin, Germany.

Riek, L. D., Adams, A., & Robinson, P. (2011). Exposure to cinematic depictions of robots and attitudes towards them. In *ACM/IEEE International Conference on Human-Robot Interaction, Workshop on Expectations and Intuitive Human-Robot Interaction.* Lausanne, Switzerland.

Riek, L. D., Hartzog, W., Howard, D., Moon, A., & Calo, R. (2015). The emerging policy and ethics of human robot interaction. In *Proceedings of the Tenth Annual ACM/IEEE International Conference on Human-Robot Interaction* (pp. 247−248). ACM.

Riek, L. D., & Howard, D. (2014). A code of ethics for the human-robot interaction profession. *We Robot, 2014*, 1−10.

Riek, L. D., Mavridis, N., Antali, S., Darmaki, N., Ahmed, Z., Al-Neyadi, M., et al. (2010). Ibn Sina steps out: Exploring arabic attitudes toward humanoid robots. In *Proceedings of the Second International Symposium on New Frontiers in Human-Robot Interaction* (pp. 88−99).

Riek, L. D., Rabinowitch, T.-C., Chakrabarti, B., & Robinson, P. (2009). Empathizing with robots: Fellow feeling along the anthropomorphic spectrum. In *3rd International Conference on Affective Computing and Intelligent Interaction (ACII)* (pp. 1−6).

Riek, L. D., & Robinson, P. (2011). Using robots to help people habituate to visible disabilities. In *IEEE International Conference on Rehabilitation Robotics (ICORR)* (pp. 1−8). IEEE.

Rizzo, A. (2002). Virtual reality and disability: Emergence and challenge. *Disability & Rehabilitation, 24*(11−12), 567−569.

Robins, B., & Dautenhahn, K. (2014). Tactile interactions with a humanoid robot: Novel play scenario implementations with children with autism. *International Journal of Social Robotics*, 1−19.

Robinson, H., MacDonald, B., & Broadbent, E. (2014). Physiological effects of a companion robot on blood pressure of older people in residential care facility: A pilot study. *Australasian Journal on Ageing, 34*(1), 27−32. Available from: http://dx.doi.org/10.1111/ajag.12099.

Robinson, H., MacDonald, B., Kerse, N., & Broadbent, E. (2013). The psychosocial effects of a companion robot: A randomized controlled trial. *Journal of the American Medical Directors Association, 14*(9), 661−667.

Scassellati, B., Admoni, H., & Mataric, M. (2012). Robots for use in autism research. *Annual Review of Biomedical Engineering, 14*, 275−294.

Shibata, T. (2012). Therapeutic seal robot as biofeedback medical device: Qualitative and quantitative evaluations of robot therapy in dementia care. *Proceedings of the IEEE, 100* (8), 2527−2538.

Shibata, T., & Wada, K. (2011). Robot therapy: A new approach for mental healthcare of the elderly − a mini-review. *Gerontology, 57*(4), 378−386.

Siciliano, B., & Khatib, O. (2008). *Springer handbook of robotics*. Springer.

Sirkin, D., & Ju W. (2014). "Using embodied design improvisation as a design research tool." In Proc. Int'l. Conf. on Human Behavior in Design, Ascona, Switzerland.

Sung, J.-Y., Guo, L., Grinter, R. E., & Christensen, H. I. (2007). *My roomba is ramboi: intimate home appliances*. Springer.

Tamura, T., Yonemitsu, S., Itoh, A., Oikawa, D., Kawakami, A., Higashi, Y., et al. (2004). Is an entertainment robot useful in the care of elderly people with severe dementia? *The Journals of Gerontology Series A: Biological Sciences and Medical Sciences, 59*(1), M83−M85.

Tanaka, M., Ishii, A., Yamano, E., Ogikubo, H., Okazaki, M., Kamimura, K., et al. (2012). Effect of a human-type communication robot on cognitive function in elderly women living alone. *Medical Science Monitor: International Medical Journal of Experimental and Clinical Research, 18*(9), CR550−CR557.

Vanderborght, B., Simut, R., Saldien, J., Pop, C., Rusu, A. S., Pintea, S., et al. (2012). Using the social robot probo as a social story telling agent for children with ASD. *Interaction Studies, 13*(3), 348−372.

Wang, L., Rau, P.-L. P., Evers, V., Robinson, B. K., & Hinds, P. (2010). When in rome: the role of culture & context in adherence to robot recommendations. In *Proceedings of the Fifth ACM/IEEE International Conference on Human−Robot Interaction* (pp. 359−366). IEEE Press.

Waytz, A., Cacioppo, J. T., & Epley, N. (2010). Who sees human? The stability and importance of individual differences in anthropomorphism. *Perspectives on Psychological Science, 5*, 219−232.

CHAPTER 9

Public Health Surveillance: Predictive Analytics and Big Data

Chris Poulin[1], Paul Thompson[2] and Craig Bryan[3]
[1]Patterns and Predictions, Portsmouth, NH, USA
[2]Institute for Security, Technology, and Society, Dartmouth College, Hanover, NH, USA
[3]Department of Psychology, The University of Utah, Salt Lake City, UT, USA

INTRODUCTION

Similar to findings in military and veteran samples, the majority of individuals who die by suicide deny suicidal ideation or intent in the period of time immediately preceding their deaths. Unfortunately, progress in the accurate detection and identification of at-risk individuals has been limited by the absence of studies supporting the ability of any suicide prevention screening method to reliably and accurately predict future suicide. If progress is to be made in public health problems such as suicide prevention, both within and external to the military, new tools and technologies will need to be developed and tested. Because suicide is a relatively uncommon outcome, solutions will require very high-frequency data collection to ensure sufficient information is available to detect emerging risk before a suicide attempt occurs. Furthermore, because most individuals who die by suicide are not actively engaged in mental health care at the time of their deaths, solutions will need to be implemented outside of the healthcare system. Automated linguistic analysis of social media posts meets both of these requirements.

As we will discuss, our "Durkheim Project" addresses this critical public health problem within the military and veteran communities, it also directly targets three of the National Action Alliance for Suicide Prevention's (NAASP) Research Prioritization Task Force highest priority goals in suicide research: determining the degree of suicide risk among individuals in diverse populations through feasible screening and assessment approaches; assessing who is at risk for attempting suicide in the immediate future; and preventing the emergence of suicidal behavior. It is the application of these ever-improving analytical tools that will improve understanding of public health (especially mental) in the twenty-first century.

Artificial Intelligence in Behavioral and Mental Health Care.
DOI: http://dx.doi.org/10.1016/B978-0-12-420248-1.00009-X

THE CURRENT STATE OF INFORMATICS

Emerging trends in data analysis have been augmented by the proliferation of supercomputing-related technologies, otherwise known as 'high-performance computing' systems. The tools used in supercomputing, which dates to the early Cold War era, bear a striking similarity to many of the tools used in big data analysis, albeit now with a greater emphasis on functionality and ease of use. For example, many nuclear research programs required complex simulation capabilities that outstripped simple computing resources. Combined with an explosion in the amount of information available to scientists in other areas, such as astronomical science, researchers pushed for the development of tools that could do more with less. In the 1990s, these software tools found their way to commodity machines (or personal computers), which formed the basis for the generation of modern grid computing tools.

Commercially, Google was one of the first large companies to embrace commodity distributed computing. For Google's founders, a primary goal was to provide better search engines, both in scope and sophistication, while spending fewer resources to process the data. Their initial attempt was a set of tools for distributed computing on low-cost machines. In 2004, Google launched a series of internal initiatives to develop a reliable big data infrastructure. These findings were subsequently published in a series of high-profile research papers (Dean & Ghemawat, 2004; Fikes et al., 2006).

Many researchers took interest when these Google papers were released. One researcher, Doug Cutting, was inspired to write his own implementation of a distributed storage system, eventually called Hadoop. This influential system, with its open-source grid tools and systems similar in functionality have further driven the rise of what has been known recently as "big data," thereby effectively allowing researchers to utilize resources across multiple machines with ease.

OVERVIEW OF RECENT APPLICATIONS

If you collect enough information, you can perceive many things. For example, if given access to enough data about an anonymous individual, you can likely identify that individual. With enough information over time, you can predict events in that individual's life, and if you observe how an individual reacts to these events, you could potentially predict that individual's future behavior. Most importantly, within this information lies tremendous opportunity to help individuals avoid unnecessary hardships and live better lives.

These opportunities are especially apparent in the field of medicine. With the ability to collect and view more patient data, researchers and physicians are able to better quantify risks to individuals. They can view details that previously slipped past clinical practice and can identify potential medical problems *before* they happen. With the deployment of systems in both research and clinical medical practice, the elusive promises of preventive medicine are closer to being realized.

Our team has spent over a decade researching the cues in language and the correlations between combinations of words and outcomes. While teaching a machine to understand language is widely considered to be a "hard AI" problem — that is, requiring an advanced level of artificial intelligence — many have proven that increasingly sophisticated computer systems can predict correlations of language with events. We recently applied this system to the challenge of estimating suicide risk among US veterans. Assessing suicide risk is a particularly difficult clinical task for healthcare professionals, and one that is highly amenable to data systems, as well as being socially worthwhile (Ungerleider, 2013).

It is not just our team, but many researchers, private corporations, and public institutions that now have the capability to collect and analyze data on an immense scale (Duhigg, 2012). With this increasingly powerful analysis capability, the question therefore arises: What is truly best practice in this area?

Data Workflow

We will discuss six important implementation areas, drawing examples from a hypothetical human subjects study using private medical data. We will also draw lessons from our past and present work at the Durkheim Project.

1. Collection

    First, data must be collected. Gathering medical data generally requires informed consent in the form of an opt-in procedure, usually a formal consent agreement. In our project, we follow clinical standards, even when not strictly needed, in order to maintain the utmost trust in the data collected by our system.

2. Storage

    Datasets are usually stored in large databases following collection. The individual or institution storing the data may or may not have a data governance or data privacy policy. In brief, a data governance policy determines what to do with the data, while a data privacy policy determines who can view the data. In the case of medical data, the information requires more careful handling. For example, proper procedure restricts access to the dataset and requires that data be stored securely behind an IT firewall. In our project, we first aggregate the data from social media and mobile applications worldwide on secure cloud services (e.g., Amazon Web Services), and then transmit the data to our medical center partner for final storage using encryption.

3. Processing

To analyze the datasets, we must process the data using some sort of computing cluster. This cluster may be in a secure data center, or it may not. The transmissions between the analyst who is sending the data and the machines that are processing the data may or may not be encrypted. The data processing machines may or may not be secure themselves. In fact, standards in the field of data processing are only now emerging. For example, our project's facilities have a Cray supercomputer behind a firewall that processes the data, before transmitting the results to another system that can be accessed by medical analysts directly via the Internet.

4. Query

Once an initial data analysis has been conducted, it is necessary to specify who has access to the data. The question now becomes, who has rights to query the system? In the case of medical risk analysis, the issue of query is strongly related to the privacy of the individual. At the Durkheim Project, our medical protocol dictates that the raw data contained in medical records of those who are suicide-positive are not seen by non-Veterans Affairs staff. However, once the data are "de-identified" and analyzed, our internal team (bound by nondisclosure agreements and HIPAA regulation compliance rules) can access the information.

5. Reporting

Analytics reports are usually a combination of numbers, qualitative visualizations, and written narratives intended to describe tested outcomes. The end consumer might be a scientific journal, government research agency, or a health policymaker. This leads to the question, can the consumer of the report trust the data? Does this consumer or decision-maker understand how the data were collected? Do they know whether the data were stored and processed securely? How will the dissemination of the analytic report impact the people, places, and things that were analyzed? In the case of our medical data, only de-identified data are disseminated outside of the direct researchers. We shared our preliminary, de-identified, results with other organizations under nondisclosure agreement, as well as with our funding agency (DARPA). Final publication of results was in a peer-reviewed journal (PLoS One). Any further sharing of our patient related data would have required restrictions. Dissemination of final results will vary highly by project, depending on the type of intended analysis.

6. Intervention

In the medical case the proper use of risk metrics can enable triage of clinical resources and produce recommendations for risk reduction or lifestyle changes. In considering these scenarios, it is important to ask, should the person entrusted with these decisions also be trusted with their analysis? We argue the answer is only if they know (with great certainty) how the information was collected, stored, processed, queried, and reported. Making use of our own analysis, our systems are currently engaged in intervention efforts related to suicide and other mental health risks. Effective clinical interventions must first be based upon validated, peer-reviewed medical research. No responsible clinical decision-maker would assume otherwise. In our case, although we have published comprehensive methods, we have only begun the validation of our methodology. This process is ongoing.

The Durkheim Project

The Durkheim Project was a successful DARPA-sponsored program that established both validated risk metrics for suicide risk and a capability to scale to larger opt-in networks (both social and mobile). The various data and revised indicators are then fed into an analytics environment, which enables both accurate and timely interventions by clinicians via a secure communication network.

The project is currently advancing the state-of-the-art in suicide risk detection and *intervention* for US veterans, specifically by providing an end-to-end solution to isolate risks and provide a novel upstream intervention. Our methods are at the intersection of advanced predictive analytics, psychology, financial analysis, and network computing. Our team members have previously applied these methods to successfully study psychiatric event risk in suicide, and we are now expanding our effort to enable *interventions triage* based on validated risk values. We have had prior success in applying 'big data' to the differentiation of suicide from nonsuicide cases, and have demonstrated 14% more accurate classification of suicide outcomes as compared to the clinician standard

(Poulin et al., 2014). Recently, we began exploring the use of this predictive capability in facilitating intervention (Poulin et al., 2014). Finally, as part of this effort, we are planning to track outcomes via the new VA/DOD Suicide Data Repository.

This is a first-time capability to detect (proven) suicide risk in real-time and then act with an effective clinical triage resource. This dramatically improves capabilities to effectively manage mental healthcare resources for US veterans.

Background

Suicide is a leading cause of death in the United States, and is the second most common cause of death in the United States military (Department of Defense, 2011; Ritchie, Keppler, & Rothberg, 2003). Despite considerable efforts by military and civilian organizations to address this problem, military suicide rates have continued to rise. In response to these trends, attention has been focused on improving suicide prevention screening to enhance early detection and connection of at-risk individuals with appropriate treatment and support services. The considerable bulk of these screening efforts has occurred across the full spectrum of health care, to include primary care clinics, mental health clinics, and emergency departments. Unfortunately, the majority of individuals who subsequently make a suicide attempt or die by suicide are "missed" by current screening methods (Busch, Fawcett, & Jacobs, 2003; Coombs et al., 1992; Hall, Platt, & Hall, 1999; Kovacs, Beck, & Weissman, 1976). In other words, most individuals who die by suicide deny that they are suicidal or do not explicitly verbalize suicidal intent during their last medical appointment or screening immediately preceding their deaths. The problem of screening in medical settings is especially pronounced for military personnel and veterans, for whom self-disclosure of mental health problems in general, and suicidal intent in particular, is influenced by pervasive mental health stigma. As a result, expanded suicide prevention screening has not noticeably affected military suicide trends.

Overall, accurate mental health diagnosis and the prediction of negative events such as suicide or suicide ideation is limited by: (i) a lack of understanding of the true differentiating risks of suicide (Department of the Army, 2010) and (ii) a lack of near real-time reaction capability to large volumes of data. There is a need for broader coverage suicide risk detection and a better understanding of the expression of suicide ideation through data mining of text and images. The Durkheim Project's solution is to provide continuous monitoring of text-based information, such as those found in social network user behavioral intent enabling intervention; facilitated by social/online data sources, powered by a medically validated suicide risk classifier.

Related Work

There are many non-real-time linguistic approaches to analyzing suicide risk (Barak & Miron, 2005; Jones & Bennell, 2007; Lester, 2008a, 2008b; Lester, 2010a, 2010b; Lester, Haines, & Williams, 2010; Lester & McSwain, 2010; Stirman & Pennebaker, 2001). Of this literature base, only Barak and Miron (2005) previously considered online text. Most other text analysis suicide research studies have focused on the analysis of suicide notes or literary writing. For example, there are studies of the writings of suicidal poets (Lester & McSwain, 2010; Stirman & Pennebaker, 2001) and studies involving distinguishing genuine and simulated suicide notes (Jones & Bennell, 2007; Lester, 2010a).

Recent work in the military has focused on the concept of the "suicidal belief system," which posits that suicidal individuals hold certain beliefs and assumptions about themselves that distinguish them from non-suicidal individuals (Bryan et al., 2014). For example, highly suicidal individuals often perceive themselves as a burden on others, as fundamentally flawed or defective, and as incapable of solving problems or managing distress. Because these suicidal beliefs manifest in spoken and written forms of communication, they provide clues to heightened suicide risk, even when the individual denies overt suicidal intent. Assessment of these suicidal beliefs has been shown to differentiate military personnel who have attempted suicide from those who have thought about suicide, but not acted upon these thoughts, and has been shown to predict future suicide attempts regardless of a service member's level of suicide ideation (Bryan et al., 2014). The measurement and quantification of this suicidal belief system, expressed in writing on social media platforms, could therefore contribute to significant advances in the detection of emerging suicide risk in real-time, *before a suicide attempt occurs*. This objective is the primary aim of the Durkheim Project.

Overview

The Durkheim Project consisted of three phases. During the first phase, a clinician's dashboard was built and a Veterans Affairs (VA) predictive risk

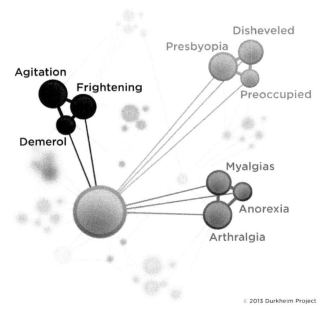

Figure 9.1 Research phase 1: Veterans Affairs medical records study.

medical records study was completed, based on an analysis of the narrative, or free text, portions of VA medical records. Also during the first phase, the initial software infrastructure to collect and analyze the social media data for phase 2 was designed and implemented. During the second phase, now underway, opt-in social media postings are being collected and analyzed. During the third phase, a pilot program will isolate serious suicide risk for individuals in real-time and develop a prediction triage model for improved suicide intervention

During phase 1, linguistics-driven prediction models were developed to estimate the risk of suicide. These models were generated from unstructured clinical notes taken from a national sample of United States VA medical records. The protocol for this study was approved by the Institutional Review Board (IRB) of the VA Medical Center where the study was conducted. We created three matched cohorts: veterans who completed suicide, veterans who used mental health services and did not complete suicide, and veterans who did not use mental health services and did not complete suicide during the observation period ($n = 70$ in each group).

From the clinical notes we generated datasets of single keywords (Figure 9.1) and multi-word phrases, and constructed prediction models using a supervised machine-learning algorithm based on a genetic

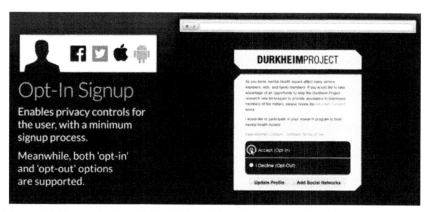

Figure 9.2 Research phase 2: Predicting risk with opt-in social media postings.

programming framework, MOSES (Goertzel, Geisweiller, Pennachin, & Ng, 2013; Looks, 2006, 2007). MOSES can be described as a variant of a decision-tree forest, with certain genetic and maximum entropy techniques mixed in: maximum entropy to apply pressure to minimize tree size and genetic to ensure tree species diversity. In our prior research we have found that MOSES consistently outperforms standard text classification approaches such as support vector machines (SVMs). The primary hyperparameter that we used was the dynamic feature size. The resulting inference accuracy was at first 65% and then consistently 67% or more. This was the prediction accuracy for assigning a patient to the correct cohort. These data suggest that computerized text analytics can be applied to unstructured sections of medical records to estimate the risk of suicide (Poulin et al., 2014). The resulting system could potentially allow clinicians to screen seemingly healthy patients at the primary care level, and to continuously evaluate suicide risk among psychiatric patients.

Although opt-in data collection and analysis for phase 2 is now underway (Figure 9.2), the software development required for this data collection and analysis was completed during phase 1. A phase 2 protocol for collecting and analyzing opt-in social media postings and presenting predictions to clinicians via the Durkheim Project's Clinicians' dashboard has also been approved by our IRB. When the system is fully operational (see phase 3), a clinician will see predictive models of suicide risk for a given patient, which are constructed from the patient's medical records and the patient's opt-in social media postings. Subjects are currently being recruited via targeted efforts in collaboration with Facebook (PR Newswire, 2013).

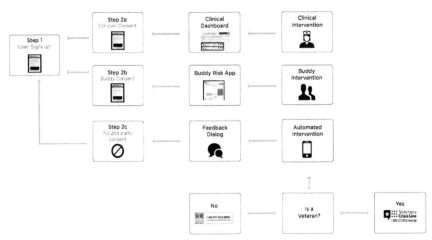

Figure 9.3 Research phase 3: Intervention.

A Facebook applications window is being used to recruit people that Facebook has identified as being military personnel or veterans. The resulting system can collect data and provide risk scores for thousands of users at Internet scale.

For phase 3, a protocol has been recently completed. This protocol includes an un-blinded, three-cohort design for a pilot program that proposes to detect serious suicide risk for individuals in real-time and to develop a prediction triage model for improved suicide intervention (Figure 9.3). Plans are also in place to use and improve upon the linguistically based prediction capabilities of the model developed during phase 1, which was able to predict suicide with limited accuracy before the suicides occurred. The theoretical assumption is that words chosen by those at-risk for suicide vary at different levels and stages of risk. Building from ongoing observations from the phase 2 study and feedback obtained during the conduct of the phase 3 study, the primary aim is to adjust the linguistics-driven model to predict suicide risk within a critical period for intervention at various levels of risk severity.

In this protocol, ongoing monitoring of the network allows continuous updating and change in value of risk alert levels among the green-to-red color coding. When the predictive system detects postings that exceed a certain threshold level of potential suicide risk, risk alerts are triggered in real-time and sent to either a monitoring clinician or a pre-identified buddy monitor, or to an automated system that generates supportive messages that are sent immediately to the at-risk individual.

To better characterize the risk for the population of active-duty military and veterans, the analysis for this study is limited to primary participants. These primary participants may be newly recruited via the dedicated Facebook and mobile applications or, using the same dedicated application, from those already participating in the phase 2 study. In either case, all primary participants must provide informed consent for this specific study. That is, those already involved in the phase 2 study must provide separate consent to participate in the phase 3 study. However, outside of the context of this study, the computerized intervention is open to members of the general public who might wish to take advantage of the program's intervention potential. Primary participants are active-duty US military or veterans with English as a primary or secondary language who agree to post to social media using English. The age limit for primary participants in the phase 3 study, as with the phase 2 study, targets the age group most likely to actively use social media, i.e., those between the ages of 18 and 45.

RESULTS

To date, results are only available for the phase 1 study. For single-word models, the predictive accuracy was approximately 59% (the average for 100 models), and scores for individual candidate models ranged from 46 to 67% (Figure 9.4). Because our training sets are balanced cohorts, we have used accuracy as a surrogate for precision and recall metric. Accuracy was computed using five-way cross-validation. Models that used certain word pairs had significantly better scores than single-word models, although they are far less human-readable. For example, the phrases "negative assessment for PTSD" and "positive assessment for PTSD" carry different meanings. This phrase-based approach was more accurate than a single-word approach. For preselected word pairs, the individual model scores ranged from 52 to 69%, with an average of 64% (for 100 models). In the final experiments, the combined cohorts "1v2v3 classifier" had a peak performance of 70%, and an average performance of 67%.

Implications

Our analyses were successful at determining useful text-based signals of suicide risk. We obtained accuracies of greater than 60% for ensemble averages of 100 models, and our individual model accuracies reached 67–69%. Given the small size of the dataset and the fragmentary nature of the clinical notes, this performance level represents a significant achievement.

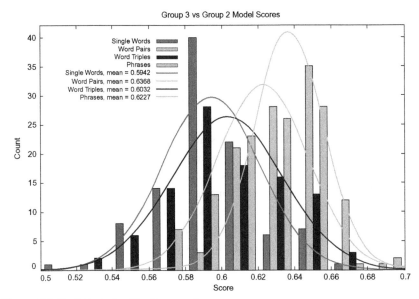

Figure 9.4 Statistical classification results.

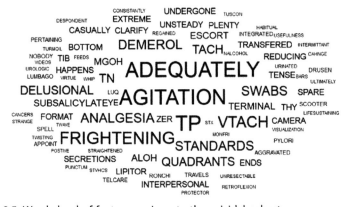

Figure 9.5 Word cloud of features unique to the suicidal cohort.

For a classifier, these results represent a statistically significant "signal." Meanwhile, we showed that, methodologically, word pairs are more useful than single words for model construction on electronic medical record (EMR) data. Furthermore, the predictive feature words that distinguished each group were highly revealing, especially for the suicidal cohort, and were consistent with the existing medical literature on suicide. See Figure 9.5.

Many medical conditions have been associated with an increased risk for suicide, but these conditions have generally not been included in suicide risk assessment tools. These conditions include gastrointestinal conditions, cardiopulmonary conditions, oncologic conditions, and pain conditions. Also, some research has emerged that links care processes to suicide risk. The word "integrated" emerged as a key term in our study and is also reflected in the integrated care literature (Bauer, Chan, Huang, Vannoy, & Unützer, 2013).

Although the text on which our predictive model was based for the phase 1 medical records study was text written by a physician or other healthcare provider, our hypothesis is that some of the highly predictive features learned during phase 1 carry over to the predictive modeling of opt-in social media postings during phase 2, in which the text is written by the patient. We expect that some of the features or concepts will be the same among physician-written and individual-written text due to the ability to do software-based synonym matches. Additionally, a physician or other healthcare worker may sometimes quote or paraphrase what a patient said when adding a note to the clinical record. A key predictive feature, such as the word "anxiety," may be used either by a clinician or a patient. We believe that the use of specialized text-analytic resources such as linguistic inquiry and word count (LIWC) may (or may not) also help improve our results (LIWC, 2014).

In future research we plan to scale up the phase 1 medical records study from our current study, in which each cohort had 70 subjects, to a study using the same protocol, but with at least 1,000 subjects in each cohort. We also plan to transfer the predictive model built from the phase 1 study to the analysis of phase 2 opt-in social media postings. Once our phase 3 protocol has IRB approval, we plan to begin phase 3 of the Durkheim Project, informed by the results and ongoing follow-on research, of our phase 1 and 2 studies. In our future research we plan to use additional features from the structured portions of the medical record, as well as to use other data filters (e.g. LIWC). In both our medical records and social media research we plan to use temporal analysis.

Although the phase 1 study was successful in distinguishing the cohort of completed suicides both from the control group cohort and the psychiatric cohort, it was difficult to distinguish text-based noise from signal with high accuracy in our initial results. We expect that our planned follow-on study with 1,000 subjects in each cohort will have much less problem in distinguishing signal from noise. Suicide risk prediction is a very difficult problem, but we believe that studies such as our phase 1 and 2 studies, which use supervised machine learning techniques, can uncover predictive risk factors that are not immediately obvious to healthcare providers. At the same time, we also believe that more effective suicide risk prediction systems can be built based on the integration of machine learning methods and the expertise of suicidologists. In particular, integrating an understanding of military culture into our methods is deemed to be important.

LARGER COHORTS (CURRENT WORK)

Suicide Data Repository: For tracking and evaluating program effectiveness, we started the application for access to this new outcomes tracking database. Specifically, the Repository says "have mortality data for all Veterans who separated from active-duty military service between 1979–2011, and for users of VHA services between the years 1999–2011. Data is to be updated annually as they are available from the CDC, and are currently available to all VA and DOD staff." As such, we plan to utilize this database for our validation efforts, as a retrospective study component of the larger validation effort. As a second subtask we also enable *prospective* tracking of specified individuals. The use of third-party tools has been authorized for an initial cohort study size of up to 3,000 individuals (or 1,000 in each of three cohorts).

The Durkheim Project Architecture

Our architecture is the answer to the question of how to build a system that collects, stores, analyzes, and allows clinicians to react to suicide risk at Internet scale. As such, our machine learning technology is a real-time environment for the isolation of risk and the exploration of risk factors. Further utilizing a unique and patented 'unsupervised learning' approach to statistical learning, we are able to detect the seemingly undetectable factors of mental health risk across cohorts at scale. Finally, we have programmed a robust collaborative environment for clinical interaction (e.g., secure risk dashboards); a true "big data" infrastructure. Existing components include (Figure 9.6):

1. *An Opt-In Interface Layer:* As discussed above, this is the Data Collection App that allows for data permissions, to data storage and analytics services (Figure 9.7).
2. *A Data Collection Layer:* In the current Durkheim architecture, this component runs on Amazon EC2 (Figure 9.10). This architecture is discussed in greater detail in the conference presentation by Krugler (2013).

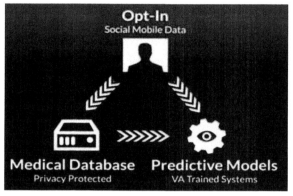

Figure 9.6 Overview of the informatics network.

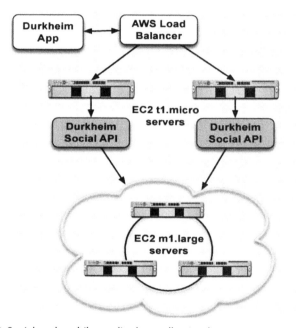

Figure 9.7 Social and mobile media data collection layer.

3. *A Storage Layer:* In the current Durkheim architecture, this HIPAA compliant component is housed by Dartmouth Hitchcock Medical Center (Figure 9.8). Best practices from this effort are to be transferred for use on any new hosted data network.

4. *A Machine Learning (Basic) Core:* As discussed above, these are the predictive results described in the journal PLoS One (2014).

5. *A Scalable Machine Learning Core:* As part of our DARPA program, we built a secondary classifier (B-Counts) that allowed for linear scalability and real-time classification (Figure 9.9).

Figure 9.8 Medical database (behind the data security firewall). *Poulin et al., 2014.*

Figure 9.9 Intervention, and associated partner institutions.

6. *Automated Intervention Network Events*: The Durkheim team is building out these network alerts (Facebook, email, SMS messages) to enable real-time intervention.

IMPACT

Ours has been a leading team in the prediction of risk for suicide and the scaling of systems for the detection of risk. We assert that clinical personnel immediately gain an unprecedented real-time capability to see risks at various levels through further field tests. This enables a first-time triage of clinician-directed interventions with patients. For example, if we see that a VA system user is at an elevated risk (red indicator), the clinician can put him or her on a watchlist filter. If those on a watchlist filter then escalate to a highly critical level of risk (black indicator), resources can be focused where they are most needed. Other specific impacts include:

1. Continued understanding of the *how* and the *when* of suicide risks
   a. Continued refinement of predictive models of suicide's *time sequence*
   b. Big data research on the *correlative relationships* between many negative events
      − e.g., validated events of mental health risks, with financial distress
2. Interventions protocols for intelligent *resource matching*. Specifically;
   a. Development of systems that provide *the right aid, at the right time*
   b. Use of a secure Dashboard technology to *view those at risk in real-time*
   c. *Secure and data-audited communications* with those thought to be at risk
      − e.g., via a Secure Support Network
3. First-time application of real-time financial information to the problem of suicide
   a. Hone in on *financial stress factors* that might correlate to suicide
   b. Designed to support continuous monitoring of populations of up to *tens of millions*.
4. Fundamental understanding of mechanisms underlying suicide
   It is readily apparent that there is both heterogeneity and complexity to the various mechanisms of mental health and suicide risk. This lends itself to an important question: Are there upstream (latent) mechanisms that are common to multiple negative personal events? Or are there multiple negative conditions that are produced under similar environments? What differentiates each? Though we understand that current subject matter experts (SMEs) have strong opinions on these subjects, we propose quantifying what appears to *happen at scale*. This has yet to be accomplished in suicide research.
5. Immediate improvement of suicide risk
   Although there is a tendency to de-correlate fundamental research with operational systems, we believe such a 'status quo' approach is one we should avoid. There is in fact sufficient evidence to build systems that detect and resolve risks in *real* and *appropriate time* by following a treatment triage based on the severity of perceived risk (see Figure 9.10).
6. Increasing innovation
   As many (successful) international science efforts have proven, central leadership and an affirmation of a direction *towards rapid solutions* is needed. In our prior efforts, this conclusion precipitated our awareness efforts with large data content partners such as Facebook,

Time Series Classifications for Optimal Interventions

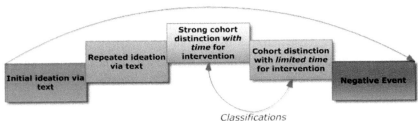

Classifications

Figure 9.10 Time series of various events requiring differing interventions.

Inc. Now with dedicated mobile resources, we anticipate a uniquely rich dataset combined with data communications.

7. In addition to meeting an urgent need for the veteran's health, the project therefore addresses several of the 12 goals identified by the National Action Alliance for Suicide Prevention's (NAASP) Research Prioritization Task Force as being of greatest priority for suicide-focused research:

   a. *Goal #2*: "Determine the degree of suicide risk (e.g., imminent, near-term, long-term) among individuals in diverse populations and in diverse settings through feasible and effective screening and assessment approaches."

   b. *Goal #3*: "Assess who is at risk for attempting suicide in the immediate future."

   c. *Goal #11*: "Prevent the emergence of suicidal behavior by developing and delivering the most effective prevention programs to build resilience and reduce risk in broad-based populations."

By combining efficacious broad data analysis with the care of clinical human subject study, multiplied with the *power of big data networks* to bring resources together, we propose a potentially *high-impact* solution to intervention around the mental health risk of suicidality.

APPLICABLE ETHICAL CONSIDERATIONS

If current technologies can enable us to predict events, then the actions of large corporations, NGOs, and governments have the potential to affect behavioral change on those populations whose future behavior is predicted. In the cases described above, there are clear advantages to this predictive potential. Just consider a situation in which an unregulated medical insurance company understands individual risk values and adjusts its pricing accordingly, thus adversely affecting the unhealthy population. These capabilities, combined with other tools like geo-location from mobile phone data, are incredibly powerful: they can predict where an individual will go and what they will do.

At the Durkheim Project, in our own behavioral modification studies, we hope to enable interventions for individuals – not only "just before" a negative event occurs, but also well before. For example, if an individual has acute risk of suicide within days, then emergency services might need to be involved. However, if an individual is exhibiting early stages of a suicidal thought process, an intervener can offer softer cues that a more positive outcome is possible, thus avoiding later acute risk. This is, in fact, our current research effort.

Consent

Careful implementation of opt-in/consent-based data collection saves a great deal of confusion and institutional heartache down the line. In this context, careful means explicit – for example, avoiding long contracts with fine print, and clearly describing the data's current and future use. At the Durkheim Project, we have made a concerted effort to ensure our consent process is easy to understand. In the medical case, the underlying data are already regulated and protected, but the analysis of meta-data is a legal gray area.

Privacy

A core social function of privacy is to spare us from embarrassment and societal exclusion. Privacy is also a protected right in many developed nations. Privacy protection in the world of big data will increasingly mean the difference between fair treatment and discrimination, or in many cases, life and death. In suicide risk prediction, we are fully aware of the implications of false-positive signals – for example, we might embarrass our users. In many cases, even a true positive might exacerbate an individual's risk if the data are treated with improper care.

Transparency

While some subjects are certainly sensitive or private property, it is the transparency of the underlying process that will win the trust of big data consumers. Trust in systems is critical to maintaining a stable infrastructure, and systems must have checks that are formal and procedural to instill trust. Furthermore, transparency on the part of data leaders is needed for trust in data systems. Data leaders should seek to assure the public, as customer or constituent, that their analysis will be used for constructive purpose. The Durkheim Project team understands that trust is the core function of our effort to reach out to, and stay in contact with, enough individuals to make a difference in public mental health.

Discussion

Artificial intelligence in mental health care offers truly a world-changing paradigm. The same technology that initially drove much of the growth of companies such as Google is now diffusing into the mainstream. However, we are only beginning to see the potential applications. Like the powerful paradigms before increasingly intelligent systems will offer applications for the benefit of mankind, as well as applications that control others and harm societies. For example, we are already beginning to witness some of the implications of deep privacy and behavioral tracking.

As such, we advocate more transparent and consent-based data systems. We hope that with the Durkheim Project, we lead with a positive example. We believe that systems with this design philosophy can truly change the world for the better, while systems without this philosophy tend to be adversarial and exploitive. Researchers and clinicians should be aware of both the upside and downside risks of these new data systems.

FUTURE PROSPECTS IN THE TOPIC AREA

Next-Generation Inference

Statistical inference accuracy is critical to next-generation artificial intelligence systems and medical predictive analytics more generally. Powered by recent advances in applied mathematics, we have reached an exciting place in the convergence of understanding of learning and pattern recognition systems.

A key unifying idea is attention to invariants and regularities across abstract processes. These processes can be either representational (Deep Learning), functional (Compressed Sensing), or algorithmic (Meta-learning). Briefly, these three areas of learning are:

- *Meta-learning*: Learning about (machine) learning systems to produce more efficient machine learning as a runtime and discipline. What one learns is presumably regularity in features or representations about learning systems and their input (features) data (Brazdil, Carrier, Soares, & Vilalta, 2008).

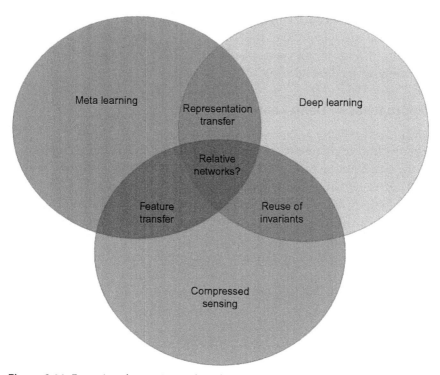

Figure 9.11 Emerging themes in machine learning.

- *Deep Learning*: A prominent form of hierarchical machine learning that uses many deep layers of abstract representation, inspired by human visual processing capabilities. It is currently the dominant classifier approach (Hinton, Srivastava, Krizhevsky, Sutskever, & Salakhutdinov, 2012), and has a long history (Hinton, Sejnowski, & Ackley, 1984).
- *Compressed Sensing/Sampling*: A recent development related to finding better than Nyquist-Shannon rates for measuring information in a signal, using invariants used in encoding (Candès & Plan, 2010).

Given common theoretical intersection points in the machine learning space, we might speak of high-level concept of "Relative Networks," a term that captures the many common aspects of modern learning (Figure 9.11).

The recurring theme for relative networks is the repeated use of structured signal similarity and intersection (A ∩ B) and the unstructured noise dissimilarity/symmetric difference (A Δ B). It is a focus on invariant representations, and *their own* meta-spatio-temporal relationships as further invariants, that will allow learning to be better understood.

This is a true meta-learning, based upon "ontology of degree" or "positionals" to paraphrase the scientist Vannevar Bush. We are currently building systems of this type of brain-like model representation, to enable downstream medical decision.

Approaches in Deep Learning

Deep learners are a type of neural network that uses feed-forward optimization of parameters to attain a hierarchical distribution of objects. It is the simplification of feed-forward networks that enables effective abstractions of many layers of conditional probability trees (CPTs) – hence the term "deep." They were first introduced by Geoff Hinton in the 1980s, under the paradigm of Restricted Boltzmann machines. Later, the concept of Convolutional Networks was introduced, which preserve the essential elements of the paradigm, but have actually gone on to reach the current apex of machine learning classification quantitative performance, e.g., object recognition (Hinton et al., 2012). They have been highly successful recently, and are considered the state-of-the-art in machine learning.

Limitations of Deep Learning

At a high level, we assert that the hierarchical, yet ultimately linear, properties of individual Deep Learning networks invariably converge to local minima: this over-fitting is powerful for powering computational efficiency in the representation, but has an inherent limitation for robustness. In physics terms, connecting many networks (i.e., closed systems) primary input mechanisms, where the input is relatively regular, produces a thermodynamic reduction of the total system to the least energy state. In mathematical terms, chaining together neural networks will produce a mathematical homology, subject to the mean of the permutations on the network as a whole. It is a known practical problem with neural networks, and one that the pioneers (Hinton et al., 1984) of Deep Learning have started to address in their implementations (Hinton et al., 2012). While we actually proposed this understanding as a basis for optimization of a machine learning process in the past, similar work has been proposed by others more formally (Watanabe, 2009), and has even recently been seen experimentally by the authors.

Latest Extensions of Deep Learning

As recently as over the last year there have been successful attempts to rectify the current problem by introducing a form of "bagging" or parameter seeding of values across nodes of networks (Boedecker et al., 2014). And the most recent success story builds on this work to introduce what we would argue is noise introduction (via what is known as L2 pooling) into Deep Networks. In a further overlay, Riedmiller and colleagues at Deep Mind went on to publish a highly visible paper (Mnih et al., 2015), where they formally mentioned using a reinforcement learning paradigm (reinforcement learning is the assumption that the network has "agency," and that its actions should produce, or penalize, rewards). The claim that really got people's attention recently was "We apply our method to seven Atari 2600 games from the Arcade Learning Environment, with no adjustment of the architecture or learning algorithm. We find that it outperforms all previous approaches on six of the games and surpasses a human expert on three of them." Ultimately though, we would argue that this works so well because it is what a neuro-anatomist would say is a feedback suppression overlay on a feed-forward learning network. The brain has been experimentally shown to have these attributes (Seidler et al., 2004), so it is in fact "As we may think" (Bush, 1945).

Technical Steps, Challenges, and Risks

The computational complexity of adding functions on top of functions introduces increased computational runtime of Deep Learning systems, but there is also the practical problem of an increasingly poor understanding of design in the heterogeneity of the systems themselves. What we have, therefore, is a (machine) learner that encapsulates both the attributes of Deep Learning and the benefits of Reinforcement Learning. Such a system is, in theory, more conceptually simple, yet as powerful as the state-of-the-art, has more scalability in the face of heterogeneity of problem types, as well as a far more efficient computational runtime.

Deep Learning, a Discussion

As the recent success of Deep Learning illustrates (Krizhevsy, Sutskever, & Hinton, 2012) significant machine learning performance gains are possible using neurological-inspired learning models, leveraging both hierarchical and associative learning. Neuromorphic learning technology will increasingly support both indexing and search tasks with state-of-the-art levels of performance (both in robustness qualitative and standard quantitative metrics), while simultaneously having a more elegant theoretical model informing the design. Today's Deep Learning systems are among the top-performing machine learning classifiers, but their use has largely been restricted to visual object recognition. Meanwhile, the lack of heterogeneous functionality precludes these implementations from broader application. By implementing further associative methodologies, we antici-pate that improved Deep Learners can enable artificial intelligence with more *agency*. A similar design has recently made big news in the machine learning community (Mnih et al., 2015), where a system was able to learn both the patterns and the rules of a video game without instruction. The long-term impact will be an advance in the general understanding of infor-mation processing in the field of artificial intelligence, and its none-too-ironic application to advancing medical decision-making and understanding the depths of the human mind.

CONCLUSION

We have discussed the vexing problem of suicide, and how informatics could potentially help. A brief history of big data informatics and big data surveillance, was then discussed. We then turned to how a successful big data project should be structured. Next, we discussed our solution, the Durkheim Project. Finally, we explored the application of a new class of inference system with the potential to further revolutionize both the scale and accuracy of modern medical decision-making. It is our hope that we have conveyed the technical extent to which these systems can operate, as well as ethical best practice.

REFERENCES

Barak, A., & Miron, O. (2005). Writing characteristics of suicidal people on the internet: A psychological investigation of emerging social environments. *Suicide and Life-Threatening Behavior, 35,* 507–524.

Bauer, A. M., Chan, Y.-F., Huang, H., Vannoy, S., & Unützer, J. (2013). Characteristics, management, and depression outcomes of primary care patients who endorse thoughts of death or suicide on the PHQ-9. *Journal of General Internal Medicine, 28,* 363–369.

Boedecker, J., Springenberg, J. T., Wülfing, J., & Riedmiller, M. (2014). Approximate real-time optimal control based on sparse Gaussian process models. In *Adaptive Dynamic Programming and Reinforcement Learning* (ADPRL-2014).

Brazdil, P., Carrier, C. G., Soares, C., & Vilalta, R. (2008). *Metalearning: Applications to data mining (cognitive technologies)* Berlin: Springer.

Bryan, C. J., Rudd, M. D., Wertenberger, E., Etienne, N., Ray-Sannerud, B. N., Morrow, C. E., et al. (2014). Improving the detection and prediction of suicidal behavior among military personnel by measuring suicidal beliefs: An evaluation of the suicide cognitions scale. *Journal of Affective Disorders, 159,* 15–22.

Busch, K. A., Fawcett, J., & Jacobs, D. G. (2003). Clinical correlates of inpatient suicide. *Journal of Clinical Psychiatry, 64,* 4–19.

Bush, V. (1945, July). As we may think. *The Atlantic.*

Candès, E. J., & Plan, Y. (2010). A probabilistic and RIPless theory of compressed sensing. *IEEE Transactions on Information Theory, 57*(11), 7235–7254.

Coombs, D. W., Miller, H. L., Alarcon, R., Herlihy, C., Lee, J. M., & Morrison, D. P. (1992). Presuicide attempt communications between parasuicides and consulted caregivers. *Suicide and Life-Threatening Behavior, 22,* 289–302.

Dean, J., & Ghemawat, S. (2004). *MapReduce: Simplified data processing on large clusters.* Google, Inc. http://static.googleusercontent.com/media/research.google.com/en/us/archive/mapreduce-osdi04.pdf.

Department of the Army. (2010). Health promotion risk reduction suicide prevention. *U.S. ARMY HP/RR/SP REPORT.* Washington, DC: Department of the Army.

Department of Defense. (2011). *Department of defense suicide event report calendar, year 2010.* Washington, DC: Department of Defense.

Duhigg, C. (2012). How companies learn your secrets, New York Times. <http://www.nytimes.com/2012/02/19/magazine/shopping-habits.html?pagewanted=1&_r=2&hp&> Accessed 17.03.14.

Fikes, A., Wallach, D. A., Chang, F., Dean, J., Burrows, M., Gruber, R. E., et al. (2006). *Bigtable: A distributed storage system for structured data.* Google Inc. http://static.googleusercontent.com/media/research.google.com/en/us/archive/bigtable-osdi06.pdf.

Goertzel, B., Geisweiller, N., Pennachin, C., & Ng, K. (2013). Integrating feature selection into program learning. In *Proceedings of AGI-13,* 2013, 799 (pp. 31–39).

Hall, R. C., Platt, D. E., & Hall, R. C. (1999). Suicide risk assessment: A review of risk factors for suicide in 100 patients who made severe suicide attempts. Evaluation of suicide risk in a time of managed care. *Psychosomatics, 40,* 18–27.

Hinton, G. E., Sejnowski, T. J., & Ackley, D. H. (1984). *Boltzmann machines: Constraint satisfaction networks that learn.* Pittsburgh, PA: Carnegie Mellon University.

Hinton, G. E., Srivastava, N., Krizhevsky, A., Sutskever, I., & Salakhutdinov, R. R. (2012). Improving neural networks by preventing co-adaptation of feature detectors. <http://arxiv.org/abs/1207.0580>.

Jones, N. J., & Bennell, C. (2007). The development and validation of statistical prediction rules for discriminating between genuine and simulated suicide notes. *Archives of Suicide Research, 11,* 219–233.

Kovacs, M., Beck, A. T., & Weissman, A. (1976). The communication of suicidal intent. *Archives of General Psychiatry, 33,* 199–201.

Krizhevsy, A., Sutskever, I., & Hinton, G. (2012). ImageNet classificaation with Deep Convolutional Neural Networks. In *Proceedings of the Neural Information Processing Conference.*

Krugler. (2013). C* Summit 2013: Suicide risk prediction using social media and cassandra. <https://www.youtube.com/watch?v=vB2S5NcOcEM>.

Lester, D. (2008a). Computer analysis of the content of suicide notes from men and women. *Psychological Reports, 102,* 575–576.

Lester, D. (2008b). Differences between genuine and simulated suicide notes. *Psychological Reports, 103,* 527–528.

Lester, D. (2010a). Linguistic analysis of a blog from a murder-suicide. *Psychological Reports, 106,* 342.

Lester, D. (2010b). The final hours: A linguistic analysis of the final words of a suicide. *Psychological Reports, 106,* 791–797.

Lester, D., Haines, J., & Williams, C. (2010). Content differences in suicide notes by sex, age, and method: A study of Australian suicide notes. *Psychological Reports, 106,* 475–476.

Lester, D., & McSwain, S. (2010). Poems by a suicide: Sara Teasdale. *Psychological Reports*, *106*, 811−812.

LIWC. Linguistic Inquiry and Word Count. (2014). <http://www.liwc.net/> Accessed 28.04.14.

Looks, M. (2006). Competent program evolution (Unpublished doctoral dissertation). St. Louis, MO: Washington University.

Looks, M. (2007). Meta-optimizing semantic evolutionary search. In H. Lipson (Ed.), *Genetic and Evolutionary Computation Conference*, GECCO 2007, Proceedings (pp. 626). London, England, UK.

Mnih, V., Kavukcuoglu, K., Silver, D., Rusu, A., Veness, V., Bellemare, M., et al. (2015). Human-level control through deep reinforcement learning. *Nature*, *518*, 529−533. Available from: http://dx.doi.org/10.1038/nature14236.

Poulin, C., Shiner, B., Thompson, P., Vepstas, L., Young-Xu, Y., Goertzel, B., et al. (2014). Predicting the risk of suicide by analyzing the text of clinical notes. *PLoS One*, *9*, e85733.

PR Newswire. (2013). "The Durkheim Project" will analyze opt-in data from veterans' social media and mobile content − seeking real-time predictive analytics for suicide risk. *PR Newswire*. Retrived April 28, 2014 from: <http://www.prnewswire.com/news-releases/the-durkheim-project-will-analyze-opt-in-data-from-veterans-social-media-and-mobile-content----seeking-real-time-predictive-analytics-for-suicide-risk-213922041.html>.

Ritchie, E. C., Keppler, W. C., & Rothberg, J. M. (2003). Suicidal admissions in the United States military. *Military Medicine*, *168*, 177−181.

Seidler, R. D., Noll, D. C., & Thiers, G. (2004, August). Feedforward and feedback processes in motor control. *Neuroimage*, *22*(4), 1775−1783.

Stirman, S. W., & Pennebaker, J. W. (2001). Word use in the poetry of suicidal and nonsuicidal poets. *Psychosomatic Medicine*, *63*, 517−522.

Ungerleider, N. (2013). This may be the most vital use of 'Big Data' We've ever seen. *Fast Company*. <http://www.fastcolabs.com/3014191/this-may-be-the-most-vital-use-of-big-dataweve-ever-seen>.

Watanabe, S. (2009). *Algebraic geometry and statistical learning theory*. Cambridge: Cambridge University Press.

CHAPTER 10

Artificial Intelligence in Public Health Surveillance and Research

Yair Neuman

Department of Education, Ben-Gurion University of the Negev, Israel

INTRODUCTION

On April 20, 1999, two high school students, Eric Harris and Dylan Klebold, entered the Columbine High School, which they attended, and launched a bloody terror attack targeted mostly against other students. At the end of what has become known as the Columbine High School Massacre, 15 people were dead, including Harris and Klebold who died by suicide, and 21 people were injured. In retrospect, we know that this shocking attack didn't come out of the blue. Several years earlier, Harris had created a website in which he publicly presented his disturbed intentions. Numerous complaints had been filed at the Jefferson County Sheriff's Office concerning Harris but nothing had been done. Both Harris and Klebold continued to document their intentions and their wish to initiate a terror attack that would compete with the Oklahoma City bombing. The copycat pattern was evident in this case, and Harris and Klebold were quite explicit about their disturbed source of inspiration. Their declared intentions were transformed into deeds and the two boys freely purchased firearms and prepared bombs. A FBI task force later determined that Harris was a "clinical psychopath" and Klebold was "a depressive" (Cullen, 2004). A psychopath and a depressive, who had criminal records for theft, drew their source of inspiration from a mass murderer, published their violent intentions, and freely purchased firearms, should and could have been treated differently. The Columbine incident was not the last one. The Sandy Hook Elementary School Shootings, that took place in 2012, was the deadliest mass shooting at a grade school in the United States, and the second deadliest mass shooting following the Virginia Tech shootings in 2007 (Effron, 2012). In 2014, 22-year-old Elliot Rodger conducted a mass shooting leaving a manifesto titled "My Twisted World." The perpetrators of all of these mass shootings were known to be mentally disturbed and suspected of being a threat to others.

Artificial Intelligence in Behavioral and Mental Health Care.
DOI: http://dx.doi.org/10.1016/B978-0-12-420248-1.00010-6

One example of what could have been done to prevent these crimes is using an artificial intelligence (AI) tool that searches a database of criminal records and credit card transactions for purchasing weapons or chemicals used to build homemade bombs. Given a teenager's criminal record and a record of firearm purchases, the system could also identify texts written by the teen in one of the social media platforms (e.g., Twitter) so as to analyze it through algorithms of natural language processing (NLP) and machine learning (ML) and extract from it relevant psychological features. In the case of Harris, the system could have inferred that the same person who had a criminal record and bought firearms is also a psychopath. Putting aside ethical issues of privacy, the benefits of such a tool are clear. In the case of Columbine, preventive actions could have immediately been taken by mental health experts (e.g., psychiatrists or clinical psychologists) and the school administration (e.g., the school counselor) by notifying law enforcement agencies to check whether the signal sent by the automated system was a warning signal or a false alarm.

I have chosen these high-profile cases as a starting point for a discussion on AI in public health surveillance and research because these incidents are a painful memory for many Americans and clearly illustrate the need for screening technologies in public health surveillance.

My aim is to discuss the potential of several such technologies so as to expand our abilities in the realm of public health, from screening for depression to searching for mental health problems to prevent violent acts among teenagers. However, before discussing the main issue of this chapter, a few words must be shared on the meaning of the term "artificial intelligence."

AI is defined as "the technology designed to perform activities that normally require human intelligence" (Luxton, 2014). According to this definition, even a simple calculator used by a schoolboy is an example of AI, as the execution of an arithmetic calculation is a unique skill of educated human beings. Implementing this skill *in silico* is, therefore, an example of AI in action.

Personally, I find it easier to use the term intelligence amplification (IA), which refers to the effective use of information technology for augmenting human intelligence. This approach was described many years ago by Engelbart (1962, p. 8) who wrote: "The conceptual framework we seek must orient us toward the real possibilities and problems associated with using modern technology to give direct aid to an individual in comprehending complex situations, isolating the significant factors and solving problems."

The term IA doesn't restrict us to mimicking "human intelligence" in designing technologies that may support the cognitive activities of human beings. For instance, NLP is a field with remarkable achievements and with high relevance to public health surveillance and research. However, arguing that NLP is AI obliges us to prove that the algorithms used by the NLP community validly represent the way human beings actually process language and perform complex cognitive computations. While cognitive scientists may be very interested in examining computational models of the human mind, this is not the main issue in NLP, which is guided by a more pragmatic approach, *suggesting the evaluation of the quality of algorithms* by measuring their performance, putting aside the issue of how well these algorithms may simulate the human mind.

Briefly, the approach adopted in this chapter is basically a pragmatic approach. Public health surveillance and research would benefit from the use of technologies that augment the cognitive tasks performed by human beings in this field. These technologies may draw on ideas and models of human psychology, but they are not restricted to these models or to their verification. Such technologies should be judged by a pragmatic criterion only; the degree in which they effectively support human activity. Henceforth, I use the term AI in the sense of IA.

After presenting the general approach, we will illustrate the various ways in which technologies can help us improve public health to include screening for suicidal intentions or even depression, screening for potential mass shooters, and the early identification of neurodegenerative diseases such as the Alzheimer's disease (AD). This chapter does not aim to review or summarize either the emerging field of AI in public health or the more specific field of technology and psychology. Readers who are interested in these fields may refer to papers written by Luxton (2014) for instance. The aim of the current paper is much more focused: to present several cases illustrating the benefits of using IA technologies for public health issues that involve a significant mental health dimension.

Living in a Dark Tunnel of Pain: Automatic Screening for Depression

Most people have experienced periods in their life in which they felt moody, suffered from low levels of energy, and lacked interest in what they usually considered enjoyable activities. If there is no physical external reason or a biological explanation for this subjective experience, and if it persists beyond temporal mood fluctuations, we name the condition "depression." While there are various forms of depression differing in their intensity, characteristics, and causes, the general experience of feeling depressed is familiar to many people or can at least easily be imagined. The World Health Organization (WHO) describes depression as "a common illness worldwide, with an estimated 350 million people affected." However, this "common illness" "may become a serious health condition as it can cause the affected person to suffer greatly and function poorly at work, at school, and in the family. At its worst, depression can lead to suicide. Suicide results in an estimated 1 million deaths every year."

Depression has an important diagnostic dimension as "Even in some high-income countries, people who are depressed are not always correctly diagnosed" (http://www.who.int/mediacentre/factsheets/fs369/en/). In this context, it is important to understand depression better and to provide the public health system with AI tools that may support the valid diagnosis of depressed people.

The DSM-IV (American Psychiatric Association, 1994) defines a major depressive episode as a period characterized by low mood and a loss of interest or pleasure in everyday activities, but let us better explain the meaning of depression. Millon et al. (2004) explain that depression may either be a symptom or a term used to describe the personality (i.e., depressive personality). Whether as an illness or as a personality type, depression is experienced in terms of a deep sadness, hopelessness, helplessness, a belief of self-worthlessness, self-criticism, pessimism, and guilt. Major depression, termed clinical depression, is a disorder that represents one extreme form of the depressive experience and is associated with suicide and severe implications for the quality of life.

While expert mental health practitioners such as psychiatrists and psychologists are able to diagnose depression by using acceptable diagnostic manuals such as the DSM, it is clear that diagnosing the level of depression of a subject is both time- and energy-consuming. The inevitable result is that too many people are left undiagnosed or receive the diagnosis too late at a stage where the depression has negatively influenced their quality of life. Can applications in AI help us to address this problem?

While putting the burden of diagnosis entirely on the computer is unreasonable, we can definitely use intelligence applications for a preliminary screening for depression. Such an intelligent application would be proactive in the sense that the subject would not have to take any steps to benefit from it. The application may, for instance, analyze the subject's Facebook page or his voice to identify the "warning signals" of depression.

When such signals are identified, the system can inform the subject or those who are legally responsible for him (e.g., the parents) that signs of depression have been identified and that an in-depth diagnosis is highly recommended. In other words, such an intelligent system may be used for the unobtrusive but highly important task of screening for signs of depression and raising the awareness of the individual and of the health system of a depressive state. For example, let's imagine Judy, who is a 16-year-old girl. For several weeks, she sneaks into her room immediately after returning from school and avoids any contact with her worried parents. When asked about her behavior, Judy responds with various justifications that do not satisfy her parents. Is she experiencing a normal phase of development or should she be examined by an expert? Automatically analyzing Judy's search queries in Google or correspondences in Twitter may provide us with significant information about her mental state and whether or not there is a place for worry. The question, of course, is how this procedure can actually be applied.

In a previous paper (Neuman, Cohen, Assaf, & Kedma, 2012), we proposed an NLP approach to the recognition of depression in people. Before presenting our approach, let me review different NLP approaches addressing similar challenges.

The assumption underlying all NLP approaches to the recognition of depression through texts is that the language used by the person is indicative of his psychological state. This assumption is both trivial and not trivial at the same time. On one hand, language as the major medium of communication both between people and to oneself (i.e., inner speech) is indicative of our subjective experience. When someone says "I'm feeling lost. There is no point in living this life," we may immediately suspect him/her of being depressed. On the other hand, the complexity of language is such that it cannot be considered simply a mirror of our mind. Language is used for rhetorical aims, to manipulate others, and to reflectively and paradoxically examine itself, such as in the case of humor. In other words, language is not the simple and straightforward mirror of our mind or of our mental and emotional states.

Because of the complexity of language, the recognition of depression in a person through text becomes a challenge. One major and dominant approach for identifying "depressed" texts is the ML approach. ML entails the design of systems that can "learn" from data to perform various intelligent tasks such as classification. The system identifies and formalizes the relationship between input features and output products that are of interest to the researcher. For example, let us assume that we have a corpus of texts written by both depressed and nondepressed people. How can we use these texts to "teach" our system to automatically and successfully classify future texts as written either by depressed or nondepressed people? After all, if we have some information about the mental state of the writers in advance, why do we need the NLP algorithms? For understanding the relationship between the input (e.g., texts) and the output criteria (i.e., depressed vs nondepressed), we must have a tagged and labeled corpus saying that some texts were written by depressed people and others texts by nondepressed people. In practice, obtaining high-quality data, though not an easy task, is essential, as the ML algorithm has to be trained on a corpus. In our study, we may ask a group of depressed patients to write an essay describing their experiences and compare these essays with essays written by nondepressed individuals. The two datasets will be matched by variables, such as gender and age, so that the groups, or more accurately the two groups of texts, are "equal" except for being written by depressed versus nondepressed people. Our task now is to "teach" a system to differentiate between depressed and nondepressed, so that when examining texts from a different corpus in the future, the system will successfully classify texts with a high level of accuracy. A common approach in ML is to split the dataset into two — a training and a test set. In the training set, we define a set of potentially differentiating features/cues. For instance, we count the number of "sad" words in the text and ask whether this particular number or percentage of sad words in the text can be used to predict whether a text was written by a depressed or nondepressed individual. Here, we use single words as our basic unit of analysis, but the use of combinations of two words (i.e., bigrams such as "high school"), three words (i.e., trigrams), and so on may improve the performance of the system in classifying subjects as has been recently illustrated in the screening for posttraumatic stress disorder (He, Veldkamp, & de Vries, 2012).

The set of features we choose for the classification task can be enormous and the role of the learning phase is to find a model — usually statistical — that best differentiates between depressed and nondepressed subjects based on that given set of features. For example, by using the training set and a list of word categorizations, we may find that what differentiates between depressed and nondepressed people are "sad" words but not words that indicate "anger." A statistical model that we may use for the analysis of such a case is a Bayesian model that may ask what the probability is of being a depressed person/text *given* that the text is characterized by a certain percentage of "sad" words.

After the training phase has been completed, we can move on and test our model with the test set. The reason for testing the model again is that while using the training set, we have fitted our statistical model to the data, that is, we have developed a model that best differentiates between the values of the dependent variable (i.e., depressed vs nondepressed) based on the values of the independent variables (i.e., the linguistic features such as the percentage of "sad" words). In fact, we can always fit a function to our data as there is no set of relations between input/output data that cannot be mathematically formalized. However, to estimate the extent to which the model we have imposed on the data can be generalized, which is the real challenge, we must test it on the test set.

This approach to the identification of depression has been recently used by Resnik, Garro, and Resnik (2013). These researchers used a collection of essays that were collected from 124 college students who were asked to describe their "deepest thoughts and feelings about being in college." Each essay was accompanied by the Beck Depression Inventory (BDI) score. Setting a threshold for depression, 12 students were defined as depressed and the remaining 112 as nondepressed; therefore, the prevalence of depressed subjects/texts in the sample is approximately 10%. For each essay, the researchers calculated the number of words in each of the 64 word categories that were used by LIWC (Tausczik & Pennebaker, 2010) such as the "affect category" (e.g., negative emotion) and the "topic category" (e.g., health, religion) plus a list of topics that were identified for each text.

It was found that this algorithm was able to classify the subjects with 0.50 precision and 0.50 recall. The precision score means that in 50% of the cases in which the system identified a text as depressed, the text had been written by an individual already diagnosed with depression. The recall score means that the system correctly identified 50% of the previously diagnosed depressed people. Now, let us assume that we would like to randomly guess who is depressed in our sample of college students. Randomly "hitting" our targets has a 10% chance of success. However, the chance of identifying our depressed students by using our model is significantly higher at 50%. These results are impressive, but because the model uses essays in which the students were deliberately asked to describe their "deepest thoughts and feelings" in a reflective way, which is just a step away from asking them outright if they are depressed, identifying depression was relatively easy. The generalization of the model to real world data is thus questionable. In addition, using a predefined dictionary of words/features for screening for depression has its own problems. The fact that researchers limit themselves to a predefined set of features may blind them to other significant cues that characterize the "phenomenology" or the subjective experience of the specific phenomenon under inquiry. This difficulty has another aspect.

We may identify depression in texts by seeking symptoms of depression such as a lack of appetite, a sharp decrease in libido, insomnia, and so on. However, this "symptomology," which is forced in a top-down manner, probably does not exhaust the whole spectrum of linguistic means ordinary people may use to express their subjective experience of depression, i.e., the phenomenology of depression.

To address the challenge of screening for depression by taking into account the subjective experience of ordinary human beings and their way of using language, we have chosen another approach. Our point of departure is the importance of metaphorical language in people's description of depression. We assume that ordinary people do not use expert terminology to describe the experience of depression, but instead describe depression by drawing on other semantic fields. More specifically, we were interested in *simile* — a figure of speech involving the explicit comparison of one thing with another — being used to describe depression. We were interested in the ways ordinary people describe depression and therefore we searched the Web for the pattern "Depression is like *," where "*" is a "wild card" used to signify any relevant word or phrase. We automatically analyzed the phrases people used to describe depression, added a manual expert analysis, and built a "depression lexicon" of words and phrases.

To test the benefits of using the lexicon for screening for depression, we have analyzed a corpus of blogs comprising 398,691 posts of 17,031 bloggers, and scored each text according to the number of words from the depression lexicon that were evident in it. To test the screening ability, we identified 83 posts that showed signs of depression. The posts were identified by searching for the root word "depress" and by manually verifying that the author testifies that she/he is in a state of depression. It goes without saying that the root word "depress" has been removed from all of the linguistic analyses we have performed on the texts. In addition, we manually identified 100 posts in which no sign of depression was evident. These posts were used as a control group. As a statistical model, we used a binary logistic regression analysis with depression as the dependent variable and our depression score (DepScore) as the independent variable.

The regression analysis was statistically significant with 84% accuracy. This is a 30% improvement over the base-rate of depressive text in our sample (55%). There are some necessary qualifications accompanying these results, but the bottom line is that by using NLP tools we may actually "understand" the way ordinary people describe the experience of depression in layman terms and to use this understanding for automatically screening for depression through text analysis.

There are significant improvements that can easily be made to the very simple logic of the system we have developed, and the future development of IA tools for depression screening must support the public health system in this important task. In any case, the idea of automatically screening for depression is highly relevant for both individuals and for health systems. For the individual, such a system may provide a "looking glass" through which she/he may mirror and monitor his/her mental states. The famous legendary Baron von Munchausen was able to pull himself out of a swamp by grabbing his own hair and pulling himself outside. Many times, we need assistance from the outside and technology may offer it. For the public health system, a tool providing screening for depression would be highly efficient and economical and may provide the health system with the ability to take important preventive steps before the individual sinks into despair. Technology may not necessary function as a lifeguard, but it can definitely be used as a life belt.

Neurodegenerative Diseases and the e-Health Challenge

The increase in life expectancy is a blessed outcome of the economic, scientific, and political advancements that have been achieved in modern societies. However, a byproduct of this increase is the appearance of neurodegenerative diseases that were almost unknown in societies where life expectancy was shorter.

In this context, AI technologies may be used for detecting early warning signs indicating the onset of a neurodegenerative disease. This early detection is relevant only if it is accompanied by preventative steps or interventions that may at least impede the progress of the disease.

At this point, there is no scientific cure for the main neurodegenerative diseases we know. However, there are some promising directions for the technological identification of the behavioral symptoms preceding and accompanying the disease. For instance, in a recent competition organized by Kaggle and the Michael J. Fox Foundation for Parkinson's research (http://www.kaggle.com/c/predicting-parkinson-s-disease-progression-with-smartphones-data), the competitors were asked to identify symptoms of Parkinson disease (PD) by analyzing data collected through subjects' smartphones. It was an interesting competition as the idea of collecting data through individuals' smartphones is unintrusive, "natural," and holds the promise for efficient screening. In addition, the challenge is scientifically intriguing as it involves the efficient separation of "signal" from "noise." For instance, tremors are an indicative "signal" of PD but this symptom can be noisy and result from normal hand movements, etc. Separating the signal from the noise is not a trivial task and accompanies many eHealth applications.

The winners of the competition were four Italian computer scientists who used a ML approach for differentiating between the PD subjects and a control group.[1] This achievement proves that movement-related symptoms of PD (e.g., shaking) can be collected from passive mobile phone data and used for identifying PD patients.

Similar achievements may be gained with regard to AD, a common form of dementia characterized by a significant loss of cognitive ability, which is much more severe than in the usual aging process *per se*.

AD is characterized by confusion, memory loss, irritability, aggression, and problems with language. Variability of the symptoms and their progression make it extremely difficult to identify the eruption of the disease in its salient form and forecast the course of development in the individual's total decline. In other words, in the predementia phase, it is quite difficult to provide a differential diagnosis and to differentiate between symptoms of stress or aging and symptoms of AD. The potential warning signals, such as a decline in abstract thinking, cannot be easily differentiated from background noise.

Language problems are of specific interest for the early identification of AD. The AD patient may suffer from a decrease in verbal fluency, naming, and discourse-level processing, with emphasis on lexical-semantic processing (Taler & Phillips, 2008). Semantic loss is therefore a powerful warning signal of the onset of AD. Other studies propose additional aspects of language use, such as "propositional density" (Engelman, Agree, Meoni, & Klag, 2010), nonliteral language comprehension

---

[1] http://www.reuters.com/article/2013/04/24/mjff-lionsolver-chall-idUSnPNDC01009+1e0+PRN20130424.

(Rapp & Wild, 2011), and the quality of the spoken narrative (Murray, 2010), as relevant for the diagnosis of the AD.

The ability to identify signs of AD through automatic text analysis has been illustrated through the case study of the novelist Iris Murdoch. In an interesting analysis of Iris Murdoch novels (Garrard, Maloney, Hodges, & Patterson, 2005), the ratio between the numbers of words overall (number of word tokens) and the number of distinct words (word types) was found to be indicative of her late-onset AD. This study was followed by the automatic analysis of grammatical complexity (Pakhomov, Chacon, Wicklund, & Gundel, 2011) that was extended to the analysis of other novelists (Le, Lancashire, Hirst, & Jokel, 2011) with results indicating a decline in lexical richness as indicating approaching AD (van Velzen, Nanetti, & de Deyn, 2013).

These studies suggest that the automatic analysis of texts may have a significant contribution to the screening of AD symptoms at an early stage of the disease. The question is what would be the reason to attempt this analysis. After all, AD has no cure and therefore identifying "early warning signals" of AD seems to be pointless. However, this is not quite true. Jelcic et al. (2012) point to the fact that semantic memory declines many years before the diagnosis of the disease and argues that lexical-semantic stimulation may improve episodic memory. If this is the case, then screening for early warning signals of AD may be used for clinical interventions that do not provide a solution to the disease but may effectively delay its development.

However, here I would like to make a "tricky" move. If we can use a variety of linguistic features for the automatic diagnosis of AD through text and even speech analysis and know that it is quite difficult to differentiate between AD in its early phase and contextual situation of stress, why not use the same tools for screening for stress among "normal" people?

The idea is simple and its implications are important. All of us have a dynamic pattern of behavior with ups and downs. The ups and downs can result from different sources such as a work load and/or a cognitive load associated with negative feelings of strain and pressure. As stress has well-known implications for both physical and mental health, it may be helpful to provide people with a personal "stress barometer" that automatically measures their stress level by analyzing their written texts in the posts they send through Twitter or those published on their Facebook page, and by analyzing their spoken language as they use their smartphones. In other words, while identifying the onset of a neurode-generative disease is highly important, the same technology may be used to monitor stress.

I would like to present an application that I have been thinking about for a couple of years as the result of serving as the head of my department. In life, there are certain social interactions that fortify your level of energy. When interacting with certain individuals, you might feel as if your energy level has been refueled. In contrast, there are certain interactions that might sap you of your energy. You end such interactions with a feeling of exhaustion and lassitude. I humorously call individuals involved in such interactions "energy vampires." However, it is only in retrospect and after certain reflections that a person can understand that she/he has been robbed by interacting with these individuals. The application that I have been considering would be able to "read" a person's stress level and map his/her social interactions by pointing to those interactions that are most destructive. Such an application may give us the "view from within" on our unconscious mental state but from the technological outsider's point of view. It can even politely suggest that if the interaction is not necessary, it is healthier to avoid the company of these "vampires." Let us consider one possible practical application of such a "stress barometer" technology. A former member of the military forces arrives at a therapist with complaints that raise the suspicion that the person is suffering from PTSD. We may provide the person with an app that monitors stress levels through text, voice, and the analysis of various biomarkers. The data collected by the app may be organized on temporal, geographical, and social dimensions and provide the therapist with valuable information on the time, locations, and social contexts in which the stress levels are high. The therapist may use this information to advise the patient to avoid certain stressful contexts until his/her mental condition is stabilized.

Mass Shooters and the Challenge of Screening for Harmful Offenders

I opened this chapter by discussing the Columbine High School Massacre and the benefits of screening for mental pathologies that might have devastating consequences on society. In fact, the phenomenon of "civilian mass murderers" is statistically marginal. In terms of priorities, it is better to invest in preventing alcohol and drug abuse. However, murderers such as school shooters gain unproportional media coverage that, in turn, creates social anxiety. In this context, an AI screening tool is a social must as its relevance goes far beyond the task of identifying a potential murderer in the haystack of disturbed individuals. The act of school shooting is the end product of a pathological and social process and individuals who are identified as "potential shooters/murderers" should be treated mentally, educationally, and socially for their own benefit and for the benefit of the society in which they are a part. In this context, an automatic screening procedure should identify candidates for (i) in-depth personal diagnosis and (ii) therapeutic and preventive steps to be taken by mental health practitioners and law enforcement agencies. The problem is that, to identify these individuals, we must better understand the mind of a mass shooter. Again, I emphasize the fact that the civilian mass murderer is a relatively rare phenomenon that may teach us a lesson about the more frequent cases of vengeful and violent behavior to which many other people belong. Identifying those people is of high importance. The problem facing us is that there is no agreed diagnosis for mass murderers. For instance, it was argued that the psychological diagnosis of mass shooters is often based on symptoms that are shared with other diagnoses (Dutton, White, & Fogarty, 2013, p. 548). In this case, it is quite difficult to reach a consensual diagnosis. This difficulty can be illustrated through the analysis of Seung-Hui Cho, who murdered 23 students and faculty members at Virginia-Tech on April 16, 2007. Reviewing the different diagnoses of Cho, one may encounter a supermarket of pathologies as he was diagnosed as a paranoid-schizoid (Knoll, 2010a,b), depressive (Dutton et al., 2013), schizophrenic (Langman, 2009), and as suffering from selective mutism (Freedman, 2013). In a "manifesto" that Cho sent to the media before executing his vicious deed, he compared himself to Moses; therefore he can also be diagnosed as a disturbed narcissist (Mullen, 2004).

In addition to the above-mentioned diagnoses of Cho, his documented social detachment may also lead us to diagnose him with a schizoid personality disorder (ScPD), which is characterized by a "pervasive pattern of detachment from social relationships" (Triebwasser, Chemerinski, Roussos, & Siever, 2012). It was found that ScPD is firmly linked to "unbearable and inescapable loneliness" (Martens, 2010, p. 38), which is a repeating theme evident in the writings of Cho and other mass murderers. ScPD was found to be correlated with violent behavior (Pulay et al., 2008) and is a precursor of violence toward self and/or others (Loza & Hanna, 2006). This knowledge leads us to add the ScPD aspect to the other diagnoses presented above. However, the salient majority of people suffering from ScPD do not commit violent acts. These nonconverging expert opinions should not be interpreted as a sign of professional confusion. It is well known, both in medicine and psychology, that a primary disorder is usually accompanied by one or more additional disorders. This phenomenon is described as "comorbidity" and, therefore, there is an inherent difficulty in providing a differentiating diagnosis and producing an informative profile of a mass shooter.

Despite the intensive clinical and forensic work on the subject of mass murderers (e.g., Declercq & Audenaert, 2011; Ferguson, Coulson, & Barnett, 2011; Levin & Madfis, 2009; Meloy, 1997), there is no solid "profile" of mass shooters that can be used for screening and prevention. As a first step, one should try to provide a theoretical and empirical grounded profile of a mass shooter. This challenge has been addressed in one of my recent papers (Neuman, Assaf, Cohen, & Knoll, 2015) as described below. To introduce our approach, it is necessary to first understand the idea of vector space models and their relevance for automatic personality analysis (Neuman & Cohen, 2014).

Vectorial Semantics and Personality Analysis

How do we understand the meaning of words? This question has puzzled intellectuals since antiquity. While philosophical and psychological approaches are indispensible, vector space models of semantics suggest that the meaning of a word and the concept it represents can be *pragmatically* identified by analyzing words co-occurring with our target word in a given context. Our aim in understanding the meaning of the word "paranoid," for example, is practical, as we plan to automatically analyze a text and measure to what extent the symptoms of paranoia are evident in the text. As a first step, we analyze a very large and representative corpus of the English language to identify the adjectives co-located with "paranoid" in texts. The assumption is that the semantic neighborhood of the word can give us the sense of the word. In this hypothetical example, we may find that the two adjectives most frequently co-located with the word paranoid are: *suspicious* (frequency = 3) and *angry* (frequency = 6). Ignore the small numbers as they are used for illustration only. The numbers actually mean that, in the texts we have analyzed, the word paranoid is accompanied by the word suspicious three times and by the word angry six times. The shaded area in Table 10.1 shows these data.

We can now consider the words suspicious and angry as two *dimensions* defining the *semantic space* of paranoid. In this semantic space, the

Table 10.1 Adjectives Co-Located with Suspicious and Angry

	Paranoid	Histrionic	Narcissistic
Suspicious	3	3	3
Angry	6	3	2

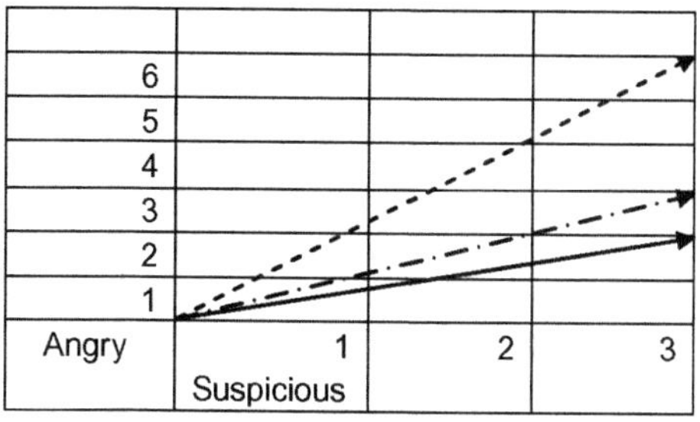

Figure 10.1 A graphical representation of Table 10.1.

meaning of paranoid is represented as a *vector* in a two-dimensional space defined by suspicious and angry, as represented in Figure 10.1. Next, we find that *narcissistic* and *histrionic* are two other words residing in this semantic space, as presented in Table 10.1.

Figure 10.1 is a graphical representation of Table 10.1. The X-axis signifies the dimension of "Suspicious" and the Y-axis signifies the "Angry" dimension.

In this space, "Paranoid" is represented by the dashed vector whose coordinates are $X = 3$ and $Y = 6$. Along the same line, the bold vector represents histrionic and the third vector narcissistic. We can see that the vector of histrionic is closer, and therefore closer in similarity to the vector of narcissistic than to the vector of paranoid. Measuring the similarity of vectors is a simple but rigorous procedure that relies on the cosine between them and provides us with a lead as to how close the words/concepts are to each other.

We have just learned how the meaning of words can be represented as a vector in a semantic space and how to measure the semantic similarity of words. In practice, the situation is much more complex than what is described above, for several reasons. First, each word is accompanied by many other words that co-occur with it in a linguistic corpus. Therefore, instead of a simple two-dimensional space, as appears in Figure 10.1, we have to deal with a multi-dimensional space. In addition, in some cases, we plan to measure the similarity of texts comprising many words rather than the semantic similarity of isolated words only.

Putting complexities aside, the basic idea of representing the meaning of words as a vector in a high-dimensional semantic space and measuring the similarity between words/texts by measuring the distance between the vectors has proved to be extremely effective and may be used for personality analysis.

Let us now return to our example of the word paranoid. To recap, we would like to measure the degree in which a certain text "expresses" paranoia (e.g., *I suspect that the government is responsible for this conspiracy*). Using the vectorial semantic approach, we represent the relevant words in the text — in our case, the sentence — as a vector in a high-dimensional semantic space and measure the distance between the vector comprised of these words and the vector of words representing the paranoid personality disorder (PPD; e.g., suspicious, angry). The closer the vectors are, the more analogous the sentence is to the personality vector and, therefore, our hypothesis that the sentence represents the paranoid personality becomes stronger.

In summary, the first step in the vectorial semantics approach to personality analysis is to identify words that are the best representatives of a certain personality dimension or disorder such as the PPD. My basic assumption, which is deeply grounded in psychological research, is that experts can characterize personality types — specifically PDs — by using a minimal set of words that grasp the essence of the disorder. For example, the adjective "suspicious" is a prototypical keyword in describing a PPD. Using a set of adjectives that describe a PD, we may automatically analyze a given text by simply representing it as a vector and measuring its similarity to predefined vectors of PDs.

The vectorial semantic approach to personality assessment can thus be summarized as follows (Neuman & Cohen, 2014): (i) based on theoretical and/or empirical knowledge, select a set of words that represent a psychological trait; (ii) represent this set as a vector; (iii) choose a text you would like to assess and represent its words as a vector; and (iv) measure the similarity between the vectors. The similarity score is indicative of the degree in which the personality trait is represented in the text.

Analyzing the Texts of the Mass Shooters

Texts written by mass murderers are few and difficult to find. To identify the profile of mass shooters, I have selected eight texts written by mass murderers. Most of the texts were downloaded from a site dedicated to the study of mass shooters. The texts were:

1. The manifesto written by Seung Hui Cho, who murdered 23 students at the Virginia Tech Massacre
2. The manifesto of Christopher Dorner, a former police officer who murdered four people in a series of shooting attacks
3. The suicide note of Wellington de Oliveira, who murdered 12 children at the Rio de Janeiro school shooting
4. The documents of Pekka Eric Auvinen, who murdered eight people at the Jokela High School Massacre in Finland
5. The writings of "Kip" Kinkel, the perpetrator of the Dawson College Shootings, who murdered four people
6. The suicide note of Marc Lépine who murdered 14 women at the "Montreal Massacre"
7. The writings of Luke Woodham who murdered three people, and
8. The manifesto of Jiverly Wong, who conducted the Bingham shootings and murdered 13 people.

These texts present a variety of stylistic forms of different lengths, but, following the proposal to focus on the "phenomenology" of the perpetrator, as described, for example, in their diaries (Dutton et al., 2013), all of the chosen texts represent the murderer's first-person perspective before the murder took place.

I have explained the importance of analyzing the phenomenology of a mental disturbance in the context of screening for depression (Neuman et al., 2012) and here I apply it to the analysis of mass shooters. To profile the mass shooters, we must compare them to the same kind of reference group. I have used the Blogs Authorship Corpus (Schler et al., 2006) and, for comparison, selected blogs written by males aged 15−25, collapsing the posts written by the same person into a single text. Overall, I have analyzed the blogs written by 6,050 individuals and compared them to the texts written by mass murderers.

Preprocessing of the Text and Analysis

First, I have used Stanford Part-of-Speech Tagger (Toutanova, Klein, Manning, & Singer, 2003) and extracted *four* part of speech categories from the text: nouns, verbs, adverbs, and adjectives. This procedure allows us to focus our analysis on the main categories of words and to avoid what is known as "stop words" (e.g., "such"). From each text, I have automatically chosen the 10 most frequent nouns, the 10 most frequent verbs and the 10 most frequent adjectives. Overall, we used 30 words to represent each blogger and each murderer. For the analysis of the texts, we followed the idea of the vectorial semantic approach to personality analysis as presented above.

More specifically, we use the dual-space model developed by Turney, Neuman, Assaf, and Cohen (2011) and Turney (2012). This model allows us to measure the semantic similarity of words and texts by using the "dual space," examining the "domain" similarity of words (i.e., "topic" similarity) and the similarity in their "function" (i.e., role or usage). This model is implemented in a vectorial semantic space constructed by Turney, which allows us to measure the similarity between texts. We measured the semantic similarity between each of the texts and word vectors representing four personality disorder traits that were preselected based on our theoretical knowledge of the psychology of mass murderers: PPD, narcissistic personality disorder (NPD), schizotypal personality disorder (ScPD), and depressivity (DEP). The vectors were as follows:

1. PPD: suspicious, hypersensitive, wronged, hostile
2. NPD: arrogant, manipulative, egocentric, insensitive
3. ScPD: detached, avoidant, lonely, indifferent
4. DEP: sad, lonely, hopeless, worthless.

In addition to the four personality vectors mentioned above, and based on Neuman's (2012) recent theory of revenge, we used nine additional word vectors:

1. Hopeless: hopeless, desperate
2. Lonely: lonely, lonesome
3. Helpless: helpless, defenseless
4. Pain: pain, misery, agony
5. Revengeful: revengeful, vengeful, vindictive
6. Chaotic: chaotic, disordered
7. Unsafe: unsafe, insecure
8. Abandoned: abandoned, deserted
9. Humiliated: humiliated, shamed.

These vectors aim to represent different facets of vengeful behavior that may contribute to the screening procedure. Overall, we have analyzed 13 vectors and each text was automatically analyzed and received its similarity score to the above vectors/variables.

Analysis and Results

First, we compared the scores of the mass murderers' texts to the bloggers' texts. We used the Mann-Whitney U test with a Monte Carlo simulation of 10,000 samples and 0.95 confidence interval. The use of the Monte Carlo simulation allows us to gain a better and more valid estimation of our measures.

It was found that the mass murderers scored higher than the comparison group on the following vectors:

1. Vengeful ($z = 2.64$, $P = 0.003$)
2. Helpless ($z = 2.6$, $P = 0.01$)
3. PPD ($z = 2.28$, $P = 0.01$)
4. NPD ($z = 2$, $P = 0.02$) and
5. Humiliated ($z = 1.83$, $P = 0.03$).

These findings allow us to build a "narrative" or to profile the mass murderers as follows: The murderer is a suspicious and angry person (i.e., a paranoid) whose grandiosity (e.g., *I'm Jesus*) aims to cover a fragile self. When this personality encounters a humiliating situation, it experiences what is described in the literature as *narcissistic injury and rage* that threatens the integrity of his ego. Normal people may find different ways to cope with this injury, but our personality feels helpless and the result is vengeful intentions that aim to recover the degraded self. The profile described so far is the bomb waiting for a trigger to explode and bring about a bloodbath. This profile is visually described in Figure 10.2.

The Screening Procedure

Despite the importance of providing a profile for mass murderers, the real challenge is the automatic screening for potential mass murderers. Given the negligible number of mass murderers, it is unrealistic to develop a procedure for identifying this needle in a haystack without the unbearable cost of too many false alarms. However, to adopt a more practical perspective, we may ask if there is a procedure that an expert can use to better search the corpus of texts to find potential mass murderers. Analogically, this is the same as developing algorithms to reduce the search space of missing survivors at sea. As we cannot guarantee a perfect

Figure 10.2 The profile of a mass-murderer.

"hit" in the target, we must define a reasonable search space (e.g., the ship was lost 200 km north of Cape Town) and try to reduce this search space as much as we can. In our mass murderer texts, given the profile portrayed above, we can try to rank the cases according to their personality disorder scores, and start searching for the potential mass murderers starting with those ranked at the top. This approach is similar to the automatic identification of sexual predators (Inches & Crestani, 2012), in which a ranked list of suspects is automatically created to prioritize the investigation. However, the method presented below can be used only for priorization. Our basic assumption is that an expert forensic investigator can identify the texts written by murderers as a "red flag," in a similar manner to a psychologist who may identify symptoms of depression in a given text. An effective screening procedure may significantly reduce the number of texts the expert must read to identify these red flags.

For ranking the texts, we first used a Binary Regression Analysis. The independent variables were the measures described in the profile and the dependent variable was whether the text was written by a murderer or not. Moreover, our analysis produced the *Leverage Value* that measures the relative influence of each observation (e.g., text) on the model's fit. We rank the texts in a descending order for providing the expert with an optimal search strategy and start searching for the murderers' texts from the highest scores and counting the number of texts the expert should read in order to identify them. This amounts to a strategy of screening for the texts by searching from the top-scored texts to the bottom. Interestingly, Cho's manifesto ranked 2, Lepine 49, Kinkel 84, Donner 198, Pekka 363, Luke 479, Wong 1162 and de Olivieti 1473.

Now, let us assume the expert is skimming the texts for clues at a common reading speed of 700 words per minute. It would take him 1,142 h to skim the whole corpus but only 134 h if he is using our procedure. The bottom line is that, to use the proposed screening procedure, we would need 5% of the time needed for reading the whole corpus, which is an improvement by a factor of 20. This result is impressive but very far from providing a real-world advantage as the number of texts in Big Data repositories are too big even for our impressive improvement. In practice, a real-world application should include more data from various sources so as to improve our screening. Adding medical records, criminal records, financial transactions, school reports, and other sources of information may significantly improve the performances and establish a working screening system that may provide red flags to those needing treatment. However, one should consider the ethical implications of an automatic screening technology. Most people who will be screened for a professional inspection would never commit a murder. By automatically "marking" them as suspects we are using a stigma rather than a valid diagnosis. This unfortunate result is inevitable given the low prevalence of offenders in the population and the limitations of the automatic screening tool. The ethical considerations of using a screening tool go far beyond the limited case of the mass murderers. Screening a child for suicidal thoughts may be a legitimate move but when we analyze an adult who may want to defend his/her privacy or even his/her right to die by suicide, things get much more complicated. These ethical issues go beyond the individual case. The same depression screening technology may be used to inform parents about the mental condition of their teenager but the same technology may be used by the government in order to analyze how depressed a given population is in order to manipulate it for strategic aims. This chapter does not aim to fully discuss these difficult ethical considerations or to present a ready-made solution. It is important, however, to consider these issues as the ethical and legal aspects of emerging technologies should always be taken into account.

CONCLUSION

In this chapter, I have introduced several ideas and case studies illustrating the potential of AI for augmenting the cognitive abilities of human beings in public health surveillance and research. If the current technological trajectory is going to proceed along the same pattern of development, we anticipate the emergence of technologies that are far beyond our imagination. The development of these technological tools sometimes precedes the development of their potential uses and, in contrast to some linear conceptions, actually invites new ideas for innovation and research and begins new dialogs and promotes the use of novel applications, extending the limit of our understanding. In this context, people interested in health surveillance and research should be sensitive and attentive to emerging technologies, determining how these technologies can improve the way we operate in the world. For instance, the prevalence of social media invites the use of screening tools for analyzing platforms such as Facebook or Twitter through automatic tools of personality analysis. A recent methodology I have developed can automatically extract various personality dimensions of a text (Neuman & Cohen, 2014) even when the data involve only the last 100 Tweets of the user.

Current limits and the tyranny of ideas should not constrain the technological venture described above. David Ben-Gurion, the first Prime Minister of Israel, and a visionary thinker who laid the foundation of the Zionist state, had a dream of turning the Israeli desert into a flourishing garden. In one of his tours in the Negev, he arrived at the Ramon Crater and considered turning it into a lake. His escorts explained that it is impossible. "Who said so"? asked Ben-Gurion. "The experts," they answered. To this, Ben-Gurion retorted, "So, replace the experts." While this story might present Ben-Gurion in a negative light, it must be remembered that he established the basis for Israeli scientific studies and technology and that, in a period where most Israelis did not own a telephone or a refrigerator, the Weizmann Institute of Science was involved in building one of the first computers in the world. The lesson we learn from this anecdote is of the importance of visionary thinking and the way human vision and technology should be brought together − with all the inevitable risks − to the benefit of mankind.

REFERENCES

American Psychiatric Association. (1994). *Diagnostic and statistical manual of mental disorders: DSM-IV* (4th ed. Washington, DC: American Psychiatric Association.
Cullen, D. (April 20, 2004). The Depressive and the psychopath. Slate. Retrieved from: <http://www.slate.com/articles/news_and_politics/assessment/2004/04/the_depressive_and_the_psychopath.html>.
Declercq, F., & Audenaert, K. (2011). Predatory violence aiming at relief in a case of mass murder: Meloy's criteria for applied forensic practice. *Behavioral Sciences & the Law, 29,* 578−591.
Dutton, D. G., White, K. R., & Fogarty, D. (2013). Paranoid thinking in mass shooters. *Aggression and Violent Behavior, 18,* 548−553.
Effron, L. (2012). *Mass school shootings: A history.* ABC News. Retrieved 23.06.14.
Engelbart, D. C. (1962). Augmenting human intellect: A conceptual framework. Summary Report AFOSR-3223 under Contract AF 49 (638)-1024, SRI Project 3578 for Air Force Office of Scientific Research. Stanford Research Institute. Retrieved 01.03.07.
Engelman, M., Agree, E. M., Meoni, L. A., & Klag, M. J. (2010). Propositional density and cognitive function in later life: Findings from the Precursors Study. *The Journals of Gerontology Series B: Psychological Sciences and Social Sciences, 65*(6), 706−711.
Ferguson, C. J., Coulson, M., & Barnett, J. (2011). Psychological profiles of school shooters: Positive directions and one big wrong turn. *Journal of Police Crisis Negotiations, 11,* 141−158.
Friedman E. (2013). *Va. Tech shooter Seung-Hui Cho's mental health records released.* ABC News. Available from: <http://abcnews.go.com/US/seung-hui-chos-mental-health-records-released/story?id=8278195>. Accessed 30.09.13.

Garrard, P., Maloney, L. M., Hodges, J. R., & Patterson, K. (2005). The effects of very early Alzheimer's disease on the characteristics of writing by a renowned author. *Brain, 128*(2), 250−260.

He, Q., Veldkamp, B. P., & de Vries, T. (2012). Screening for posttraumatic stress disorder using verbal features in self-narratives: A text mining approach. *Psychiatry Research, 198*, 441−447.

Inches, G., & Crestani, F. (2012). Overview of the international sexual predator identification competition at pan-2012. In P. Forner, J. Karlgren, & C. Womser-Hacker (Eds.), *CLEF 2012 Evaluation Labs and Workshop − Working notes papers*. Italy: Rome.

Jelcic, N., Cagnin, A., Meneghello, F., Turolla, A., Ermani, M., & Dam, M. (2012). Effects of lexical−semantic treatment on memory in early Alzheimer disease an observer-blinded randomized controlled trial. *Neurorehabilitation and Neural Repair, 26* (8), 949−956.

Knoll, J. L. (2010a). The "pseudocommando" mass murderer: Part I, The psychology of revenge and obliteration. *Journal of the American Academy of Psychiatry and the Law Online, 38*, 87−94.

Knoll, J. L. (2010b). The "Pseudocommando" mass murderer: Part II, The language of revenge. *Journal of the American Academy of Psychiatry and the Law Online, 38*, 263−272.

Langman, P. (2009). Rampage school shooters: A typology. *Aggression and Violent Behavior, 14*, 79−86.

Le, X., Lancashire, I., Hirst, G., & Jokel, R. (2011). Longitudinal detection of dementia through lexical and syntactic changes in writing: A case study of three British novelists. *Literary and Linguistic Computing, 26*(4), 435−461.

Levin, J., & Madfis, E. (2009). Mass murder at school and cumulative strain A sequential model. *American Behavioral Scientist, 52*, 1227−1245.

Loza, W., & Hanna, S. (2006). Is schizoid personality a forerunner of homicidal or suicidal behavior? A case study. *International Journal of Offender Therapy and Comparative Criminology, 50*, 338−343.

Luxton, D. D. (2014). Artificial intelligence in psychological practice: Current and future applications and implications. *Professional Psychology: Research and Practice, 45*(5), 332−339. Available from: http://dx.doi.org/10.1037/a0034559.

Martens, W. H. (2010). Schizoid personality disorder linked to unbearable and inescapable loneliness. *The European Journal of Psychiatry, 24*, 38−45.

Meloy, J. R. (1997). Predatory violence during mass murder. *Journal of Forensic Sciences, 42*, 326−329.

Millon, T., Millon, C. M., Meagher, S., Grossman, S., & Ramnath, R. (2012). *Personality disorders in modern life*. New York: John Wiley & Sons.

Mullen, P. E. (2004). The autogenic (self-generated) massacre. *Behavioral Sciences & The Law, 22*, 311−323.

Murray, L. L. (2010). Distinguishing clinical depression from early Alzheimer's disease in elderly people: Can narrative analysis help? *Aphasiology, 24*(6−8), 928−939.

Neuman, Y. (2012). On revenge. *Psychoanalysis, Culture & Society, 17*, 1−15.

Neuman, Y., & Cohen, Y. (2014). *A vectorial semantics approach to personality analysis*. Scientific Reports. Available from: <http://dx.doi.org/10.1038/srep04761>.

Neuman, Y., Cohen, Y., Assaf, D., & Kedma, G. (2012). Proactive screening for depression through metaphorical and automatic text analysis. *Artificial Intelligence in Medicine*.

Neuman, Y., Assaf, D., Cohen, Y., & Knoll, J. L. (2015). Profiling school shooters: Automatic text-based analysis. *Frontiers in Psychiatry, 6*, 86.

Pakhomov, S., Chacon, D., Wicklund, M., & Gundel, J. (2011). Computerized assessment of syntactic complexity in Alzheimer's disease: A case study of Iris murdoch's writing. *Behavior Research Methods, 43*(1), 136−144.

Pulay, A. J., et al. (2008). Violent behavior and DSM-IV psychiatric disorders: Results from the national epidemiologic survey on alcohol and related conditions. *The Journal of Clinical Psychiatry, 69*, 12−22.

Rapp, A. M., & Wild, B. (2011). Nonliteral language in Alzheimer dementia: A review. *Journal of the International Neuropsychological Society, 17*(2), 207.

Resnik, P., Garron, A., & Resnik, R. (2013). Using topic modeling to improve prediction of neuroticism and depression in college students. In *Proceedings of the 2013 conference on empirical methods in natural language processing*, (pp. 18−21). Seattle, WA.

Schler, J., Koppel, M., Argamon, S., & Pennebaker, J. W. (2006). Effects of age and gender on blogging. *AAAI Spring Symposium: Computational Approaches to Analyzing Weblogs, 6*, 199−205.

Taler, V., & Phillips, N. A. (2008). Language performance in Alzheimer's disease and mild cognitive impairment: A comparative review. *Journal of Clinical and Experimental Neuropsychology, 30*(5), 501−556.

Tausczik, Y. R., & Pennebaker, J. W. (2010). The psychological meaning of words: LIWC and computerized text analysis methods. *Journal of Language and Social Psychology, 29*, 24−54.

Toutanova, K., Klein, D., Manning, S., & Singer, Y. (2003). Feature-rich part-of-speech tagging with a cyclic dependency network. In *Proceedings of HLT-NAACL 2003*, (pp. 252−259).

Triebwasser, J., Chemerinski, E., Roussos, P., & Siever, L. J. (2012). Schizoid personality disorder. *Journal of Personality Disorders, 26*, 919−926.

Turney, P. D. (2012). Domain and function: A dual-space model of semantic relations and compositions. *Journal of Artificial Intelligence Research, 44*, 533−585.

Turney, P., Neuman, Y., Assaf, D., & Cohen, Y. (2011). Literal and metaphorical sense identification through concrete and abstract context. In *Proceedings of the 2011 conference on empirical methods in natural language processing*, (pp. 680−690). Edinburgh, Scotland, UK, July 27−31.

van Velzen, M. H., Nanetti, L., & de Deyn, P. P. (2013). Data modelling in corpus linguistics: How low may we go? *Cortex*. Available from: http://dx.doi.org/10.1016/j.cortex.2013.10.010.

CHAPTER 11

Ethical Issues and Artificial Intelligence Technologies in Behavioral and Mental Health Care

David D. Luxton[1,2], Susan Leigh Anderson[3] and Michael Anderson[4]
[1]Naval Health Research Center, San Diego, CA, USA
[2]Department of Psychiatry and Behavioral Sciences, University of Washington, Seattle, WA, USA
[3]Department of Philosophy, University of Connecticut, Stamford, CT, USA
[4]Department of Computer Science, University of Hartford, West Hartford, CT, USA

INTRODUCTION

Each chapter of this book has demonstrated the many practical uses of artificial intelligence (AI) technologies and techniques in mental health care. These include applications across diverse mental healthcare domains and activities including therapeutic interventions, clinical decision-making, self-care, education, public health surveillance, healthcare administration, research, and more. While AI technologies can provide numerous practical benefits, there are also important ethical issues that require careful thought and consideration by the designers, manufacturers, and end users (i.e., clinicians and healthcare organizations) of these technologies. The use of new technologies in health care, including many of the AI technologies and approaches described in this book, can cause new ways that existing ethics requirements (and laws) can be violated or challenged. Some of the issues concern additional risks that impact patient privacy, safety, autonomy, and trust. The use of autonomous intelligent care providers is an emerging opportunity that requires particular attention. Consider a virtual human or robot that is designed to provide treatment interventions and monitoring of the symptoms of psychiatric patients. The system will need to be able to make decisions and select appropriate courses of action that are consistent with applicable professional ethics codes and standards during interactions with care seekers. The system must also be capable of resolving complex ethical dilemmas that it encounters during the course of care. The designers,

Artificial Intelligence in Behavioral and Mental Health Care.
DOI: http://dx.doi.org/10.1016/B978-0-12-420248-1.00011-8

manufacturers, and end users of these technologies must be aware of the ethical issues in order to optimize the design and use of these technologies.

In this chapter we discuss ethical issues associated with AI technologies that are applied to behavioral and mental health care. We specifically focus on the application of intelligent autonomous systems, such as virtual humans and robots that interact with care seekers. For the purposes of this chapter, we use the term intelligent autonomous care providers (IACPs) to describe these systems. Other terms that have been used to describe autonomous artificial intelligent systems include intelligent autonomous machines and artificial intelligent care providers (AICPs; Luxton, 2014).[1] We begin by providing a brief overview of ethics in health care and how the use of intelligent technologies poses new risks. We then present methods for designing and testing the ethical decision-making and behavior of intelligent machines. While the topic of ethics is our focus, applicable legal requirements (e.g., privacy laws) are considered, as these are also important for the design and ethical use of these technologies for real-world applications.

OVERVIEW OF ETHICS CODES AND ETHICAL BEHAVIOR IN HEALTH CARE
Background

Modern medical ethics are concerned with the application of fundamental values and general ethical principles to medical practice and research. In general, medical ethics are intended to help guide the behavior of healthcare professionals and organizations towards the benefit and protection of patients and others who may be affected by their behavior. Thus they protect not only patients but also care providers and their institutions by setting standards of conduct that ultimately promote the trust of patients, professional colleagues, and the general public.

The four cornerstones of medical ethics are *respect for autonomy, beneficence, nonmaleficence,* and *justice. Respect for autonomy* affirms patients' right to think freely and decide and act on their own free will. This includes patients' rights to self-determination and full disclosure of information so that patients can make informed decisions and choices regarding their care. *Beneficence* means that healthcare providers will promote patients' general wellbeing.

---

[1] The autonomy of a system can be thought of as residing on a continuum ranging from some level of control from external influence to no causal intervention at all.

Nonmaleficence requires that the actions of care providers do not harm the patient involved or others in society. This includes providing treatments known to be effective and assuring competence of care. *Justice* refers to the principle that holds that patients in similar situations should have access to the same care, and that in allocating resources to one group we should assess the impact of this choice on others. These are considered *prima facie* principles because each principle is considered binding unless it conflicts with another principle, and if it does, it requires us to choose between them (Gillon, 1994).

Medical ethics are formalized and communicated by established codes and oaths, the origins of which can be traced back thousands of years (e.g., Babylonian Code of Hammurabi, Oath of Hippocrates). The first formal ethical code of a medical professional organization was published in 1847 by the American Medical Association (AMA Code of Medical Ethics). The British Medical Association followed suit by publishing its first code of Medical Conduct of Physicians in 1858. After the Second World War, the World Medical Association was established as a forum where national medical associations could discuss the ethical concerns presented by modern medicine. The World Health Organization (WHO) issued the International Code of Medical Ethics, the first worldwide medical ethical code, in 1949. The code was based on the Declaration of Geneva, which was adopted by the General Assembly of the World Medical Association in 1948 in response to the medical crimes of Nazi Germany.

The American Psychiatric Association (APA), American Psychological Association (APA), and the American Counseling Association (ACA) are examples of several of the largest mental healthcare professional organizations in the United States that have published ethical codes and guidelines for their respective professions (see ACA, 2014; APA, 2002, 2013). The American Psychological Association organizes its guidelines by standards, which range in topic areas including the resolution of ethical issues, competence, psychological assessment, and those specific to therapy. The American Psychological Association's Ethics Code preamble and general principles are aspirational in intent, whereas its ethical standards are enforceable rules of conduct. That is, the code's preamble and general principles describe the goals to which psychologists aspire, whereas the code's ethical standards describe the rules by which psychologists must abide. Violators of ethical standards may thus be subject to sanctions such as expulsion from the professional organization. The overarching intent of codes and guidelines, such as those of the American Psychological Association are thus to provide mental healthcare professionals with direction to help guide their behavior and justify their decisions and courses of action including the resolution of ethical dilemmas that they encounter.

It is important to note that ethics and legal principles differ in that ethics are guiding principles whereas laws, while sometimes based on ethical or moral principles, are enforceable rules and regulations that have penalties if violated. Sometimes, however, the law may be in conflict with ethical principles. Many medical organizations, such as the American Medical Association, specify that when the professional believes a law is unethical, they should work to change the law (AMA, 1994). Ethical principles also differ from societal values or moral values, the latter two being dependent on personal or societal standards of what is important and thus could be in conflict with ethical principles or with the law.

Technology-Associated Ethics Codes and Guidelines

Several mental healthcare professional organizations have included provisions pertaining to the use of current technology embedded in their ethical guidelines or as supplements. Topics include electronic data security, use of the Internet for providing care services, and the use of electronic communication (e.g., email, social media) with patients. The American Telemedicine Association (ATA) is one organization that has published several guidelines specifically for the use of technology to provide care (ATA, 2012). Other organizations that have published ethics codes or guidelines include the International Society for Mental Health Online's Suggested Principles for the Online Provision of Mental Health Services (https://www.ismho.org/suggestions.asp) and the eHealth Code of Ethics (http://www.ihealthcoalition.org/ehealth-code/).

Established professional ethics codes and practice guidelines do not presently address the emerging ethical implications associated with IACPs. However, several organizations and individuals have proposed guidelines regarding the ethical use and design of intelligent machines. In 2011, the Engineering and Physical Sciences Research Council (EPRSC) and the Arts and Humanities Research Council (AHRC) (Great Britain) published a set of ethical principles for designers, builders, and users of robots along with seven "high-level messages intended to be conveyed" (see Table 11.1). Riek and Howard (2014) also proposed ethical guidelines specific to robots (see Chapter 8), and Luxton (2014) has

Table 11.1 Engineering and Physical Sciences Research Council (EPRSC) and the Arts and Humanities Research Council (AHRC) Principles of Robotics

1. Robots should not be designed solely or primarily to kill or harm humans.
2. Humans, not robots, are responsible agents. Robots are tools designed to achieve human goals.
3. Robots should be designed in ways that assure their safety and security.
4. Robots are artifacts; they should not be designed to exploit vulnerable users by evoking an emotional response or dependency. It should always be possible to tell a robot from a human.
5. It should always be possible to find out who is legally responsible for a robot.

The messages intended to be conveyed

1. We believe robots have the potential to provide immense positive impact to society. We want to encourage responsible robot research.
2. Bad practice hurts us all.
3. Addressing obvious public concerns will help us all make progress.
4. It is important to demonstrate that we, as roboticists, are committed to the best possible standards of practice.
5. To understand the context and consequences of our research, we should work with experts from other disciplines, including: social sciences, law, philosophy, and the arts.
6. We should consider the ethics of transparency: are there limits to what should be openly available?
7. When we see erroneous accounts in the press, we commit to take the time to contact the reporting journalists.

provided recommendations specifically for ethical use and design of AICPs (see Tables 11.2 and 11.3).

Science fiction has also broached the topic of ethics and intelligent machines, most famously Isaac Asimov's Three Laws (and a "Zeroth Law" that was added later) of Robotics (Asimov, 1942). The laws are:

1. A robot may not injure a human being or, through inaction, allow a human being to come to harm.

2. A robot must obey the orders given it by human beings, except where such orders would conflict with the First Law.

3. A robot must protect its own existence as long as such protection does not conflict with the First or Second Law.

0. A robot may not harm humanity, or, by inaction, allow humanity to come to harm.

Although quite popular, these laws have been questioned as being inconsistent, incomplete, and advocating an absolute hierarchy that can

Table 11.2 Summary of Considerations and Recommendations for Ethical Codes, Guidelines, and Use of Artificial Intelligent Care Provider (AICP) Systems

1. Ensure appropriateness of the use of AICPs for intended clinical populations and the individual needs of patients.
2. Disclose what services and limits of services will be provided by AICPs.
3. Ensure that system users understand the capabilities, scope of use, and limitations of AICP systems and describe these to patients as part of the informed consent process.
4. Require human supervision and monitoring for adverse patient reactions and clinical contraindications when these may be a risk.
5. Display credentials and qualifications of both AICPs and care provider users.
6. Describe and disclose data use including extent of data collection, access limitations, and disposition of data records.
7. Follow applicable privacy laws and rules.
8. Ensure that AICP system capabilities follow the latest established clinical best practices.
9. Ensure that the end of the patient–AICP interaction provides continuity of care and sensitivity to the emotional nature of patient–AICP interactions.
10. Provide a mechanism for patients to ask questions and report complaints.

Source: (Luxton, 2014).

Table 11.3 Summary of Recommendations for the Design of Artificial Intelligent Care Provider (AICP) Systems

1. Design to follow the appropriate ethical codes and guidelines consistent with domain of use.
2. Identify and provide specifications of use and limits of autonomy of AICP systems to end users.
3. Test safety and ethical decision-making of AICP systems in diverse ethical situations encountered in all applicable clinical contexts.
4. Include capability for data logs/audit trails to track and explain AICP decision-making.
5. Provide built-in safeguards to assure that systems are only able to provide services within established boundaries of competence and domain of use.
6. Consider the level of human realism of AICPs including appearance and other behavioral characteristics as appropriate for intended application.
7. Consider cultural sensitivity and diversity in design of AICPs.

Source: (Luxton, 2014).

not be defended and is unacceptable for advanced robots (Clarke, 2011). Asimov himself appears to reject the Laws in his short story "The Bicentennial Man" (Asimov, 1976).

Roboethics (Veruggio, 2007) is an emerging field that is concerned with the ethical behavior of humans when it comes to designing, creating, and interacting with artificially intelligent agents (i.e., robots). Some of the topics discussed in roboethics might concern ethical obligations for how people should treat robots, such as whether any rights they may have are respected or whether, even if they have no rights themselves, they are treated respectfully so that cruel behavior towards them will not lead to treating humans badly since they are likely to resemble humans in form and function (Anderson, 2011a,b).

Machine ethics is concerned with developing ethics for autonomously functioning machines (e.g., robots and artificially intelligent agents) in contrast to developing ethics for human beings who use machines. Machine ethics involves *giving* machines ethical principles or a procedure for discovering a way to resolve the ethical dilemmas they might encounter, enabling them to function in an ethically responsible manner towards the humans they interact with (and other machines) through their own ethical decision-making (Anderson & Anderson, 2011). Building IACPs that act in an ethically responsible fashion has the advantage of not putting the burden of determining the ethically correct use of the machine on the user. Moreover, because it is difficult to anticipate every situation where it is important that an IACP behave correctly, it is better to have ethical principles built into them to ensure that they act correctly, no matter what situation they might find themselves in, rather than trying to program them to do so in an *ad hoc* manner.

PARTICULAR ETHICS CHALLENGES

Therapeutic Relationships and Emotional Reactions

The ethics codes and guidelines of professional healthcare organizations generally advocate maintaining a professional relationship between the healthcare professional and patient. The professional relationship or *therapeutic relationship* refers to the relationship between a provider of care (e.g., a psychotherapist) and a patient, whereby the care provider hopes to engage with and achieve goals with a patient (Bordin, 1979). Professional medical providers are in a position of power in their relationship with patients and thus there is potential for exploitation of, and causing harm to, patients. In mental health care, highly charged emotional interactions are intrinsic in the process of psychotherapy; thus respect for the emotional vulnerability of patients is a requirement. The professional relationship between supervisors and trainees is also addressed in many ethical codes and guidelines as supervisors are in a position of power over their trainees and ethical violations have the potential to damage the trust between supervisors and trainees.

Designers and end users (i.e., healthcare organizations and healthcare professionals) of virtual humans, robots, or other forms of IACPs that interact with humans must consider the ethical obligations associated with the therapeutic relationship. This includes issues regarding the emotional bond between patients and providers and the expression and experience of emotions that occur during the therapeutic process. It is necessary for psychotherapists, for example, to monitor the experience emotions, attenuate emotional interaction, and create a safe therapeutic environment for the patient to express and experience emotions. It is also necessary to consider the appropriate way to end the therapeutic relationship, a process that can be quite emotionally charged. Failure to be sensitive to these issues is an ethical problem. Strong emotional reactions that are not appropriately dealt with could lead to behavior that brings harm to the patient or others' safety.

Empathetic understanding between the care provider and care seeker is essential for establishing the therapeutic relationship and for achieving effective therapeutic outcomes. The *ELIZA effect* refers to when users of machines (i.e., computers) perceive them as having intrinsic qualities and abilities, such as understanding or emotions (Hofstadter, 1996). The Eliza effect is named after Joseph Weizenbaum's 1966 chatterbot program ELIZA that, when running its DOCTOR program, was capable of simulating a Rogerian psychotherapist. Weizenbaum observed that even when people consciously knew that they were conversing with a computer program, they seemed to experience their interaction with the simulated psychotherapist as if it was a real person. Weizenbaum explains that this is because the user assigns meaning and interpretation to what the simulation communicates, which "confirms the person's hypothesis" that the system understands them (Weizenbaum, 1976).

Advances in affective sensing and computing are enabling intelligent machines to interact with people in a very human-like empathetic and caring way. Even when a patient is consciously aware that the IACP is a machine, the patient can be expected to experience intense emotions during the interaction and toward the simulation. The experience of emotions would be desirable for many therapeutic purposes; however, it is important to consider how this might also be undesirable. Some patients may become overly attached to a virtual human or humanoid robot in a less than desirable manner or become emotionally upset and cause harm to self or collaterals after interacting with it (Luxton, 2014).

To address these issues, it will be necessary to update professional ethical codes and guidelines to consider the therapeutic relationship between IACPs and patients. Provisions that include requirements for human supervision of IACPs, whereby clinicians are responsible for monitoring and addressing therapeutic relationship issues, emotional reactions, and adverse patient reactions that may pose a risk to patient safety should be considered. Requirements for supervision or monitoring should depend on the context and clinical application of IACP systems. For example, IACPs that are used for simple assessment of symptoms, educational coaching, and training purposes may not require the level of supervision or monitoring that more intensive clinical interactions and treatments would require.

Competence of Intelligent Machines

Mental healthcare professionals conduct many activities that require general and specific training and skill. For example, they need to know how to appropriately apply therapeutic methods and treatments based on established best practices and standards of care. Competence refers to their ability to appropriately perform these tasks. Competence is of ethical significance because providing services outside of the boundaries of trained skill or expertise could put patients at risk of harm — what may be a violation of the ethical principle of beneficence.[2] Furthermore, professional care providers who act outside of their competence can cause damage to the perception of their profession (i.e., trust) when examples of inappropriate or harmful behavior become public. For example, a psychologist who lacks knowledge about how to appropriately administer a psychological test may repeatedly misdiagnose his or her clients and make inappropriate recommendations for treatment. The incompetent behavior of the psychologist could thus cause harm to the patient and potentially result in an entire community not trusting the psychologist and ultimately the profession.

Many ethics codes of professional healthcare organizations include specific provisions regarding professional competence. The American Psychiatric Association code, for example, states "A psychiatrist who regularly practices outside his or her area of professional competence

---

[2] It can be argued that causing harm in some scenarios is not absolutely wrong. For example, assisting a person to die by suicide who has a terminal illness and who is in terrible pain may be viewed as ethically justifiable when respect for autonomy outweighs "doing no harm."

should be considered unethical. Determination of professional competence should be made by peer review boards or other appropriate bodies" (APA, 2013, p. 5). In the healthcare professions, competence is generally determined and maintained through formal education, licensure, specialty training, and continuing education requirements.

The use of IACP systems can present a significant ethical problem if they are not adequately designed to perform tasks in a competent manner or controlled based on the scope of their tested capabilities. Highly autonomous systems would need to demonstrate core competence in the application of interpersonal techniques, treatment protocols, safety protocols (e.g., plan for how to manage situations where care seekers indicate intent to self-harm or harm another person), and cultural competencies. Virtual care providers that become accessible on the Internet and that claim to provide clinical services or benefits when they are not adequate or appropriate to do the stated services may be a particular problem.

Professional users of IACPs (i.e., mental healthcare providers, companies that provide IACP services) must have an understanding of the appropriate use of, and limitations of, the systems. Future guidelines should include requirements to demonstrate that system users understand the capabilities, scope of use, and limitations of these systems. Ideally, it is best if the burden is not placed on the users of the system, but on the design of the system, with medical ethicists involved, to ensure that it acts in an ethically responsible manner towards the humans it interacts with. Mental healthcare providers who augment their work with these systems should have training and knowledge regarding the use of IACPs and in the domain and population that the IACP is to be used. For example, IACPs should only be accessible to care seekers with major depressive disorder when the IACP is designed to provide care to this clinical population. It should also be a requirement for IACP systems to be updated to keep current with the latest clinical best practices. Built-in safeguards to assure that systems are only able to provide services within the boundaries of competence for the intended domain of use may also be required (Luxton, 2014).

Also, the honest and obvious display of credentials and representation of qualifications and competencies of IACPs and their operators should help consumers make informed decisions and help protect them from harm resulting from incompetence or unauthorized practice. The American Psychological Association Ethics Code explicitly states: "Psychologists make available their name, qualifications, registration number, and an indication of where these details can be verified" (APA, 2002). The lack of display of the credentials and qualifications of IACP systems and their operators could be damaging to end users and the mental healthcare profession. Patients should also have a way to voice concerns regarding patient safety or quality of services provided by IACPs and to have those issues reviewed and resolved (Luxton, 2014).

Patient Safety

Another way that healthcare providers can cause harm to patients is by not adhering to patient safety protocols, standards, or procedures. Some of the principal things that can go wrong include significant worsening of psychiatric symptoms, adverse emotional reactions (e.g., anger outbursts), self-harm, or unexpected medical emergencies. Under certain circumstances, the professional healthcare provider is also responsible for taking steps to help assure the safety of third parties, such as when patients threaten physical harm to another person or when evidence of child or elder abuse becomes known. Take, for example, a patient who discloses intent to cause physical harm to their spouse. Duty-to-warn statutes require healthcare professionals to notify authorities (law enforcement) and, in some cases, the spouse (or other third party) when a patient makes a threat to another person. Taking actions to assure the safety of patients can sometimes raise significant ethical dilemmas, such as when duty-to-warn requirements require healthcare providers to break patient confidentiality when they notify the police or other third party. Resolving ethical dilemmas involves determining how to correctly balance competing *prima facie* ethical duties (Anderson, 2011a,b).

In order for IACP systems to function optimally, they will need to be capable of monitoring risks of harm to the patient or others. This would include monitoring of content of what the patient discloses and ongoing assessment of risk factors, such as significant worsening of symptoms and indication of violent behavior toward the self or others. These systems will also need to be able to apply clinical judgment (e.g., assessing intent, weighing clinical and other factors) to make decisions regarding the most ethically justifiable or acceptable course of action. There should also be a back-up plan if the IACP experiences a malfunction during a session or is unavailable (e.g., a network failure occurs). If a human care provider is to step in when an IACP is unavailable, the credentials of that care provider need to be established (e.g., professional licensure requirements, appropriate training).

Also, in the healthcare profession, professional licensure requirements and laws regarding practice jurisdictions are intended to help assure the public that the healthcare professional meets particular standards to protect the public. Laws regarding duty-to-warn and other requirements may vary from one jurisdiction to another (i.e., state to state in the United States). Unregulated deployment of IACP systems, such as on the Internet, will undoubtedly present significant ethical and legal implications if expectations for competence and patient safety, and jurisdictional requirements are not enforced. For IACP systems that are accessed remotely (i.e., via the Internet), we should expect adherence to the same guidelines for assuring patient safety and overall clinical best practices that are used in the field of telemedicine (Luxton, 2014). These include; assessment of whether remote care is appropriate to begin with, assessment of safety risks, the gathering of information regarding emergency services at the patient's location, and involvement of third parties who may assist during emergencies (see Luxton, Nelson, & Maheu, in press).

Respect of Privacy and Trust

Respect of privacy reflects the right to autonomy and dignity and it is seen as essential to individual wellbeing (Moore, 2005). Betrayal of trust due to privacy invasion or unauthorized use of information damages the trust of both individual healthcare providers and their profession. Possible misuse of private data can result from haphazard handling of data (e.g., leaving a lap-top with patient data unsecured in a coffee shop) or unauthorized access to electronic data by hackers. While threats to patient privacy (electronic data security) remain common to many types of technologies used in the practice and management of health care, current and emerging technological capabilities, such as psychological signal detection (e.g., via visual, voice, psychological data collection) as well as recorded conversations (audio, video, or text) between patients and IACPs create the potential for much more data to be collected about individuals, and without individuals being aware of the collection (Luxton, 2014). In traditional "in office" conversations between healthcare professionals and patients, the discussion stays in the room and is not recorded (unless consent is obtained to record a session). Patients can be expected to willfully share very personal information with IACP systems, which can cause significant harm to individuals if that information is misused.

Social robots used for health care also pose particular risks to privacy due to the capability for direct surveillance (onboard sensors could allow for third-party observation) and their capability to be in places that are normally reserved as private, such as the home (Calo, 2011). Moreover, Ryan Calo has discussed concerns about artificially intelligent agents that can stand in for a human *as subject* (Calo, 2011). For example, corporations and governments are now making use of social machines and software to stand in for marketers, recruiters, and spokespersons in order to gather information and influence consumers and everyday citizens. He suggests that the mere presence of a humanoid robot will signal to individuals that they are not alone, even if the robot is neither collecting nor evaluating information on behalf of a human. People can be expected to react to social machines as though they were human beings, including with respect to the sense of being observed. He suggests that we may experience a change of attitudes towards increasing discomfort of widespread machine custodianship of personal information.

Dual-use is another issue that should be considered. Dual-use is a term to describe the application of a technology for more than one use, such as the use of drones for aerial observation of wildlife in public parks and the use of the same basic technology to fire missiles at enemy combatants during war. Dual-use of technologies may also be a threat to the trust that people have of these systems and the helping professions. As noted by Luxton (2014), it is feasible that the same psychological signal detection systems designed for mental healthcare purposes can be used for prisoner interrogation objectives. Awareness of this may impact the public's willingness to use the technology for healthcare purposes. Also, the possibility that data collected while interacting with IACPs may also be used by corporations, governments, or other entities for making predictions about a person's behavior that have implications, such as for future employment, may also increase distrust and apprehension regarding their use.

To address these concerns, full disclosure of what the system(s) does, its purpose, its scope, and how people use the information from it needs to be provided to end users. How and when data collected by IACPs will be shared must be disclosed to patients so that they can make an informed decision about seeking care from an IACP or other alternatives. This disclosure should also describe whether the system(s) meets requirements of applicable privacy laws (i.e., HIPAA in the United States). Rules that specify requirements for maintenance and destruction of IACP data records, including conversation logs, should be developed and disclosed to end users.

Deception and Appearance

Miller (2010) and Riek and Watson (2010) have discussed "Turing deceptions," whereby a person is unable to determine whether they are interacting with a machine or not. The Wizard-of-Oz effect refers to when a person (usually an experimenter or a confederate) remotely controls a robot that appears to be operating on its own. These issues pose an ethical problem, especially when working with intellectually challenged and psychologically vulnerable persons. For example, certain types of patients, such as those with dementia or delusional or psychotic psychopathologies, may be especially at risk of harm. Even when disclosure is made that the system is "just a machine," some patients may believe that the machine is "alive" or that there is a person, or some other malevolent force, behind the simulation. In all situations, it should be disclosed whether the machine functions autonomously or there is actually a person behind it.

The level of human likeness of a simulation is also an important ethical consideration, because how realistic it appears may have bearing on how people will psychologically experience their interaction with it (Luxton, 2014). This notion is supported by research that has examined the phenomenon of the "uncanny valley." More than 40 years ago, Masahiro Mori, a robotics professor at the Tokyo Institute of Technology hypothesized that as the appearance of a robot is made more human, some people's emotional response to the robot will become increasingly positive and empathic, until a point is reached when the response quickly becomes that of unsettling revulsion. However, as the robot's appearance continues to become less distinguishable from that of a human being, the emotional response becomes positive once again and approaches human-to-human empathy levels. This u-shaped response curve is called the "uncanny valley" (Mori, 1970). What level of realism would be most tolerable and preferable by patients is a question that requires further research. This topic has important ethical ramifications as the level of realism may influence the clinical effectiveness of the simulation as well as be harmful for care seekers who experience adverse reactions.

Responsibility

Another important question is: who should be responsible for the decisions and actions of IACPs? Should responsibility be tied to the designers of the technologies, the end user, or some combination of both designers and end users? What about when intelligent machines are designed and put to use as autonomous agents capable of making independent decisions about the care of patients?

Sullins (2011) describes a theoretical standard user, tool, victim model. In this model, technology (the tool) mediates the situation between the actor (person who uses the technology) and the victim. Take, for example, a scenario where a psychiatrist with the best of intentions designs a website that provides his or her patients with a method for tracking daily regimens of medication use. If the psychiatrist has made a programming error that provides inaccurate information to a patient and a patient suffers harm due to misuse of medications, the psychiatrist (or potentially the designer of the software) would be seen as at fault, not the website. In this example, the user (the psychiatrist) has moral agency, whereas the website has none. This issue becomes more complex when the tool (e.g., an IACP) has a level of agency for decision-making. Take, for example, another scenario whereby an IACP that is capable of functioning autonomously is responsible for monitoring and adjusting medication prescriptions for patients. If the IACP is truly autonomous, then should it be held responsible if it makes an error and a patient is harmed?

Sullins proposes that intelligent machines are indeed moral agents when there is a reasonable level of abstraction under which the machine has autonomous intentions and responsibilities. If the machine is seen as autonomous, then the machine can be considered a moral agent. If this is the case then the machine may also be seen as responsible, at least in part, for the actions "it makes." However, it can be argued that autonomous behavior is not enough to hold an intelligent machine responsible for its actions. Another requirement is that the entity would have to have acted freely. Clearly, the concepts of autonomy, intentionally, and moral responsibility of machines have deep philosophical considerations.

One of the ways that current IACPs are fundamentally different from human care providers is that they cannot accept appropriate responsibility for their actions nor do they have the moral consequences that humans do (Luxton, 2014). Machines will not experience humiliation, stress, or the pain associated with loss of clinical privileges at hospitals, professional reprimand, expulsion from professional organizations, loss of their license to practice, or other legal sanctions. While this topic is open to philosophical debate, it may make most practical sense for legal liability to be explicitly linked to human designers of these systems. However, the burden of responsibility can extend to the end user (the mental healthcare professional or organization that uses the technology) when the end user does not use the technology appropriately, such as using IACPs with patient populations for which they may be contraindicated. We must be very careful about putting IACPs into practice if there is the potential that they could behave unethically.

If the ethics of a mental healthcare professional (or their employer) are ever called into question, they must demonstrate that their actions were reasonable and consistent with what is typically expected by peers in the same profession, ethical codes, laws, and guidelines. As autonomous intelligent agent systems, such as IACPs, increase in computational complexity, it will become increasingly difficult to know how these systems derived their decisions. If an IACP system exists as a mysterious "black box," it may be considered unethical to use it without the capability to demonstrate how the system derived its decisions for a particular course of action (Luxton, 2014). According to Anderson and Anderson (2011), for ethical decision-making, the intelligent machine must be able to justify its actions by not only citing the principle used, but also the cases from which it is derived. Moreover, liability risks may increase significantly with the use of highly autonomous intelligent systems as it may become increasingly difficult to predict the actions of IACP systems in every situation. Requirements for an audit trail with a minimum level of detail to describe the decision process may be one way to address the "black-box" issue. Formal specifications of limits of use as well as limits of autonomy of the systems might also be needed. Moreover, legal restrictions on the use of IACPs when presented to the public in untested and unregulated manner may also be required.

DESIGN AND TESTING RECOMMENDATIONS
Ethical (Moral) Turing Test

Named after Allan Turing, the "Turing test" is a machine's ability to exhibit intelligent behavior that is indistinguishable from that of a human. A basic description of the Turing test is as follows: A remote human interrogator must distinguish between a computer and a human subject based on their replies to various questions posed by the interrogator. The human interrogator cannot see or hear the robot or human subject, but can only communicate via text. By means of a series of such tests (within a certain timeframe) a computer's success at "thinking" can be measured by inability of the interrogator to distinguish between the computer and the human subject.

Allen, Varner, and Zinser (2000) discuss a Moral Turing Test (MTT) to judge the success of an automated moral agent (AMA). Allen, Varner, and Zinser note that a language-only test based on just moral justifications would be inadequate; they consider a test based on moral actions, rather than just description of reasons. "One way to shift the focus from reasons to actions might be to restrict the information available to the human judge in some way. Suppose the human judge in the MTT is provided with descriptions of actual, morally significant actions of a human and an AMA, purged of all references that would identify the agents. If the judge correctly identifies the machine at a level above chance, then the machine has failed the test" (p. 206). While they are careful to note that indistinguishability between human and automated agents might set the bar for passing the test too low, such a test by its very nature decides the morality of an agent on the basis of appearances. Others have argued that the MTT is not enough to explain a machine as moral. Parthemore and Whitby (2013) propose three building blocks that any successful candidate for moral agency must have: the concept of self, the concept of morality, and the concept of concept.

The Andersons (2011a,b) argue that one must make a distinction between a *full moral agent*, that is an agent that can be held morally responsible for its actions, and an *ethical agent* that consistently performs morally correct actions and can justify them if asked. It is possible to be an ethical agent and yet one should not be held morally responsible for one's actions. An ethically trained, autonomously functioning machine is a prime example. Ideally, the machine should be trained to follow general ethical principles that allow it to determine the ethically correct action even in situations that were not part of its training.

The Andersons have devised a variant of the MTT that simply compares the ethically preferable action specified by a machine, following its principle(s), in an ethical dilemma with that of an *ethicist* faced with the same dilemma. If a significant number of answers given by the machine match the answers given by the ethicist, then it has passed the test. Such evaluation holds the machine-generated principle(s) to the highest standards and, further, permits evidence of incremental improvement as the number of matches increases.

GenEth: A General Ethical Dilemma Analyzer

Developing ethical principles for the guidance of autonomous machine behavior clearly is a complex process that involves determining ethically relevant features, their incumbent duties, and how to weigh them when they pull in different directions. To help contend with this complexity, the Andersons have developed GenEth (2014), a general ethical dilemma analyzer that, through a dialog with ethicists, helps codify ethical principles from information concerning specific cases of ethical dilemmas in any given domain. GenEth uses inductive logic programming (Lavrac & Džeroski, 1997) to infer a *principle of ethical action preference* from these cases that is complete and consistent in relation to them. As the principles discovered are *most general specializations*, they cover more cases than those used in their specialization and, therefore, can be used to make and justify provisional determinations about untested cases. These cases can also provide a further means of justification for a system's actions through analogy: as an action is chosen for execution by a system, clauses of the principle that were instrumental in its selection can be determined and, as clauses of principles can be traced to the training cases from which they were abstracted, these cases and their origin can be ascertained and used as justification for a system's actions.

To validate the system, GenEth was used to abstract principles from cases in a number of domains in which autonomous systems might be likely to be deployed and these principles were then subjected to the Andersons' version of the MTT. The test was administered to five ethicists comprised of 28 multiple-choice questions in four domains, using for each a principle that was codified by their general ethical dilemma analyzer, GenEth. Of the 140 instances, the ethicists agreed with the system's judgment on 123 of them or about 88% of the time. It is of note that of the 17 responses in which ethicists were not in agreement with the system, none was a majority opinion. It could be argued that majority agreement in all dilemmas with the responses given by principles abstracted using GenEth begins to validate the system.

GenEth could easily be applied to technology used in mental health domains where there are clearly ethically relevant features of decisions that must be made leading to *prima facie* duties and decision-principles required to correctly balance them. Imagine, for instance, a mental health advisory system that must weigh respect for the autonomy of the patient, against the possibility of harm to the patient or others and possible good that can come from therapy, along with the preservation of trust between the care provider and patient. From clear cases where an ethicist familiar with the domain can say which ethically relevant features are involved, to what extent, whether they should be maximized or minimized (which determines the *prima facie* duties), and which action is correct, decision-principles can be learned that machines can be trained to follow.

What Can Ethical Machines Teach Us?

Intelligent machines capable of providing optimal solutions to ethics questions may be favorable over humans and could one day serve as role models for us. McCorduck (1979) suggests that artificial intelligent judges should be used because they would be impartial and not have self-serving personal agendas. Luxton (2014) suggests that IACP systems will not have personal problems that interfere with their competence to perform work-related duties, nor be susceptible to other ethical pitfalls such as dual relationships outside of the therapeutic relationship or worse, sexual intimacies with patients or their family members. Thus, these systems could be advantageous over humans from an ethics perspective. Others, however, have recommended caution. The late scientist Joseph Weizenbaum (Weizenbaum, 1976) raised concern about the use of computer technology in place of humans in professions that involve caring, interpersonal respect, understanding, and important decision-making, because computers lack the qualities of compassion and wisdom. He was concerned that decision-making would be reduced to a computational metaphor and lead to a mechanistic expectation on important decisions that would ultimately devalue the human experience and dignity. A potential consequence of the widespread and systematic use of technology in place of humans may be the risk that patients will be seen as a commodity rather than as people with individual needs. These concerns, as well as broader concerns about the psychosocial impact of relationships with machines in place of people, have been echoed by others (Luxton, 2014; Turkle, 2007).

Although many people are concerned with the lack of emotions, particularly empathy, in machines (at least as they exist at present), Susan Anderson has argued that while it is important to be sensitive to others' emotions to act morally, it is not essential for a machine to have emotions itself. It "could be trained to take into account the suffering of others in calculating how it should behave in an ethical dilemma." Furthermore, she argues "having emotions can actually interfere with a being's ability to determine and perform the right action in an ethical dilemma. Humans are prone to getting 'carried away' by their emotions to the point where they are incapable of following moral principles" (Anderson, 2011a,b).

Throughout the history of human kind we have harmed and caused suffering unto each other as the result of conflicting ethical beliefs. The ethical values held by individuals and societies (including those that are reflected in professional ethical codes and guidelines) are influenced by culture as well as personal values and the situation of the person who is making the decision (e.g., a care provider). While individuals and societies may have different ethical values, this does not mean that they are necessarily equally acceptable. As described by Anderson (2011c), ethicists are concerned with the values that people *ought to have*, rather than with the values people *happen to have*. Ethicists believe that in any ethical dilemma, there is only one right way to behave, although this does not imply that all ethical issues are resolved at this time. The optimal ethical decision is thus something to strive for and when there is no agreement yet among ethicists as to correct ethical behavior in certain domains, we should not permit machines to function autonomously in those domains. Perhaps the development of ethical machines is part of our own evolution towards universally accepted ethical values that will inspire us to behave more ethically towards one another. There is hope that abstracting from input given by ethicists about particular clear cases may lead to the discovery of decision principles to guide machine behavior that also can be used to resolve disputes between human beings. This can happen as a result of the computational power of today's machines that can keep track of more information and be more consistent than the human mind. Machines that always act in accordance with the ethical decision principles learned through this process can be good role models for humans, teaching us how to behave more ethically. These machines can not only aid us in many ways, but also show us how we need to behave if we are to survive as a species.

CONCLUSION

Professional healthcare organizations and regulatory boards must stay current with technological developments and take a proactive approach to address issues before they become a problem. End users, researchers, developers, and healthcare professionals, regardless of their professional discipline, must all remain aware of the ethical issues involved and be active participants in discussions and decision-making regarding the current and future use of these technologies. The development of AI technologies in behavioral and mental health care also brings opportunities for psychologists and other mental health professionals to collaborate with ethicists, engineers, and technological visionaries in the development of these technologies to assure that they are developed to function in an ethically responsible manner. It is a brave new world for the mental healthcare professions.

REFERENCES

Allen, C., Varner, G., & Zinser, J. (2000). Prolegomena to any future artificial moral agent. *Journal of Experimental and Theoretical Artificial Intelligence, 12*, 251–261.

American Counseling Association. (2014). *ACA code of ethics*. Retrieved from: <http://www.counseling.org/Resources/aca-code-of-ethics.pdf>.

American Medical Association. (1994). *Opinion 1.02 – The relation of law and ethics*. Retrieved from: <http://www.ama-assn.org//ama/pub/physician-resources/medical-ethics/code-medical-ethics/opinion102.page>.

American Psychiatric Association. (2013). *The principles of medical ethics with annotations especially applicable to psychiatry*. Retrieved from: <http://www.psych.org/File%20Library/Practice/Ethics%20Documents/principles2013--final.pdf> Accessed 03.11.14.

American Psychological Association. (2002). *American psychological association ethical principles of psychologists and code of conduct*. Retrieved from: <http://www.apa.org/ethics/code2002.html> American Psychiatric Association. Accessed 09.02.14.

American Telemedicine Association (ATA). (2012). Telemedicine Practice Guidelines, Retrieved from: <http://www.americantelemed.org/resources/telemedicine-practice-guidelines/telemedicine-practice-guidelines#.VXuTZflVhBc>.

Anderson, S. L. (2011a). Machine metaethics. In M. Anderson, & S. L. Anderson (Eds.), *Machine ethics* (pp. 21–27). New York, NY: Cambridge University Press.

Anderson, S. L. (2011b). The unacceptability of Asimov's three laws of robotics as a basis for machine ethics. In M. Anderson, & S. L. Anderson (Eds.), *Machine ethics* (pp. 285–296). New York, NY: Cambridge University Press.

Anderson, S. L. (2011c). How machines might help us achieve breakthroughs in ethical theory and inspire us to behave better. In M. Anderson, & S. L. Anderson (Eds.), *Machine ethics* (pp. 285–296). New York, NY: Cambridge University Press.

Anderson, M., & Anderson, S. L. (Eds.), (2011). *Machine ethics*. New York, NY: Cambridge University Press.

Anderson, M. & Anderson, S. L. (2014). GenEth: A general ethical dilemma analyzer. In *Proceedings of the twenty eighth AAAI conference on artificial intelligence*, Quebec City, Quebec, CA July 2014.

Asimov, I. (1942). *Runaround. Astounding science fiction*. New York: Street and Smith Publications, Inc.

Asimov, I. (1976). *The bicentennial man*. New York, NY: Doubleday.

Bordin, E. S. (1979). The generalizability of the psychoanalytic concept of the workingalliance. *Psychotherapy: Theory Research & Practice, 16*(3), 252–260.

Calo, R. (2011). Robots and privacy. In *Robot ethics: The ethical and social implications of robotics*. MIT Press. Available from: <http://ssrn.com/abstract=1599189>.

Clarke, R. (2011). Asimov's Laws of Robotics: Implications for information technology. In M. Anderson, & S. L. Anderson (Eds.), *Machine ethics* (pp. 285–296). New York, NY: Cambridge University Press.

Gillon, R. (1994). Medical ethics: Four principles plus attention to scope. *BMJ, 309*, 184.

Hofstadter, D. R. (1996). Preface 4 the ineradicable Eliza effect and its dangers, Epilogue. *Fluid concepts and creative analogies: Computer models of the fundamental mechanisms of thought* New York: Basic Books.

Lavrac, N., & Džeroski, S. (1997). *Inductive logic programming: Techniques and applications*. Ellis Harwood.

Luxton, D. D. (2014). Recommendations for the ethical use and design of artificial intelligent care providers. *Artificial Intelligence in Medicine, 62*. Available from: http://dx.doi.org/10.1016/j.artmed.2014.06.004.

Luxton, D. D., Nelson, E., & Maheu, M. *A practitioner's guide to telemental health*. Washington, DC: American Psychological Association Books, in press.

McCorduck, P. (1979). *Machines who think* (1st ed.). New York: W. H. Freeman.

Miller, K. W. (2010). It's not nice to fool humans. *IT Professional, 1,* 51–52.

Moore, A. (2005). Intangible property: Privacy, power and information control. In A. Moore (Ed.), *Information ethics: Privacy, property, and power.* Seattle, WA: University of Washington Press.

Mori, M. (1970). The uncanny valley. *Energy, 7*(4), 33–35.

Parthemore, J. L., & Whitby, B. (2013). What makes any agent a moral agent? Reflections on machine consciousness and moral agency. *International Journal of Machine Consciousness, 05*(105). Available from: http://dx.doi.org/10.1142/S1793843013500017.

Riek, L. D., & Howard, D. (2014). A code of ethics for the human-robot interaction profession. In *Proceedings of we robot.* Available at: http://robots.law.miami.edu/2014/wp-content/uploads/2014/03/a-code-of-ethics-for-the-human-robot-interaction-profession-riek-howard.pdf.

Riek, L. D., & Watson, R. N. (2010). The age of avatar realism: When seeing shouldn't be believing. *IEEE Robotics & Automation Magazine, 17*(4), 37–42.

Sullins, J. P. (2011). When is a robot a moral agent? In M. Anderson, & S. L. Anderson (Eds.), *Machine ethics.* New York, NY: Cambridge University Press.

Turkle, S. (2007). Authenticity in the age of digital companions. *Interaction Studies, 8*(3), 501–517.

Veruggio, G. (2007). EURON roboethics roadmap. Available at: <http://www.roboethics.org/index_file/Roboethics%20Roadmap%20Rel.1.2.pdf>.

Weizenbaum, J. (1976). *Computer power and human reason: From judgment to calculation.* San Francisco, CA: W. H. Freeman.

GLOSSARY

AI Artificial intelligence. Machines or software designed to resemble and/or behave similarly to natural intelligent beings. The actual "intelligence" of machines labeled as AI varies greatly.

AI framework A combination of multiple algorithms to produce an artificially intelligent system.

Actuator The mechanisms that enable a robot to move.

Affective computing Computing techniques and applications involving emotion or affect.

Agent Sometimes referred to as an "intelligent agent." This is an autonomous entity — either natural (e.g., an animal) or artificial (e.g., a robot or AI) — that can sense its environment, think about what to do, and act upon it in some way. For a physical agent, that may be through the use of muscles or motors. For a software agent, that may be computationally.

Agent-based modeling & simulation (ABM, ABMS) A category of modeling and simulation concerned with replicating the inputs, behaviors, and actions of autonomous agents. ABMS are generally used for computational experiments on communities of agents that act as surrogates for their real world counterparts.

Ambient Intelligence (AmI) Environments with embedded electronics that are sensitive and responsive to the presence of people within them.

Ambient persuasive technologies Ubiquitous systems embedded within one's everyday environment that are intended to aid in behavior and lifestyle change.

Artificial general intelligence A machine that exhibits behavior at least as skillful and flexible as humans do.

Artificial life The simulation of biological life with technology.

Artificial neural network An interconnected group of artificial neurons using computational, mathematical, or technological models.

Attentional computing Computing techniques and applications involving attention.

Belief state Probabilistic estimation of current conditions, used by AI when direct observation of the actual state of the world is inaccessible or missing. In a health setting, this can be used to maintain beliefs about a patient's health status in the absence of direct clinical observation, or when underlying disease status must be inferred indirectly from symptoms.

CDSS Clinical Decision Support System. A tool, typically computerized, designed to enhance clinical decision-making by providing information or recommendations at the point-of-care.

Cloud Computing Process whereby computer processing and storage are accessed on the Internet rather than on a local computer.

Cognitive computing An approach to software/hardware computer architecture that attempts to replicate certain aspects of natural cognition, e.g., Hebbian learning and emergent behavior. The approach fundamentally differs from the traditional von Neumann computing architecture, which virtually all computer technology in the world today relies upon.

Cognitive load The total amount of mental effort used by the working memory.

Cognitive scaffolding The use of tools in the environment to enhance human cognition by offloading certain cognitive tasks.

Convolutional networks Hierarchical classification system utilizing dynamic levels instead of a rigidly fixed structure.

Cray grid A supercomputer manufacturer.

DARPA Defense Advanced Research Projects Agency.

Data mining Process of discovering meaningful patterns in data. Typically used for classification, clustering, and prediction. Although the term has some subtle differences in usage from machine learning, in reality the two often employ many of the exact same algorithms and approaches.

Deep learning Algorithms in machine learning that attempt to model high-level abstractions in data.

Digital avatar Digital representation of a person, taking on the characteristics (e.g., appearance, personality, clinical attributes) of that person within the digital world. Such avatars enhance our ability to create more realistic simulations of the real world.

Durkheim Emile Durkheim (April 15, 1858–November 15, 1917). Author of *Suicide 1897*.

Dynamic feature size The ability to change the feature input size in a statistical classification workflow.

EC2 Amazon's Elastic Cloud web service.

EHR Electronic Health Record. A computerized system for storing and maintaining patient health data.

Expert system A computerized system that attempts to replicate the decision-making capabilities of human experts. Traditional expert systems relied on a knowledge base of probabilistic rules and an inference engine utilizing those rules for prediction. In modern AI and machine learning, a variety of algorithms/approaches could be seen as embodying the spirit of "expert systems," though they may not fit the traditional definition.

Firewall A security barrier between two networks.

GENETH General ethical dilemma analyzer. A program that, through a dialog with ethicists, helps codify ethical principles from information concerning specific cases of ethical dilemmas in any given domain.

GSP Three human value trees known as Goals, Standards, and Preferences that are utilized to appraise both events occurring in the world and action choices about how to behave.

Hadoop A distributed file system, also a catchphrase for a suite of software tools for cloud computing.

Health Information Exchange (HIE) Computerized system for integrating patient health data across multiple organizations/providers.

HIPAA Health Insurance Portability and Accountability Act of 1996.

Human–robot interaction A multidisciplinary "field of study dedicated to understanding, designing, and evaluating robotic systems for use by or with humans."

Hyper-parameter A vector that distinguishes a plane in the support vector machine.

IACP Intelligent autonomous care providers.

Internet of Things (IoT) The interconnection of mobile and computerized devices (e.g., sensors) that can communicate with each other via the Internet.

Learning agent An agent that can operate in unknown environments and improve through learning by using feedback from its environment.

LIWC A program for linguistic content analysis, first written by James Pennebaker and colleagues.

Machine learning A branch of artificial intelligence that attempts to create artificial systems that can "learn" from data. Typical tasks include classification, clustering, and prediction. A related term is data mining.

MHSUITRY A variable of the NSDUH survey dataset covering suicide attempts.

Mind wandering Involuntary lapses in attention from the task at hand to thoughts unrelated to the task.

Moral Turing Test (MTT) A method to judge the success of an automated agent.

Morphology The physical form a robot may take. Robot morphologies include mechanical-looking (functional), animal-looking (zoomorphic), and human-looking (anthropomorphic). In terms of physical capability, robots of various morphologies can exhibit *limb-like motion*, such as walking, running, climbing, turning, grabbing, shaking, gesturing; *face-like motion*, such as facial expressions, gazing, nodding; and other forms of *biological motion*, such as flipping, flying, and undulating.

MOSES A machine learning library.

Multi-agent system (MAS) A computerized system composed of multiple interacting intelligent agents. Multi-agent systems are useful for solving certain distributed problems and for modeling systems with interacting, sometimes conflicting, sometimes synergistic components (as many clinical scenarios are comprised).

NSDUH National Survey on Drug Use and Health sponsored by the US government.

Online agent An AI system (either hardware or software) that is constantly reevaluating its decisions and plans as it interacts with the world and new information/observations are received. This is in contrast to agents that determine a plan (e.g., optimal policy) *a priori* based on some static set of data.

Performance moderator function (PMF) An evidence-based, quantified relationship between some moderator or stimuli (e.g., no sleep, adrenaline, a fright) and a specific aspect of human performance (perception, memory, problem solving, etc.). These are also called dose−response functions.

PMFserv A computational library that serves up PMFs as needed by an autonomous agent trying to reason through its responses and reactions to various stimuli it is encountering.

Roboethics This is an emerging field that is concerned with the ethical behavior of humans when it comes to designing, creating, and interacting with artificially intelligent agents (i.e., robots).

Robot A physically embodied system capable of enacting physical change in the world. Robots enact this change with effectors that move the robot itself (i.e., locomotion) or move objects in the environment (i.e., manipulation).

Robotics technology Primarily refers to robots, but also includes affiliated technological systems, such as sensor systems, algorithms for processing data, decision-making software, etc.

Serious games Computer games developed for training and learning purposes.

Serious mental illness (SMI) A diagnosable mental, behavioral, or emotional disorder of sufficient duration and persistent or recurring functional impairment so as to meet criteria associated with medical categorization defined more formally in the US Federal Register and subscribed to by agencies such as NIMH, CMS, etc.

Smart home An approach for creating a network of interacting technologies within people's living environments. From a health standpoint, this typically entails use of in-home sensor networks for monitoring/improving a person's activity and functioning levels.

Socially assistive robots (SARs) Robots that attempt to aid people through social interaction and engagement, having measurable behavioral, cognitive, or therapeutic effects on people. The effects are similar to those seen from pets, for instance.

StateSim A simulation of a region, district, or state that emulates the organizations and population members and their daily routines of living, working, socializing, exercising, etc. This operates like a SimCity style of program, except it seeks to emulate real life.

Strong AI Machines that can think in the same ways as humans do.

Support vector machines A type of machine learning relying on high numbers of linear dimensions to approximate a classification.

Transition models In many temporal modeling approaches, these are matrices of probabilities of transitioning from one state (e.g., a patient's current outcome measure value) to another state, given certain actions (e.g., treatments). These allow us to calculate the probability of certain outcomes/costs (for a patient) for sequences of potential actions/observations over time.

Turing deceptions Situations when a person is unable to determine if they are interacting with a machine or not.

Turing test A test of a machine's ability to impersonate intelligent behavior equivalent to, or indistinguishable from, that of a human.

Virtual affective agents Intelligent virtual agents capable of affective interaction, such as expression of "emotions" and recognition of human emotions.

Weak AI Machines capable of narrow intelligent tasks.

WHODAS A variable of the NSDUH survey and dataset which specifically covers the World Health Organization Disability Assessment Schedule of six domains of functioning.

Wizard-of-Oz Refers to a person, usually an experimenter or confederate, remotely operating a robot or virtual agent without the knowledge of the person(s) co-present with the robot/agent. The Wizard may control a number of things about the robot, including its navigation, movement, gestures, speech, etc.

INDEX

Note: Page numbers followed by "*f*" and "*t*" refer to figures and tables, respectively.